THE NEGLECTED IMPACT OF NON-ECONOMIC FACTORS ON THE DEVELOPMENT OF FINANCIAL CRISES AND GOVERNMENTAL RESPONSES

The Mexican and Malaysian Cases of the 1990s

Fahrettin Sümer

Foreword by Donald J. Puchala, Ph.D.

T0290711

University Press of America,® Inc.
Lanham · Boulder · New York · Toronto · Plymouth, UK

Copyright © 2012 by
University Press of America,® Inc.
4501 Forbes Boulevard
Suite 200
Lanham, Maryland 20706
UPA Acquisitions Department (301) 459-3366

Estover Road
Plymouth PL6 7PY
United Kingdom

British Library Cataloging in Publication Information Available

Library of Congress Control Number: 2011933100
ISBN: 978-0-7618-5646-7 (paperback : alk. paper)
eISBN: 978-0-7618-5645-0

⊖™ The paper used in this publication meets the minimum
requirements of American National Standard for Information
Sciences—Permanence of Paper for Printed Library Materials,
ANSI Z39.48-1992

For my family

TABLE OF CONTENTS

Preface

Financial crises are significant economic, political and international events. In today's financial affairs, the world cannot ignore financial crises occurring in a particular country or region due to their multiple economic, financial and political implications at domestic, regional, and international levels. Nor can those countries or regions dealing with their own crises ignore their network of linkages with the outside world. Despite the broad literature on financial crises, the causes and consequences of financial crises and governmental policy responses have not been sufficiently explained.

This book is mainly concerned with two major questions: (1) how does a financial crisis develop and (2) how does a government respond to a financial crisis? In an attempt to shed light on these questions, it closely examines two cases: Mexico during the Mexican Peso Crisis of 1994-1995, and Malaysia during the Asian Financial Crisis of 1997-1998. It argues that economic explanations of financial crises are lacking in answering these questions, since they do not pay enough attention to non-economic factors stemming from a county's political, societal, institutional and external contexts.

The examination of the Mexican and Malaysian cases evidence this argument and shows that multiple non-economic factors—domestic political, societal, institutional, and psychological/ ideological factors as well as external influences and pressures—can play as significant roles as economic ones. Interplay of these non-economic factors with economic ones brought these financial crises and shaped the Mexican and the Malaysian governments' policy behaviors.

The research of this book was completed before the recent global financial crises that allegedly started in the US. Even though the book does not discuss this crisis, readers will be able to draw parallels between this and the crises of the 1990s in terms of affects of non-economic factors on the development of a crisis and governmental responses.

The successful completion of this book was due to so many people's help and support. Although I cannot list all of their names, I would like to extend my heartfelt thanks to all of them, in particular my family, whose enduring patience and support enabled me to complete my Ph.D. and work on this book.

My graduate education in the United States started at Rutgers University and continued at the Department of Government and International Studies (currently the Department of Political Science) as well as the Department of Economics at the University of South Carolina (USC). I am very thankful to my professors at these institutions for providing me with a great learning and academic experience.

The topic of this book was first inspired by Professor Donald J. Puchala at USC during our discussions on globalization. My curiosity in regards to different dimensions and implications of globalization and my talks with various other professors involved me in the topic of financial crises in the aftermath of the Asian financial crisis. It was professor Puchala's inspirational teaching, advice, and guidance, and the very helpful comments of professors Donald E. Weatherbee, Harvey Starr, Robert Angel, and Mona M. Lyne, and Dr. Douglas P. Woodward's great help and support, who is the Director of the Division of Research at the Moore School of Business of USC, which enabled me to complete my research and write this book. I owe all of them more than a short thank you. You will always be remembered.

I also would like to thank Professors Betty Glad and Roger A. Coate for their very helpful comments and advice. I would like to express a special thanks to my wife, Sheima Salam. She helped with the editing of my book greatly and patiently. In addition, her family, in particular her dear mother Sultana Salam, has always been very encouraging and supportive to both of us.

During my research, I received the John C. West Fellowship and a Research Fellowship via the Department of Political Science. I am very grateful for the providers of these supports, which financially enabled me to complete my research.

Richmond, 2010   FS

Foreword

By Donald J. Puchala

This perceptive study by Fahrettin Sümer could not have been completed at a more propitious time. As the world in 2010 haltingly recovers from the worst economic crisis since the Great Depression, Dr. Sümer significantly extends our understanding of why such crises periodically humble global capitalism. He focuses on the Mexican financial crisis of 1994 and the Malaysian predicament during the Asian meltdown of 1997. His findings, however, echo in scores of similar situations and notably in the recent American-precipitated Great Recession of 2007-2009. *The Neglected Impact of Non-Economic Factors* summarizes much of what is known about the origins and unfolding of financial and economic crises and adds to this all that Sümer's careful research has uncovered.

The Neglected Impact of Non-Economic Factors is a treatise in international political economy. Its central message is that governments responding to economic crises do not always do what is economically timely or even economically rational. This is because governments and their leaders are constrained by the pressures of office and imperatives connected with staying in office to attend to the demands of crucial constituencies. Political pressures, social contracts, or even cultural mores determine governments' priorities and sometimes lead to less than optimum economic policy choices. In the cases of smaller countries or weaker ones, international pressures can also weigh heavily upon domestic policy choices.

"Governments," Sümer posits, "do not simply react to macroeconomic variables and/or market forces with an economics rationale, but their behaviors are shaped within a political process that is influenced by multiple domestic and international, economic and non-economic factors." Yet, if this infinitely sensible proposition is true, Sümer then wonders, why is it so frequently passed over in the explanations of financial crises offered in the literatures of Economics? Trained as both a political scientist and an economist, Sümer displays considerable respect for, as well as sophisticated understanding of, the writings of the many economists who have looked into crises of capitalism. But the economists' explanations tend to be incomplete because, all too often in the social sciences, academic disciplines become walled intellectual domains, and those searching for insights seldom venture beyond the walls. To his credit, and very much to the enlightenment of his readers, Sümer disregards the walls between Economics and Political Science and works comfortably and fruitfully in both domains. To understand financial and economic crises and their handling, one must grasp both the complexities of the economic forces at play and the policy options governments are obliged to consider because they are political organizations.

Yes, the Mexican peso was over-valued in 1994, and yes the Mexican government should have devalued the currency much sooner. But the Salinas government in 1994 confronted an array of imperatives that rendered the economic right thing to do politically all but impossible. An election was imminent:

the strong peso abetted the import tastes of the rising middle class that also happened to be an important segment of the electoral base for the PRI. The exchange rate also spurred the influx of foreign capital and kept Mexican business very much in the PRI camp. Mexico was looking as well toward the boom that would expectedly follow the establishment of NAFTA. Therefore, the year 1994, when a fiercely divided the U.S. Congress could have easily sent NAFTA into oblivion, was hardly the time to devalue the peso and display Mexico as an unreliable partner. Added to this, it may be recalled that the insurrection in Chiapas led by the Zapatista National Liberation Army began in January, 1994, so that it is perhaps understandable that President Salinas' attention was not entirely focused on the plight of the peso.

Yes, the Malaysian economy in 1997 was much weaker than Prime Minister Mohamad Mahathir acknowledged, or perhaps even recognized. The exchange rate was overvalued, the current account was chronically imbalanced, mobile capital was building up rapidly in relation to the level of international reserves, the savings to investment gap was widening and indebtedness was soaring. Under these conditions Malaysia was hardly immune to the contagion effects of the spreading Asian Financial Crisis that began in Thailand. Yet Mahathir and his close political supporters did little to stave off the collapse of the ringgit despite sound counsel from economists in Malaysia as well as from the IMF. Why? Because, Mahathir's political stature was built upon the dominant Malaysian business class, some particularly prominent families also among the business elite, and a nationalistically mobilized populace. Easy money, high rates of government spending, huge and costly public works, heavy borrowing and a public rhetoric of growth and ascendance bought the support of the Malaysian elites. Anti-western diatribes and indictments hurled at foreign financiers roused the masses. Within this political context, doing the right things economically were not realistic options.

The Neglected Impact of Non-Economic Factors should be read most carefully. Its lessons concern not the "whats" of governments' responses to economic crises but rather the "whys." The "whats" of course are in the statistics — the rates, ratios, balances and imbalances that often predict what is about to happen and then tellingly expose what is happening as bubbles burst, investors flee, and workers suffer. Governments intervene. What they do is often economically inappropriate. Why they do it is what Dr. Sümer's book is about. This is a first book by a promising scholar. I look forward to the next.

Acronyms

APEC	: Asia-Pacific Economic Cooperation
ASEAN	:Association of Southeast Asian Nations
BIS	: Bank for International Settlements
BA	: *Barisan Alternatif* (Alternative Front, in Malaysia)
BN	: *Barisan Nasional* (National Front, in Malaysia)
BNM	: *Bank Negara Malaysia* (Malaysian Central Bank)
BOM	: *Banco de Mexico* (Bank of Mexico , the Central Bank of Mexico)
CA	: Current Account
CB	: Central Bank
CPI	: Consumer Price Index
CTM	: Mexican Workers Confederation
DAP	: Democratic Action Party (in Malaysia)
EMS	: European Monetary System
EOI	: export-oriented industrialization
EPF	: Employees Provident Fund (in Malaysia)
EZLN	: The Zapatista National Liberation Army (in Mexico)
FDI	: foreign direct investment
FED	: The U.S. Federal Reserve Board
GATT	: General Agreements on Tariffs and Trade
IMF	: International Monetary Fund
ISI	: import substitution industrialization
KLSE	: Kuala Lumpur Stock Exchange
MCA	: Malaysian Chinese Association (the UMNO's coalition partner)
MIC	: Malaysian Indian Congress (the UMNO's coalition partner)
NAFTA	: North American Free Trade Agreement
NDP	: National Development Policy (in Mexico)
NEAC	: National Economic Action Council (in Malaysia)
NEP	: New Economic Policy
NERP	: National Economic Recovery Plan
NIC	: newly industrialized country
OECD	: the Organization for Economic Cooperation and Development
PAN	: *Partido Acción Nacion (*National Action Party, in Mexico)
PAS	: the Malay-based Party Islam (Parti Islam SeMalaysia—PAS)
PDR	: the Party of the Democratic Revolution
PEMEX	: Mexican Petroleum
PI	: portfolio investments
PMR	: *Partido de la Mexicana Revolución* (Mexican Revolution Party)
PNR	: *Partido Nacional Revolucionari* (National Revolutionary Party, in Mexico)
PRI	: *Partido Revolucionario Institucional* (Institutional Revolutionary Party, in Mexico)
UEM	: United Engineers Malaysia
UMNO	: United Malay National Organization
WB	: World Bank
WTO	: World Trade Organization

CHAPTER I: ABOUT THE BOOK

WHAT IS THIS BOOK ABOUT?

Financial or currency crises as we know today have been the repetitive feature of the international economy since the replacement of gold and silver coins with paper money,[1] even though economic downturns/crises reoccurred throughout history. As a result of financial and economic globalization, financial crises have arguably become more prevalent during the last two decades. Among the recurrent international economic events of the 1990s and 2000s have been devastating financial crises. The well-known Asian financial crisis of 1997-1998 was preceded by a major crisis of the European Monetary System (EMS) in 1992-1993 and the devastating Mexican Peso crisis of 1994-1995. Financial crises have also hit Russia (1998), Brazil (1999), Turkey (2001), Argentina (2001), and several others. The world is still dealing with the ramifications of the global financial crisis of 2008-2010. As Blinder (1999) writes, "financial conflagrations have become too frequent, too devastating, and too contagious to be ignored."[2]

Financial crises are significant economic, political and international events for the following reasons: (1) they often cause huge output losses and a radical reduction of GDP growth in the affected countries for a year or much more—the EU countries were mostly able to avoid this. (2) Their financial and economic repercussions spread beyond the borders of affected countries due to globalization, the integration of financial markets and the network of economic linkages, and they threaten regional and global economic stability. (3) They usually generate radical domestic political and societal events and stimulate or discourage some international political developments along with economic ones. In today's financial affairs, the world cannot ignore financial crises happening in a particular country or region due to their multiple economic and political implications at domestic, regional, and international levels, nor can those countries or regions dealing with their own crises ignore their network of linkages with the outside world.

There is not a consensus definition of a financial crisis. Also, the terms "currency crisis," "balance of payments crisis," and "financial crisis" are often used interchangeably in the literature. "Financial crisis" is a larger term that contains currency crises and other types of financial crises. Eichengreen and Portes (1987) define a financial crisis as "a disturbance of financial markets, associated typically with falling asset prices and insolvency among debtors and intermediaries, which ramifies through the financial system, disrupting the market's capacity to allocate capital within the economy. In an international financial crisis, disturbances spill over national borders, disrupting the market's capacity to allocate capital internationally."[3] The term "financial crisis" in this book mostly refers to currency crises, since the cases examined in this book are currency crises. But the arguments of the book apply to all kinds of financial crises.

A financial/economic crisis is a process that can be divided into three time periods: development, occurrence and recovery. During the first period, a financial crisis develops within a country (or countries) as it (or they) becomes increasingly vulnerable to financial and economic shocks, due to long and short-term economic policies as well as domestic and external financial/economic developments, and political, societal, and institutional factors. The depth of economic vulnerabilities and how they evolve is determined by both economic and non-economic factors. At one point during this period, the government of the vulnerable country usually starts to deal with these vulnerabilities in order to prevent a possible crisis. When and how the government starts dealing with the country's economic and financial vulnerabilities depend not only on the depth of the vulnerabilities but also on domestic political, societal, and legal/institutional factors as well as external developments and influences. In order for a government to be able to deal with its vulnerabilities, it has to be aware of them, prioritize them over other issues or concerns, and have the ability to deal with them. Otherwise, governments are usually unable to take the necessary measures in enough time to prevent a crisis situation. They often prioritize political concerns over economic ones, misperceive the economic situation, and make mistakes.

During the second period, the financial crisis occurs and forces the government to deal with the crisis in a more profound way, with or without outside help. As the government shapes its response policies, the concerned domestic and international parties and interest groups become involved in the process of dealing with the crisis situation, and affect how the government responds. Governments shape their response policies within an interaction process involving multiple domestic and international actors, and they may either lean toward domestic influences and pressures or international ones, or may attempt to balance the contradictory domestic and international pressures.

The third period starts after governments determine their response policies. This is the policy implementation and recovery period, and decision-makers either implement the chosen policies or revise them as they observe trends and are pressured by the demands of domestic and external actors as well as political and societal developments. This period lasts until the financial crisis fades away as it is dealt with.

This book is mainly concerned with two major questions: (1) how does a financial crisis develop and (2) how does a government shape its response policy during a financial crisis? In an attempt to shed light on these questions it closely examines two cases: Mexico during the Mexican peso crisis of 1994-1995, and Malaysia during the Asian financial crisis of 1997-1998. Therefore, what is to be explained includes: (1) the development of the Mexican peso crisis of 1994-1995 and the Mexican government's response to it, and (2) the development of the Asian financial crisis in Malaysia and the Malaysian government's response. In terms of the aforementioned three time periods, this book is concerned partly with the first period, fully with the second period, and with the early part of the third period.

INQUIRIES, GOALS, AND PREMISES OF THE BOOK

Economics, naturally, was the first discipline that studied financial crises. Despite the long history of financial crises, economic crisis models attempting to explain the causes and consequences of crises have become a distinguished part of economics literature only during the last three decades. During this period, despite the progress made in explaining financial crises, each new experience of a crisis forced economists to revise prior models or to offer new models. "First-generation" models, referring to earlier models that were pioneered by Krugman (1979), reflected the experiences of financial crises in the 1970s. "Second-generation" models, promoted by Obstfeld (1994), came out in the early 1990s, due to the shortcomings of the first generation models in explaining the Latin American debt crises in the 1980s and the EMS crisis of 1992-1993. However, these models were not very helpful in predicting the financial crises of the 1990s, and were inadequate in explaining the causes and consequences of them. As a result, revised new models, which some call "third-generation" models, appeared following the Mexican peso crisis and the Asian financial crisis.[4] Additionally, Krugman (March 2001) and a few others offered "fourth-generation" crisis models, which emphasized the effects of capital flows on exchange rates, weaknesses in balance sheets of companies, and quality of institutional infrastructure for financial intermediation, which in turn affects the levels of financial development, trust in the financial system, and credit risks. The literature based on fourth generation models recognized some non-economic factors, such as quality of financial policies, rule of law, property rights, as well as culture and politics at large as important variables because of their impacts on efficiency of decision making, level of uncertainty, and transaction costs.[5]

Despite these multiple models of economics and the broad literature on the causes and consequences of financial crises, the questions of how financial crises develop and how governments shape their response policies have not been adequately addressed. Every new crisis repeatedly demonstrated the shortcomings of economic crisis models, in terms of their ability to predict and explain the causes and consequences of a different financial crisis. In addition, economics literature has either ignored the question of explaining government behavior during a crisis or governments are assumed to react to economic variables with an economic rationale.

Economic explanations of a financial crisis or crisis models are based on establishing relationships between certain economic variables and certain economic and financial outcomes. They either ignore the impact of non-economic factors or treat them as not as significant as economic factors. Therefore, economists are inclined to attribute the weaknesses of economic crisis models to their inability to appreciate the causes and consequences of some economic variables adequately. However, as the financial crises in the 1990s and the 2000s demonstrated, non-economic factors play significant roles in how financial crises emerge and develop and how governments respond to them. Governments do not simply react to macroeconomic variables and/or market forces with an economics rationale, but their behaviors are shaped within a political process that is influenced by multiple domestic and international, economic and non-economic factors. One must consider domestic political, societal/cultural, and legal/institutional factors, as well as external links and influences in assessing the causes of financial crises and explaining governmental responses. As mentioned before, although some economists do refer to some domestic political and societal events, as well as external developments, they do so in a rather limited way. Their analyses are usually short in evaluating how these non-economic factors interplay in bringing about financial crises, and in shaping governmental responses.

One goal of this book is to demonstrate that economic explanations of financial crises are lacking in answering the questions of how financial crises develop and how governmental policy responses are shaped, since they do not pay enough attention to non-economic factors, stemming from a county's political, societal, and institutional as well as external contexts. *Another goal* of this inquiry is to illustrate the impact of these various non-economic factors on the development of the Mexican peso crisis and the Mexican government's policy behavior as well as on the development of the Asian financial crisis and the Malaysian government's policy behavior. *A third goal* is to offer an analytical framework in order to explain the impact of multiple non-economic factors as well as their interplay with economic variables in bringing financial crises and in shaping governmental policy responses.

With these goals, the book consists of the following chapters. Chapter II introduces readers to economic crisis models and explanations and their assumed, prescribed, or predicted government behavior. It investigates the kinds of economic variables that economic crisis models look at in order to explain and predict a financial crisis, and how these models perceive governmental policy behavior during a crisis. Chapter III questions why economic crisis models were short of predicting the Mexican peso crisis based on the country's economic indicators, surveys *ex-post* economic explanations of the crisis and their conceptions of the Mexican government's policy behavior, and discusses the shortcomings of such explanations. The chapter proposes that one major short-coming of the economic explanations is their failure to pay enough attention to the impact of various external and domestic non-economic influences and pres-sures. Then, Chapter IV identifies, traces, and assesses the impact of multiple non-economic factors on the development of the peso crisis and on the Mexican government's policy behavior, and demonstrates the interplay of economic and non-economic factors during the crisis. Chapters V and VI pursue the same patterns of investigation as Chapters III and IV with the Asian financial crises and the Malaysian case.

The examination of the Mexican and the Malaysian cases shows that eco-nomic crisis explanations based on economic indicators are short in explaining the crises and these governments' policy behaviors. Non-economic factors can play as significant roles as economic factors in bringing financial crises and in shaping governmental policy responses. An interplay of economic and non-economic factors brought these financial crises and shaped these governments' policy behaviors. Having reached these conclusions, the next question is how do various external and domestic non-economic factors interplay with economic variables in bringing financial crises and in shaping governmental responses? How can we explain the impacts of these multiple non-economic factors as well as similarities and differences between the cases? Chapter VII offers an analyti-cal framework in order to explain the impact of non-economic factors as well as their interplay with economic factors based on the findings of the previous chap-ters and the relevant literature. It discusses the nature of the causal mechanism that leads to financial crises and shapes governmental responses. It also com-pares the cases to a certain extent, and assesses the variations across the cases in terms of the relative impact of economic versus non-economic factors and do-mestic versus external factors. This chapter concludes the book.

The book contributes to the financial crisis literature in several ways. The topic of this book is somewhat at the interface of comparative politics, interna-tional relations, and political economy, as well as economics and global finan-cial relationships. Thus, it bridges various fields of studies to a certain extent. Even though financial/monetary affairs at domestic and international levels draw the attention of researchers from many different fields of study,[6] the question of how financial crises develop has not been addressed extensively by analysts other than economists. As this book argues, economic explanations do not in-corporate adequately the impact of non-economic factors on the development of financial crises. The book bridges economic explanations of financial crises with political economy, political science/comparative politics, and international rela-tions literature, which are helpful in explicating the impact of non-economic factors on markets, government behaviors and economic policies. It also offers an alternative explanatory framework to economic explanations that considers non-economic along with economic factors in determining the causes and con-sequences of financial crises as well as governmental responses. It aims to further illuminate how multiple non-economic and economic variables interplay in bringing financial crises and in shaping governmental policy responses.

A broad body of literature from political science, international studies, and political economy as well as economics can be related to how governments respond to financial crises. However, there are not many studies that deal specifically with the impact of non-economic factors on how governments handle financial crises politically. A few examples of such studies that address similar questions are: Gourevitch (1986), *Politics in Hard Times,* Horowitz and Heo's (2001) edited book, *The Political Economy of International Financial Crisis,* and Weintraub (2000), *Financial Decision-Making in Mexico.* However, these works do not ask the same questions nor do they have the same goals of this inquiry. In addition, a few comparative studies, like Gourevitch's (1986) *Politics in Hard Times* compare governmental responses to economic/financial crises in countries with similar domestic and external contexts, namely democratic Western countries. A good deal more work needs to be done concerning non-western and semi-autocratic countries, and variations of governmental responses in different domestic and external contexts need to be explored further. This book is a contribution to fill this gap as well.

AN INTRODUCTION TO THE CASES

Mexico and the 1994-1995 Peso Crisis

Mexico gained its independence from Spain in 1821. Mexican society was composed through a process of "racial mixing" of Spanish and indigenous Indian communities during the colonial period. For the first fifty years of its independence, the Mexican economy was stagnant and politics were unstable as forty-five administrations came and went. During the mid-1840's Mexico lost about half of its territories to the United States. Mexican history marked another period with Porfirio Díaz's dictatorship, known as *Porfiriato* (1875-1911). During this period, although a considerable industrial development was achieved, the majority of the population did not benefit much from this economic development, and they were excluded from political participation. This "unfair" political and economic system generated a series of grievances among workers and peasants, and incited the "first great social revolution of the twentieth century" in 1910.[7] The revolution had multiple actors with different goals. As a result, the revolution was followed by a civil war, which lasted until 1919. Nonetheless, the revolution and the subsequent civil war gave birth to the contemporary Mexican state. You may see the details of Mexico's historical background in Appendix A.

Challenges to the revolution and political instabilities in the 1920s were resolved in 1929 with the leadership of Plutarco Elías Calles (1929-1934), who created a new political body, the National Revolutionary Party, PNR,[8] which later became the PMR,[9] and was the precursor of today's Institutional Revolutionary Party, PRI.[10] Calles was able to bring competing interests under the PNR and to establish a set of formalized rules to govern the political game. The PNR was pragmatically designed to play the role of a broker among different segments of the revolutionary elite and to constrain the nature of opposing demands. These initial legal, institutional, and political developments have shaped Mexican political life up to today. The PNR/PRI ruled the country until 2000. The political system has been based on a massive concentration of power in the presidency with a prohibition of reelection for presidents. Presidents through the bureaucratic apparatus have had dominance over both the state and the party, and the state-party network has dominated the society.[11]

The Mexican revolution represented a coalition of interest groups and produced an ideology that held the government responsible for social justice. Influenced by the revolutionary ideology, Mexico's political economy evolved toward a "corporatist system" of interest representation. In the 1990s, the Mexican regime has been given different names by different people, such as a "one-party-democracy," "selective democracy," "presidentially centered" system, and authoritarian regime.[12] Nonetheless, the Mexican system has been politically stable from the late 1920s to the early 1990s. Political stability in Mexico provided the country with a macroeconomic context that was conducive for economic growth. Its location next to the U.S. also indirectly supported the regime by providing economic relief in the form of investment and emigration.[13]

From the 1940s to the early 1980s Mexico had a mixed economy and followed Import Substitution Industrialization (ISI) strategies. Mexican economic growth was both higher than the world average and relatively stable until the 1970s. The ISI model faced new challenges in the 1970s. During the last year of presidents Luis Echeverría (1970-1976) and José López Portillo (1976-1982), Mexico had a devaluation of the peso and an economic collapse. During the President Miquel de la Madrid (1982-1988) term, Mexico was burdened with huge foreign debt and the country's balance of payments was increasingly deteriorating. As a result, Mexico faced a deep economic crisis in 1982, had high inflation throughout the 1980s (159 percent in 1987) and another devaluation of the peso in 1988. The financial/economic crisis of the 1980s forced Mexican governments to gradually change their mixed economy of the ISI with a "neoliberal," market-oriented approach through structural adjustment programs in the late 1980s and 1990s, which aimed at liberalization, privatization, and deregulation.[14]

In the late 1980s, the political legitimacy of the regime was historically low, mostly due to economic decline and widespread corruption. By 1988, the PRI's hegemony was crumbling. In the July 6, 1988 presidential elections, the PRI had its worst performance, and won the elections with barely over 50 percent of the vote. The PRI's presidential candidate Carlos Salinas de Gortari was inaugurated on December 1, 1988. Salinas broadened the neoliberal economic policies of the preceding administration in the mid-1980s, and adopted a new anti-inflation policy. In the early 1990s, Salinas' economic policy was paying off. The Mexican economy grew on average by 3.0 percent between 1989 and

1994, and it regained the confidence of international capital by the 1990s. As a result Mexico received huge capital inflows until mid-1994.

The implementation of NAFTA on January 1, 1994 further advanced Mexico's economy in a neoliberal direction and opened the economy to the forces of global capitalism. Subsequently, Mexico has become a member of the Organization for Economic Cooperation and Development, the OECD, and the Asian-Pacific Economic Cooperation (APEC).[15] According to Loser and Williams (1997), Mexico's openness and integration into international financial markets made it more vulnerable to a reversal in market sentiments.[16] The opening of the Mexican economy and the capital inflows increased Mexico's economic interdependence with the world economy, in particular with that of the United States.

Until mid-1994, Salinas' neoliberal economic reforms seemed to be very successful and were continuously praised by the media, financial experts, academics and international financial institutions, specifically the IMF and the World Bank.[17] As Chapter III illustrates, the Mexican economy seemed to be sound until mid-1994. Inflation was low, fiscal deficits were eliminated, and the official debt was reduced to half.[18] These successes in the economic front erased the misgivings about the legitimacy of Salinas' election in 1988, and provided Salinas and the PRI with an election victory in the nationwide congressional elections in 1991. Although Mexico's economic growth slowed down in 1993 and 1994, Salinas' popularity was high, and the political stability of the regime no longer seemed fragile until late 1994. Weintraub (2000) asserts that "Salinas was widely admired, both inside Mexico and abroad, for his political and economic mastery during his initial five years, and this turned to contempt as his final year progressed. This deepened into outright hatred when the peso was devalued barely three weeks after his successor, Ernesto Zedillo, was inaugurated as president."[19]

The devaluation of the Mexican peso on December 20, 1994 shocked Mexican and international financial markets and evolved into a broader financial crunch that was felt in and out of Mexico. By March 1995, the peso lost 50 percent of its value against the dollar, and Salina's major success, the low inflation rate, was replaced by 60 percent inflation.[20] This was the fourth major currency crisis in Mexico in fewer than twenty years.[21]

What caused the "unavoidable" devaluation and subsequent financial crisis, which surprised everybody? As we shall see in Chapter III, economists point to economic variables such as real exchange rate overvaluation, excessive current account deficits, fiscal and monetary expansion, and weak supervision over the banking system, as well as excessive reliance on private short-term capital flows in the aftermath of the peso crisis. However, this book argues that causes of the devaluation and financial crisis cannot be reduced to economic variables that economists point at, and the rationale of economics cannot adequately explain the Mexican government's behavior during the crisis.

The crisis developed as the result of a combination of economic/financial factors and non-economic factors, in particular those that were political, through an interaction process within the Mexican context. Guerrilla uprisings in the southern state of Chiapas, and the political assassinations before and after the 1994 presidential election intermixed with a weakened economic/financial situation in bringing the crisis. In retrospect, most experts point out that "an earlier and large-scale devaluation would have been a much wiser course."[22] However, again, multiple non-economic factors prevented Mexican authorities from responding effectively to market signals and negative economic trends. Chapter IV will explain why.

Malaysia and the 1997-1998 Asian Financial Crisis

Malaysia gained its independence from Britain in 1957. The country inherited an ethnically divided society. Until the British colonization, the Malaysian territory consisted of indigenous *bumiputera*[23] (sons/daughters of the soil). The British brought Tamil laborers (Indians) from southern India to work in the cultivation of rubber tree plantations, and Chinese to mine the tin in Malaysia. By 1900, Chinese made up one third of the total population, and Indians 10 percent on the Malaysian peninsula.[24] In today's Malaysia, 57.8 percent of the total population, which is about 22 million, is *bumiputera* (8.8 of which are non-Malay). Chinese make up 24.9 percent, Indians are 7 percent and others are 3.1 percent of the total. Resident aliens, made up mostly of Indonesian immigrant workers, comprise a significant 7.2 percent of the total population.[25]

Malaysia's contemporary political system and its institutions were shaped during the period of independence. They evolved to today with some changes. Following the Second World War Malay leaders formed the United Malay National Organization, i.e. today's UMNO, in order to seek an independent Malaya. The Alliance Party, a coalition of three ethnic parties—UMNO, MCA (today's the Malaysian Chinese Association, established by the Chinese), and MIC (today's the Malaysian Indian Congress, established by the Indians)— won the first elections with an overwhelming majority in 1955. This coalition negotiated Malaya's independence in 1957, maintained its unity after the independence, and won the elections held in 1959, 1964 and 1969 as well.[26]

In 1962, Malaya became Malaysia with the cooperation of Singapore, Sarawak, and North Borneo (today's Sabah). Singapore became a separate state in 1965. The Malaysian federation faced its first and maybe biggest challenge in 1969 when ethnic riots broke out on May 13, 1969 (three days after the election), as a result of widespread dissatisfaction with the government among the ethnic groups, in particular Malays. The riots showed the vulnerability of the Malaysian multi-racial unity that had been believed to prevail, and ended the Alliance among the three ethnic parties.[27] By 1974, the UMNO, under Abdul Razak's leadership, was able to bring its coalition partners the MCA and MIC back in order to establish a coalition called the National Front, *Barisan Nasional* (BN) along with other smaller parties. In 1974, the BN (the former Alliance) came in power again, and has not lost any election so far. The UMNO and its leaders have been playing the major role in the coalition.[28] You may see the details of these historical developments in Appendix B.

Ethnic/communal politics has been the major ingredient in Malaysia's political life. The ethnic division has been "the predominant factor shaping political alignments, determining the structure and roles of institutions, and defining the basic priorities of public policy."[29] Economic policies were also affected by ethnic concerns. The New Economic Policy (NEP) was adopted to bring equality between Malays and other ethnic groups in 1974.[30] Malaysian economic development and the subsequent expanding economic pie enabled all the ethnic communities to improve their standard of living. This provided the BN with a "performance legitimization" and helped the coalition leaders in their manipulation of politics and policies with considerable public support.[31] Each Prime Minister developed his own technique and leadership style in creating and managing inter-ethnic coalitions and the bonds among them.[32] For the last two decades, Malaysia's most powerful political figure has been the Prime Minister and the UMNO leader Mohamad Mahathir.[33] Since he came to power in 1981, Mahathir has been an economic modernizer and "an ideologue of the state-sponsored constructive protection."[34] Over the years, he articulated an anti-British and an anti-Western ideology, which is often referred to as *Mahathirism*. Mahathir had a vision of transforming Malaysia into a newly industrialized country, NIC, under genuine *bumiputera* capitalist entrepreneurship.[35]

As we shall see in Chapter V, Malaysia was one of the fastest growing countries in South East Asia prior to the Asian financial crisis. However, democratic norms and principles declined during the Mahathir years. Overtime, Malaysia became a country similar to its Asian counterparts, where governmental economic tutelage, a capitalist economy, and an authoritarian government existed together.[36] Although formal institutions of democracy have always existed, the Malaysian political system has essentially been authoritarian due to extensive restrictions on civil liberties and opposition. Mahathir denied the necessity to advance toward a Western model of liberal democracy and defended an Asian type of democracy, in which the Malaysian regime would fit.[37]

The Asian financial crisis started in Thailand on July 2, 1997, when the Bank of Thailand announced that it would no longer defend the peg system. By December 1997, the crisis engulfed the Philippines, Malaysia, Indonesia and Korea. The Philippine peso was the first to come under serious attack, and other regional currencies, including the Indonesian rupiah, the Malaysian ringgit, and the Korean won, followed the peso. These attacks forced these countries to devalue their currencies, and the devaluation triggered a disastrous financial crisis, the implications of which were felt around the globe, in particular in Japan. The World Bank, in a 1993 research report, *The East Asian Miracle*, praised "the miraculous economic growth" of the regional countries for their prudent macroeconomic management, and a unique combination of market and government-led policies.[38] The crisis came as a surprise and halted this "miraculous economic growth" of the regional countries. Almost a half-century of economic progress came to a crashing halt with the crisis.

As Chapter V demonstrates, economists pointed to economic variables such as overvaluation of the real exchange rate, chronic current account imbalances, rapid build-up of mobile capital in relations to the level of international reserves, worsened savings-investment gaps, and soaring indebtedness, as the causes of the crisis. In Malaysia, the economy was overheated and the health of the financial system was deteriorated. Domestic loan advances as a proportion of GDP rose beyond sustainable levels by the mid-1990s.[39] As Chapters V and VI explain, economic explanations of the Asian financial crisis in the region and in Malaysia are not sufficient, since they are inclined to ignore the non-economic sources of economic vulnerabilities. The collapse of the Thai baht was contagious, and these countries, including Malaysia, had some economic weaknesses. However, the economic weaknesses and the Thai "trigger" do not adequately explain the occurrence of the financial crisis and the regional governments' responses to it, as argued in Chapters V and VI. Sources of economic weaknesses are not purely economic but also political, legal/institutional, and societal. These non-economic factors along with economic ones affect investors' perception of countries and their behavior as well as policy behaviors of governments. Economic explanations cannot explain the Malaysian government's policy behavior, which was quite different than that of the regional countries. Unlike other regional countries PM Mahathir rejected an IMF bailout package and its policy prescriptions, used domestic resources in order to overcome the crisis situation, and brought capital control. Chapter VI explains why.

METHODOLOGY

This inquiry does not build on a theory, and aims to neither verify a theory, nor test hypotheses. Rather, it aims at demonstrating, assessing, and explaining significant roles that non-economic factors play in bringing a financial crisis and in shaping governmental response policies along with economic factors. It illustrates how the non-economic factors interplay with economic variables and affect the behaviors of market participants and responses of governments with two cases. It also attempts to explain the causal mechanism that exists between non-economic factors and a financial crisis as well as governmental responses, in the light of relevant literature, and offers an explanatory framework that incorporates economic explanations with the analysis of non-economic factors. Based on the empirical evidence provided by two cases, it reaches "suggestive" conclusions. For its purposes, this inquiry uses a comparative methodology and case study approach that requires an in-depth analysis of each case. Case studies and similar comparative methodology are used in many earlier studies.

As Charles Tilly in his 1984 book, *Big Structures, Large Processes, and Huge Comparisons*, indicates, there are four different types of comparisons. One is the "universalizing" comparison, which identifies common properties among all instances of a phenomenon. The second type is the "individualizing" comparison, in which a researcher compares the specific instances of a given phenomenon by contrasting cases/instances, in order to grasp the peculiarities of each case. The third type is the "variation-finding" comparison, in which a researcher studies the systematic differences among cases/ instances in order to establish a principle of variation in the character or intensity of a phenomenon. The fourth type of comparison is the "encompassing" one, such as Wallerstein's brand of world system analysis, in which researchers place different instances at various locations within the same system, and explain the system with the characteristics of the instances as a function of their varying relationships. Tilly adds that comparative studies are usually not purely universalizing, individualizing, variation finding, or encompassing, but are combinations of all of these.[40]

The cases represent different external and domestic contexts, as well as some similarities, such as the semi-autocratic governments that both Mexico and Malaysia had during their financial crises. The differences between the cases are useful in order to explain how dissimilar contexts of a financial crisis and governmental policy making affect the development of financial crises and policy responses to them. In particular, the cases are useful for demonstrating what difference the contrasts in the external involvement of each case make. As Tilly indicates, attempting to show that the environment/context shapes the policy responses of each country naturally leads to the individualizing comparison. Therefore, this research uses individualizing comparisons combined with a degree of variation-finding comparisons in explaining the development of the financial crises and governmental response policies of each country within its domestic and external contexts.

Tilly is not alone in legitimizing "individualizing" comparisons as a worthwhile social scientific endeavor. David Collier, based on Arend Lijphart's 1971 article, lists five types of case studies, one of which is hypothesis generating case studies along with analytical, interpretative, theory confirming, and deviant case studies. He also asserts that comparative studies may aim at "the examination of two or more cases in order to highlight how different they are, thus establishing a framework for interpreting how parallel processes of change are played out in different ways in different contexts. This contrast of contexts is central [for this type of comparison]."[41] Ragin asserts that the case-oriented approach examines the cases as wholes, "which means that causal significance of an event or structure depends on the context,"[42] and on other features of the case. Comparativists in this tradition compare how different conditions or causes fit together in one setting and contrast that with how they fit together in another setting.

Individualizing case studies are fruitful in several ways. They are essential for insightful descriptions of complex events, such as governmental responses to financial crises within complex domestic and external contexts, and good explanations depend on good descriptions and vice versa.[43] Another advantage of case studies is the development of good causal hypotheses as complements to good descriptions. Moreover, case studies encourage and facilitate theoretical innovations and generalizations.[44] Nonetheless, comparative case studies must be conducted in a systematic way for description and explanation. For example, framing a case study around an explanatory question could lead to a more focused and relevant description, explanation and comparison.[45]

This inquiry proceeds in accordance with these methodological concerns and recommendations. The book research is constructed around two questions: how financial crises develop and how governments shape their response policies. It first investigates in what ways and why economics cannot offer adequate answers to these questions. Then, the book closely examines the cases in order to answer these questions and find out which non-economic factors played significant roles along with economic variables in bringing financial crises and in shaping government response policies in Mexico and Malaysia. Then, it discusses how different non-economic factors played different roles in the Mexican and Malaysian contexts, and assesses the relative impact of economic versus non-economic factors and external versus domestic factors to a certain extent in these countries' different contexts. The fact is that not only the cases but also the financial crises that this book examines are different. However, this fact does not adversely affect the research, since the questions this book asks apply to both cases and financial crises.

SOURCES

As mentioned earlier, there is plenty of literature on financial crises, although the amount of literature that deals with similar topics of this inquiry is limited. As the literature review in the upcoming chapter reveals, the literature both on the Mexican peso crisis of 1994-1995 and the Asian financial crisis of 1997-1998 is abundant. This study used mostly firsthand literature for the discussion of economic crisis models and explanations of these crises in the subsequent chapters. For the case studies, this inquiry resorted to multiple resources. Along with library resources such as books, journals, and other printed materials, electronic sources such as Lexis-nexis and internet sources, publications of the IMF and the World Bank, annual and special reports, newsletters from regional news agencies, regional newspapers and magazines that publish in English as well as U.S. newspapers and magazines are used. The Internet also made available some additional information sources such as the web pages of the central banks of Mexico and Malaysia as well as other governmental and international institutions. The case narratives and explanations are based on primary and reliable sources as much as possible.

Availability of multiple information sources enabled this inquiry to uncover how the financial crisis developed in each case country, what were the relationships between response policies and their economic and non-economic causes, and how the various initial conditions were translated into certain outcomes. By resorting to multiple sources of information, it was possible to cross-check and therefore to verify observations as well as claims based on those observations. Qualitative descriptions of case studies are supported with quantitative data to the extent of their availability.

NOTES

---

1. Paul R. Krugman,"Introduction," in *Currency Crises* (Chicago and London: The University of Chicago Press, 2000), 1.

2. Alan S. Blinder, "Eight Steps to *New* Financial Order," *Foreign Affairs* 78, No. 5 (September /October 1999), 50.

3. Baryy Eichengreen and Richard Portes, "The Anatomy of Financial Crisis," in *Threats to International Financial Stability* (New York & Cambridge: Cambridge University Press, 1987), 10.

4. Krugman, "Introduction," 2, 4.

5. Udaibir S. Das, Plamen Iossifow, Richord Podpiera, and Dmitriy Rozhkov, "Quality of Financial Policies and Financial System Stress," *IMF Working Paper* WP/05/173 (August 2005), 5-6.

6. See Peter Dombrowski, "Haute Finance and High Theory: Recent Scholarship on Global Financial Relations," *Mershon International Studies Review* 42 (1998), 1-28 for a broader review of the literature on global finance.

7. Miguel Ángel Centeno, *Democracy within Reason: Technocratic Revolution in Mexico,* 2nd ed. (University Park, PA: The Pennsylvania State University Press, 1997), 6.

8. *Partido Nacional Revolucionario.*

9. *Partido de la Mexicana Revolución.*

10. *Partido Revolucionario Institucional.*

11. Centeno, *Democracy within Reason,* 7-8; Stephen D. Morris, *Political Reformism in Mexico: An Overview of Contemporary Mexican Politics* (Boulder and London: Lynne Rienner Publishers, 1995), 17, 18.

12. Dan A. Cothran, *Political Stability and Democracy in Mexico: The "Perfect Dictatorship?"* (London, Westview, Connecticut: Praeger, 1994), 233.

13. Ibid.

14. Manual Pastor Jr.,"Pesos, Policies, and Predictions: Why the Crisis, Why the Surprise, and Why the Recovery?" in *The Post-NAFTA Political Economy: Mexico and the Western Hemisphere* (University Park, PA: The Pennsylvania State University Press, 1998), 121, 122; Nora Lusting, *Mexico: The Remaking of an Economy* (Washington, D.C. Brookings Institution Press, 1992), 1; David M. Gould, "Mexico's Crisis: Looking Back to Assess the Future," in *Changing Structure of Mexico: Political, Social, and Economic Prospects* (New York and London: M.E. Sharpe, 1996), 17-38, 38.

15. Sidney Weintraub, "Mexico's Foreign Economic Policy: From Admiration to Disappointment," *Changing Structure of Mexico: Political, Social, and Economic Prospects* (New York & London: M.E. Sharpe, 1996), 43; Jonathan Heath, *Mexico and the Sexenio Curse: Presidential Successions and Economic Crisis in Modern Mexico* (Washington, DC: The CSIS Press, 1999), 35; Centeno, *Democracy within Reason,*16, 17; Jorge I. Domínguez, "The Transformation of Mexico's Electoral and Party System, 1988-1997: An Introduction," in *Toward Mexico's Democratization: Parties Campaigns, Elections, and Public Opinion* (New York and London: Routledge,1999), 4, 206-208; Lusting, *Mexico: The Remaking of an Economy,* 2; Al I. Pérez, "Free Trade with Mexico and U.S. National Security," in *Mexico Faces the 21st Century,* (Westport, CT: Greenwood Press, 1995), 119.

16. Claudio M. Loser and Ewart S. Williams, "The Mexican Crisis and Its Aftermath: An IMF Perspective," in *Mexico 1994: Anatomy of an Emerging-Market Crash* (Washington, DC: Carnegie Endowment for International Peace, 1997), 268.

17. Sebastian Edwards, "Bad Luck or Bad Policies? An Economic Analysis of the Crisis," in *Mexico 1994: Anatomy of an Emerging-Market Crash* (Washington, DC: Carnegie Endowment for International Peace, 1997), 99.

18. Robert L. Bartley, "The Peso Folklórico: Dancing Away From Monetary Stability," in *Mexico 1994: Anatomy of an Emerging-Market Crash* (Washington, DC:Carnegie Endowment for International Peace, 1997), 147.

19. Sidney Weintraub, *Financial Decision-Making in Mexico: To Bet a Nation* (Pittsburgh, PA: University of Pittsburgh Press, 2000), 31.

20. Gould, "Mexico's Crisis: Looking Back to Assess the Future,"16.

21. Previous three devaluations took place in 1976, 1982, and 1988. Bartley, "The Peso Folklórico: Dancing Away From Monetary Stability," 141.

22. Peter H. Smith, "Political Dimensions of the Peso Crisis," in *Mexico 1994: Anatomy of an Emerging-Market Crash* (Washington, DC: Carnegie Endowment for International Peace, 1997), 39.

23. The term *bumiputera* does not refer to one ethnic group, but refers to Malays and other indigenous people. In today's Malaysia, the *bumiputera* segment of Malaysian society consists of dominantly Malay Muslims, but also includes those non-Malay ethnic groups in Sarawak and Sabah. See Francis Kok-Wah Loh, "State-Societal Relations in a Rapidly Growing Economy: the Case of Malaysia, 1970-1997," in *Economic Liberalization, Democratization and Civil Society in the Developing World* (New York: St. Martin's Press, Inc., 2000), 65.

24. Jomo K.S., *Growth and Structural Change in the Malaysian Economy* (New York: St. Martin's Press, 1990), 2; Steven Schlossstein, *Asia's New Little Dragons: the Dynamic Emergence of Indonesia, Thailand, and Malaysia* (Chicago: Contemporary Books, 1991), 224; Rajah Rasiah, "Class, Ethnicity and Economic Development in Malaysia," in t*he Political Economy of the South-East Asia: An Introduction* (Melbourne: Oxford University Press, 1997), 123.

25. Subramaniam S. Pillay, "The Malaysian Model: Governance, Economic Management and the Future of the Development State," in *the East Asian Development Model: Economic Growth, Institutional Failure and the Aftermath of the Crisis* (The U.K.: Macmillan Press Ltd. and the U.S.: St. Martin's Press, Llc., 2000), 204, 205; Abdul Rahman Embong,"Pluralism in Post-Colonial Malaysia," in *the Politics of Multiculturalism: Pluralism and Citizenship in Malaysia, Singapore, and Indonesia* (Honolulu: University of Hawai'i Press, 2001), 59.

26. Schlossstein, *Asia's New Little Dragons . . .* , 224-228; Pillay, "The Malaysian Model . . . ," 205-206.

27. Edmund Terence Gomez and Jomo K.S., *Malaysia's Political Economy: Politics, Patronage and Profits*, Updated ed. (New York & Cambridge: Cambridge University Press, 1999), 21, 22; R.S. Milne and Diane K. Mauzy, *Malaysian Politics under Mahathir* (London and New York: Routledge, 1999), 21; Pillay, "The Malaysian Model . . . ," 206.

28. Schlossstein, *Asia's New Little Dragons . . .* , 224-28; Pillay, "The Malaysian Model . . . ," 206.

29. Gordon P. Means, *Malaysian Politics: The Second Generation* (Singapore: Oxford University Press, 1991), 310.

30. Milne and Mauzy, *Malaysian Politics under Mahathir*, 21.

31. Means, *Malaysian Politics: The Second Generation*, 275, 279.

32. Ibid., p.284.

33. Schlossstein, *Asia's New Little Dragons . . .* , 229.

34. Khoo Boo Teik, *Paradoxes of Mahathirism: An Intellectual Biograph of Mahathir Mohamad* (Kuala Lumpur: Oxford University Press, 1995), 9.

35. Jomo K.S., *Growth and Structural Change in the Malaysian Economy*, 201; Teik, *Paradoxes of Mahathirism: An Intellectual Biograph of Mahathir Mohamad*, 337-338.

36. Schlossstein, *Asia's New Little Dragons . . .* , 6.

37. See Ibid.,; Frances Loh Kok Wah and Joel S. Kahn, "Introduction: Fragmented Vision," in *Fragmented Vision: Culture and Politics in Contemporary Malaysia* (Honolulu: University of Hawaii Press, 1992), 4; Kok-Wah Loh, "State-Societal Relations in a Rapidly Growing Economy: the Case of Malaysia, 1970-1997," 84-85; Edmund Terence Gomez and Jomo K.S., *Malaysia's Political Economy: Politics, Patronage and Profits* (New York & Cambridge: Cambridge University Press, 1997), 121; Milne and Mauzy, *Malaysian Politics under Mahathir*, 2, 3.

38. Callum Henderson, *Asia Falling: Making Sense of the Asian Crisis and Its Aftermath* (New York: McGraw Hill, 1998), xv, 2.

39. Prema-chandra Athukorala, *Crisis and Recovery in Malaysia: The Role of Capital Controls* (Cheltenham, UK and Northampton, MA: Edward Elgar, 2001), 58, 59; *Financial Times* (Special Report-Asia in Crisis), January 13, 1998, 08.

40. Charles Tilly, *Big Structures, Large Processes, and Huge Comparisons* (New York: Russell Sage Foundation, 1984).

41. David Collier, "The Comparative Politics," In *Political Science: The State of the Discipline II* (Washington, DC: APSA, 1993), 108.

42. Charles C. Ragin, *The Comparative Method: Moving Beyond Qualitative and Quantitative Strategies* (Berkeley, Los Angeles, and London: University of California Press, 1987), xiii.

43. Gary King, Robert O. Keohane, and Sidney Verba, *Designing Social Inquiry: Scientific Inference in Qualitative Research* (Princeton, NJ: Princeton University Press, 1994), 44.

44. Anthony M. Orum, Joe R. Feagin, and Gideon Sjoberg, "Introduction: The Nature of the Case Study," in *A Case for Case Study* (Chapel Hill and London: University of North Carolina Press, 1991), 2.

45. King, Keohane, and Verba, *Designing Social Inquiry . . .* , 45.

CHAPTER II: THE ECONOMIC EXPLANATIONS OF FINANCIAL CRISES AND OF GOVERNMENTAL RESPONSES

HOW DID A FINANCIAL /CURRENCY CRISIS OCCUR IN THE 1990S?

Mexico, as a result of market-oriented economic reforms introduced by President Salinas' administration, 1988-1994, and its entry into NAFTA, attracted large capital inflows in the 1990s. Despite the substantial success of the economic reforms, the Mexican Peso crisis of 1994-1995 occurred in the middle of this resurgence of international capital flows in the 1990s. Economists pointed to overvaluation of the Mexican peso, a high current account deficit (over 7 percent of Mexico's GDP in 1994), and increasing non-performing loans of the weak banking system associated with inadequate supervision, as some possible underlying causes of the crisis. In addition, 1994 was an election year and an uprising in Chiapas (southern Mexico) along with some political turmoil and political assassinations took place. These economic and political factors together caused investors to panic and created the Peso crisis of 1994-1995, which was not expected by many. Mexico was able to overcome the crisis only with the US-backed IMF rescue package of over $50 billion.

Similarly, in the 1990s Southeast and East Asian countries also received large capital flows and the Asian financial crisis came as a big surprise as it occurred in a part of the world that inspired success stories about the economic "miracles," or "East Asian miracles." However, things suddenly went wrong in the summer of 1997. In these countries, governments either had small fiscal deficits or surpluses, inflation was low, trade policies were outward-oriented, and private firms (and not governments) owned most of the foreign debt. Some underlying causes as proposed by economists include: an increasing number of riskier investments and rising defaults on loans due to weak banking supervisions and the lending boom, overvalued currencies and a slowdown in the growth of their exports, and high current account deficits, especially in Thailand (about 8 percent of GDP in 1996). The Asian Financial crisis started when the Thai government failed to defend its currency, the baht, and allowed it to depreciate in the beginning of July 1997.[1] In a short time, the crisis spread to the other Asian countries, including Malaysia. These countries also received large amounts of the IMF-backed bailout packages, with the exception of Malaysia, in order to overcome the crisis.

How did these crises unfold? How do similar crises unfold? This section introduces readers to some features of financial/currency crises before exploring the crisis models in the next section.

Financial/currency crises or balance of payment crises usually occur in countries with a fixed exchange rate system or an exchange rate system away from the floating system, such as managed peg, crawling peg, or hard peg (currency board) systems. Governments usually commit themselves to a currency peg as part of economic programs aiming at some long-term economic goals, such as reducing inflation. In order to keep the predetermined fixed exchange rate system of a country, the Central Bank (CB) either has to buy foreign assets in order to expand the money supply, or has to sell foreign assets in order to contract the money supply. If, for example, there is a growth in the money demand due to output expansion, and thus interest rates rise and the currency appreciates, the CB buys foreign assets and expands the money supply. When the money supply increases, interest rates fall back to their original levels, and exchange rates hold at the fixed level. If the demand for money shrinks in the country, the CB sells foreign assets and reduces the money supply in order to keep the interest rates as well as the exchange rates at their original levels. As a result, the CB's monetary policy becomes dependent on the goal of maintaining the fixed exchange rate, and cannot be used for domestic purposes, such as to fight unemployment. When a government commits itself to a pegged exchange rate, it implicitly accepts to pay some short-term prices, such as a lower level of employment, possibly a loss of competitiveness in the international markets, and a recession.[2]

A balance of payments or devaluation crisis unfolds when a market participant's expectation about the future exchange rate changes with a belief that the CB could not or would not maintain the fixed rate due to reasons such as its declining foreign reserves, currency appreciation and current account deficits, or increasing unemployment. The key element in all currency crises is that investors flee the pegged currency due to their fear that the government might decide to devalue it for the aforementioned reasons. Ironically, much of the pressure for such devaluation comes from these capital flights.[3]

In normal times, ignoring the risks and liquidity problems associated with investments as well as the purchase of foreign assets, the following conditions must hold in foreign exchange markets. According to the interest parity condition, "the foreign exchange market is in equilibrium when deposits of all currencies offer the same expected rate of return"[4]

In the short run "an increase in a country's money supply causes its currency to depreciate in the foreign exchange market . . . and a reduction in a country's money supply causes its currency to appreciate in the foreign exchange market."[5] Let us assume that there is an increase in the current account deficit of a country due to an appreciation in the real exchange rates or a decline in the country's exports and increase in its imports. The growing current account deficit after a certain level (a deficit above 5% of GDP is usually considered high by economists) will create an expectation of devaluation in the foreign exchange markets.

This expectation shift will cause an increase of expected domestic currency return on foreign currency deposits. As long as interest rates stay below the new expected return on foreign assets, speculators/investors will shift their investments from domestic assets to foreign assets, and pull their short-term or portfolio capital from the country. In this situation, the CB must sell its foreign reserves in order to keep the fixed exchange rate at the same level. However, this action by the CB will shrink the domestic money supply and raise the interest rates. As speculators continue to buy foreign assets, the CB will face a sharp fall in its reserves and a rise in home interest rates above the world interest rates. This reserve loss will increase the devaluation expectation and cause further capital outflows, eventually creating a balance of payment crisis. In sum, when there is not enough private capital to offset a current account deficit, the CB reserves will decline, and this decline will create devaluation expectations, which in turn cause speculative attacks and further reduce CB reserves. As the CB's foreign reserves become too low to defend the fixed exchange rate, speculators may further attack the country's currency by borrowing in-home currency and buying foreign assets with an expectation that the home currency will be devalued. Eventually, the CB will be forced to devalue its currency, maybe by a larger amount than planned.[6]

Most economists are likely to agree broadly on how a financial/currency crisis unfolds. However, not only the impact of non-economic factors on the development of financial crises has been ignored, but also the economic causes and consequences of financial crises have long been disputed among economists. More specifically, one disputed issue is which or what kinds of domestic and international macroeconomic weaknesses cause a shift in expectations of speculators/investors and start the mechanism described above? How long and to what extent would a country's central bank or monetary authorities defend the currency and at what point would they decide to devalue it? In addition, how governments behave and shape their policy responses during financial crises has not been adequately addressed.

The next section explores the first and second-generation crisis models that preceded the cases under consideration in terms of causes and consequences of financial crises and government behavior. The causes of financial crises according to these models, how they conceive government behavior and to what extent they consider non-economic factors in explaining financial crises are questioned. The discussion here will be utilized in the upcoming chapters in investigating the shortcomings of economic crisis models in explaining and predicting the Mexican peso crisis and the Asian financial crises as well as in assessing the Mexican and the Malaysian governments' policy behaviors. Although this chapter only discusses first and second generation crisis models, the subsequent chapters survey particular economic explanations of the financial crises, as the cases are examined. The last chapter critiques the recent economic crisis explanations and models (which some analysts refer to as third and fourth-generation crisis models) in terms of their inadequacy in incorporating the impact of non-economic factors into their analyses and explanations. Therefore, you may expect more economic discussion throughout the book.

CRISIS MODELS THAT PRECEDED THE MEXICAN PESO CRISIS AND THE ASIAN FINANCIAL CRISIS

Causes and Consequences of Financial Crises According to the First and Second-generation Crisis Models

The financial and banking crises in the 1970s, 1980s and the 1990s in different parts of the world have created a large literature on financial crises. Crisis models or explanations in the literature would agree on how a crisis unfolds in a similar way and that expectation of devaluation make devaluation more likely. However, despite these two decades of research, causes and consequences of financial crises, or what determines whether and when a currency or banking crisis occurs have not been resolved yet or have required a fresh look after each crisis.[7] In addition, neither has the impact of non-economic factors on the development of financial crises, nor the causes and consequences of government behavior during a financial crisis been addressed enough.

In the terminology of Eichengreen, Rose, and Wyplosz (1996), first-generation crisis models, inspired by the Latin American style currency crisis of the 1970s, came in the late 1970s. These early models, as exemplified by Krugman (1979) and Flood and Garber (1984), viewed "a central bank's efforts to peg an exchange rate using reserves as being similar to a commodity agency's efforts to peg a resource price using its stockpile. In each case, the resource price or exchange rate will prevail as long as there is enough stock of resources or foreign exchange to be sold. However, if there is a long run upward trend in the 'shadow price' of foreign exchange, the peg will not hold."[8] In these models, the key is the shadow price. If the shadow price exceeds the peg, rational, fully informed speculators, as they seek arbitrage, will rapidly buy out the stocks ahead of the expected crisis date, and thus quicken the occurrence of it. The channel for occurrence of a financial crisis is a mechanical one: speculation leads to depletion of foreign exchange reserves and thus forces the central bank to give up its defense of the original parity.[9] Thus, an upward trend in the shadow price of foreign exchange causes speculators to change their future expectations of devaluation, and start the mechanism described in the previous section. What causes the upward trend in the shadow price of a foreign exchange?

These models blame bad macroeconomic fundamentals and therefore poor government policies as the root cause of the crisis. The upward trend in the shadow exchange rate is due to the government's need for seigniorage, i.e. funding available to the government through printing money due to persistent deficits with an exchange rate peg and the pursuit of inconsistent policies. It is assumed that all budget deficits are financed with domestic credit in these models. Money-financed, unsustainable fiscal deficits lead to a persistent loss of international reserves and ultimately start a currency crisis. In order to prevent and/or solve a crisis situation, fiscal problems must be addressed.[10] Later, first-generation models were extended to include deviations from purchasing power parity, capital controls (as lengthening the defense of the currency peg), uncertainty about monetary and fiscal policies (as causing faster reserve depletion), and portfolio optimization by investors (as they shift their investments toward foreign assets and accelerate the losses of the central bank reserve). These extensions point to additional regularities, such as overvalued real exchange rates, higher real wages, rising relative unit labor costs, current account deficits, accelerating reserve losses, and significant policy uncertainty as indicators accompanying fiscal expansions.[11]

One of the weaknesses of these models is that they assume passive governments during a crisis, as the speculative attacks force the CB to act in a certain way. Authorities peg the exchange rate until their reserves are exhausted, and are forced to float the currency.[12] These models explain how rational financial markets respond to unsustainable macroeconomic policies but ignore the policy options available to authorities and "the ways in which marginal costs of exercising these options are balanced."[13] Since the conjectural response of governments affects the actions of the rational speculators, these models are short of illuminating the factors that generate crises and the outcomes of crises.[14] Secondly, a crisis was considered to be inevitable given the "bad" government policies, and the timing of it can be more or less predictable, although in practice it would be very hard to predict. Therefore these models are deterministic. However, they failed to predict later crises. Thirdly, these models do not see that the crisis would harm the economy, since a crisis would just reveal the weaknesses of an economy, and they do not expect a post-crisis recession. Crises are monetary events with few real consequences.[15] However, later crises did not necessarily occur due to bad fundamentals that the first generation models pointed to and usually had severe impacts on economic growth or output.

The Latin American debt crisis in 1982 and the EMS crisis of 1992-1993 depart from these models' explanations and predictions. Although currency runs were part of the story in the Latin American crisis, it was mainly about a sovereign debt crisis, and was followed by a real-side slump. The EMS crisis on the other hand was a result of a series of speculative attacks on the European currencies and seigniorage was not an issue. It was hard to claim irresponsible policies in any of the countries involved in the EMS system. In addition, there were no long-trend disequilibrium exchange rates and there was not a mechanical linkage between capital flight and abandonment of the peg, but it was simply a matter of policy choice.[16]

The way the EMS crisis occurred inspired the "second generation" crisis models, whose assumptions and predictions are different from those of the "first generation" models. There are several variants of the second-generation model, and two of them in particular are presented in the Obstfeld (1994) paper. Assuming that governments can borrow international reserves or exercise other policy options to defend exchange rates during a currency crisis, Obstfeld (1994) asks, "what factors determine a government's decision to abandon a currency peg or hang on?"[17] According to one variant of these models, "high nominal interest rates associated with devaluation expectations can force a government to devalue a currency whose peg would have been viable under another set of private expectations."[18] In this model, devaluation expectations feed into interest rates and thus weaken a government's commitment to the peg. High interest rates may affect government policy through their impact on the banking system, firms' balance sheets, or in some other ways. According to another variant of these models, governments may abandon the peg with a desire to offset shocks to competitiveness and employment. These time devaluation expectations feed into wages and competitiveness, and weaken the government position by raising unemployment. Instead, they may decide to float the peg from the predetermined fixed exchange rate to a new depreciated level. In both of these models, "crisis and realignment result from the interaction of rational private economic actors and a government that pursues well-defined policy goals."[19] In these models, causality does not flow exclusively from fundamentals to market expectations, but increases in devaluation expectations can become self-fulfilling, and interactive causality can generate multiple equilibria.[20] Arbitrary expectation shifts "can turn a fairly credible exchange-rate peg into a fragile one."[21] Thus, these models provide us with the possibilities of self-fulfilling speculation and multiple equilibria modeling. Multiple equilibria is consistent with the view that speculations can be motivated by many factors, and not necessarily and primarily with economic fundamentals. These models do not necessarily reject the relevance of economic fundamentals, but bring the nature of their fundamental relationship with speculation to our attention. In other words, first-generation and second-generation models are not mutually exclusive. A currency's vulnerability to self-validating speculation depends on the fragility generated by some economic fundamentals. However, the occurrence and timing of a crisis may not be predicted solely based on fundamentals due to self-fulfilling and multiple equilibria features of a currency crisis.[22] Any random event could trigger a shift from an unlikely devaluation situation to a very likely one in the view of markets. These kinds of shifts might be accompanied by a sharp rise in domestic interest rates and a loss in foreign reserves (which is not a factor that ultimately leads to devaluation). The question is not that the crises are a result of "fundamentals" or "purely self-fulfilling expectations," but could be a manifestation of possible multiple equilibria,[23] according to these models.

One example of the second-generation model is Ozkan and Sutherland's (1994) model of the ERM crises. In this model, a country's government commits itself to a currency peg because of some long-term economic goals. When the peg loses its credibility, investors will ask for higher interest rates in order to keep their assets in the country's currency. According to this model, there might not be any monetary and fiscal imbalances in the period preceding the crisis, and macro policies might be consistent with the maintenance of the currency peg. The government's irresponsible policies are not necessarily the root cause of a crisis, and therefore the model is not deterministic, but a crisis may occur unexpectedly. Governments have much more freedom of action in terms of deciding whether to defend the parity or abandon the defense. This model assumes that governments have the ability to defend fixed exchange rates indefinitely by raising interest rates and borrowing from outside. However, worsening domestic conditions might induce governments to abandon the peg. For example, if the peg system is associated with high and rising unemployment due to some reasons, which could originate outside of a country, a government's defense of the peg will create financial distress and worsen unemployment, and negatively affect the government's popularity. In this situation, a government may decide to focus on reducing unemployment and increasing output. Speculators anticipating the policy shift may attack the currency in advance. A government may defend the peg in the absence of a speculative attack, but might not defend in case of an attack, when the cost of defense is greater than the cost of abandoning the defense in terms of political fallout and credibility. In fact, doubts about the government's willingness to defend and speculators' belief that some other speculators are about to attack encourage an attack, and thus "self-fulfilling crises of confidence" emerge.[24]

Like first-generation models, second generation-models do not see the abandonment of the peg in a devaluation crisis as a negative shock to employment and output, since it could actually be positive. Due to macroeconomic payoff to devaluation, real economic performance should if anything improve following the devaluation, as it happened in Britain at the end of the 1992 crisis,[25] according to these models.[26]

What Should One Expect in Order to Predict a Financial Crisis According to These Crisis Models?

First-generation models are clearer than second-generation models in terms of what we should expect before the crisis. According to the first-generation models, what we should observe includes fiscal deficits and expansionary fiscal and monetary policies, overvaluation of the real exchange rate, current account deficits, higher real wages, inflation, and accelerating reserves losses along with significant policy uncertainty prior to speculations.[27] According to Eichengreen, Rose, and Wyplosz (1995), these models' predictions and explanations fit quite well with what happened in a few countries with high inflation, i.e. Mexico and Chile in the 1970s, and France and Italy in the early 1980s. As it was mentioned in the previous section, these models are short in explaining the Latin American debt crisis in 1982 and the crisis of the EMS in 1992-1993. Most of the countries affected by the EMS crisis did not have significant monetary and fiscal imbalances as Eichengreen and Wyplosz (1993) argue.[28] When it comes to the second-generation models, what we would expect before a crisis is not clear-cut. There are many possibilities in terms of what to expect before a crisis.

According to these models, financial crises need not be preceded by expansionary monetary and fiscal policies, or by the imminent depletion of reserves, even though some evidence of monetary and fiscal imbalances might be observed. What we should observe instead are rising unemployment or interest rates, or some other domestic economic developments that concern the government. However, government concerns change from one country to another, there are no objective critical points of these indicators, and speculators' anticipation of government behavior also change from one country to another. Political factors and labor market conditions are important for these models.[29] There are many different avenues for a crisis to develop and persuade optimizing governments to abandon the peg, according to these models. During the 1992-1993 EMS crisis, European countries experienced the deepening recession and rising unemployment. A speculative pressure on a country's currency would push its government to raise interest rates in order to defend the peg. In turn, this would lead to the deterioration of unemployment and the current account, and make that country more vulnerable to a devaluation crisis. Also, unemployment and interest rates may rise not only due to domestic reasons, but also due to developments in other countries. As Gerlach and Smets (1994) assert, a speculative attack that led to devaluation in one country might worsen the competitiveness of that country's trading partners and thus weaken the willingness of the governments of those countries to keep the peg. Thus, a currency crisis may develop through channels of contagion.[30] For example, the collapse of one currency may cause the collapse of some other currencies by revealing information about the weaknesses of those economies, by functioning as a wake up call, and by panicking investors. In short, there may be no evidence of budget deficits, monetary expansion, reserve losses, overvaluation, or current account deficits, but the events happening outside of a country may lead to a crisis, due to contagion effects. Thus, a speculative attack may proceed rather than follow imbalances in domestic fiscal policies and current accounts.[31]

Another possibility that could trigger a crisis is the existence of multiple equilibria in foreign exchange markets. According to the Flood and Garber (1984b) and Obstfeld (1986) models, the contingent nature of the macro-policy rule generates multiple equilibria in the foreign exchange markets. While there is nothing that precludes the maintenance of the prevailing peg, and monetary and fiscal policies are in balance, if the currency will be attacked, the monetary policy may shift toward a more expansionary direction with a lower level for the exchange rate. A collapse of one currency could change investors' expectations and shift markets from one equilibrium to another. A small shock that pushes a currency out of its zone or peg may induce traders to initiate a speculative attack. Raising interest rates in a speculative attack situation in order to defend the currency would increase unemployment rates, which in turn would further increase the speculators' expectations of devaluation. Indeed, a small increase in the unemployment rate may trigger a self-fulfilling currency crisis by making the defense of the peg more costly for the government officials. According to these models, a speculative attack that leads to a self-fulfilling currency crisis may occur for different reasons in different places, even when there are not any strong positive indicators in the macroeconomic data. A disturbance in the foreign exchange market or a successful attack in another country or devaluation in a neighboring country may serve as a focal point for coordinating speculators' actions.[32]

Table 2.1.Symptoms and Leading Economic Indicators

Symptoms	Indicators
Fiscal and Monetary Imbalances	M1 (increasing) M2 (increasing) Public Sector Fiscal Deficit (high) Central Governments' Budget Deficits (high) Public Debt (increasing) Inflation (high, or increasing) Domestic Credit (increasing)
Problems with Current Account	Current Account Deficit (high) Real Exchange Rate (overvalued) Exports (decreasing or not increasing as much as imports) Imports (increasing) Trade Balance (negative, increasing)
Problems with Finance Account	Reserves (declining) Reserve Losses (accelerating) Foreign Debt (increasing) Short-term Foreign Debt (increasing) Capital Flight (yes, possibly increasing)
Growth Slowdown and Other Governmental Concerns	GDP (declining) GDP Growth (declining) Stock Prices (declining) Real Wages (increasing) Unemployment (increasing) Domestic Real Interest Rates (increasing)

Source: Own elaboration inspired by *Currency and Banking Crises: The Early Warnings of Distress*. Graciela L. Kaminsky, IMF Working Paper, WP/99/178, December 1999.

As Kaminsky (December 1999) asserts, theory does not provide an unambiguous answer to the causes of currency crises, and/ or what economic indicators should be looked at in order to detect an upcoming crisis. As we may have witnessed from the preceding discussion, the crisis literature sometimes refers to indicators and sometimes refers to symptoms created by those indicators. Given the preceding discussion, the symptoms and indicators in the table on the previous page could be associated with the first and second-generation crisis models.

Having listed what to expect in terms of possible economic symptoms and indicators before an upcoming crisis, we can examine the cases under consideration on whether they had these symptoms and indicators, and if so to what extent. Were they sufficient to bring a financial crisis, unless some non-economic, political factors intervened? What kinds of non-economic factors contributed to the emergence of these crises? However, before we start examining the cases in the subsequent chapters, let us reconsider what are the described, assumed, or expected government behaviors according to these crisis models. Then we can discuss how far the actual Mexican and Malaysian government responses to their crises reflected these kinds of behaviors.

Government Behavior According to These Crisis Models

As we have seen, the first generation models assume that governments or monetary authorities responsible for fixing the exchange rate react passively to the monetary disruption caused by an attack. In other words, the supply of base money in the country being attacked plunges as a result of reserve losses during the attack. However, in actual experience, as Flood, Garber, and Kramer (1996) demonstrate: "the monetary base implications of the attacks are usually sterilized."[33] In addition, when governments are responding to disturbances in markets and are determining policies to handle them, they have many other political as well as economic considerations and their responses are influenced by non-economic factors, such as the legal framework in which they have to operate. According to the second-generation models, governments do not passively react to markets, but interact with them. They suggest that a crisis evolves through a complicated interaction process among the domestic financial and non-financial sectors, international investors, banks and governments.[34] Literature in this tradition opens the door to the possibility that political variables rather than economic variables might play a more critical role in speculative attacks. Left-wing governments and governments with small parliamentary majorities might be more sensitive to the unemployment rates than the right-wing governments and governments with large parliamentary majorities. Crises may occur before the elections if governments need to follow an expansionary monetary policy to enhance their chances of victory. In fact, political variables could be affected by and affect economic variables.[35] Both the market participants and governments are assumed to be acting in order to maximize their gains. Governments have to consider not only their commitments to the exchange rate and some long-term economic goals associated with it, but also other economic variables, such as unemployment and rising interest rates, and their political implications. Rational governments, worried about their popularity and reelections, may not tolerate increasing rates of unemployment, interest rates, and decreasing output after a certain level.

Although the second-generation models consider the political factors, they do so in a rather limited way. What affects a government's behavior is usually not limited to these considerations. There are multiple other factors, non-economic in their nature and stemming from a county's external and domestic-political, societal, and legal contexts, which affect how a government behaves during a crisis. Expected and unexpected political and societal events happening within a country affect not only its government's policies, but also domestic and international macroeconomic trends and perceptions and reactions of market participants, and therefore how a financial crisis develops. Neither first-generation nor second-generation models explicitly incorporate these actual and potential non-economic influences in explaining financial crises and assessing government behavior. The examination of the Mexican and the Malaysian cases in the subsequent chapters illustrates that there are multiple non-economic influences intermixing with economic variables in causing these countries' financial crises and shaping their governments' behaviors. The next two chapters examine the Mexican case and the subsequent two chapters examine the Malaysian case.

NOTES

1. Thomas A. Pugel and Peter H. Lindert, *International Economics* (New York: Irwin McGraw-Hill, 2000), 4, 607-609.

2. Paul R. Krugman and Maurice Obstfeld, *International Economics: Theory and Policy* (New York: Addison-Wesley, 2000), 500-529; Graciela L. Kaminsky, "Currency and Banking Crises: The Early Warnings of Distress," *IMF Working Paper* WP/99/178 (December 1999), 6.

3. Krugman, "Introduction," 1.

4. Krugman and Obstfeld, *International Economics: Theory and Policy,* 347.

5. Krugman and Obstfeld, *International Economics: Theory and Policy,* 376.

6. Ibid., 500-529.

7. Krugman,"Introduction," 1; Paul R. Krugman, *Crises: The Next Generation?* Draft, March 2001, http://www.stern.nyu.edu/globalmacro, (accessed July 12, 2001), 2, 3.

8. Ibid., 3; Kaminsky, "Currency and Banking Crises: The Early Warnings of Distress," 6.

9. Krugman, *Crises: The Next Generation?,* 4; Krugman,"Introduction," 2,4.

10. Krugman, *Crises: The Next Generation?,* 4.

11. See Barry Eichengreen, Andrew K. Rose, and Charles Wyplosz, "Exchange Market Mayhem: The Antecedents and Aftermath of Speculative Attacks," http://www.haas.berkeley.edu/~arose/RecRes.htm, (accessed August 12, 2001), 11, 12 for details.

12. Krugman, *Crises: The Next Generation?,* 4.

13. Maurice Obstfeld, "The Logic of Currency Crises," *NBER Working Paper* No. 4640 (February 1994), 16.

14. Ibid., p.16.

15. Krugman, *Crises: The Next Generation?,* 4; Krugman,"Introduction," 2,4,5;

and Kaminsky, "Currency and Banking Crises: The Early Warnings of Distress," 6.

16. Obstfeld, "The Logic of Currency Crises," 2,3.

17. Obstfeld, "The Logic of Currency Crises," 2, 23.

18. Ibid., p. 4.

19. Ibid., p. 2, 3, 23.

20. There is demand and supply in the foreign exchange markets. Private parties supply their dollars, and how much the central bank demands usually determines the price. Multiple equilibria refers to a market situation in which the slope of the supply curve is in general not decided, and the supply curve bends several times, creating more than one equilibrium exchange rate price. See Rodseth (2000), p. 22.

21. Obstfeld, "The Logic of Currency Crises," 4.

22. Olivier Jeanne, *Currency Crises: A Perspective on Recent Theoretical Developments*, Special Papers in International Economics No. 20 (Princeton, NJ: Princeton University Press, Department of Economics, 2000), 2-4.

23. Obstfeld, "The Logic of Currency Crises," 48, 49.

24. Krugman, *Crises: The Next Generation?*, 5-7; Krugman,"Introduction," 2, 3,5, and Eichengreen, Rose, and Wyplosz, "Exchange Market Mayhem: The Antecedents and Aftermath of Speculative Attacks," 8, 20,13,14.

25. Krugman. in *Crises: The Next Generation?*, indicates that there are reservations about this assertion in the literature since it is based on only one comparison (Britain versus France).

26. Ibid., 7; Krugman,"Introduction," 2, 3, 5.

27. Eichengreen, Rose, and Wyplosz, "Exchange Market Mayhem: The Antecedents and Aftermath of Speculative Attacks," 11.

28. Ibid., p. 12, 13.

29. Eichengreen, Rose, and Wyplosz, "Exchange Market Mayhem: The Antecedents and Aftermath of Speculative Attacks," 14.

30. There are three types of contagion explanations in the literature, all of which are compatible with the second-generation crisis models. One type, e.g. Bikhchandani, Hirshleifer, and Welch (1992), emphasizes "information cascades," in which subsequent investors acquire information from the actions of the preceding investors, and follow them. Another type of contagion explanation, e.g. Gerlach and Smets (1994), and Eichengreen et al. (1997), points to the channel of "spillover" in which a devaluation in one country due to a speculative attack causes trade and current account deficits, and a decline in reserves in its trading partners, making those countries' currencies vulnerable to a speculative attack. Rijckeghem and Weder (1999) blame bank lending as a source of spillover, as opposed to trade linkages and country characteristics. They find evidence "in favor of a common lender effect in the Mexican, Thai, and Russian crises . . . " Van Rijckeghem and Beatrice Weder, "Sources of Contagion: Finance or Trade?" *IMF Working Paper* WP/99/146 (October 1999), 1. The third type of contagion models, e.g. Masson 1998, defines the contagion as simultaneous occurrences of currency crises due to multiple equilibria and self-fulfilling speculative attacks, rather than being linked to macroeconomic fundamentals. See Allan Drazen, "Political Contagion in Currency Crises," in *Currency Crises* (Chicago and London: The University of Chicago Press, 2000), 50-52 for a summary of these explanations.

31. Eichengreen, Rose, and Wyplosz, "Exchange Market Mayhem: The Antecedents and Aftermath of Speculative Attacks," 15.

32. Eichengreen, Rose, and Wyplosz, "Exchange Market Mayhem: The Antecedents and Aftermath of Speculative Attacks," 16-21.

33. Therefore, they broaden the standard attack model to include the effect of sterilization on other markets, in particular bonds markets. They argue that a fixed exchange rate policy gets even more fragile when the monetary authorities also target the base money supply through sterilization. See Garber and Kramer (1996), p. 223, 225, 233.

34. Guillermo A. Calvo, "Balance of Payments Crises in Emerging Markets: Large Capital Inflows and Sovereign Governments," in *Currency Crises* (Chicago and London: The University of Chicago Press, 2000), 71.

35. Eichengreen, Rose, and Wyplosz, "Exchange Market Mayhem: The Antecedents and Aftermath of Speculative Attacks," 21.

CHAPTER III: THE SHORTCOMINGS OF THE ECONOMIC EXPLANATIONS: THE MEXICAN CASE

One purpose of this chapter is to question why economic crisis models that were discussed in the previous chapter were short of predicting the Mexican peso crisis. Another purpose is to survey *ex-post* economic explanations of the crisis and their perceptions of the Mexican government's policy behavior in order to demonstrate their inadequacy in integrating the impact of non-economic factors into their analyses. The chapter proposes that one major shortcoming of the economic explanations is their failure to pay enough attention to the impact of various external and domestic non-economic influences and pressures. The next chapter will identify, trace, and assess the impact of various non-economic factors in order to support this proposition.

   This chapter starts with some background information about Mexican economic developments prior to the crisis. Then, it questions why the Mexican peso crisis was not predicted and prevented. In the meantime, Mexico's macroeconomic conditions before and during the crisis are explored in light of the crisis models and relevant literature. Finally the chapter critically surveys the ex-post explanations of the peso crisis.

ECONOMIC DEVELOPMENTS PRIOR TO THE PESO CRISIS

From the 1940s to the early 1980s Mexico had a mixed economy with a strong elite consensus on the state's role in the economy. During this period, Mexican governments followed Import Substitution Industrialization (ISI) strategies, characterized by protectionism in foreign trade, state subsidies to local production, and direct foreign investment by transnational companies. Mexican economic growth was both higher than the world average and relatively stable until the 1970s. Real GDP growth in Mexico was annually 2.9 percent on average between 1930 and 1940. Starting from the 1940s, the "Mexican miracle" occurred, with an annual real GDP growth that averaged 6.9 percent between 1940-1950; 5.6 and 7.0 percents growth rates between 1950-1960 and 1960-1970 respectively; and 5.5 percent between 1970-1980, a relatively slowed growth rate.[1]

However, great inequality accompanied the high rates of growth. Large segments of the population, particularly the working class and peasants, were not getting their share of the economic growth. In 1970, the bottom 50 percent received 17 percent of national income while the top 10 percent captured 50 percent.[2] The ISI model faced new challenges in the 1970s: agricultural production stagnated, the trade deficit was increasing, and the overprotected industry reached its limits in terms of growth and productivity. Mexican governments attempted to recapture the magic of the "Mexican miracle" in the 1970s and the early 1980s by increasing government intervention in the economy through higher federal spending and a larger number of public sector firms.[3] President Luis Echeverría (1970-1976) followed expansionist policies financed by oil revenues and external borrowing in order to gain popular support, but he was challenged by previously acquiescent private sector and foreign firms, and his economic program was disrupted by the oil shock of 1973. The discovery of new massive oil deposits enabled his successor José López Portillo (1976-1982) to achieve renewed economic growth fueled by petrodollars. However, it did not last long. The increasing petrodollar revenues and the economic growth encouraged massive foreign borrowing and Mexico faced a debt crisis in 1981.[4]

In 1982, President Portillo handed only a "bankrupt country" to President Miguel de la Madrid (1982-1988). Mexico was burdened with huge foreign debt and the country's balance of payments was increasingly deteriorating. Mexico was greatly constrained in servicing or refinancing its debt due to its economic stagnation, the world's highest interest rates at that time, and the decrease of its major export revenue from oil because of falling oil prices. As a result, Mexico faced a deep economic crisis in 1982, inflation soared close to 100 percent, and inflation reached 159 percent in 1987. The pressures of repaying foreign debt worsened the public deficit, which was accompanied by inflation and capital flight. Toward the end of de la Madrid's term, the public deficit was consuming nearly a fifth of Mexico's GDP. The Mexican economy shrank during this period. It recorded an average negative growth rate of 0.15 percent from 1982 to 1988. Per capita income fell sharply in the 1980s, partly because of population growth along with the economic deterioration. Of course the situation for those at the bottom was worse. The De la Madrid administration's attempts to stabilize the markets and revive the economy did not bring any substantial results. In 1988, inflation started to decline from its 1987 peak, but the Mexican economy was still in stagnation and did not recover from the adverse effects of the 1982 crisis.[5] The ISI strategy that Mexico followed for decades fell apart in the 1980s. It cost Mexico high foreign debt, increased government deficits, and created a big state sector in the economy that was associated with favoritism and corruption. The government, as the director of the economy, commanded many different sectors of the economy including minerals in the ground (especially oil), electricity generation, steel mills, railroads, airlines, ports, basic petrochemicals, and even much of the food distribution.[6]

The financial/economic crisis of the 1980s forced Mexican governments to gradually change their mixed economy of the ISI with a "neoliberal," market-oriented approach through structural adjustment programs in the late 1980s and 1990s, which aimed at liberalization, privatization, and deregulation.[7] The opening of the economy was formally accepted when Mexico joined the GATT (General Agreements on Tariffs and Trade) in 1986, and continued through the 1990s by the gradual replacement of the ISI economic strategy with the neoliberal economic policies.[8] The neoliberal policies gradually reduced government intervention in the market, enhanced market allocation of goods and services, and opened the economy to international markets.

The President Salinas de Gortari administration (1988-1994) started more profound and wide-ranging liberal economic reforms in 1988, and adopted a new anti-inflation policy. These reforms included budget deficit reduction, comprehensive privatization and deregulation including the banking sector, transportation, and telecommunications, liberalization of foreign investment, and trade liberalization, i.e. the opening of the economy to international competition. Salinas' economic reforms "followed the script of what is known as the 'Washington consensus'"[9] with an export-oriented industrialization (EOI) emphasis in it. Public subsidies were substantially withdrawn, and a policy of low wages was adopted in order to make the Mexican exports more competitive and attract more foreign investment. In 1989, a law was passed that permitted 100 percent foreign ownership in most sectors of the economy. In December 1993, further deregulation of direct foreign investment was enacted in preparation for the start of NAFTA.[10] These economic reforms were accompanied by a stabilization program, which included a currency policy of the crawling peg with an adjustable band, replacing the exchange peg imposed in 1987, in order to bring exchange rate predictability. The band of exchange rate, wage increases, and some prices were decided through the *Pacto* mechanism—a broad social and economic agreement between the government, the private sector, and labor unions.[11]

In the early 1990s, Salinas' economic policy was paying off, and will be discussed in the upcoming section in more detail. Between 1988 and 1994, economic activity recovered sharply, GDP and private consumption rose about 30% and investment grew more than 70%, although growth during this period was uneven. Private capital flows from abroad began in the late 1980s and grew continually until late 1994. The initial success of the economic program accompanied by the signing of the NAFTA agreement created euphoria and by 1993 Mexico started to attract much more portfolio investment.[12] Mexico was recognized as a country successfully managing economic reform and adjustment. The Mexican economy regained the confidence of international capital by the 1990s, and the country received huge capital inflows. Mexico received net capital inflows of $102 billion between 1990 and 1994 as compared with Mexico's experience of net capital inflows of $15 billion between 1983 and 1989, which reflected the impact of the 1982 debt crisis. In fact, Mexico was the leader among LDCs in 1993 with $31 billion of capital inflows, which accounted for 20 percent of the net capital flows that went to all LDCs in that year.[13] As a result of this trend, Mexico's reserves increased to over $25 billion by 1994 from under $10 billion in 1990.

MACROECONOMIC INDICATORS OF MEXICO: WHY WAS THE MEXICAN PESO CRISIS NOT PREDICTED AND PREVENTED?

With the aforementioned economic trends, it did not seem that a devaluation and a subsequent financial crisis would take place in Mexico at the beginning of 1994. The classic symptoms of devaluation, such as rising inflation, large fiscal deficits, and growing official debt (which was reduced to half) were not there.[14] As it may be seen in Appendix C, the public sector's fiscal (financial) balance as a percentage of GDP declined from -5.6 in 1989 to -2.1 in 1993, and increased to -3.9 in 1994. The central government's budget deficit as a percentage of GDP declined from -5.0 in 1989 to -0.7 in 1994. Gross public debt as a percentage of GDP was under the OECD countries' average and declined steadily from 1989 to 1994. Although money markets in Mexico had been volatile throughout 1994, an OECD report at the beginning of December 1994 was optimistic about Mexico's economy—predicting a 3.8 percent GDP growth for Mexico in 1995. However, three weeks later, on December 20, 1994, international financial markets were shocked by the devaluation of the Mexican peso, which evolved into a broader financial crunch that was felt in and out of Mexico. By March 1995, the peso lost 50 percent of its value against the dollar, and Salinas' major success, the low inflation rate (7.1% in 1994), was replaced by over 50% inflation.[15] What went wrong? Was this crisis predictable given the Mexican macroeconomic indicators (presented in Appendix C)?

In fact, Mexico began 1994 with strong economic fundamentals. As mentioned earlier, the Mexican economy was growing at an average of 3 percent between 1989 and 1994 compared to an average of 0.1 percent between 1982 and 1988. 159.2 percent inflation in 1987 was brought down to 8 percent in 1993 and the public sector budget deficit of 16 percent in 1987 was almost eliminated. In addition, Mexico's economy was liberalized and opened. By 1994, about 1,000 state-held industries were privatized, tariffs were cut back, and many barriers for foreign investment had been eliminated. Moreover, the NAFTA agreement went into effect starting from January 1, 1994, and Mexico became a member of the Organization for Economic Cooperation and Development (OECD) in that year.[16]

On the negative side, although Mexico's GDP significantly grew on average 3 percent between 1989 and 1994, economic growth steadily declined from 4.5 percent in 1990 to 2.8 percent in 1992 and to only 0.6 percent in 1993.[17] It jumped back to 3.5 percent in 1994, but this was mainly due to the government's expansionary fiscal policies before the elections. Through a fiscal consolidation in the 1980s, fiscal deficits were transformed into a fiscal surplus of 1.8 percent of GDP in 1990. However, the fiscal stance deteriorated thereafter as the capital inflows mounted, and in 1994 it deteriorated to the surplus of only 0.5 % of GDP. In the meantime, the Mexican peso was overvalued about 30.2 percent, if 1994 is compared with the 1985-1989 average. International reserves substantially grew between the 1990 and 1993 period, but 1994 witnessed a drastic reversal with a loss of almost $19 billion. Although in the early 1990s almost all monetary aggregates grew quickly, domestic credit grew very rapidly in 1994, as the Mexican authorities attempted to sterilize the effects of the reserve outflow. Credit to the private sector as a share of GDP also grew rapidly, from 15.1% in 1989 to 46.3% in 1994. The ratio of M2 to GDP increased substantially in the same period as well. At the same time, the quality of bank portfolios was deteriorating as revealed after the crisis. Non-performing bank loans rose from 9% in December 1994 to 17% in September 1995.[18]

With the opening of the economy and the signing of NAFTA, Mexican exports surged, but so did Mexican imports. Mexico had massive current account deficits, as imports steadily exceeded exports during the early 1990s. CA deficits increased systematically from 1.4% of GDP in 1988 to 7.6 % in 1994, driven by a decrease in private savings, even though public savings were actually increasing and overall investment was going up slightly. Relaxation of credit constraints on domestic borrowing allowed a rise in consumption and a fall in savings, along with an increase in imports due to real peso appreciation and trade liberalization. In the early 1990s, U.S. interest rates were low, and investors were unusually willing to move their funds to Mexico and to some other developing countries in hopes of higher return. The current account deficit (and the trade deficit) was covered by this inflow of foreign capital. Thus, Mexico's balance of payments was dependent on a continuation of the inflow of foreign capital. For example, roughly $2 billion a month in foreign capital flowed into the country during the first half of 1994. From 1989 to 1994, the accumulated capital account surplus totaled $109.5 billion. However, the problem was that most of this capital came in the form of short-term speculative portfolio investments (PI) rather than longer-term foreign direct investments (FDI). PI substantially exceeded FDI from 1991 through 1993, but sharply fell in 1994, especially in the second half.[19] Although capital inflows increased Mexico's foreign exchange reserves, the Mexican economy became dependent on almost $30 billion net capital inflows per year, and therefore probably became vulnerable to shocks. The current account deficit (and the trade deficit) was covered by the inflow of foreign capital, which came mostly in the form of portfolio capital. In addition, the Mexican government did not put in place enough measures to minimize risks associated with huge capital inflows, following the bank privatization and financial liberalization in Mexico.[20] The increase of Mexico's international reserves gave the government and investors a false sense of security, even though the Mexican current account deficits widened.[21] Nonetheless, Mexico was attracting enough capital until 1994, and the current account deficit was seen as sustainable by most investors. The U.S. House of Representatives ratified NAFTA after November 17, 1993, and it was expected that Mexico would receive sufficient foreign investment in 1994 to pay for its imports and deficits. Even U.S. officials were expecting that Mexico would receive sufficient foreign investment in 1994 to pay for its imports and deficits.[22]

When we evaluate these economic trends all together, we see some negative trends but also positive ones. Based on these economic indicators and the crisis models, the Mexican crisis could hardly have been predicted. In fact, the Mexican crisis and its depth were not predicted, even though a few analysts pointed to the real appreciation of the exchange rate.[23] As Sachs, Tornell, and Velasco (1996a) assert, many analysts pointed to Mexico's growing current account deficit in 1994 as well as the real appreciation of its currency, as it halted the capital inflows and prompted the collapse of the Peso, after the crisis. But they argue Malaysia and Thailand, with equally large current account deficits (as a percent of GDP), did not suffer from capital outflows that time. Moreover, the Peso crisis caused adverse market reactions in Argentina and Brazil in early 1995, but not in Chile and Colombia. Therefore, economic fundamentals alone do not explain the causes and implications, nor the depth of the crisis.[24] No one expected an immediate financial crisis due to the weaknesses in the Mexican economy. According to Edwards and Savastano (2000, p. 188), "this inability to grasp the seriousness of the Mexican situation (both before and after the collapse) clearly illustrates the shortcomings of the models commonly used both by private sector and academic analysts. . . ." However, they think that these shortcomings are due to inadequately appreciating some of the economic variables, such as real appreciation of the currency.

The argument of this chapter is that although the shortcomings of these crisis models might partly be due to not appreciating the importance of some domestic or international economic variables, they are also partly due to the fact that markets react to economic variables differently in different external and domestic-political, societal, and legal contexts. In addition, governments react to or interact with economic variables and market participants within these contexts, and how they react or respond to these variables differ from one country to another. Therefore, it seems that economic analyses must assess the impact of non-economic factors, i.e. domestic-political, societal, and legal factors as well as external links and influences, sufficiently enough to explain the causes and consequences of financial crises and to understand government behavior during a crisis. Sachs, Tornell, and Velasco (1996a) also agree that macroeconomic fundamentals alone do not explain the causes, implications, and depth of the peso crisis. They argue that the Mexican crisis was a result of perceived risk of financial collapse, a self-fulfilling attack and panic along with the weak fundamentals. Countries, such as Argentina and Brazil, with similar vulnerabilities were also affected by these kinds of speculative attacks following the peso crisis. However, it is hard to tell which country is more vulnerable to a speculative attack than any other country based on economic fundamentals alone. Expected and unexpected political concerns, societal events, and legal constraints as well as countries' external commitments and obligations affect the economic trends, government behavior, and market participants' confidence in governments' commitments to the peg. In fact, we can observe these kinds of impacts in the Mexican case.

The next chapter demonstrates the impact of multiple external and domestic political, societal and legal non-economic factors on the development of the crisis and the Mexican government's policy behavior. It argues that the interplay of these non-economic factors with economic variables brought the peso crisis and impacted the government's policy behavior. If these non-economic factors such as the *Pacto* mechanism, the Zapatista uprising, and political assassinations did not exist, and the government was able and willing to choose correct policies or devalue the peso on time, would macroeconomic variables deteriorate as they did, or even had they deteriorated, would markets react to them in the same way? Would the government handle the financial crisis this way, if Mexico's political and societal contexts were different, and if there was no election in 1994, and President Salinas did not want to become candidate for the directorship of the WTO? It is highly probable that those economic indicators would not cause a crisis if they were not in the Mexican context. Although second generation crisis models and some particular explanations of the Mexican peso crisis acknowledge the impact of non-economic factors on the development of the crisis and how the government handled it, they do not sufficiently and systematically incorporate them into their economic analysis and their explanations of the crisis. In the next section, we will review some *ex-post* explanations of the Mexican Peso crisis. Then, the next chapter will illustrate that the Mexican peso crisis developed due to both economic and non-economic factors and that the Mexican government's behavior during the crisis was not a simple response to the economic variables but was shaped under multiple economic and non-economic influences within Mexico's domestic and external contexts.

EX-POST EXPLANATIONS OF THE MEXICAN PESO CRISIS

After the Mexican Peso crisis, many economists not only questioned why it was not predicted, but also offered their explanations of the crisis. Some of these explanations also refer to some political factors, non-economic events and developments as causes of the Mexican peso crisis along with the economic variables, and to the Mexican government's behavior during the crisis explicitly or implicitly. However, these explanations as well are short of integrating the non-economic influences in the development of the crisis into their analyses, and of assessing the Mexican government's behavior during the crisis. Here, a brief summary of *ex-post* explanations of the Mexican peso crisis is presented.

It is hard to argue that there is a consensus on what caused the peso crisis in terms of approximate contribution of various variables. However, it might be possible to classify these explanations into two categories. One category of explanations blames macroeconomic fundamentals and "bad" government policies, which were associated with these bad macroeconomic variables, as the underlying causes of the crisis, rather than the elements of panic or adverse and unexpected shocks. The second category blames the panic behavior, adverse, expected and unexpected shocks, and borrowing constraints as being responsible for the crisis, rather than the macroeconomic fundamentals and bad government policies. There are examples from both types of explanations in the following paragraphs. The first category acknowledges the contribution of bad government policies in worsening the macroeconomic conditions and the second category accepts the unexpected political and societal developments as a trigger to a panic and herd behavior on the investors' side. As we will see in the next chapter, both types of influences took part in the development of the Mexican Peso crisis.

In the first category, one conventional explanation blames bad fiscal and/or monetary policy. This explanation might seem baseless, given that the inflation declined to 8 percent in 1993 and to 7.1 percent in 1994, and the Mexican government had budget surpluses in 1992 and 1993 and only a 0.7 percent deficit for 1994. The analysts who held bad fiscal and monetary policies responsible for the crisis argue that the budget numbers reported by the Mexican government were misleading, a large quantity of *tesobonos* (the dollar-denominated treasury bills) were issued, and that the government was actually running a substantial budget deficit. They think that the monetary policy was too loose in 1994, which was a critical year. They blame the Mexican government for selling reserve assets, and expanding domestic credit in order to cover up the hampered short-term capital inflow, after the March assassination of the presidential candidate Colosio. According to them, the Mexican government should have increased domestic interest rates in order to restrain domestic loan demand and attract additional foreign funds.[25] Also some analysts argue that "the paucity and unreliability of official data on key economic variables" was the major factor in triggering the speculative attacks on the peso.[26]

Edwards and Savastano (2000) do not think that this view is supported by evidence. According to them, Mexican interest rates, in fact, rose substantially after the March crisis and raising interest rates did not necessarily make monetary policy tighter.[27] In support of this criticism, Kamin and Rogers (1996), using econometric models of money demand, find that the substantial increase in the growth rate of Mexico's monetary base, which grew from 7% in 1993 to 21% in 1994, reflected strong positive shocks to the demand for money, rather than an excessive expansion of the money supply. They also point to the fact that monetary policy in 1994 was not significantly looser, and interest rates were close to their predicted levels in 1994.[28] The claim that a large quantity of *tesobonos* were issued is not justified as well, since they did not represent new indebtedness, but were a device for refinancing short-term *cetes* (the peso-denominated treasury bills).[29] In addition, markets were fully aware and supportive of the Mexican government's decision in April 1994 to replace maturing peso-denominated *cetes* with the dollar-linked *tesobonos*. It is also hard to argue that the official data available to foreign investors were unreliable. The academic and public debates on Mexico's external position were widespread during the first half of 1994, and the U.S. Treasury was able to keep track of the evolution of Mexico's international reserves throughout 1994, as the documents were released to the U.S. Senate Banking Committee.[30]

Another conventional explanation for the crisis, in the first category, such as Dornbusch and Werner (1994), and Kamin and Rogers (1996), points to the Mexican exchange rate policy. This approach points to Mexico's large and persistent current account deficits, which rose from $14.6 billion in 1991 to $28.8 billion in 1994, and argue that the Mexican economic crisis was building over several years. The substantially overvalued peso maintained the current account deficit, which must be financed by foreign borrowing. However, borrowing from abroad cannot go on forever. At one point, foreign lenders stopped lending further and rolling over their loans when they realized that the country's aggregate borrowing path was unsustainable. Instead they started to withdraw their capital, and the capital outflows eventually forced the Mexican government to the devaluation, which together with price increases and sudden withdrawal of foreign funds generated a severe recession. According to this explanation, the Mexican government should have corrected the policy of pegging the peso, in order to allow depreciation in the peso. The government's delay resulted in harsher and more destabilizing devaluation and a financial crisis. This view, e.g. Dornbusch and Werner (1994), asserts that the pegged exchange rate for stabilization is only good for a short time period, since an accumulation of real appreciation would eventually risk the success of the stabilization.[31]

Similarly, Kamin and Rogers (1996, 286) believe that exchange rate-based stabilization programs are inherently liable to induce currency overvaluation and therefore create current account deficits, in part because of sluggish momentum in domestic inflation after the exchange rate. In turn, these developments undermine the viability of the exchange rate peg, even if fiscal and structural policies have been appropriate. In their opinion, the devaluation was caused by real-appreciation and current account deficits endemic to the exchange rate stabilization, rather than the resumption of profligate macroeconomic policies. In addition, renewed access to international capital markets and rising private indebtedness led to over-indebtedness, problems in the financial sector, and weakening economic activity. Thus it became harder to follow a tight monetary policy in the face of a speculative attack.[32] In parallel, Kalter and Ribas (1999) assert that the real appreciation of the peso with an increased current account deficit along with a weakening banking system contributed to an underlying economic disequilibrium, and in turn reduced the authorities' policy degrees of freedom. According to them, the balance of payment crisis developed hand in hand with the banking crisis. Moreover, a marked increase in government expenditures and taxation increased production costs, caused excess demand for non-traded goods, and weakened the traded goods sector.[33]

As it might be noticed, these explanations focus on a few macroeconomic variables and do not pay sufficient attention to the impact of non-economic factors. Nonetheless, Edwards and Savastano (2000) identify a few economic policy mistakes of the Mexican authorities prior to the crisis. In their opinion, the rate at which capital flowed into Mexico in 1992-1994 was clearly not sustainable in the long run, given the magnitude of inflows and the high level of CA deficit. But the Mexican authorities largely ignored this apprehension, since the capital inflows were largely private and the fiscal accounts were in surplus. Later, approval of NAFTA in late 1993 and Mexico's expected entry into the OECD in 1994 engendered faith in the argument that Mexico's macroeconomic fundamentals were sound. As a result, the authorities further ignored the weaknesses, and announced a more ambitious program for the 1994 presidential election year. The program envisaged single-digit inflation, a pick up in output growth, and no fundamental change in the core macroeconomic policies. In addition, there was a need for adjustment in the real exchange rate due to overvaluation, to which a few analysts, e.g. Dornbush, R. (1993), pointed. However, Mexican authorities missed the chance to devalue in an orderly manner well ahead of the election. Later, the authorities found themselves in a desperate game of buy time by issuing *tesobonos*.[34] According to Espinosa and Russell (1996), however, a country may have a current account deficit and heavy foreign borrowing, not necessarily due to overvaluation of its currency, but because the country might offer attractive investment opportunities and lack enough domestic savings to finance them internally. This possibility was particularly relevant to the Mexican situation, according to them.[35] Another policy mistake, according to Edwards and Savastano (2000), is that the Mexican authorities did not realize that their debt strategy, i.e. the rapid replacement of maturing *cetes* with *tesobonos*, kept the interest rates below their equilibrium level for a prolonged period of time, instead of serving to smooth transitory hikes in interest rates. Maybe the Mexican authorities were under the impression that they had weathered the worst of the speculative pressures and that the capital inflows would resume again soon. They might also have been concerned that high interest rates and a depreciation of the peso would further deteriorate the situation of the banking system. Whatever the reason, Mexican authorities underestimated the risks embedded in their chosen course of action.[36] Although Edwards and Savastano (2000) point to a few policy mistakes, they do not question much why governments make these kinds of mistakes. Do governments only misperceive, wrongly assessing the macroeconomic conditions, or do they act this way with various political concerns and under multiple non-economic influences from the country's external and domestic contexts? As demonstrated in the next chapter, the Mexican government determined its policy responses to the crisis situation within an interaction process, under multiple domestic and external influences.

In the second category, Sachs, Tornell, and Velasco (1996b) challenge the explanations proposing that the Mexican financial crisis was the consequence of an overvalued exchange rate and a large current account deficit, coupled with the external shocks that hit Mexico in 1994. They argue that, although the exchange rate was overvalued by 20%-25% by early 1994, the extent of overvaluation had been stabilized due to a low inflation rate. In addition, the nominal exchange rate depreciated by 10% in March 1994, and the U.S. dollar itself was depreciating in real terms against European currencies and the Japanese yen. Although the current account deficit reached the level of 6.8% of GDP in 1993, and 7.9% in 1994, the Mexican public debt level at 30% of GDP in 1993 was less than half of the OECD average. Moreover, after the approval of NAFTA, as one would expect, Mexico continued to borrow internationally in 1994 to the same extent as in 1993, i.e. about 8% of GDP, leading to a consolidation of foreign investment into Mexico.[37] They also reject propositions suggesting that, like in the first generation crisis models, "excessive money growth caused reserves to decline until speculators predictably mounted an attack on the currency and caused the collapse of the peg."[38] According to them, two features of the process that led to the December panic do not fit with the predictions of the standard speculative attack models. First, behavior of interest rates on both *cetes* and *tesobonos* did not show any big jump until after the devaluation took place in December. They rose after the political assassinations in Mexico in March 1994, but fell back after the election of president Zedillo and remained basically constant until November. Secondly, although according to the standard speculative attack model, the real interest rate differential between Cetes and Tesobonos should have fallen after the devaluation, in reality both nominal and real terms interest rate differentials rose tremendously. In addition, unlike standard model expectations, a peso collapse in December was not expected, nor were there any concerns about the possibility that Mexico might default, as international press coverage strongly suggests.[39] Given this evidence, they argue that the fundamental conditions of the Mexican economy cannot account for the entire crisis, but "the December crisis was the result of a shift to a panic equilibrium."[40] In the first quarter of 1995, Mexico found itself in a financial panic, as investors fled Mexico despite very high interest rates and an undervalued currency. "A sudden shift in expectations—probably prompted by the devaluation—was the trigger for the crisis."[41] They argue that BOM was not vulnerable to a self-fulfilling attack until late 1994. The Calvo and Mendoza (1996) study shows that Mexico's ratio of reserve to short-term liabilities reached to below one in late 1994. In conclusion, they think high levels of short-term debt and low levels of reserves caused a self-fulfilling attack. This argument is compatible with the second-generation crisis models.[42]

Likewise, Calvo and Mendoza (1996) attribute the causes of Mexico's balance-of-payment crisis to large imbalances between the stocks of financial assets and foreign reserves. This imbalance made Mexico vulnerable to a speculative attack. The devaluation in such a vulnerable situation led to a massive run against financial assets, even though these outflows seemingly were inconsistent with the country's fundamentals. Anticipation of a banking-system bailout led to a speculative attack on Mexico's foreign reserves, causing investors to run away from Mexico's financial assets in a "herding behavior."[43] Mexico experienced a new kind of balance of payment crisis in the era of the global capital market, with a massive run against *tesobonos* by global investors, and with its impact on the other emerging markets worldwide.[44]

Sachs, Tornell, and Velasco (1996b) think that the Mexican government's policy mistakes caused a decline in reserves and an increase in short-term debt. After the March assassination of presidential candidate Colosio, the capital inflows that financed the CA deficit over 7% of GDP were greatly hampered. The Mexican government aimed to maintain the exchange rate and prevent further increases in interest rates by expanding domestic credit (loose monetary policy) and by converting *cetes* into *tesobonos*, and it did not tighten the fiscal policy. In the end, the capital outflow continued, the BOM's international reserves declined, and Mexico's short-term dollar-denominated debt increased. Thus, Mexico became vulnerable to a self-fulfilling speculative attack. The Mexican government could have avoided the crisis if it had devalued the currency further by lifting the ceiling and following a tighter monetary and fiscal policy, according to them.[45]

Cole and Kehoe (1996) also see the Peso crisis as a self-fulfilling debt-crisis due to the Mexican government's inability to roll over its debt in late 1994. The Mexican government attempted to convert its peso-denominated debt, *cetes*, into longer-term inflation indexed *ajustabonos,* and to short-term dollar indexed *tesobonos*, throughout 1994, in order to keep its debt service low. However, this increased the Mexican government's dollar-indexed debt relative to its foreign reserves. On the other hand, the political turmoil that Mexico was experiencing in 1994 worsened the economic situation. As Mexican and foreign investors began to move portfolio investment out of Mexico, the government's foreign reserves fell substantially because of its policy of sterilizing this outflow. By December 1994, the reserves fell down below the short-term dollar indexed liabilities of the Mexican government.[46] The December devaluation worsened the situation, as it kept the tesobonos values constant while lowering the dollar value of Mexico's GDP and government revenues. The dollar denominated short-term debt maturing in early 1995 was far exceeding the remaining foreign reserves of Mexico.[47] After this point the Mexican government could not roll over its debt since investors, fearing that Mexico would not be able to honor its commitments on the bonds, stopped buying new bonds, and thus actually disabled the Mexican government. Therefore, the Mexican government was exposed to a self-fulfilling crisis, since it could not roll over its short-term debt.[48] Andrew and Ríos-Rull (1996), however, think that the Mexican government could not roll over its short-term debt because Mexico's private and public sectors reached their borrowing limits due to "credit constraints" imposed externally.

In the second category, Espinosa and Russell (1996) emphasize the financial panic stimulated by political turmoil in 1994, instead of borrowing constraints. Their explanation acknowledges the impacts of political factors the most emphatically of all explanations. According to them, "the basic cause of the crisis was the political turmoil in Mexico that led foreign lenders to become concerned about the fate of their investment."[49] Mexico's externally financed growth strategy, the pegged exchange rate regime, and the fact that a large fraction of capital inflows were short-term capital, combined all together, prepared the conditions for a financial panic, which was similar to a nineteenth century U.S. financial panic triggered by "bad news." The adverse political events that followed the August election convinced many foreign investors that the political strife within the PRI and the country would continue during the Zedillo administration, and made them increasingly reluctant to commit or recommit funds to Mexico. The renewed uprising of the Chiapas in the South, the exhaustion of the BOM's foreign exchange reserves, and the December 20 devaluation further increased the panic. The development, structure, and practices of financial institutions made the economy vulnerable to political shocks, rather than the management of the economy. The principle cause of the crisis was excessive reliance of Mexico's commercial and financial institutions on short-term liabilities.[50] They think that if Mexico had a floating exchange regime, and the government had discouraged Mexican banks from issuing short-term liabilities, a major financial crisis would have been less likely. Similarly, Gil-Díaz and Carstens (1996), writing from their perspective at the Bank of Mexico, argue that "Mexico experienced a politically triggered speculative attack that snowballed into a financial crisis."[51] According to them, "all foreign exchange losses coincided with a political shock and not with an *ex-ante* expansion of credit. Furthermore, if authorities maintain an exchange rate band, a speculative attack cannot be resisted when the speed and amount of financial resources are overwhelming."[52]

Among these explanations, Espinosa and Russell (1996) and Gil-Díaz and Carstens (1996) point to political turmoil as an important component of the development of the Mexican peso crisis. Although the other explanations acknowledge the influence of the political factors, they do not regard them as important as macroeconomic factors and they see panic behavior and speculative attacks as being due to economic vulnerabilities. As will be seen in the next chapter, political concerns and societal events, and legal/institutional constraints, interacting with the economic vulnerabilities, had a significant impact in the development of the peso crisis.

These *ex-post* explanations also pointed to the Mexican government's policy mistakes, and implicitly or explicitly told us how the Mexican government should have behaved in order to prevent the crisis. There is some implicit assumption and expectation of government behavior along with recommendation in these explanations. It seems that if governments do not misinterpret the macroeconomic conditions and make policy mistakes, they can rationally address the macroeconomic problems and prevent or deal with a crisis situation. However, not only the development of the crisis, but also the Mexican government's behavior was shaped by multiple, expected and unexpected, external and domestic, and political and economic influences. It seems that how a government behaves during a financial crisis depends on how these influences interplay, and which of those particular governments or policy-makers prioritize. Governments react to economic variables, but not necessarily in the way as implicitly or explicitly stated by these economic theories and explanations.

As the next chapter will demonstrate, the Mexican government's policy behavior reflected the impact of multiple domestic and external non-economic influences and pressures. For example, the government acted under the influence of business and labor leaders, within the constraints of the *pacto* mechanism. It was exposed to pressures from international investors, in particular those in the United States, U.S. government officials, the IMF, and the World Bank. These various domestic and external pressures, constraints, and influences affected the Mexican government's decisions in terms of what to do next. The Mexican government's response policy, indeed, was a result of a multi-faceted interaction process.

The crisis developed as the result of a combination of economic/financial factors and non-economic factors, in particular those that were political. The uprising in the southern state of Chiapas and the political assassinations before and after the 1994 presidential election intermixed with a weakened economic/financial situation to bring the crisis. In retrospect, most experts point out that "an earlier and large-scale devaluation would have been a much wiser course."[53] However, again, multiple non-economic factors prevented Mexican authorities from responding effectively to market signals and negative economic trends, as the next chapter demonstrates. How the Mexican government handled the crisis did not reflect a simple rational reaction to the economic variables, although the concerns about the economic variables were there. If the interaction process went a different way, the Mexican government could have ended up with a slightly or largely different policy response than its actual response.

NOTES

1. Robert E. Looney, *Economic Policy Making in Mexico: Factors Underlying the 1982 Crisis* (Durham. NC: Duke University Press, 1985), 5; Wayne A. Cornelius and Ann L. Craig, *The Mexican Political System in Transition*, Monograph Series 35 (San Diego: University of California, Center for U.S.-Meixcan Studies, 1991), 105, 106; Victoria E. Rodríguez and Peter M. Ward, "Introduction: Governments of the Opposition in Mexico," in *Opposition Government in Mexico* (Albuquerque: University of New Mexico Press,1995), 4; Domínguez, "The Transformation of Mexico's Electoral and Party System, 1988-1997 . . . ," 204; Cothran, *Political Stability and Democracy in Mexico*, 61.

2. Weintraub, *Financial Decision-Making in Mexico: To Bet a Nation*, 23.

3. Centeno, *Democracy within Reason*, 8; Rodríguez and Peter M. Ward, "Introduction: Governments of the Opposition in Mexico,"4; Mauricio A. González Gómez, "Crisis and Economic Change in Mexico," in *Mexico Under Zedillo* (Boulder and London: Lynne Rienner Publishers, 1998), 37-40.

4. Centeno, *Democracy within Reason*, 9; Domínguez, "The Transformation of Mexico's Electoral and Party System, 1988-1997 . . . ," 205.

5. Looney, *Economic Policy Making in Mexico: Factors Underlying the 1982 Crisis*, xv; Domínguez, "The Transformation of Mexico's Electoral and Party System, 1988-1997 . . . ," 203, 205; Centeno, *Democracy within Reason*, 9; Lusting, *Mexico: The Remaking of an Economy*, 2, 10; Gerardo Otero, "Neoliberal Reform and Politics in Mexico: An Overview," in *Neoliberalism Revisited: Economic Restructuring and Mexico's Political Future* (Westview Press,1996), 6,7.

6. Weintraub, *Financial Decision-Making in Mexico: To Bet a Nation*, 19.

7. Pastor Jr., "Pesos, Policies, and Predictions . . . ," 121, 122; Lusting, *Mexico: The Remaking of an Economy*, 1; Gould, "Mexico's Crisis: Looking Back to Assess the

Future,"17-38, 38.

8. Otero, "Neoliberal Reform and Politics in Mexico: An Overview," 6, 7.

9. According to Naím (1997), it consists of "policy goals of fiscal discipline, tax reform, financial liberalization, a single competitive exchange rate, liberalization of trade and foreign investment, privatization, and deregulation." Moisés Naím, "Mexico's Larger Story," in *Mexico 1994: Anatomy of an Emerging-Market Crash* (Washington, DC: Carnegie Endowment for International Peace, 1997). Reprinted from *Foreign Policy* 99 (Summer 1995), 295.

10. Otero, "Neoliberal Reform and Politics in Mexico: An Overview," 6, 7.

11. Sebastian Edwards and Miguel A. Savastano, "The Mexican Peso in the Aftermath of the 1994 Currency Crisis," in *Currency Crises* (Chicago and London: The University of Chicago Press, 2000), 185; Jeffrey Sachs, Aarón Tornell, and Andrés Velasco, *Financial Crises in Emerging Markets: The Lessons From 1995*, Working Paper 5576 (National Bureau of Economic Research, May 1996a), 39-40.

12. Guillermo A. Calvo and Enrique G. Mendoza, "Mexico's Balance-of-payments Crisis: A Chronicle of a Death Foretold," *Journal of International Economics* 41 (1996), 238.

13. Douglas W. Arner, "The Mexican Peso Crisis: Implications for the Regulation of Financial Markets," http://iibf.law.smu.edu/pub/dougla.htm (accessed December 14, 2000), 6.

14. Bartley, "The Peso Folklórico: Dancing Away From Monetary Stability,"147.

15. Gould, "Mexico's Crisis: Looking Back to Assess the Future,"16. This was the fourth major crisis in Mexico in fewer than twenty years. The previous ones are the Echeverría devaluation in 1976, the López Portilla devaluation of 1982, and the devaluation in the election year of 1988. See Bartley, "The Peso Folklórico: Dancing Away From Monetary Stability," 141.

16. Weintraub, "Mexico's Foreign Economic Policy: From Admiration to Disappointment," 43; Heath, *Mexico and the Sexenio Curse . . .* , 35. Also see Lawrence H. Summers, Testimony Before the Senate Committee on Banking, Housing, and Urban Affairs on March 10, 1995. U.S. Congress. Senate. Committee on Banking, Housing, and Urban Affairs. SUDOC: Y4.B22/3:S.HRG.104-164, 1995.

17. Donald E. Schulz and Edward J. Williams, "Crisis of Transformation: The Struggle for the Soul of Mexico," in *Mexico Faces the 21st Century* (Westport, CT: Greenwood Press, 1995), 8.

18. Sachs, Tornell, and Velasco, *Financial Crises in Emerging Markets: The Lessons From 1995*, 40-41.

19. Otero, "Neoliberal Reform and Politics in Mexico: An Overview," 8; Heath, *Mexico and the Sexenio Curse . . .* , 36. See the Appendix C for the amounts of PI and FDI investments.

20. Sachs, Tornell, and Velasco, *Financial Crises in Emerging Markets: The Lessons From 1995*, 40; Heath, *Mexico and the Sexenio Curse . . .* , 36.

21. Joseph A. Whitt Jr., "The Mexican Peso Crisis," Federal Reserve Bank of Atlanta. *Economic Review* (January/February 1996), 10.

22. Weintraub, "Mexico's Foreign Economic Policy: From Admiration to Disappointment," 43, 44; Gerald M. Meier, *The International Environment of Business: Competition and Governance in the Global Economy* (New York & Oxford: Oxford University Press, 1998), 209; Whitt Jr., "The Mexican Peso Crisis," 9; and Weintraub, "Mexico's Foreign Economic Policy: From Admiration to Disappointment," 43, 44. Also

see Summers, *Testimony Before the Senate Committee on Banking, Housing, and Urban Affairs* on March 10, 1995.

23. For example, Dornbush (1993) indicated that the overvalued exchange rate was the current problem of the Mexican Economy. Rudiger Dornbush, "Mexico: How to Recover Stability and Growth," in *Stabilization, Debt, and Reform* (Englewood Cliffs, NJ: Prentice-Hall, 1993), 369. The World Bank's 1993 *Trend in Developing Economies* (325-330) pointed to slowing GDP growth in Mexico and argued that it was due to Mexico's slow productivity growth, tight fiscal and monetary policies, the real exchange rate appreciation, and a weak U.S. economy.

24. Sachs, Tornell, and Velasco, *Financial Crises in Emerging Markets: The Lessons From 1995,* 1.

25. See Marco Espinosa and Steven Russell, "The Mexican Economic Crisis: Alternative Views," Federal Reserve Bank of Atlanta, *Economic Review* (January/February 1996), 26-27 for a literature review on these kinds of explanations.

26. Edwards and Savastano, "The Mexican Peso in the Aftermath of the 1994 Currency Crisis," 189.

27. Ibid., p.189.

28. Kamin and Rogers, "Monetary Policy in the End-game to . . . ," 285, 303.

29. Espinosa and Russell, "The Mexican Economic Crisis: Alternative Views," 26-27.

30. See D'Amato (1995), and Edwards and Savastano, "The Mexican Peso in the Aftermath of the 1994 Currency Crisis," 189-190.

31. Espinosa and Russell, "The Mexican Economic Crisis: Alternative Views," 22-23.

32. Steven B. Kamin and John H. Rogers, "Monetary Policy in the End-game to Exchange-Rate Based Stabilization: the Case of Mexico," *Journal of International Economics* 41 (1996), 286, 287, 304.

33. Eliot Kalter and Armando Ribas, "The 1994 Mexican Economic Crisis: The Role of Government Expenditure and Relative Prices," *IMF Working Paper* WP/99/160 (December 1999), 3-4.

34. Edwards and Savastano, "The Mexican Peso in the Aftermath of the 1994 Currency Crisis," 187.

35. Espinosa and Russell, "The Mexican Economic Crisis: Alternative Views," 23.

36. Edwards and Savastano, "The Mexican Peso in the Aftermath of the 1994 Currency Crisis," 191-192.

37. Jeffrey Sachs, Aarón Tornell, and Andrés Velasco, "The Mexican Peso Crisis: Sudden Death of Death Foretold?" *Journal of International Economics* 41 (1996b), 265-268.

38. Ibid., p.266.

39. Ibid., pp.265-268.

40. Sachs, Tornell, and Velasco, "The Mexican Peso Crisis: Sudden Death of Death Foretold?," 268; also see their June 1995 paper.

41. Sachs, Aarón Tornell, and Andrés Velasco, "The Mexican Peso Crisis: Sudden Death of Death Foretold?," 280.

42. Ibid., p.280.

43. Calvo and Mendoza, "Mexico's Balance-of-payments Crisis: A Chronicle of a Death Foretold," 235, 262,263.

44. Ibid., 236.

45. Sachs, Aarón Tornell, and Andrés Velasco, "The Mexican Peso Crisis: Sudden

Death of Death Foretold?," 266, 280.

46. Harold L. Cole and Timothy J. Kehoe, "A Self-fulfilling Model of Mexico's 1994-1995 Debt Crisis," *Journal of International Economics* 41 (1996), 323, 325, 326.

47. Ibid., p. 336.

48. Ibid., p. 309-310.

49. Espinosa and Russell, "The Mexican Economic Crisis: Alternative Views," 34.

50. Espinosa and Russell, "The Mexican Economic Crisis: Alternative Views," 28-35.

51. Francisco Gil-Díaz and Agustín Carstens, "One Year of Solitude: Some Pilgrim Tales About Mexico's 1994-95 Crisis," *American Economic Review Papers and Proceedings* 86, No.2 (May 1996),168.

52. Ibid., p. 165.

53. Smith, "Political Dimensions of the Peso Crisis," 39.

CHAPTER IV: THE IMPACT OF NON-ECONOMIC FACTORS: THE MEXICAN CASE

As examination of the Mexican case with economic crisis models and explanations suggested in the previous chapter, the development of financial crises and how governments shape their response policies cannot be adequately addressed with the rationale of economics. One goal of this chapter is to evidence the arguments made in the previous chapter. It identifies, traces, and assesses the impacts of multiple non-economic factors on the development of the peso crisis and on the Mexican government's policy behavior. Another goal is to illustrate the interplay of non-economic and economic factors and to demonstrate the significance of non-economic factors in bringing the financial crises and in shaping governmental policy responses within Mexico's external and domestic-political, societal, and institutional/legal contexts. The chapter traces the interplay of a number of complex political, societal, and institutional factors with economic factors within the Mexican contexts, in order to demonstrate how the initial conditions translated into the next and following situations.

Since the impact of each non-economic factor is best understood within the sequence of events and within the Mexican contexts, the following story will proceed near-chronologically with references to Mexican history, culture, and external and domestic contexts. The chapter focuses on how the Mexican peso crisis developed in 1994 and how the government behaved in 1994 and early 1995.

1994, SALINAS' FINAL YEAR OF PRESIDENCY: THE ROAD TO THE PESO CRISIS

As we have discussed in the previous chapter, the Mexican economy seemed to be sound and Salinas' neoliberal economic reforms seemed to be very successful until mid-1994. However, an interplay of economic and non-economic developments within the Mexican contexts led to the devaluation of the Mexican peso on December 20, 1994 and the subsequent crisis. The following story explains why.

The Impacts of Non-Economic Factors before the 1994 Election

The impacts of historical inheritance, the corporatist system, and the pacto mechanism. As seen in more detail in Appendix A, the Mexican political regime has been marked by a close alliance between politicians (from the ruling party, PRI), technocrats, and the leaders of key groups, such as those of the labor and the peasantry, since the 1920s. Influenced by revolutionary ideology, Mexico's political economy evolved toward a corporatist system of interest representation, under which individuals and societal interest groups have been expected to relate themselves to the state through an institutionalized structure that is recognized by the state. In this corporatist system, every major interest group has had formal or informal ties with the ruling elite. Such alliances among the ruling elite and the interest groups brought social and political stability, and they were often sealed in explicit contracts, which are called *pacto*.[1] Following the debt crisis of 1982, the five years of stagflation and an abrupt devaluation in November 1987 forced the Mexican government to adopt a set of reforms, which included the creation of a formal *pacto* and the adoption of a fixed exchange rate system, along with some fiscal measures and economic liberalization. The *pacto* mechanism aimed at establishing "social consensus" on economic policies and the peso exchange rate by bringing government, labor, rural and private-sector representatives in on the contents of an economic program.[2] In 1988, the Salinas' administration modified the exchange rate system from a completely fixed exchange rate system to a system based on a pre-announced rate of devaluation (which had to be below the ongoing inflation), and later to an exchange rate band with a sliding ceiling. Salinas's stabilization program aimed at guiding prices, the exchange rate, and wage increases through predetermined exchange rate anchors supported by restrictive fiscal and monetary policies, and the *pacto*(s).[3]

At the beginning, the *pacto* was renewed annually, but after two years it started to be renewed about every three months due to uncertainty and decreasing credibility of the government. Between December 1987 and November 1994, the *pacto* was renewed a total of twelve times.[4] It became an important feature of the Mexican economic policy process from 1987 throughout the Salinas administration. The government's commitment to the peso exchange rate through the *pacto* mechanism helped to reduce inflation and created enough confidence to attract capital from abroad, since the profits made from peso interest rates could be transformed into high dollar returns. However, the *pacto* mechanism constrained the government in determining the Central Bank's intervention bands to the peso exchange rate, since any change in that regard had to be signed by business and labor leaders as well as government officials. Thus, capital flows into Mexico became highly dependent on the *pacto* along with the

Central Bank's commitment to maintain the exchange rate. Any immediate modification in exchange rate policy was difficult.[5]

The impacts of the pacto mechanism, domestic interest groups, the opposition to NAFTA within the U.S. Congress, and Mexican officials' economic ideology. Many agree that the Mexican peso was overvalued in 1994. According to some economists, it was overvalued by 30 percent at the end of 1993, when 1990 is taken as a reference year. The overvalued peso lost its competitive edge of a highly undervalued currency in 1986-1987, and became the major cause of trade and current account deficits in Mexico.[6] In October 1993, at a time when the U.S. Congress was still discussing the approval of NAFTA, the Mexican government had a *pacto* meeting. An interviewee who was present in that meeting told Weintraub (2000) that the leaders of the senior business group "suggested a prudential devaluation of the peso by 10 percent." Such devaluation was going to be a cushion for the election year of 1994, since it was going to be difficult to devalue at that time. However, bankers present at that meeting as well as the governor of the Bank of Mexico Mancera and the secretary of Treasury/Finance Aspe were against devaluation. So, a devaluation decision did not come out at that meeting.

One reason why the Mexican economic policy officials were against the devaluation at that time was the uncertainty about whether the U.S. Congress would approve NAFTA. "The opposition to NAFTA was fierce in the United States, more so than for any trade agreement in the postwar period."[7] As Weintraub (2000) notes, "had the peso been devalued then, just before the contentious issue of NAFTA approval was coming up for a final vote in the U.S. congress, that might have been enough to tilt the decision against the agreement."[8] Another reason was the senior economic officials' (in particular, Aspe's and Mancera's) preference for symbolic single-digit inflation at the cost of lower economic growth. There was no disagreement among senior policy officials on keeping the inflation low. They were also in consensus in terms of the use of the *pacto* mechanism to achieve this objective. The differences among officials concerned to what extent to prioritize low inflation over economic growth.[9] Economic growth was steadily declining from 4.4 percent in 1990 to 2.8 percent in 1992 and to only 0.6 percent in 1993.[10] The uncertainty about congressional approval of NAFTA also had a negative impact on the growth rate during the third quarter of 1993. The general perception was that a "rejection of the agreement would lead to lowered expectations about Mexico's economic future and the possibility of considerable capital flight."[11] The political leadership, in particular Salinas and Colosio, who was selected as a presidential candidate on November 28, 1993, would have been concerned about lower economic growth, or recession. However, Aspe and Mancera seemed to prioritize lower inflation over any other objective, including economic growth, which would follow later in a non-inflationary environment. According to Weintraub (2000), Mancera and Aspe constantly reflected this priority in their speeches through 1993 and early 1994.[12] With this priority they were against a devaluation, which would sour inflation even though it would help the economic growth resume again.

The impact of the upcoming presidential election and U.S. Congress's approval of the NAFTA. One interviewee told Weintraub (2000) that the recession of 1993 frightened President Salinas, particularly coming into an election year.[13] The scare of low growth and its possible effect on the upcoming presidential elections later led to an increased use of development banks,[14] which were not included in the balance of the financial budget of the public sector since the start of 1993. They were ideal mediums for increasing public expenditures without affecting the balance of the public sector.[15] The Mexican government via Mexico's central bank extended large sums of credit to development banks and these banks gave lines of credits to small and medium-sized industries. As a result, not only did the development bank deficits grow in 1994, as compared to 1993, but also the government had in fact a loose budget and followed an expansionary fiscal policy before the 1994 presidential election. According to the information given to Weintraub (2000) by knowledgeable insiders, the government's intention was to overcome the recession by lending freely before the upcoming election.[16] The government's expansionary fiscal policy, in turn, caused increases in private investments and consumption of durable goods. From the first quarter to the second quarter of 1994, private consumption of durable goods increased from —0.7 percent to 10.5 percent, current government spending increased from 4.3 percent to 10.0 percent, and private investment increased from 2.0 percent to 12.1 percent. Of course, part of the increase in the investment rates was due to the increase in foreign direct investment resulting from the implementation of NAFTA. The approval of NAFTA by the U.S. Congress changed investors' confidence. According to Bank of Mexico data, capital inflows to Mexico jumped to $7 billion in December 1993, from an around $2 billion average of the first 11 months of 1993, following the U.S. Congress approval of NAFTA. As a result of increases in government spending and investment rates, Mexico's GDP growth jumped miraculously from 2.3 percent for the first quarter to 5.6 percent in the second quarter of 1994 and averaged 3.5 percent in 1994. However, the expansionary fiscal policy was not compatible with maintaining a peg of the exchange rate within the intervention bands. The credit boom that went to consumption negatively affected the already high current account deficits.[17] The Salinas' administration followed such expansionary policies anyway before the elections in 1994 with political concerns.

The impacts of Salinas' neoliberal economic policies, poverty and income inequality, the implementation of NAFTA, the Mexican authoritarian system, and the Zapatista uprising in Chiapas. Since the initiation of more market-oriented economic policies following the 1982 crisis, poverty and income inequality across social classes and geographical regions have intensified. The benefits of the Salinas administration's economic achievements were not distributed equally as well. Although some reduction in poverty was achieved during the Salinas years, his neoliberal economic policies further increased the income inequality. From 1982 to 1994, minimum real salaries fell 67 percent, and median salaries fell more than 50 percent.[18] Salinas' neoliberal reforms included a reduction of the state's obligations to the peasantry[19] as well as removal of import barriers and more reliance on the market. Peasant organizations could not contest the pro-market reforms in agriculture, since they had already been weakened by repression, internal divisions, and the economic stagnation of the 1980s by the time Salinas assumed the presidency. The signing of the NAFTA agreement in 1993 and its implementation in 1994 brought pressure for further liberalization.[20] Sectors with strong international commercial and financial ties were concentrated in the North of Mexico, rather than the South. Thus the implementation of NAFTA was likely to benefit those in the North and the Valley of Mexico, while adversely affecting, or doing nothing for the impoverished South. Large portions of the south were "left with three choices: continuous social deterioration, migration, or rebellion" without new economic, social, and political opportunities.[21] The Zapatista National Liberation Army, EZLN,[22] in Chiapas, (a southern impoverished state of Mexico) led by its charismatic leader, Subcommandante Marcos, started an uprising on January 1, 1994, the day on which NAFTA started to be implemented. The rebellion showed that not the entire south of Mexico agreed with NAFTA.[23] According to Otero (1996), "the Chiapas uprising was but the most radical expression of discontent with growing inequality and lack of democracy in Mexico."[24]

The EZLN uprising not only showed the discontent of the South with NAFTA, but also challenged established authority and demanded political reform, reflecting popular demand in Mexico. In fact, the uprising and its leaders gained popular support all over Mexico in a short time.[25] By the 1990s, components of the authoritarian system had been weakened, but strong, new democratic institutions had not been developed. Changes during Salinas' administration in this direction were only few and piecemeal. Salinas reestablished presidential hegemony, more than introducing democratic pluralism. He worked toward enhancing presidential image and maintaining the cohesion of the political elite and the PRI's hegemony. Instead of negotiating with the opposition, in particular the Mexican left, and implementing thorough electoral reforms, he aimed at isolating them.[26] Thus, the political reforms were insufficient to defuse the political crises of 1994 and their impact on the economy. "The lack of political reform made the economic project extremely vulnerable to political upheaval, as the Chiapas uprising revealed," according to Dresser (1997).[27]

The uprising demonstrated to the world that Mexico had pressing social problems and tremendous inequalities, despite the economic reforms and highly acclaimed social programs.[28] Changes in political and social spheres were much slower than changes in the economy. Salinas' political reforms did not help to reduce the social tension, even though he attempted to make some changes to the structure of the corporatist relationship in response to his promises of political modernization and democracy. Interest mediation through the traditional corporatist sectors of the party was not replaced by a more direct popular participation.[29] Nonetheless, Salinas' economic policies weakened the traditional "populist-distributive coalition of inward-looking development." The liberalization, privatization and deregulation of the economy aimed at enhancing economic efficiency and attracting foreign investment. The Salinas administration worked toward building a support coalition around center-right, and continued state intervention and patronage in a different way, geared toward export-led growth. Salinas' coalition-building policies aimed at neutralizing organized labor, controlling and allocating discretionary credit to private-sector groups, obtaining the support of popular groups, in particular through the National Solidarity Program (*Pronasol*), and eliciting the support of the middle-class through consumption of imports. These policies were further enhanced through monetary and fiscal policies in 1994.[30] Overtime, *Pronasol* was increasingly deployed to co-opt supporters of the opposition instead of addressing the needs of the extremely poor. In the end, the compensatory, neopopulist policies as part of the Salinas coalition-building project were also proven to be insufficient to contain social disaffection. "Had the Salinas regime broadened its social base, even at the expense of the scope and pace of economic reforms, the political instability of 1994 might have been deterred," according to Dresser (1997).[31]

Although the rebellion in Chiapas did not pose a serious threat to political or economic stability, prolongation of that conflict, along with subsequent political developments, gave "a sense of uncertainty and erosion of power" in Mexico.[32] The uprising raised questions about the political and social structure of Mexico, and marked the beginning of significant developments in 1994 that led to the peso crisis, even though it did not cause immediate large capital flight and a big disturbance in the financial markets. Despite the uprising, Mexico's international reserves continued to grow from around $25 billion at the beginning of 1994 to a peak of more than $29 billion in mid-February and early March.[33] However, the uprising affected the work habits of President Salinas, according to Weintraub (2000). An insider informed Weintraub (2000) during his interviews in Mexico that "[Salinas'] priorities changed from concentrated attention on economic issues to an effort to manage the Chiapas developments and to minimize their impact on the nation as a whole. . . .Meetings of the president with his economic cabinet, which had taken place at more or less weekly intervals in 1993, occurred rarely in 1994."[34] The lack of economic cabinet meetings reduced the discussion of economic issues to a minimum in a country "where opinions from outside a small insider group were barely entertained."[35] The president was no longer seeking internal debate to obtain some form of high-level consensus on economic policy. Thus, the uprising in Chiapas partly paralyzed the government, at least in regards to economic policy, at the beginning of 1994. The president and his close associates held weekly, even daily meetings to solve this issue.[36]

The impacts of the internal quarrel within the ruling party (PRI), and Salinas' candidacy for the directorship of the WTO. Another distraction for the president was an ongoing internal quarrel within the PRI regarding the selection of Luis Donaldo Colosio on November 28, 1993 as a presidential candidate for the 1994 election. Colosio's selection alienated many, including Manuel Camacho Solís, the mayor of Mexico City and a longtime ally of Salinas, who was expected to be chosen as Salinas' successor. When he was passed over in favor of Colosio, he resigned his position and for many months acted "as if he might be chosen to replace Colosio as the presidential candidate of the PRI."[37] He was a popular political figure in Mexico and his political position and criticism of the PRI not only inflicted much damage on Colosio's campaign, but also had negative implications for the already sensitive Mexican markets. Salinas appointed him as Secretary of Foreign Relations, and later as his mediator to deal with the problem of the uprising in Chiapas.[38] Some others in the PRI, "mainly those referred in Mexico as the *dinosarios* (dinosaurs) were also not satisfied with the selection of Colosio as the presidential candidate." Colosio had held important posts in Mexico as a senator, head of the PRI, and a cabinet officer before his selection as the presidential candidate. However, the *dinosarios* did not find Colosio sufficiently dedicated to the continuation of the PRI's power, mainly due to his agenda for political reforms and his interest in social issues.[39] In the meantime, Salinas, supported by the U.S. administration, became a candidate for becoming Director General of the World Trade Organization (WTO). As we will further discuss in the later parts of this chapter, his candidacy affected his actions and policy behaviors. It also constrained him in his actions against the Zapatista uprising, since he wanted to avoid controversial actions, such as military suppression, not to lose support for his candidacy, according to many Mexican senior persons as Weintraub reports (2000).[40]

   The impacts of political assassinations and Mexico's weak banking system. Even though the Chiapas uprising did not have any immediate affect on the stability of Mexican financial markets, subsequent events did. First, Alfredo Harp Helú, president of BANAMEX, Mexico's largest bank, was kidnapped on March 9, and then the PRI presidential candidate Luis Donaldo Colosio was assassinated following a political rally in the northern border city of Tijuana on March 23, 1994. Colosio's assassination, which was the first high-level political killing since 1929, raised substantial doubts about the economic and political stability of Mexico and became the biggest shock of all in the market place.[41] There was a widespread belief in Mexico that Colosio's murder was orchestrated by senior persons in the PRI.[42] All of these events led to a drastic change in Mexico's business environment and undercut the administration's credibility. Investors who had been "overly confident" after the signing of NAFTA in November 1993 became increasingly concerned among all sorts of rumors. Following the assassination, there was a large amount of capital flight out of the country, depleting Mexico's foreign exchange reserves.[43]

   On March 29, 1994, Salinas selected Ernesto Zedillo Ponce de Leon as the PRI's new presidential candidate for the August 1994 elections. Camacho Solís' candidacy no longer seemed feasible after the assassination of Colosio. Zedillo had been serving as the Salinas' administration Secretary of Education before he left the office to become Colosio's campaign coordinator in November 1993. He met the constitutional requirement that "the candidate had to be out of office for at least six months before the date of the election" and satisfied the practice of choosing a cabinet officer as the PRI presidential candidate.[44] In regards to the uprising in the state of Chiapas, Salinas' administration declared a unilateral cease-fire, abandoning its reactive policy of repression. In addition, Salinas replaced the governor of Chiapas with former human rights ombudsman Jorge Carpizo. Later, the government opened negotiation with the rebels.[45]

After the selection of Zedillo as the PRI's presidential candidate, foreign reserves were still falling. The Central Bank's foreign reserves stood at $28.321 billion on March 23 and fell to $17.536 billion by April 21, resulting in a net loss of $10.785 billion in one month.[46] Despite the deteriorating situation, Mexico's economic policymakers downplayed the large current account deficits and the overvaluation of the peso during the first quarter of 1994. The Mexican officials in the Bank of Mexico and the Ministry of Finance discussed the situation after Colosio's assassination, but at the end, they chose not to change monetary and exchange rate policies. The assassination "was seen as a one-time event whose consequences would pass after the initial shock."[47] However, it was not transitory. Both Mexican and foreign investors "never fully recovered their earlier confidence in the financial-political stability of Mexico."[48] Beyond their wishful thinking and/or misperception of the situation as temporary, Mexican officials were also constrained by Mexico's week banking system, and were inclined to maintain the monetary base reasonably steady (instead of tightening it), in order not to upset the already weak banks. Salinas' structural reform program included the liberalization of the financial sector and the privatization of the banking industry.[49] The liberalization of the banking sector and of trade, which made available imported consumer goods together with the government's achievements in reducing the fiscal deficits, led to considerable growth of credit and a consumption boom.[50] In addition, the bank privatization was carried out haphazardly, the quality and experience of the buyers were not considered, and the proper regulatory standards and supervision were not set. In some cases, the new owners did not adequately capitalize their banks. Thus, over time, risky loans had increased and these banks had become increasingly vulnerable to market setbacks by 1994.[51] As Weintraub's (2000) interviews with officials from the Bank of Mexico and the Ministry of Finance reveal, the weaknesses of the commercial banks constrained the decisionmakers' flexibility in their monetary policy. The fear was that raising interest rates (tight monetary policy) would worsen the already weak private banks and the fragile financial system.[52]

The impacts of domestic interest groups and the presidential elections. As of the first half of 1994, the Mexican government had two choices in principle, according to Frieden (1997). It could have allowed the peso to depreciate, or it could have implemented deflationary policies (tight monetary and fiscal policies) to sustain the peso peg. However, the government did not seem to choose one or the other. Both policy options had pros and cons, and it was hard for the government to make a decision. Depreciation would reduce pressure on exporters and import-competitors, who were facing difficulties. It would also enable the government to lower interest rates, and in turn benefit indebted and borrowing firms. On the other hand, a depreciation would hurt the purchasing power of the broad voter sources of the PRI in the urban middle class and working classes.[53] In addition, some members of Mexico's business and financial community as well as some economic policy officials did not want a depreciation.

Those economic policy officials, in particular Aspe and Mancera, who priori-tized low inflation and stable low wages over an immediate resumption of eco-nomic growth, were in favor of deflationary policies. However, deflationary measures were going to hurt some other businesses and labor groups. The real appreciation of the peso put competitive pressures on the producers of tradable goods, which included many Mexican manufacturers, as reflected in a growing CA deficit.[54] Nonetheless, the government was reluctant to depreciate the peso before the election. As the elections were approaching, "the government could not afford to alienate electorally important groups, such as the urban middle class and lower middle class consumers. Adverse price pressures on manufac-turers due to the real appreciation were less urgent, as was the longer-term con-cern about the fate of public finances."[55]

Retaining the political support of the urban middle and working classes and key business groups, especially in the election year, was very important for Salinas and the PRI. The overvaluation of the peso and the capital flows in the 1990s were associated with a surge in the country's imports and contributed to the general satisfaction by increasing the consumption of the urban middle and working classes. Less expensive imported goods benefited the middle-class and some lower middle class consumers more than the poor. The capital flows en-abled businesses to borrow with less costs and to service the existing debt. The continuation of the massive capital flows and maintenance of the exchange rate policy were important for the compensation of these key groups in order to assure electoral victory of the ruling party. Foreign funds also enabled the gov-ernment to spend selectively to support politically influential sectors, such as small-and medium-size businesses, selected elements of the labor movement, and other beneficiaries of the government's "solidarity" or *paranasol* program, to ease their economic adjustment and get their political support. Salinas at-tempted to compensate "losers" of his neoliberal economic policies in order to build a support coalition, although some sectors of the economy, in particular the peasants, were left to the initiative of market forces.[56] Due to its political benefits, the Mexican government grew too dependent on the flow of foreign capital and a cheap dollar. Policymakers avoided making painful short-term decisions, such as the depreciation of the peso.[57]

Mexico's economic officials kept repeating that their main objective was to maintain the existing exchange rate policy, in order to assure the continuation of capital inflows. In the meantime, retaining the current exchange rate became a symbol of the government's overall policy credibility. Any deviation would reduce confidence, and therefore the capital inflows that Mexico's economic stability very much depended on.[58] However, Salinas' expansionary fiscal and credit policies were incompatible with maintaining the exchange rate. One way of defending an exchange rate is to tighten monetary policy. Actually, the BOM claims that it pursued a tight monetary policy during this time, but some analysts question this claim, arguing that the BOM did not push interest rates up suffi-ciently enough after Colosio's assassination. In addition, the BOM chose to sterilize the reserve losses to prevent a reduction in the monetary base. As a result, the monetary base grew more than 20 percent during most of 1994.[59] Moreover, the government resisted increasing interest rates on peso-denominated public debt. Low interest rates and the expanded monetary base enabled the financial system, in particular the official development banks, to increase their credits. Their credit outstanding increased by 35 percent in the twelve months ending in June 1994. In parallel, the fiscal policy was being relaxed.[60]

The impacts of the presidential election, governmental structure, and wishful thinking. During the second quarter of 1994, politics became the top priority for the political leadership, including Salinas, in order to assure a PRI victory in the elections. In light of the possibility that the PRI's candidate would lose an election for the first time in 65 years, devaluation became even less an option, Naím (1997) notes.[61] Zedillo was not a well known popular figure, even though he had served as a researcher in the Bank of Mexico, Secretary of Programming and Budget, and later as Secretary of Education. Weintraub's (2000) interviews revealed that even the nominally non-political, "independent" Bank of Mexico[62] was deeply influenced by the imperative of assuring Zedillo's victory, even though Miguel Mancera, then the governor of the Bank, denied this claim. Throughout 1994 "decisions of the 'independent' Mexican central bank were not sufficiently independent of political calculations."[63] The governor of the Bank of Mexico participated in the *pacto* meetings, which also made the governor "part of a team rather than an independent actor removed from daily political pressure."[64] It seems that the uncertainty of the electoral outcome was discussed many times among the top Mexican officials, including the officials of the Bank. According to Weintraub, (2000), the dominant mode of thinking, that time, was that "there would be time to resolve the underlying economic issues once Zedillo's election was an accomplished fact."[65] Thus, this political priority eliminated any possibility of currency devaluation before the election. Salinas was not for devaluation mainly for political reasons. For both Miguel Mancera and Pedro Aspe, inflation was a priority over other economic goals anyway. Guillermo Ortiz, then the Subsecretary for Treasury, was known to favor a more flexible exchange-rate policy, but was excluded from many meetings on economic policy. In the meantime, off-budget government expenditures grew via the use of development banks as intermediaries.[66] Thus, the Mexican government was neither allowing the peso to depreciate adequately, nor following policies that were compatible with sustaining the peso peg. Short-term electoral calculations, monetary expansion of more than 20 percent, and lax credit policies along with the decline in foreign investment and international reserves were worsening the economic situation.[67]

The impacts of wishful thinking and changes in the president's office. Although the capital flights out of Mexico reached alarming proportions in late March and April, as events unfolded, Mexican authorities treated them as temporary shocks, "not realizing that they were rapidly running out of time to correct the real exchange-rate overvaluation and to reduce their dependence on capital inflows."[68] In the meantime, "Salinas was left without an independent, informed, and non-threatening interlocutor with whom he could speak on a daily basis."[69] In early April, president Salinas lost a trusted advisor, José Córdoba Montoya,[70] who ran the coordination office of the President. He resigned from his position for reasons that are not fully clear. He was replaced, but the role he played in terms of managing the presentation of complex-cabinet deliberations for the president was not filled.[71] Ulices Beltran, then a technical adviser to the presidency, told Weintraub (2000) that "there was an absence of solid discussion of key economic issues at the presidential level after Córdoba left."[72] The old pattern of economic discussion between the president and many senior participants was broken down. President Salinas, having other priorities as well, thought it sufficient to meet with Aspe, and talk on the phone with Mancera, according to Santiago Oñate, who succeeded Córdoba.[73]

The impacts of the presidential election. Following the Colosio shock, Mexican officials spent reserves in order to protect the exchange rate and allowed the exchange rate to move from the bottom, 3.1, to the top, 3.4 per dollar. In addition, they allowed short-term interest rates on *cetes* (domestic short-term Treasury debt) to rise from 10% at the end of March to 17% at the end of April, in an attempt to stem the outflow of the capital.[74] In the meantime, some concerns about the sustainability of Mexico's external economic situation was expressed outside Mexico, by analysts, such as Dornbusch and Werner (1994) and Calvo (1994), the World Bank staff, and U.S. officials. In response to the capital flight and to restore confidence, the United States also extended Mexico a $6.7 billion line of credit on March 25, 1994.[75] In spite of the U.S. credit and the higher interest rates, investors' demand for *cetes* continued to lag because of their expectation of peso devaluation. Meanwhile, the Mexican stock market was teetering as private investors were taking their money out of the market and buying dollars and the stability of the peso was more in question.[76] According to Weintraub's (2000) observations, Mexican officials were deeply convinced that both a peso devaluation and its alternative course of sharply rising interest rates just prior to a contested presidential election would be fatal for the PRI. They were also concerned that a sharp rise in interest rates would worsen the situation of the already fragile banking sector.[77] However, investors were demanding even higher interest rates to compensate for the perceived political risks as well as ongoing increases in U.S. interest rates.

The impacts of Mexico's location, its relations with the U.S., and the developments in the U.S. The U.S. Federal Reserve Board (FED) raised short-term U.S. interest rates twice in the first quarter of 1994 (in February and March), and raised them again in the second quarter (in April and May) to curb inflationary pressures. A total of the four increases reached 1.25 percentage points. Throughout 1994, U.S. short-term interest rates were raised a total of six times and by March 1995, the FED funds rate reached 6.0 percent from 3.0 percent in February 1994. During a time of capital flight from Mexico in the aftermath of the Colosio assassination, the higher interest rates in the U.S. increased the attractiveness of investment in U.S. instruments. This, in turn, increased the capital flight out of Mexico (and other emerging markets), and brought upward pressure on the Mexican interest rates.[78] Naím (1997) argues that U.S. Federal Reserve Chairman Alan Greenspan's decisions to raise U.S. interest rates caused the Mexican markets to drop much more than did the news of the Chiapas uprising in the south.[79] The opening of the Mexican economy and the capital inflows increased Mexico's economic interdependence with the world economy, in particular with that of the United States. The hike of U.S. interest rates affected the capital inflows to all the emerging markets negatively, but it had even more of an effect in Mexico, which shares a long common border and is in a free trade zone with the world's biggest and most advanced economy.[80] In addition, having fixed its exchange rate to the dollar, the Bank of Mexico became dependent on the monetary policies of the Federal Reserve. Following a different monetary policy from that of the Federal Reserve brought only troubles to Mexico.[81] The Mexican officials failed to react adequately to the rising interest rates in the U.S., since they believed that the domestic political shocks were scaring investors, rather than external factors.[82]

The impacts of Mexican officials' misperceptions, expectations, and wishful thinking. According to Burki (1997), the World Bank staff conveyed to the Mexican financial authorities that the exchange rate had served its purpose and it was time to bring some more flexibility to it in order to prevent overvaluation and concurrent trade and current account deficits throughout 1994. The World Bank recommended to BOM officials that the BOM should leave the nominal exchange rate more flexible in order to absorb external shocks and continue to anchor its monetary policy according to an inflation rate target rather than the exchange rate target. Burki himself, as the incoming Regional Vice President for Latin America and the Caribbean, visited Mexico together with his predecessor and met with the cabinet and President Salinas in early 1994. He met with Secretary of Finance Pedro Aspe in April 1994 again. In those meetings as well they raised their concerns about the vulnerability of the external sector to the overvaluation of the exchange rate. The Mexican officials did not agree with the WB recommendations, according to Burki (1997).[83] They argued that the exchange rate band had enough flexibility to deal with disequilibria, and that a rapid increase in productivity, which would help to reduce the external imbalances (trade and CA deficits), was about to take place. They also argued that the long-term macroeconomic fundamentals were healthy, and the ratification of NAFTA would make things even better,[84] as they were expecting a surge in FDI. They believed that as Mexico became part of the NAFTA as well as other international treaties/organizations, such as the WTO, the OECD, and APEC, the political risks perceived by foreign investors would be decreased and the country's attractiveness to international capital, in particular FDI, increased. The Mexican financial authorities expected that Mexico's continuing attractiveness for foreign investors would eventually prevent capital flight, and the large gap between exports and imports would gradually close as the country's competitiveness improved. As these happen, Mexico's dependence on foreign capital would subside.[85] The prospect of NAFTA during late 1993 and 1994 fueled more capital flows, but in turn provoked even greater appreciation of the peso and thus worsened the current-account deficit in Mexico. Mexico's openness and integration into international financial markets made it more vulnerable to a reversal in market sentiments.[86] The WB staff warned the Mexican authorities about the increasing risk in the banking system as well. Although the Mexican government limited the open foreign-exchange positions of banks, it did not take any further step to improve the fragile banking system.[87]

The impacts of external interest groups. As the economic situation increasingly deteriorated following Colosio's assassination, frightened foreign investors, particularly those located in New York, increasingly doubted that the peso would hold within its trading band. According to one report, a fund manager from Fidelity Investments called Mexico's Central Bank officials in order to be assured that the peso would hold. Soon after the assassination, the Weston Group and a New York investment bank, which brokered peso security trades for mutual funds, organized a consortium known as the Weston Forum. The Forum members included the Weston Group, Fidelity, Trust Company of the West, Scudder, Stevens & Clark, Oppenheimer Management, Putnam Funds Management, Soros Fund Management, Salomon Brothers, and Nomura Securities International, according to the *Wall Street Journal*.[88] This was a formidable group, Weintraub (2000) asserts.[89] A couple of weeks after the assassination, the forum conveyed their "suggestions"/demands to the Mexican government. The forum members met twice with senior Mexican officials in Washington D.C. They also visited Mexico City on April 8 and April 20, and met with Mexican officials, including Guillermo Ortiz from the Treasury, Ariel Buira, a vice governor of the BOM, and Agustín Carstens, director of research at the BOM.[90] The recommendations/demands of the Forum were opposed to that of the World Bank. They "suggested" that the Mexican government curb the speed of the peso's daily devaluation, and insure foreign investors against currency-exchange losses on their $5 billion worth of peso-denominated securities, if the peso dropped below the prescribed range. The forum also demanded that the Mexican government issue long-term *tesobonos* and dollar-denominated treasury bills, and allow Mexican banks to increase their foreign currency liabilities to 25% of total assets from 20%, even though this would put the Mexican banks at greater risk if the peso were to fall. It also asked the government to back all these measures with the BOM's peso purchases to bolster the currency in order to stop the capital flight and attract new foreign capital.[91] Even though the forum members argued that these measures would assist Mexico in obtaining more investments, obviously they were after protecting their own interests. The consequences of disregarding their "suggestions" were not clear, but Mexican officials could not ignore the message by such a powerful group of foreign investors at a time when Mexico needed capital inflows the most. They were not disinterested bystanders and their demands were not negotiable. In fact, one day before they met with the Mexican authorities, they signaled to the Mexican authorities how much they would affect the Mexican markets. When they "refused to buy short-term Mexican treasury certificates in sufficient quantity to replace existing ones," short-term interest rates soared and the *Bolsa*, Mexico's stock market, plunged.[92]

After the "ultimatum" of the Weston Forum, the Salinas government lifted the exchange rate to the top of the band without changing the band, increased the interest rates, offered $10 billion in *tesobonos,* and bought up pesos on the international markets. Following these measures the *Wall Street Journal* wrote:

> So far, the fund managers have reason to be pleased with Mexico's response. Soon after the Weston Forum meeting, Mexican officials launched a peso rescue operation. They issued longer-term tesobonos as the investor group asked, and cut back on the auctions of Mexican treasury bills, or cetes, to reduce short-term rates. Then, senior Mexican finance officials flew to Washington to announce a trilateral currency support program among the U.S., Canada, and Mexico. After these meetings, Mr. Aspe, the finance minister, visited with Fidelity's fund managers.[93]

However, these measures did not prevent the outflow of over $10 billion from Mexico within six weeks after the assassination. If these measures were not there, would there have been even more capital flight? It is hard to know. But, it is quite clear that Mexican officials were taking the demands of fund managers seriously, even though the extent to which they were influenced by the forum cannot be known precisely. Smith (1997), quoting from the *Wall Street Journal* (June 14, 1994) writes that:

> We have to listen to these guys,' acknowledged Guillermo Ortiz Martínez, then Under Secretary of Finance. 'But one thing is to listen and the other is to follow their policy recommendations. It is pretty obvious that we would be in deep trouble if we were to be following the advice of investors' about how to run the economy.[94]

In response to the pressures on the exchange rate, the Mexican government continued to change the composition of government debt from *cetes* (the peso-denominated treasury bills) to *tesobonos* (the dollar-denominated treasury bills) in order to attract foreign capital.[95] Tesobono sales became the major instrument of financial policy during the second quarter of 1994. Outstanding tesobonos increased from $1.6 billion at the beginning of 1994 to $3.8 billion at the end of March, and to $13 billion at the end of June. By mid-1994, the government was able to convert much of its short-term *cetes* debt to *tesobonos*. By the end of 1994, *tesobonos* increased from 6 percent of the total foreign holding of government securities in December 1993 to 87 percent of that. The Mexican government issued approximately $30 billion in *tesobonos* throughout 1994. Because of their dollar indexing, the use of *tesobonos* allowed the Mexican government to pay less interest for borrowed capital. Large sales of tesobonos kept the interest rates lower than what they actually could have been in order to sustain the exchange rate, and delayed the pressures on the exchange rate for devaluation. Thus, "the tesobonos substituted for an actual devaluation of the peso, which had been ruled out for the time being."[96] However, this strategy proved to be risky because of its reliance on exchange rate stability. In addition, the government's short-term debt grew. $30 billion of total debt of about $160 billion was due in 1995, and more than $16 billion of this amount was in the form of *tesobonos.* [97]

The impacts of miscalculation and wishful thinking. The issues surrounding *tesobonos* were often discussed at the BOM board meetings, as one of the bank's senior officials told Weintraub (2000). The Spanish version of the Bank of Mexico's *Informe 1994* reveals the monetary authorities' thinking about the *tesobonos.* A passage in the *Informe 1994* argued the following:

> Because of the growing perception of foreign investors that there was a large exchange risk in Mexico, they demanded dollar instruments in place of those denominated in pesos; had the government refused to issue more tesobonos, it was highly probable that the Mexican public itself would have demanded foreign exchange as their cetes expired, putting pressure on foreign reserves and the exchange rate; what the authorities did was logical in order to get by what was considered to be a transitory situation. . . .[98]

But the demand for *tesobonos* was accelerating, not abating. By the middle of 1994, markets lost their confidence in the government's commitment for the exchange rate band. After July 18, 1994 the outstanding *tesobonos* overtook the level of the BOM reserves.[99] As elections were approaching, devaluation fears were still there. However, the government was using foreign exchange reserves to fill the financing gap rather than devaluing the peso, or rising the interest rates further to reduce the pressure on the exchange rate. Instead, the Salinas government eased the restrictions on credit. Interest rates on 28-day *cetes* declined from a peak of 18 percent in April to about 13.5 percent in November, while U.S. interest rates were increasing. The central bank, which was supposed to be autonomous, expanded credit by 400 percent from mid-1993 to mid-1994. Declining international reserves coincided with a more than 20 percent monetary expansion in 1994 and lax credit policies.[100]

Salinas initiated a few electoral laws before the August election, in order to contain the political effects of the Zapatista rebellion and Colosio assassination, as well as in response to the allegations of fraud in the 1988 elections.[101] But they were far from being genuinely democratic reforms. Mexico had its presidential elections in August 1994. The PRI's candidate Zedillo competed against two other candidates, as did Salinas in the 1988 elections. The PAN's presidential candidate Diego Fernández de Cevallos accepted Mexico's reorientation toward the market-oriented economy but challenged the lack of democracy. Cuauhtémoc Cárdenas ran for presidency again, as the candidate of the Party of the Democratic Revolution (PDR)[102] this time. He also accepted the reforms but criticized the democratic and social deficits of the Mexican political system. Diego Fernández seemed to be doing very well in early May, and an opposition victory seemed to be possible for the first time. However, "at precisely that point, Fernández suddenly and mysteriously stopped campaigning," according to

Smith (1997).[103] In the end, Zedillo won the elections with 48.8 percent of the officially recorded votes and was to be inaugurated on December 1. Diego Fernández came second with 25.9% votes, Cárdenas came third with 16.6% votes, and small parties gathered the rest of the votes.[104]

The Continued Impacts of Various Non-Economic Factors after the Election

The impacts of domestic interest groups and the government's credibility. Prior to the election, "the PRI could not afford a devaluation due to its impact on politically crucial middle-class and lower middle-class urban consumers."[105] Urban voters needed to be incited to vote for the PRI by maintaining the exchange rate and their access to inexpensive consumption goods through expansionary fiscal policies. This was especially important in that both the PDR and PAN were attracting considerable support from the urban middle classes.[106] Following the elections, the Salinas administration could have devalued the peso before Zedillo's inauguration on December 1. However, the Mexican government continued its pre-election policy, or its inaction, which was making the country increasingly vulnerable. Why? Several intermixed economic and non-economic factors prevented the government from a radical policy change. The following paragraphs shed some light on this issue. As we have discussed earlier, the exchange rate had become the symbol of the government's overall policy credibility prior to the elections. Monetary policy credibility was also associated with the nominal exchange rate.[107] Any change to the exchange rate could cause a collapse of confidence in policymakers. In addition, the government needed to convince participants of the *pacto* before taking a devaluation decision and accompanied policy measures, in order to maintain the support of the *pacto* members, in particular business and labor. The PRI needed the support of middle classes for the elections, but now, business and labor were more important for the government's capacity to implement any program that went with the devaluation. Therefore, labor and business leaders needed to be convinced that modest austerity measures were worth their cooperation and that they could expect to eventually be repaid for their support. However, the PRI's abilities to broker a resolution and its trustworthiness were questioned both before and after the election, due to internal divisions, political assassinations, and the deteriorating economic situation.[108] The Mexican government was also constrained by its symbiotic alliance with the business community, in particular the large firms and conglomerates that dominated substantial portions of the Mexican economy and the newly privatized banks. By the 1990s the power structure of the dominant one-party system had changed. The peasantry no longer represented significant resources, organized labor had lost its relative power, and small and medium businesses remained weak. The big businesses had become stronger and had a greater influence on government policies.[109]

The impacts of presidential succession and past experiences. After the election, investors, especially those who knew about the dynamics of presidential succession in Mexico, were already anxious about the power transition and the incoming administration. The presidential inauguration signified an instantaneous, complete, and profound interruption and transfer of power in Mexico. Political scientist Smith (1997) asserts that "the outgoing president exercised supreme authority right up to the final moment of the *sexenio*, at which point the successor instantly assumed full command."[110] Memories of the presidential successions in 1976 and 1982, which were accompanied with political tensions and financial/economic problems, were still alive. Similar to the situation in 1994, real appreciation and capital inflows were followed by a large devaluation and subsequent financial crisis, during those presidential successions.[111] Market participants, especially those who knew the repeated pattern, became more cautious and sensitive during the last years of the Mexican presidents in terms of the possibility of devaluation and economic collapse.[112] Zedillo, who was to be inaugurated on December 1, 1994, did not give confidence as well. He lacked any independent base of support in the PRI and it did not seem that he would be able "to hold together the disparate forces needed to sustain an orderly adjustment."[113] As a result, investors were worried and cautious about potential developments after the elections.

The impacts of presidential succession, the weak banking system, miscalculations, and wishful thinking. On September 24, the Mexican government, after an active debate, announced a new *pacto*, named the Pact for Welfare, Stability, and Growth (PABEC), in an effort to reassure investors. However, the pact did not bring any major policy change: exchange rate, fiscal and monetary policies were maintained and the substitution of maturing *cetes* with *tesobonos* continued.[114] It just confirmed the government's decision to retain the old policy. Thus, the Mexican government missed another opportunity to make gradual adjustments to the exchange rate and/or tighten the monetary policy by raising the interest rates. Many analysts, in particular Mexico-watchers, were mystified. The staff of the Federal Reserve Board later affirmed that the *pacto* provided an excellent opportunity "for altering the exchange rate regime and gradually eliminating the accumulated overvaluation."[115] Mexican officials were concerned that a rise in interest rates could undermine the country's weak banking system. Starting from late 1992, non-performing loans constantly increased, reaching 7.3 percent in 1993 and 8.3 percent at the end of the first quarter of 1994. However, the government's protection of the highly vulnerable financial system and failure to make adjustments after the elections later resulted in an even higher ratio of non-performing loans.[116] The government's attempts to strengthen the weak banks did not bring any substantial improvement.[117]

According to Weintraub (2000), president Salinas and the Secretary of Treasury/Finance Aspe[118] were behind the continuation of the old policies, especially the no-devaluation policy. For different reasons they did not want to devalue the peso before the inauguration of the new administration, as will be discussed further in the following paragraphs. The president-elect Zedillo supported the *pacto*, even though he was not a partisan of the policy and his advisers believed that exchange-rate policy should be more flexible. Zedillo said to

Weintraub (2000) in his interview "that the government could have acted on the exchange rate anytime between September 1 and November 20, not by an abrupt change, which would have been disruptive, but by beginning a gradual correction." It did not happen and Zedillo did not pressure Salinas to do so. Weintraub (2000) speculates that Zedillo did not want to offend Salinas and "assumed there was time enough once he became president himself to alter economic and financial policy."[119] Weintraub (2000) thinks that "the essence of the decision taken in the *pacto* meeting of September 24—was that corrective action [for the peso overvaluation and the growing current account deficit] could wait until the new administration was in office."[120] The Mexican officials wanted to buy time. They were optimistic that investors would see that the heightened turbulence was temporary and additional funds would flow into the country once again.[121] Indeed, the elections and the pact in September seemed to ease turbulence in financial markets for a short while, until the assassination of the PRI Secretary General and subsequent developments.[122]

The impacts of political assassinations, domestic interest groups, and miscalculations. Four days after the announcement of the *pacto* (on September 28), José Francisco Ruiz Massieu, PRI Secretary General and the leader of the PRI caucus in the Chamber of Deputies was assassinated in Mexico City as he left a political gathering. This second major political killing shook again the already volatile markets.[123] Some speculated that his assassination was a warning to Zedillo not to push ahead with his reform plans, which were supported by José Francisco Ruiz Massieu. Another speculation was that it was in retaliation against his brother, the deputy attorney general, Mario Ruiz Massieu, who was threatening to imprison the country's largest drug lords by the time Salinas left office. In the 1980s and 1990s international drug cartels grew to the extent of posing a serious threat to legal authority. Mexico had about a half dozen truly international drug cartels, in cities such as Tijuana, Sinaloa, Ciudad Juárez, and Guadalajara, and they were seriously threatening the governability of the country.[124] Mario Ruiz Massieu resumed the investigation of the assassination, but resigned from his job on November 23 (a week before Salinas was to step down from the presidency) without completing the investigation amidst accusation that the attorney general and PRI officials were obstructing his investigation. The assassination cast more doubts about the PRI's integrity and ability to maintain support for the *pacto*. It seemed that at the highest levels of the political establishments, violence and murder were coming to replace bargaining, negotiation and co-optation. It meant that Mexico's political elite lost its coherence (internal discipline), which had been the persistent feature of political stability in Mexico.[125]

The policy stance of the Mexican government remained the same after the assassination, even though investors became more nervous. In mid-October, major Mexican corporations, including telecommunication giant Telmex (Teléfonos de México), announced lower third-quarter earnings than expected. The stock market declined, and the weakened peso moved to the top of the band. The authorities intensified the substitution of *tesobonos* for *cetes* in order to attract more foreign capital.[126] Mancera gave a speech to the banking convention in Cancún on October 19. That time, the BOM's international reserve level was around 17.3 billion. In his speech, he argued that the reserves were adequate to defend the peso. The BOM was able to keep the reserves around $17.2 billion until the end of October. On November 1, Salinas gave his sixth and the last *Informe,* "state of the union" address, to the Mexican Congress. He listed the main accomplishments of his *sexenio,* and did not comment much about the "real" economic/financial problems that Mexico was facing. However, he revealed that the international reserves fell from about $28 billion at the beginning of 1994 to $17 billion at the beginning of November 1994. Like Mancera, he also assured that reserves were enough to defend the value of the peso. But markets reacted differently. Following his reassurance, the reserve level started to go down on November 3. The Bank of Mexico started to intervene in the markets on November 14, and spent $3.5 billion by the end of the month, and reserves declined to $12.5 billion. The Bank of Mexico, in its annual report, attributed the reserve losses to the resignation of Mario Ruíz Massieu as assistant attorney general with the aforementioned accusations. This was partly true, but there were more reasons.[127] Things were not going well. Capital was not flowing into Mexico, except via the continued sale of *tesobonos,* which reached around 70% of short-term public debt in excess of $27 billion. On November 15, the U.S. Federal Reserve raised short-term interest rates again, by 0.75 percent this time. This made things even more difficult for Mexico to attract capital. Mexican interest rates were not raised further due to persistent concerns about the weak conditions of commercial banks.[128]

The impacts of President Salinas' personal ambitions and commitments, wishful thinking, and the opposition to NAFTA within the U.S. Congress. Thus, toward the end of Salinas' presidency, the peso was overvalued, the stock market was depressed and Mexico's reserves were still declining. In November, newly elected president Zedillo wanted Salinas to devalue the peso before he was to be inaugurated on December 1, 1994. On November 20, Salinas administration officials and Zedillo's team[129] had a meeting at the presidential residence on a possible devaluation of the peso. Weintraub(2000)'s interview with Serra, who replaced Aspe with the inauguration of Zedillo, as well as Aspe's communications with the press show that the discussion of the meeting covered a 10-15 percent devaluation of the peso, or a drastic rise in interest rates to obviate the need to devalue.[130] However, a consensus was not possible, and at the end the Salinas group rejected any devaluation before he left office. The spokesman for the prevailing *pacto* expressed support for the decision on the same day.[131] Allegedly, Salinas refused to make the devaluation decision mainly because of his candidacy for the directorship of the WTO, for which he had President Clinton's support. He did not want to hurt his chances by admitting that his economic policy was flawed. He was eager to finish his term with a good reputation, in order to sanctify his place in history and to promote his candidacy for the WTO. Devaluation decisions by previous outgoing presidents had been deathly for their prestige. Young and ambitious Salinas was determined to challenge the destiny that the previous presidents faced as they left the office with disrepute and/or disgrace along with a degrading retirement and minor positions in the bureaucracy. A devaluation would put Salinas in a similar position. He wanted to avoid all these. Smith (1997) argues that securing "the legacy and popularity of the outgoing president" and maintaining "patronage and discipline within the PRI" were the real reasons behind the expansionary policies as well as the Salinas government's refusal to devalue throughout 1994, rather than the presidential election in August 1994. Zedillo's team was not that insistent as well. Salinas, Aspe, Zedillo and Serra thought that once the new administration was established, the adjustment could be made smoothly. Weintraub (2000)'s interviews with government insiders support his point. In addition, Salinas' advisers were worried that devaluation might have led to a stock market crash.[132]

Moreover, Salinas was implicitly under the obligation not to devalue the peso before, during or just after the ratification of NAFTA. In 1993, the pro-NAFTA forces in the U.S. insistently argued that the implementation of the NAFTA treaty would stimulate American exports and create new jobs, before the Congress cast its vote. This argument was based on the assumption that the peso would stay strong. On the other hand, the opponents of NAFTA, like Representative John LaFalce of New York, suspicious of the Mexican government, argued the opposite, i.e. the Mexican government was withholding its intention to devalue. In fact, Salinas' political reputation and destiny were closely bound with NAFTA and a stable peso.[133]

As long as he could, Salinas was not going to make devaluation for all of these reasons. Salinas placed economic policy at the service of his own political interests, and perhaps, he was not fully aware of the deleterious economic implications of that decision. His economic policies, free from any effective institutional checks, were not questioned in terms of their soundness.[134] In addition, the president was occupied with other issues—first the elections, then emotional issues concerning his marriage, and the murder of Ruíz Massieu, who had been married to his sister. Therefore, Onate, then the Chief of Staff, was not sure about the depth of Salinas' desire to head the WTO, Weintraub (2000) reports.[135] Salinas' no-devaluation decision "meant that he would have to court additional foreign investment [in order to finance CA deficits], whatever the cost; and this, in turn, required maintenance of a stable currency. Ironically enough, his efforts brought about precisely the result that he was seeking to avoid," Smith (1997) notes.[136]

The impacts of the Mexican officials' economic ideology/policy approach, political ambitions, and domestic and external interest groups. Salinas' finance minister Pedro Aspe also declined to make a devaluation plan in order to prepare the road for the Zedillo administration, and left the incoming finance minister Serra uninformed. There are several speculative explanations for Aspe's inaction. According to Weintraub (2000), Aspe did not believe in the 15 percent devaluation, or that gradual devaluation would solve the problem without losing the credibility of the government and foreign confidence. He also believed that a devaluation decision had to be embedded within an overall economic package, which should be put together by the incoming Zedillo team. Another speculation about Aspe's inaction is that Aspe wanted to stay as the Secretary of Treasury/Finance in the incoming cabinet and refused other positions offered. Since he was not going to get the position he wanted, he left the burden of the devaluation on the incoming Secretary of Finance. Miguel Mancera, the governor of the Bank of Mexico, supported by the BOM's four vice-governors, prioritized anti-inflation policies that were incompatible with a devaluation decision. However, although his voice counted much, any decision to change the exchange rate was not up to him, but was up to Aspe who had the decisive vote in the board established for this purpose. In addition, investment bankers in the money centers wanted the continuation of the policy and much more as we have discussed. They were very influential, due to Mexico's need for the capital inflow to finance its large current account deficit. U.S. officials in the Treasury and the investment bank officials who were engaged in Mexican affairs at that time informed Weintraub (2000) that Aspe was on the telephone frequently assuring bankers that the peso would not be devalued. It is hard to know how influential the investment bankers and the Weston Group were in the decision-making process, but Aspe was attentive to them, and he was trusted by them. Aspe assured and reassured them on the phone that there would be no devaluation. It seems that he assumed that the continuation of the policy would lead to continuation of much needed capital inflows.[137] The exchange rate decisions were delayed until the new year. Postponement of any devaluation decision until the beginning of the new year "would also have been more convenient for the investment bankers engaged in Mexico, because then the devaluation would come after they received their year-end bonuses."[138] Of course, it is hard to know to what extent the interests of foreign investment bankers played a role in the delay of a devaluation decision until the end of 1994.

The impacts of wishful thinking, domestic interest groups, and the pacto mechanism. Mexico's foreign reserves increasingly declined throughout November 1994, as investors with their eyes on political and economic developments in Mexico pulled their money back. The BOM continued to use its increasingly scarce dollars to defend the peso. Salinas' team was still inclined to see the instability of the financial markets as temporary and thought that normalcy would prevail in the markets once confidence was restored and political turmoil subsided. The government believed that a renewal of the *Pacto* would be enough to show the incoming government's commitment to its exchange rate policy and be adequate to shore up investor confidence. Negotiation for the Pact for Economic Growth and Stability (PECE) was on the way. Salinas and his economic team usually negotiated the content, timing and the implementation of economic/financial goals first with representatives of business associations and then informed and bargained with labor at the forum provided by the *pacto* mechanism. During this *pacto* negotiation, devaluation was debated within the context of the *pacto* mechanism, and thus some privileged groups were provided with the information of a possible devaluation. This information enabled them to "exit" the financial markets before devaluation actually occurred and, ultimately, was to exacerbate the upcoming financial crisis.[139]

The impacts of the presidential transition and miscalculations. On November 30, Zedillo's cabinet was announced, and Secretary of Finance Pedro Aspe was replaced by Jamie Serra Pucha, who had served as Secretary of Commerce under Salinas' administration and represented Mexico in the NAFTA negotiations. Mexico's stock markets (*Bolsa de Valores*) dropped 50 points, in particular as a reaction to Pedro Aspe's leave. Aspe's leave shook investor confidence, which was closely tied to Aspe's constant assurances of no devaluation, and the trust that developed between the investment bankers and Aspe.[140] Although the Zedillo administration was going to start anew on December 1, Zedillo could have reappointed Pedro Aspe as Secretary of Finance. He acted according to rules of political logic, but it was a serious mistake, according to Smith (1997). It seems that "Zedillo and his associates did not understand the extent to which the investment community identified macroeconomic stability not with the system but with Aspe himself."[141] Although Zedillo brought a member of the PAN into his cabinet as the attorney general (the first time in Mexican history) and pledged to step up efforts to solve the Colosio and Ruiz Massieu cases, and also agreed to cooperate with the opposition, these actions were not very helpful in changing the deteriorating financial economic situation.[142]

THE PESO CRISIS AND PRESIDENT ZEDILLO ADMINISTRATION

The impacts of presidential transition, the bad image of the Zedillo Administration, and administrative priorities. Zedillo was inaugurated on December 1, 1994. Zedillo, himself, told Weintraub (2000) that "when he was nominated, there were capital outflows and a fall in the stock market (*bolsa*); when he won the election, the reaction was similar; and after his inaugural address, the same thing happened."[143] Zedillo's inaugural address was not inspirational and did not touch on the sensitive financial issues. Although one day after his inauguration, Zedillo had dinner with private-sector leaders, emphasized "stability," and assured the markets that the peso would not be devalued, his assurances did not do much. Zedillo's cabinet was not well received and was referred to as a cabinet of vice-ministers in Mexico, a phrase that captured the perception of the business community as well as the popular perception. In addition, Zedillo's cabinet included many old-guard members of the ruling Institutional Revolutionary Party (PRI), who were not seen as committed as the young members of the Salinas team to further market reforms.[144] Weintraub (2000) was repeatedly told during his interviews that "the briefings of the new cabinet secretaries by the outgoing ones were largely superficial." As insiders informed Weintraub (2000), relations between the outgoing secretary of finance Aspe and the new secretary of finance Serra were cool and they were seen as rivals. Serra was not well informed about the key details that surrounded his main responsibilities at that point, and he did not find any contingency plan when he took office. Aspe's description of the meeting on November 20 implied that there was a Plan B, which would be carried out if foreign reserves fell below $10 billion.[145] In addition, during his early days Serrra was occupied with preparing the budget for 1995, which he was required to submit to the Congress by mid-December. He was busy with getting detailed briefings for his congressional testimony. He had much less time for, which turned out to be more pressing, financial and monetary issues that led to a financial collapse just five days after the legal deadline for the budget submission. If he had had time, he may have discussed the exchange rate, capital flights, the value of the peso, and listened to different views, even though the result might not have been different, since the exchange rate decisions were already deferred until the new year.[146]

On December 9, Serra announced an economic policy package and the budget for 1995, which was not compatible with the real situation. His macroeconomic policy framework called for a 4.0 percent growth in GDP, 5.0 percent inflation, and a current account deficit of 7.8 percent of GDP, and did not change the exchange rate policy and the fiscal policy. By December, Mexico's current account deficit had already reached 7.0 percent of GDP and Mexico's deteriorating economic indicators were calling for a radical change in the economic policy. As a result, the unrealistic budget, on which Serra worked hard, did not convince the markets and damaged his credibility. In retrospect, it seems that Serra did not set his priorities right. A week after the announcement of the budget and the economic policy, capital flight started again, and the foreign exchange reserves fell an additional $1 billion. Mexico's reserves were down to $11.1 billion by December 16. $4 billion dollars fled the country between mid-November and mid-December.[147] In fact, the financial crisis was about to come.

The impacts of history, nationalism, and culture. No one predicted the upcoming crisis. According to *the Washington Post,* the World Bank, IMF, and U.S. officials had warned Mexican authorities throughout 1994 to change their course of action and to make economic reforms,[148] but no one was expecting an immediate crisis. Nonetheless, as we have discussed, the Mexican authorities did not act upon recommendations for multiple non-economic reasons and stuck to their policies. Burki (1997) argues that the World Bank did not publicly criticize the Mexican government's economic policies not to upset financial markets. In early December 1994, the World Bank staff suggested a high level meeting on Mexico's macroeconomics and exchange rate policy among the senior officials of the World Bank, the IMF, and the new economic authorities of Mexico. The Mexican authorities first agreed to have the meeting between Christmas and the New Year, but later decided to postpone the meeting until February 1995.[149]

Weintraub (2000) stresses three types of historical influence (political and cultural) on how the Mexican leaders behaved in 1994. One is a *defensive variety of nationalism* as reflected in official Mexican statements and actions. The Mexican officials "repeatedly admonished other nations—really the United States—to stay out of internal Mexican affairs just as Mexico promised to stay out of the internal affairs of others."[150] Even though Salinas changed the tenor of

Mexico's relationship with the U.S., Mexican officials constantly rejected outside advice even though their economic policies were on a collision course. From his interviews, Weintraub (2000) got an impression that Mexican officials acted as if they knew "the true situation in their own country much better than officials from international financial institutions who parachuted into Mexico for negotiations." The U.S. and IMF officials he spoke to also told him that "it was a trying experience to negotiate with Mexicans, more so than dealing with the officials of most other countries."[151] In the end, Mexico had to be bailed out again with conditions imposed by external lenders, especially the IMF and the U.S. Treasury. The second type of historical influence is the Mexicans' preference for *strong national leaders*, with a belief that the country needed a firm hand to prosper. Salinas was attuned to authoritarianism and firm leadership rather than democracy, and he was popular until 1994. Many within the PRI criticized Zedillo for "his lack of forceful leadership." [152] The third one is related to the way Mexican leaders conducted the daily business of governance in the one-party rule system that lasted from 1929 until late 2000. Secrecy, arrogance, and corruption were the legacy of one-party dominance in Mexico. Transparency in conducting public affairs had been generally lacking and the public's main source of information had been the government's own explanations until the late 1990s.[153] In parallel, the level of international reserves was disclosed only three times a year by the BOM. In the aftermath of the crisis, some argued that "the lack of current information on Mexico's reserves position played an important role in magnifying the crisis. Once it was realized that the country's financial situation was much weaker than it had been led to be believed, confidence in the authorities disappeared, and a massive withdrawal of funds took place."[154]

The Mexican Government Facing the Crisis

The impacts of the rebellion in Chiapas, the pacto mechanism, and domestic interest groups. Zedillo approached the rebellion in Chiapas by hardening the government's stance with the EZLN, and armed conflict resumed in Chiapas on December 18. The next day (on December 19), already cautious investors dumped Mexican stocks and bonds following a false announcement by the Zapatista rebels that they had slipped through the military's cordon and occupied thirty-eight municipalities in Chiapas. On the same day, the Mexican foreign reserves started to decline fast again, down to $10.5 billion, a level close to the arbitrary $10 billion threshold that was set by Aspe to reconsider a policy change. That time the exchange rate was 3.47 pesos per dollar.[155] The government finally admitted that the current situation was not sustainable under severe currency trading pressures and called for a *pacto* meeting, since any change in the exchange rate policy had to be approved by the *pacto* mechanism. The meeting, at which government officials met with labor and business leaders, took place on December 19-20.[156] The discussion was lengthy. About half of the full *pacto* membership (around 60-75 people) attended and Zedillo was out of Mexico City, in Sonora. The key government player was Serra at the meeting, since he represented the decisive vote, as the Secretary of Treasury/Finance. Mancera had a bad cold and was not feeling well during the meeting.[157] In the meeting, government officials and the BOM were in consensus to abandon the exchange rate band and float the peso. However, their proposition was negotiated and overridden by the business leaders who opposed floating the peso. As a result, the government officials reached a "compromise" decision of 15% devaluation, which was suggested by then president of the Mexican banker's association, José Madariaga Lomelín. Thus, the outcome of the *pacto* meeting was strongly influenced by private bankers, a powerful interest group. With 15% devaluation, the upper limit of the intervention band of the peso increased from 3.5 to 4.0 points. Before he agreed with the outcome, Serra consulted with Mancera and with Zedillo (by phone) in order to get their full consents.[158] Later, some analysts argued that the business leaders asked for the 15 percent increase in the intervention band as a temporary measure to give them time to change their liquid assets into dollars before the implementation of the float.[159] Serra announced the devaluation decision, in a rather informal way on radio and television the morning of December 20. However, the announcement did not quell speculative attacks on the peso, but rather caused angered investors to rush their money out of the country on December 21. On that day, the BOM spent $4.5 billion to defend the peso, and the reserves fell under $6 billion. The same day, Zedillo confirmed the government's commitment to the new exchange band. But the next day the government was forced to abandon the whole exchange rate mechanism (crawling peg with band), which had been operating for three years, and announce a full float of the peso on December 22.[160] This announcement caused an almost 40 percent loss in the peso's value in a week and a crash in the Mexican stock market. The crisis in Mexico created turbulence in foreign exchange markets and huge losses throughout Latin American Stock markets, in particular those of Argentina and Brazil,[161] as well. Mutual funds that were invested in Latin America lost an average of 15.6 percent in their net asset value in a week. In Mexico, the Zedillo administration imposed a 60-day wage and price freeze with inflationary fears.[162] The United States and Canada made about a $7 billion credit ($6 billion and $1 billion respectively) available for Mexico via activation of the swap lines among these countries.[163] However, all these did not prevent Mexico from sliding into a big financial/economic crash.

The impacts of the new administration's inexperience and inadequate policy measures. Aspe was proven right; Mexico was unable to get over with a small devaluation. Whether it would have made any difference if the devaluation decision was not an isolated decision, but was accompanied by an economic policy package, we cannot know for sure.[164] According to Quiroga (2001) "the devaluation, in conjunction with the failure by Mexican economic authorities to implement complementary fiscal and monetary adjustments, resulted in a high level of uncertainty and economic dislocation."[165] In addition, not only Zedillo's inaugural address, but also the official economic program, which was the General Economic Policy Criteria (CGPE) that was set forth for 1995, did not sufficiently address how the growing economic problems were going to be solved. The CGPE, for example, acknowledged that the current account deficit would increase from $28 billion in 1994 to more than $30 billion in 1995, but did not address how such a deficit was going to be financed. This amount would require Mexico to receive over 50 percent of total foreign portfolio investments available to Latin America. In 1994, Mexico only received 18 percent of such resources. Therefore, the CGPE targets did not seem viable and realistic by both domestic and foreign market participants.[166] The devaluation decision was taken in this atmosphere. From the beginning this 15 percent devaluation did not seem sustainable without any significant supporting measures. Moreover, a few days after the devaluation, "the Bank of Mexico carried out open market operations with government bonds at interest rates of over 30 percent, sending a clear signal to the markets that the 15 percent devaluation was insufficient."[167]

The way the devaluation was handled during the week of December 19 made the new government appear inexperienced and confused. It did not seem that the Mexican government was really capable of managing the economy. In addition, the government suffced with a public announcement of the devaluation decision, without reaching out and explaining it directly to major U.S. institutional investors. "One persistent complaint of New York investment bankers was that Serra did not respond to their telephone calls after the devaluation was announced," Weintraub (2000) reports.[168] The lack of communication was an element in the investors' reaction to the devaluation and the economic breakdown, especially when it is considered that the government devalued the currency despite its repeated promises throughout 1994. The peg's failure not only exacerbated the loss of confidence in the government's capacity to handle economic problems, but also inflicted severe damage on the credibility of the Zedillo administration. In the eyes of the U.S investors the government had lost control of the situation, and the Mexican government severely lost its reputation. As a result of the breakdown of communications between the Mexican government and the investors, all kinds of speculations filled the gap. For example, devaluation implied that dollar-indexed obligations would exercise considerable pressure on the public finances. Since the Mexican government failed to announce an economic policy package to address this and similar issues, it was not clear what the Mexican government was going to do next. Some even speculated that the Mexican government could impose capital controls, or default from its obligations.[169] Rumors led to panic and Mexico's deteriorating financial/economic situation turned into a deep crisis situation.

Serra was blamed "for not having the experience and savvy in dealing with money market players in New York and elsewhere." His reactions were slow for the fast-breaking market developments in the financial sector.[170] He went to New York in order to meet with investors on December 22, but received a cold reception. He failed to convince top money managers and banking executives, who already had lost their confidence, to remain confident about Mexico and to stay as investors. A few days later, Serra and his team also met with Alan

Greenspan and other Fed officials in Washington, D.C. This meeting led to the Fed's purchase of some amount of pesos in order to strengthen it. But, the peso continued to slide. Serra scheduled a news conference on December 26 in order to provide information about the government's plans, but later cancelled it. By December 27, the Peso depreciated to 5.1 per dollar. An auction of dollar-dominated government bonds failed to attract investors, as well. Only $27.6 million was collected from the total $74 million worth of bonds. Prices began to rise and labor leaders pushed for wage negotiations.[171] On December 28, the interest rate on a 28-day *cetes* increased by 15 points and reached 31 percent. By the first quarter of 1995, it reached 80 percent and remained above 50 percent until the summer of 1996. Serra resigned, after less than a month in his job as the secretary of Finance, and Guillermo Ortiz Martínez[172] became the new secretary of Treasury/Finance. On December 29, Zedillo announced the government's will to implement an emergency economic plan, which was scheduled to be revealed on January 2, 1995.[173]

Non-economic and economic factors and intermixed domestic and external factors. The crisis surprised many in Mexico and abroad. No one predicted that the devaluation of the peso would trigger a financial/economic disaster in Mexico. Warnings from the World Bank, the IMF, and the U.S. Treasury officials did not go beyond expressing some concerns about the deteriorating economic situation of the country, in particular growing issuance of *tesobonos*. No one was overly concerned, and no one was contemplating a disaster.[174] Naím (1997) argues that "although the Mexican crisis undoubtedly had Mexican origins, it was not simply the result of government mistakes, corruption, and electoral politicking. All of these elements were present, but Mexico's crisis was as much a story about the new international financial system as it was a story about Mexico. At each of the situation's crucial turning points, external factors helped to shape the outcome."[175] Michel Camdessus, then managing director of the IMF, called the peso crisis "the first crisis of the twenty-first century." The reversal of the unprecedented volume of short-term private capital outflows, facilitated by the new integrated financial world, struck the Mexican economy very badly.[176] The boom in foreign portfolio investments in Mexican stocks and bonds was an outcome of transient financial conditions abroad more than that of the neoliberal reforms in Mexico. The huge capital inflows initially helped the Mexican economy, but later they exacerbated the Mexican peso's overvaluation, stimulated imports, and masked the gravity of Mexico's CA deficits. In 1994, they became a burden by constraining the government's policy options. The continuation of capital inflows until the second half of 1994, together with domestic political concerns and restrictions, clouded the government's vision. Conflicting imperatives of economic adjustment and political survival caused the economic policy officials to design a set of constantly contradictory policies, which were not suitable to handle the volatile international capital. The Mexican government was not prepared to handle "the consequences of Mexico's financial integration into volatile world capital markets."[177] The Mexican government, after the financial crisis, took further measures that would decrease uncertainty in financial markets, prevent capital flight, strengthen its financial system, facilitate capital inflows again, and restore its net international reserves.[178]

Dealing with the Crisis Situation

The impacts of inexperience, miscalculations, and new trials and errors. Zedillo's emergency economic plan, the Agreement of Unity to Overcome the Economic Emergency, was announced on January 3, 1995, after a one-day delay. It attributed the crisis to unsustainable current account deficits. That time, the foreign exchange position of Mexico was around $6.2 billion. The program had optimistic assumptions and expectations, but it contained more realistic measures than the December budget goals. It projected 1.5 percent GDP growth, a 19.5 percent inflation target, and a reduction of the external current-account deficit from $29 billion to $14 billion. The major objectives were to contain the inflation and to reduce the current account deficit. It also included measures that aimed at stabilizing financial markets, decreasing exchange rate volatility, and reducing interest rates gradually. In addition, a fiscal surplus of 0.5 percent of GDP was to be achieved along with a cut in government expenditures equal to 1.3 percent of GDP. Further privatization of state-owned assets was expected to yield $12-14 billion. However, Zedillo's emergency economic plan[179] was hurriedly put together and was considered by many as insufficient. The program did not schedule a rollover amortization of payments. Although the IMF endorsed the program, it did not help much in stabilizing the financial markets of Mexico. The stock market and peso continued to fall. The next day (January 4), Ortiz went to New York to present the new program to a crowd of banking and brokerage officials in the ballroom of the Pierre Hotel and to appeal to investors to continue to roll over their *tesobonos*. There he stated that he was going to meet with Michael Camdessus, managing director of the IMF, in order to negotiate a standby agreement to begin immediately.[180]

    The impacts of the IMF, the U.S. government, and opposition to the NAFTA within the U.S. Congress. During the last week of December, the IMF sent a small mission group to Mexico to discuss a new IMF program, but at that time the Mexican officials were reluctant to agree on the IMF proposals. There were different proposals for Mexico's course of action after the fall of the peso. Some analysts even suggested a unilateral suspension of debt payments until the Mexican markets were restored. The Mexican government rejected these views and was inclined to adopt a market-based economic stabilization program in close consultation with the IMF (and U.S. officials) in early January 1995. Meanwhile, the situation was getting out of control, and as we discussed earlier, a large amount of short-term debt, most of which was composed of *tesobonos*, was due in early 1995.[181] After the Mexican government determined its course of action to address the crisis situation, the details of its response policy were shaped in negotiation with U.S. and IMF officials. Eventually, the government's policy choice enabled Mexico to receive a large-scale international financial rescue package, sponsored by the U.S. and the IMF. Early January 1995 was a turning point for the Mexican government's policy choice, as the government decided to shape its response policies to the crisis under the international influences, especially those of the IMF and the U.S., rather than domestic concerns or influences. The following paragraphs first review how the government's response policy was shaped, and discuss further why the government chose an IMF-style market oriented policy.

Mexico's economic and political stability has been a great concern for U.S. administrations due to the two countries' long and multifaceted economic and financial relations. The implementation of NAFTA further advanced these historic ties between Mexico and the U.S. In addition, the effects of the Mexican financial turmoil were also felt in U.S. markets to a much lesser extent than that of the Latin American markets and the dollar fell against the German mark.[182] Of course, the spread of the peso crisis would adversely affect U.S. trade relations not only with Mexico, but also with the Latin American countries. For all these reasons, the Clinton administration was concerned with the crisis situation in Mexico. However, there was little immediate reaction from officials in Washington to the Mexican financial turmoil. It was the Christmas season and Congress was in recess. Moreover, Treasury Secretary Lloyd Bentsen had resigned and the new Treasury Secretary Robert E. Rubin had not resumed his job yet. The White House did not act until after Serra' s failure to persuade the investors in New York. In the meantime, pressures from the financial community over the White House had been building up since the devaluation of the peso.[183] After President Zedillo's announcement of his economic emergency plan, the White House publicly started to advocate U.S. support in order to restore economic stability in Mexico. In early January, Mexican and U.S. officials reached an agreement in principle that the U.S. would sponsor an $18 billion international loan package and pay for half of it.[184] Canada was to provide $1.5 billion, the Bank for International Settlements (BIS) in Switzerland was to pay $5 billion, and about $3 billion was to come from a group of about a dozen international commercial sources. But this amount was not sufficient for Mexico's immediate needs, since some $28 billion[185] in short-term Mexican treasury bills were scheduled to fall in 1995.[186] This initiative died in the week following the announcement. A couple days later, the IMF provided some loans, upon the Mexican government's request, on a standby basis (allowing Mexico to draw it down as needed). The IMF loan increased Mexico's foreign exchange reserves about $2.5 to $3.5 billion.[187] In the meantime, it was becoming clear that Mexico's markets were not going to be stabilized without a more comprehensive effort. After the White House realized that an $18 billion credit line for Mexico was insufficient to stem the crisis, the Clinton administration announced its intention of proposing legislation to Congress in order to provide a credit of $40 billion in U.S. loan guaranties for Mexico around mid-January. The amount was to be used as needed in the event of a Mexican default to pay debts.[188] The Mexican government supported the initiative and declared that the package would not cost U.S. taxpayers anything because Mexico would pay all the fees involved. The reaction of the Republican leadership to the president's loan announcement was initially positive. A proposal of loan guarantees that would range from $25 billion to $40 billion was quickly prepared. However, congressional opposition, mostly composed of those who had opposed NAFTA one year earlier, soon challenged the proposal.[189] The opponents claimed that their argument—that Mexico would devalue its currency after the agreement took effect in order to gain a competitive advantage vis-à-vis the U.S.—was proven right. The congressional opposition was supported by environmental, human rights, and pro-democracy groups in the U.S. as well. "The pro-NAFTA coalition was unable to prevail this time around because the rescue package was so intimately linked by its opponents to NAFTA."[190] The Clinton administration used many arguments to convince Congress. Robert Rubin, the Secretary of Treasury, argued before the House Committee on Banking and Financial Services on January 25 that continued growth of U.S. exports, the prevention of augmented illegal immigration from Mexico, and avoidance of financial spillovers across the globe were at stake.[191] After long discussions in Congress, it became doubtful that the proposal would pass. The Clinton administration withdrew it at the end of January.[192]

In the meantime, Mexico's financial crisis was deepening. On January 10, Mexico's overnight interest rates rose from 40 percent to 60 percent, and Mexico's stock market suffered its worst loss in more than five years. The value of the U.S. dollar also kept declining as the peso crisis continued.[193] As these developments were happening, two main opposition parties were considering a criminal action against former president Salinas and two of his top advisers for their role in the financial crisis. A survey of 114 business leaders and economists by a Mexican independent newspaper, *Reforma*, indicated that 38 percent blamed Salinas, 8 percent blamed Zedillo, and 29 percent thought that both governments were responsible. While Zedillo was working hard to overcome the peso crisis, Salinas was working hard to rescue his reputation and his campaign to head the WTO. Salinas blamed the Zedillo administration for their "mishandling" of the devaluation, and defended his economic policies.[194]

After the Clinton administration gave up the fight to get congressional approval for the $40 billion guarantee, Clinton announced a $48.8 billion multilateral assistance package on January 31, 1995.[195] Under this package the U.S. would provide up to $20 billion to Mexico. The U.S. administration provided this amount from the Treasury Department's Exchange Stabilization Fund, ESF, and the Federal Reserve's swap network, in order to avoid the need for congressional approval. One day later, the IMF concluded an 18-month standby arrangement with Mexico, which consisted of a $17.8 billion credit. Canada had already provided $1 billion in December. In addition, the central banks of the Group-10 countries provided $10 billion in short-term support, channeled through the BIS.[196] Later, the total bailout package surpassed $50 billion with some other additions.[197]

The Clinton administration had several reasons for intervening, including the dollar's drop to record lows due to the peso crisis. According to *the Journal of Commerce*, if America's efforts failed to boost the Mexican peso, the U.S. would lose $24.7 billion in GDP in 1995, as its exports would fall sharply.[198]

According to Purcell (1998), Mexico's economic crisis would involve the U.S. even if NAFTA had not existed; however, it raised America's stake in the Mexican economy. The accelerating economic integration between Mexico and the U.S. had increasingly blurred the line between domestic and foreign policies on both sides of the border. The Clinton administration's bailout decision was "the first clear post-NAFTA example of Mexico's enhanced impact on U.S. domestic politics."[199] In addition, the Clinton administration's reputation in the foreign-economic policy was pretty much tied to the success of the NAFTA agreement. Mexico's financial/economic failure would hurt all the NAFTA members if the Administration did not intervene. Non-intervention would have also caused significant financial losses on the part of U.S.-based mutual and pension funds, which heavily invested in Mexico.[200]

On February 21, the U.S. Secretary of Treasury and Mexican officials signed their $20 billion loan agreement. The U.S. made $3 billion immediately available, another $7 billion was to be provided within the next four mounts, and the remaining $10 billion was going to be expanded beginning July 1995. Both the IMF stabilization program and the U.S. support package required Mexico to take steps to tighten the monetary policy, have a budget surplus, achieve greater transparency, reduce public expenditure and not use the development banks as an alternative means to expand public expenditure. In other words, they were asking for IMF-style austerity measures. Conditions of the U.S.-Mexico loan agreement also included limitation of Mexico's credit expansion to 10 billion pesos for all of 1995, maintenance of substantially positive interest rates, and raising $12 to $14 billion in income from privatization over the next three years. Moreover, Mexico was to take tough economic measures to curb inflation and to defend the peso. Up to $10 billion of the U.S. loan was allowed to be used to bail out the troubled companies. The oil income from the Mexican state-run oil company, PEMEX, was to be forwarded to the Federal Reserve Bank of New York. If Mexico defaulted on loans, the U.S. Treasury was to seize that money.[201] The day after the agreement, interest rates on 28-day *cetes* were allowed to rise to 59 percent, the highest level in seven years. Mexican stocks gained 1.73 percent on the same day, and the peso closed at 5.845 to the dollar, which represented a loss of 40.7 percent of its value since December 20.[202]

By early March, markets were not fully stabilized yet, and the peso exchange rate fell to 8.00/dollar. After finalizing the negotiations of the international loan package with the U.S. and the IMF, the Secretary of Finance Guillermo Ortiz announced a new and more comprehensive stabilization program, called the Action Program for Reinforcement of the Unity Accord to Overcome the Economic Emergency, on March 9, 1995. Until this program, the extent of the economic collapse was underestimated. By March 10, the peso fell to 7.59/dollar and the worse seemed over. The program was a strict "orthodox" stabilization plan, which called for a very small current account deficit, tight fiscal policy, and increased the value-added tax (VAT) from 10 percent to 15 percent. It realistically anticipated a real GDP decline of 2 percent and 42 percent inflation in 1995. Since the PRI still controlled the majority of the congress, the government was able to pass these extremely unpopular measures.[203] The Clinton administration supported the program by releasing $3 billion more from the agreed $20 billion U.S. loan on March 10.[204]

Further Questioning the Mexican Government's Policy Choice

The impacts of economic ideology, external influences, and interest groups. Thus, the Mexican government shaped its response policy in consultation with the U.S. and the IMF on the basis of neoliberal economic policies, or what is known as the Washington Consensus. The Mexican government chose to stick to the neoliberal economic reforms that started in the 1980s and continued during the Salinas administration, despite the crisis situation. The policy choice of the Mexican government reinforced Mexico's neoliberal economic reform movement and opened the way for political reforms as well. Although, as we have explored, various non-economic factors greatly influenced the development of the peso crisis as well as the Mexican government's reactions to it, the push of the IMF and the U.S. apparently overwhelmed mostly domestic non-economic influences in the months after the crisis. It seems that domestic concerns were more consequential than external ones in 1994, and after the crisis the Mexican government was more receptive to external "recommendations," especially those of the IMF and the U.S. Actually, several reasons affected the Mexican government's policy choice after the crisis. One of these factors was of course the urgency of the economic/financial situation, and Mexico's need for a large international rescue package. Mexico's ties with the U.S. and its NAFTA membership probably had some affects as well on how things developed. But these reasons are short of explaining the Mexican government's policy choice.

One may ask why the 1994 crisis was not a backlash against the neoliberal economic reforms. One important factor was the Mexican leaders' ideological commitment to the neoliberal economic model. Quiroga (2001) notes that "both liberalizing economic policies and democratization itself were implemented as a result of a backlash against the interventionist policy-induced crises of 1976 and 1982."[205] Reversing the liberalizing policies toward the old policies was not an option for the Mexican elite and for the Zedillo administration. As Pastor (1998) writes, "Mexican policy makers underwent a sharp ideological shift during the de la Madrid and Salinas presidencies."[206] However, the Mexican leadership's "firm embrace of the so-called Washington consensus, a view that held that markets could do little wrong," had caused the Mexican leaders to downplay the large trade imbalance (and therefore current account imbalances) before the crisis, according to Pastor (1998). This pro-market orientation made Mexican leaders believe that, "if the government budget was balanced, then large trade imbalances simply reflected foreign optimism and willingness to finance excess investment opportunities." The Mexican economic policy makers repeatedly revealed this economic ideology in numerous interviews conducted in 1993 and 1994, Pastor (1998) argues. Since the Mexican budget was balanced, and foreign capital was clearly interested in Mexico, the overvalued exchange rate was a reflection of the approval of the government's economic policy and the trade imbalances were only temporary.[207] However, as we have discussed, things did not develop as the Mexican leadership hoped or wished.

Zedillo and his economic policy team demonstrated a strong commitment toward the IMF and the U.S. prescribed "Washington consensus" policies, when they were dealing with the crisis. The Salinas administration's policies targeted to maintain its support coalition were set aside, and new measures that aimed at enhancing economic efficiency and attracting foreign capital were taken. Even though it was very unpopular, tight monetary and fiscal policies were adopted in order to stabilize financial markets, normalize the influx of foreign capital, contain inflation, and generate a fiscal surplus.[208] However, the Mexican leadership's ideological commitment to neo-liberal policies does not explain the whole story. Liberalization of the economy during the De la Madrid and Salinas administrations created new winners and losers of the economic system as well. The Mexican government's polices gained the backing of the "winners" of the market- oriented economic policies.

Sectors oriented toward the international markets, in particular large industrial and financial conglomerates associated with foreign capital, were in favor of reducing trade barriers and retaining a market-oriented economic strategy. The substantial gains of the economic liberalization went to big businesses since the 1980s. The liberalizing policies and the privatization of banks reduced governmental subsidies to big businesses, which instead benefited greatly from joint ventures, technology transfers, and their acquisition of new industries and financial institutions through privatization. The Salinas administration encouraged the formation of large holding companies, and authorized the establishment of financial groups, which included bank and non-bank financial institutions, in order to compete with foreign capital. "By 1992 large consortiums which included 15 groups had taken control of the financial system, with a total activity estimated at 350 billion pesos, equivalent to 35.6 percent of GDP, and more than triple the tax earnings expected in 1992," according to Kleinberg, (2000, 227). Companies that had prepared themselves for the international markets, by modernizing, upgrading their plants, and re-training their personnel were also in favor of neoliberal economic policies. They have been mostly located in the north and west of the country. They represented about 60-70 percent of industrial production, even though they employed about 30-40 percent of labor. These groups tended to be supported by the middle classes and export-oriented farmers (concentrated in the North).[209]

Sectors whose production was oriented toward domestic markets and mostly protected and subsidized small and medium-sized firms wanted to maintain trade barriers and continue subsidies. Companies that came from old import-competing industries (generated by the ISI strategy) were heavily dependent on government subsidies and protection from imports. Therefore, they were against further liberalization of the economic policies. Such companies, located mostly in the South, employed about 60 percent of labor. These subsidized, inwardly oriented manufacturers tended to be supported by unorganized labor and home-market oriented peasants, especially in the Center and South.[210]

Thus, Mexico had both pros and cons of the pro-market economic policies. The Mexican government's response policies favored the pro-market groups over the others. Why? Of course, as we have discussed, the U.S. and the IMF exerted strong influences on the Mexican government's policy response. Beyond this and the Mexican policy makers' commitment to neo-liberal policies, few other domestic factors contributed to the policy outcome. The pro-market reform camp had been more concentrated, organized, and had closer ties to the economic policy makers since President de la Madrid's term. They had a political advantage over the dispersed inwardly oriented sectors. In addition, their policy choices and the foreign creditors' demands for economic reforms fell into the same category, i.e. the continuation of neo-liberal economic policies. On the other hand, the sectors oriented toward domestic markets were less concentrated and were much weaker. The economic liberalization weakened them economically and financially, and diminished their representation and bargaining power. Moreover, a clear majority of these dispersed interest groups, i.e. lower middle classes, unorganized labor, and peasants, still had the memories of the economic debacle of the 1970s and early 1980s and were unwilling to push toward old policies. The Zedillo administration needed the support of the pro-market concentrated groups, rather than the dispersed groups. The concentrated groups, given their financial and economic power,[211] dominated the media outlets and were able to mobilize some electoral support among the dispersed peasants, unorganized labor, and especially middle class groups, along with their own support.[212] The dispersed groups "did not dominate the broader public opinion to an extent that delegitimized liberal policies, and did not share the same clout with the president's team and foreign creditors," Quiroga (2001) notes.[213] As a result, "the 1994 crisis reinforced rather than reversed the trend in favor of market reforms and reduced the executive discretion. The program of trade liberalization, free convertibility, and deregulation continued. . . ."[214] The economic and political implications of the Mexican government's policy choice is summarized in the next section.

Recovery from the Crisis and the Continuation of Neo-Liberal Reforms

Economic, societal, political, and institutional implications of the crisis and the Mexican government's policy response. By mid-1995, the Mexican government's response policies to the crisis seemed to be working. Interest rates were declining, and the peso was holding around 6.0 to the dollar.[215] In the first four months of 1995, Mexican exports grew by 32 percent and imports fell by 5 percent. Although the export growth benefited a handful of Mexican export companies the most, it also led to the economic recovery. In fact, Mexico came out of the crisis faster than it did from the previous ones.[216] The Mexican reserves reached 10.65 billion by June 15. By July 1995, Mexico returned to the international public bond markets and made the loan payments successfully on its short-term government debt, in particular *tesobonos*. On July 11, the Mexican government's bond sales attracted $2 billion from private lenders. Mexico had a $7.4 billion current account surplus in 1995, as compared to an $18.5 billion deficit in 1994.[217]

However, Mexico's economic recovery process was not smooth and easy. During the first quarter of 1995, output contracted almost 10 percent. The GDP contraction peaked in the second quarter, and started to decline in the third and fourth quarters.[218] Thus, Mexico's GDP fell 6.9 percent and per capita GDP fell 8.2 percent in 1995. The crisis and the 1995 recession deteriorated income distribution, lowered the purchasing power of salaries, increased extreme poverty, and decreased tax revenues as a percentage of GDP. Real average wages in manufacturing dropped 13.6 percent and minimum wages lost 50 percent in real purchasing power. In 1995, close to a million workers became unemployed. The numbers of street vendors and the size of informal economy grew vastly. Both consumption and investment fell severely due to heavy debt loads of the private sector combined with the absence of capital flow in 1995. Not only the flow of portfolio capital dropped sharply, but also FDI fell from $11 billion in 1994 to $9.5 billion in 1995, although it increased to over $12 billion in 1996. Large firms turned their faces to export, but small and medium- sized companies suffered the most from the crisis. In 1995, consumer price inflation grew 7 times as compared to that of 1994. In addition, the peso exchange rate continued to fall in the second half of 1995. In October 1995, the peso slid to 7.30 to the dollar and on November 4, the peso dropped to 7.90 to the dollar, partly due to rumors of a possible military coup. On November 8, it fell to a 8.20-8.30/dollar ratio.[219]

In the meantime, the output contraction along with the devaluation and the higher interest rates caused many Mexican debtors to ask for suspension of their loan payments and this, in turn, increased non-performing loans sharply and led to bank failures. Only four out of the eighteen Mexican banks avoided bankruptcy.[220] In response to the banking crisis, the Mexican government converted some non-performing loans into public debt by exchanging non-performing loans for bonds via the mediation of FOBAPROA (Fondo Bancario de Protección al Ahorro), which was then operated by the Ministry of Finance.[221] The government also provided loans to the banks to fulfill their financial obligations, help them re-capitalize, and create further debt relief mechanisms.[222] The Standard & Poors estimated that the total cost of rescuing the Mexican banks would reach a total of 12% of the country's GDP, or $30 billion. The cost reached 14.5 percent of the GDP in 1998.[223] Nonetheless, Mexico's GDP started to recover in the second half of 1995 and Mexico recorded 5.1 percent GDP growth in 1996 and 6.8 percent in 1997, which was the best growth rate since 1981. By 1997, Mexico's consumer price inflation dropped to the low two-digit range again, private investment grew 25.7 percent, the fiscal budget was balanced, and FDI reached a record high of $12.5 billion. By January 1997, the government also paid its remaining balance to the U.S. and accumulated more than $10 billion in foreign exchange reserves.[224]

Mexico was faced with not only economic implications of the crisis and the government's response policies, but also with social and political implications. As we have mentioned, the crisis and the subsequent economic policies increased the poverty and the gap between rich and poor dramatically. Dresser (1997) notes that "the Zedillo team neglected socially beneficial microeconomic intervention by the state and dismantled many of the compensatory mechanisms Salinas had successfully implemented."[225] The social consequences of the crisis and the economic policies of the Zedillo administration convinced "large segments of the urban poor and the middle class that welfare gains under the new economic model are indeed limited to a few."[226] According to *Reforma*,[227] a Mexican newspaper, 64 percent of Mexicans opposed the government's economic policy. According to Kleinberg (2000):

> The changing role of the state in Mexico and its withdrawal from the economy under economic liberalization has led to a transformation in traditional state-society relations, and the erosion of the "social pact," a historical arrangement that allowed for co-optation, some distribution, some compromise, and social stability. It has been suggested that the resulting new economic relationships would lead to the dismantling of non-democratic or semi-democratic political arrangements. However, by shifting (as it did) the control and direction of the economy over the private sector, the state's capacity to act in the interest of the "weaker" groups has diminished, risking coercion, and not co-optation or compromise as its main instrument or control.[228]

Political liberalization has not been the immediate outcome of economic liberalization in Mexico. Powerful private sectors took advantage of the new economic policies, redefined their corporatist linkages with the state and the labor, and became the most influential sectors in the economic policymaking process. Under these conditions, income inequalities grew and caused social unrest and political instability. The Zedillo administration's liberalizing economic policies continued "to make concessions to business over concessions to the labor and peasant sectors."[229]

The Mexican government's fiscal and monetary policies helped Mexico not to be affected by the Asian financial crisis of 1997-1998. However, Mexico's ongoing crisis of the institutional authority was deepened due to public reaction to the crisis and the subsequent economic policies, which reflected the preferences of the new alliance between big business and the state. The PRI faced increasingly deep divisions and its grip over organized sectors of civil society further declined. The coherence and capacity of the state was weakened. There were rumors that president Zedillo might not be able to finish his term. One public opinion poll in early 1995 showed that 48 percent of respondents believed that a military coup was possible. The economic costs of the crisis also produced a considerable backlash against NAFTA, and the opponents both in Mexico and the U.S. renewed their attacks on the agreement. In the meantime, former president Salinas, in an effort to save his own prestige, blamed Zedillo for the peso crisis. On February 28, 1995, Salinas' brother was arrested in connection with the assassination of José Francisco Raúz Massieu, and there were rumors about the former president's involvement. These rumors along with the peso crisis damaged Carlos Salinas' prestige and popularity, and led him to withdraw his candidacy for the directorship of the World Trade Organization.[230]

The Zedillo administration survived through the hard times of the peso crisis. Resignations of Serra Puche, then the Secretary of Treasury/Finance, in late December 1994, and Fausto Alzati, then the Secretary of Education, on February 24, 1995 were the two incidents that suggested some disarray within the Zedillo administration. During the first half of Zedillo's *sexenio*, the Mexican government focused on overcoming short-term problems caused by the crisis. During the second half, the Mexican government dealt with the demands for better income distribution and political reforms.[231]

In terms of political reforms, broad consensus across Mexican society existed. The main concentrated interest groups, including peak business chambers, associations of exporters, and associations of international traders, were in favor of political/institutional reforms to constrain the president's power along with market-oriented economic policies. They preferred a smaller state apparatus with constrained/reduced discretionary spending power for the president. Sectors oriented toward the domestic market, import-competing producers, and subsidized service providers also preferred a smaller state that would be less aggressive and more predictable, and that would support them with trade protection and other forms of governmental assistance. A broader consensus existed in favor of measures that would guarantee a transparent electoral system and clearly separate judicial, executive, and legislative powers. There were also demands for a greater representation of minorities in the congress.[232]

Thus, the post-crisis era witnessed further democratization and decentralization in Mexico. The PRI's hegemony in the country's political life was reduced. The rebellion in Chiapas, the crisis and the subsequent economic policies undermined the PRI's support. It was the beginning of the end of the PRI's reign in Mexico for 70 years. The opposition parties as well as civil society grew stronger and "anti-institutional actors" such as the Zapatista army and organized crime persisted.[233] The PAN candidate Vicente Fox, who later won the 2000 presidential election, won governorship of Guanajuato on May 28, 1995. The PRI also lost the state of Jalisco to the PAN in the election for governor. In the mid-term elections of July 6, 1997, the PRI failed to maintain a majority in the Chamber of Deputies. In addition, the leader of the PRD (a left party), Chautemoc Cardenas, became the first non-PRI Mayor of Mexico City in that election, with the support of weakening social sectors as well as small businesses, who were not happy with the increasing free trade and liberalization. The most powerful business interests maintained their support for the PRI, but some others were involved in politics via the PAN. The PRI lost the presidential election of 2000, for the first time since the late 1920s, and the PAN candidate Vicente Fox became the current president of Mexico. The rebellion in Chiapas persisted until after Fox became the president.[234] Fox's presidency began a new era in Mexico's history, and as the accepted modes of behavior of public officials change, over time, Mexico will become more democratic.

CONCLUSIONS

In sum, this chapter has demonstrated that non-economic factors affected the Mexican government's policy behavior as well as market participants' behavior (therefore the Mexican markets) as significantly as the economic factors did. An interplay of economic and non-economic factors led to the crisis and shaped government behavior during the crisis within Mexico's external and domestic-political, societal, and institutional contexts. In this process, not only these non-economic events and developments are important, but also the sequence of them is.

As this and the previous chapters demonstrate, there are discrepancies between economic crisis models and explanations on the one hand and how crises actually emerge and evolve on the other hand. There are also discrepancies between actual government responses to crises and the government behaviors that are assumed, expected, or prescribed by the crisis models and particular economic explanations. Explanations of financial crises and governmental policy responses should integrate both economic factors and non-economic factors in order to grasp the whole picture. One must consider domestic political, societal/cultural, and legal/institutional factors, as well as external links and influences in assessing the causes of financial crises and explaining the governmental responses to crises. The next two chapters examine the Malaysian case just as the last two chapters have examined the Mexican case. Then, Chapter VII will offer an analytical framework for considering both economic and non-economic factors when assessing the causes and consequences of financial crises and governmental responses. In the meantime, it will further comparatively discuss the findings of the last two chapters and the upcoming two chapters.

NOTES

1. Smith, "Political Dimensions of the Peso Crisis," 33.
2. Francisco Gil-Díaz and Agustín. Carstens, "Pride and Prejudice: The Economics Profession and Mexico's Financial Crisis," in *Mexico 1994: Anatomy of an Emerging-Market Crash* (Washinton, DC: Carnegie Endowment for International Peace, 1997), 165.
3. Edwards, "Bad Luck or Bad Policies? An Economic Analysis of the Crisis," 98, 103.
4. Gil-Díaz and Carstens, "Pride and Prejudice: . . . ,"165.
5. Heath, *Mexico and the Sexenio Curse . . .* , 36-37; Edwards, "Bad Luck or Bad Policies? An Economic Analysis of the Crisis," 98, 103.
6. Edwards, "Bad Luck or Bad Policies? An Economic Analysis of the Crisis," 98, 103.
7. Weintraub, *Financial Decision-Making in Mexico: To Bet a Nation*, 45.

8. Ibid., p.41.

9. Weintraub, *Financial Decision-Making in Mexico: To Bet a Nation,* 41-42.

10. Schulz and Williams, "Crisis of Transformation: The Struggle for the Soul of Mexico," 8.

11. Weintraub, *Financial Decision-Making in Mexico: To Bet a Nation,* 45.

12. Ibid., p.42.

13. Ibid., p.40.

14. Development banks were designed to promote development in particular regions and sectors. Three major development banks are Nacional Financiera (Nafin), Banco Nacional de Comercio Exterior (Bancomext), and Banco Nacional de Obras y Servicios Públicos (Banobras) See Weintraub, *Financial Decision-Making in Mexico: To Bet a Nation,* 71.

15. Ibid., 41.

16. Ibid., p.72, 73.

17. Heath, *Mexico and the Sexenio Curse . . . ,* 38, 40; Weintraub, *Financial Decision-Making in Mexico: To Bet a Nation,* 43; Rogelio Ramírez de la O, "The Mexican Peso Crisis and Recession of 1994-1995: Preventable Then, Avoidable in the Future?" in *The Mexican Peso Crisis: International Perspectives* (Boulder and London: Lynne Rienner Publishers, 1996), 13.

18. Francisco Zapata, "Mexican Labor in a Context of Political and Economic Crisis," in *Changing Structure of Mexico: Political, Social, and Economic Prospects* (New York and London: M.E. Sharpe, 1996), 128.

19. The Article 27 of the Constitution, which was one of the main gains of the agrarian movements of the 1910-1917 Revolution, was amended and a new Agrarian Law was passed in 1992. Neil Harvey, *The Chiapas Rebellion: The Struggle for Land and Democracy* (Durham and London: Duke University Press, 1998), 2.

20 Ibid., 2; Otero, "Neoliberal Reform and Politics in Mexico: An Overview," 1.

21. Guillermo Trejo and Claudio Jones, "Political Dilemmas of Welfare Reform: Poverty and Inequality in Mexico,"*Mexico Under Zedillo* (Boulder & London: Lynne Rienner Publishers, 1998), .68; Aldo Flores Quiroga, "Mexico: Crises and the Domestic Politics of Sustained Liberalization," in *The Political Economy of International Financial Crisis: Interest Groups, Ideologies, and Institutions* (New York and Oxford: Rowman & Littlefield Publishers, Inc., 2001), 189.

22. EZLN stands for Ejercito Zapatista de Liberación Nacional, named after Emiliano Zapata, the hero of the peasant movement in the Mexican revolution.

23. Quiroga, "Mexico: Crises and the Domestic Politics of Sustained Liberalization,"193. Domínguez, "The Transformation of Mexico's Electoral and Party System, 1988-1997 . . . ," 5. For more information about the Zapatista rebellion in Chiapas, see Tom Barry, *Zapata's Revenge: Free Trade and the Farm Crisis in Mexico* (Boston, Massachusetts: South End Press, 1995); and Harvey, *The Chiapas Rebellion: The Struggle for Land and Democracy.*

24. Otero, "Neoliberal Reform and Politics in Mexico: An Overview," 10.

25. Smith, "Political Dimensions of the Peso Crisis," 40.

26. Luis Rubio, "Coping with Political Change," in *Mexico Under Zedillo* (Boulder and London: Lynne Rienner Publishers, 1998), 35-36; Centeno, *Democracy within Reason,* 16, 17; Schulz and Williams, "Crisis of Transformation: The Struggle for the Soul of Mexico," 4-5; Pérez, "Free Trade with Mexico and U.S. National Security," 45; Denise Dresser, "Falling From the Tightrope: The Political Economy of the Mexican Crisis," In

Mexico 1994: Anatomy of an Emerging-Market Crash (Washington, DC: Carnegie Endowment for International Peace, 1997), .62, 64.

27. Ibid., 76.
28. Edwards, "Bad Luck or Bad Policies? An Economic Analysis of the Crisis," 110.
29. Roderic A. Camp, *Politics in Mexico: The Decline of Authoritarianism*, 3rd ed. (New York and Oxford: Oxford University Press, 1999), 129,152; Centeno, *Democracy within Reason*, 18.
30. Dresser, "Falling From the Tightrope: The Political Economy of the Mexican Crisis," 56-59.
31. Ibid., p.76.
32. Smith, "Political Dimensions of the Peso Crisis," 40.
33. Weintraub, *Financial Decision-Making in Mexico: To Bet a Nation*, 50.
34. Ibid., p. 48.
35. Ibid.
36. Ibid., p. 48, 49.
37. Weintraub, *Financial Decision-Making in Mexico: To Bet a Nation*, 49.
38. Schulz and Williams, "Crisis of Transformation: The Struggle for the Soul of Mexico," 14, 15; Domínguez, "The Transformation of Mexico's Electoral and Party System, 1988-1997 . . . ," 5; Weintraub, *Financial Decision-Making in Mexico: To Bet a Nation*, 50.
39. Weintraub, *Financial Decision-Making in Mexico: To Bet a Nation*, 53.
40. Weintraub, *Financial Decision-Making in Mexico: To Bet a Nation*, 49.
41. Quiroga, "Mexico: Crises and the Domestic Politics of Sustained Liberalization," 193; Peter H. Smith and Robert L. Bartley, "Mexico: A Chronology of Financial, Economic, and Political Events," in *Mexico 1994: Anatomy of an Emerging-Market Crash* (Washington, DC: Carnegie Endowment for International Peace, 1997), 316; Morris, *Political Reformism in Mexico: An Overview of Contemporary Mexican Politics*, 104; Domínguez, "The Transformation of Mexico's Electoral and Party System, 1988-1997 . . . ," 5.
42. Weintraub, *Financial Decision-Making in Mexico: To Bet a Nation*, 56.
43. Heath, *Mexico and the Sexenio Curse . . .* , 40.
44. Weintraub, *Financial Decision-Making in Mexico: To Bet a Nation*, 56.
45. Morris, *Political Reformism in Mexico: An Overview of Contemporary Mexican Politics*, 107; Schulz and Williams, "Crisis of Transformation: The Struggle for the Soul of Mexico," 15.
46. Heath, *Mexico and the Sexenio Curse . . .* , 40.
47. Weintraub, *Financial Decision-Making in Mexico: To Bet a Nation*, 57.
48. Ibid., 58.
49. In 1989, controls on interest rates and on the term structure of traditional types of bank deposits were eliminated. The Mexican Congress amended the constitution and changed the law in order to allow private-sector majority ownership of Mexican banks and to permit the sale of the nationalized banks, in 1990. Foreign investment was permitted up to a total of 30 percent of equity. Shalendra Sharma, "The Missed Lessons of the Mexican Peso Crisis," *Challenge* 44, No.1 (January/February 2001), 74.
50. Financing from private-sector banks expanded at an annual rate of 25 percent between 1989 and 1994. It was only 13.4 percent of GDP in 1988, but reached 50.7 percent of GDP in 1994. Sharma, "The Missed Lessons of the Mexican Peso Crisis," 75.
51. Commercial bank credit increased by over 100 percent in real terms between

1987 and 1994. During the same period, credit for housing grew by almost 1000 percent, and credit for consumption by over 450 percent. Sharma, "The Missed Lessons of the Mexican Peso Crisis," 76.

52. Weintraub, *Financial Decision-Making in Mexico: To Bet a Nation,* 58.

53. Jeffry A. Frieden, "The Politics of Exchange Rate," in *Mexico 1994: Anatomy of an Emerging-Market Crash* (Washington, DC: Carnegie Endowment for International Peace, 1997), 89-90.

54. Ibid., p.89, 90.

55. Frieden, "The Politics of Exchange Rate," 90.

56 Dresser, "Falling From the Tightrope: The Political Economy of the Mexican Crisis," 61, 64, 65; Frieden, "The Politics of Exchange Rate," 89.

57. Dresser, "Falling From the Tightrope: The Political Economy of the Mexican Crisis," 76.

58. Ibid., p.66.

59. Whitt Jr., "The Mexican Peso Crisis," 12-13.

60. Edwards, "Bad Luck or Bad Policies? An Economic Analysis of the Crisis," 112.

61. Naím, "Mexico's Larger Story," 300.

62. In 1993, the Mexican Parliament enacted a legislation that gave the Banco de Mexico full independence legally, effective at the start of April 1994. The legislation set out the Bank's primary objective as the maintenance of the purchasing power of the national currency—that is, to control inflation. Weintraub, *Financial Decision-Making in Mexico: To Bet a Nation,* 63.

63. Naím, "Mexico's Larger Story," 297.

64. Weintraub, *Financial Decision-Making in Mexico: To Bet a Nation,* 63.

65. Ibid., 62.

66. Ibid., 60, 61, 63, 69.

67. Naím, "Mexico's Larger Story," 297.

68. Shahid Javed Burki, "A Fate Foretold: The World Bank and the Mexican Crisis," in *Mexico 1994: Anatomy of an Emerging-Market Crash* (Washington, DC: Carnegie Endowment for International Peace, 1997), 257; Loser and Williams, "The Mexican Crisis and Its Aftermath: An IMF Perspective," 262.

69. Weintraub, *Financial Decision-Making in Mexico: To Bet a Nation,* 76.

70. He had graduate education at Sorbonne (France) in Philosophy, and at Stanford University in Economics. He provided Salinas with advice on political as well as economic matters. Weintraub (2000), p.76.

71. Weintraub, *Financial Decision-Making in Mexico: To Bet a Nation,* 75,76.

72. Ibid., p.76.

73. Ibid., p.77.

74. Bartley, "The Peso Folklórico: Dancing Away From Monetary Stability," 150.

75. Smith and Bartley, "Mexico: A Chronology of Financial, Economic, and Political Events," 316. Arner reports that a trilateral agreement, achieved through a consultative body consisting of the finance ministers and central banks of the U.S., Canada, and Mexico in connection with NAFTA, made a short-term credit facility of $6 billion from the U.S., and Can$1 billion from Canada possible. Arner, "The Mexican Peso Crisis: Implications for the Regulation of Financial Markets," 7.

76. Ibid.; Pastor Jr., "Pesos, Policies, and Predictions . . . ," 123-125.

77. Weintraub, *Financial Decision-Making in Mexico: To Bet a Nation,* 62.

78. See Smith and Bartley, "Mexico: A Chronology of Financial, Economic, and

Political Events," 316; Weintraub, *Financial Decision-Making in Mexico: To Bet a Nation*, 2, 63, 64.

79. Naím, "Mexico's Larger Story," 296.

80. The economies of Mexico and the United States had already become intertwined by the end of the 1920s, and the Great Depression was easily transmitted to Mexico. In the 1930s, the Mexican government's efforts to reduce its economy's dependence on the United States failed, and US-Mexican economic relations further developed after World War II to the extent that Mexico became the third largest trading partner with the U.S. after Canada and Japan by the 1990s. As the Mexican government tried to attract foreign capital and Mexican businesses sought foreign capital for joint ventures and to expand plant facilities, Mexico became a preferred site for US-based multinational corporations over time. Subsidiaries of U.S. companies produced around half the manufactured goods exported by Mexico in the early 1990s. In 1991, 66.9 percent of foreign investments were U.S. investments (14 percent in France, 3.4 percent in Holland, 2.1 percent in Germany, 2.1 percent in Canada, and 2.1 percent in Japan). See Philip L. Russell, *Mexico under Salinas* (Austin, TX: Mexico Resource Center, 1994), 157. Original source is Banco de México. Besides the large amounts of investments made by U.S. companies, U.S. commercial banks loaned huge amounts to both the Mexican government and private companies. Cornelius and Craig, *The Mexican Political System in Transition*, 5-6, 18-20. The implementation of the NAFTA agreement further intensified United States-Mexican trade ties as well as accelerated Mexico's neoliberal adjustment process. Carol Wise, ed., *The Post-NAFTA Political Economy: Mexico and the Western Hemisphere* (University Park: Pennsylvania State University Press, 1998), 24-25.

81. Bartley, "The Peso Folklórico: Dancing Away From Monetary Stability,"160-161.

82. Naím, "Mexico's Larger Story," 300.

83. Burki, "A Fate Foretold: The World Bank and the Mexican Crisis," 251-252.

84. Ibid., 252.

85. Naím, "Mexico's Larger Story," 299-300.

86. Dresser, "Falling From the Tightrope: The Political Economy of the Mexican Crisis," 65; Loser and Williams, "The Mexican Crisis and Its Aftermath: An IMF Perspective," 268.

87. Burki, "A Fate Foretold: The World Bank and the Mexican Crisis," 251.

88. *Wall Street Journal*, June 14, 1994, A1.

89. Weintraub, *Financial Decision-Making in Mexico: To Bet a Nation*, 77.

90. *Wall Street Journal*, "Some Mutual Funds Wield Growing Clout in Developing Nations," June 14, 1994, A1; Weintraub, *Financial Decision-Making in Mexico: To Bet a Nation*, 78.

91. Smith, "Political Dimensions of the Peso Crisis," 41; Naím, "Mexico's Larger Story," 305; *Wall Street Journal*, June 14, 1994, A1.

92. Naím, "Mexico's Larger Story," 305; Weintraub, *Financial Decision-Making in Mexico: To Bet a Nation*, 78.

93. *Wall Street Journal*, June 14, 1994, A6.

94. Smith, "Political Dimensions of the Peso Crisis," 41.

95. Whitt Jr., "The Mexican Peso Crisis," 12-13.

96. Weintraub, *Financial Decision-Making in Mexico: To Bet a Nation*, 65.

97. See Pastor Jr., "Pesos, Policies, and Predictions . . . ," 125; Smith, "Political Dimensions of the Peso Crisis," 40; Smith and Bartley, "Mexico: A Chronology of Financial, Economic, and Political Events," 316, and Otero, "Neoliberal Reform and Poli-

tics in Mexico: An Overview," 8-9 for more information.

98. Weintraub, *Financial Decision-Making in Mexico: To Bet a Nation*, 81.

99. Ibid., 77.

100. Smith, "Political Dimensions of the Peso Crisis," 42.

101. Domínguez, "The Transformation of Mexico's Electoral and Party System, 1988-1997 . . . ," 5. Following the controversy over the 1988 elections, several changes took place in the Mexican electoral system during the Salinas administration. Between 1989 and 1993, several constitutional amendments affecting the electoral process were made, an independent Federal Electoral Institution (IFE) was created, and a new electoral law that doubled the number of Senate seats from 64 to 128 was passed along with some other changes in order to promote pluralism within the congress. Subsequent laws established campaign spending ceilings and prohibited political contributions by government agencies and officials, the private sector, religious institutions, and foreign individuals and organizations, and expanded rules promoting equal access to media coverage of political parties. In 1994, several additional changes were made. These changes included having external audits of voter registry, a special prosecutor for electoral crimes, serial numbering of ballot stubs, acceptance of international 'visitors' during federal elections, a constitution of Citizen Counselors on IFE General Council, and suspension of party-paid advertisement and government promotion programs, respectively 10 and 20 days, before federal elections, along with some additional changes. See V.Jorge Alcocer, "Recent Electoral Reform in Mexico: Prospects for a Real Multiparty Democracy," in the Challenge of Institutional Reform in Mexico (Boulder and London: Lynne Rienner Publishers, 1995), 59.

102. He founded the PDR from the smaller parties that backed his candidacy in 1988. It is an odd mix of the PRI defectors and a collection of left-wing parties, from the Mexican Communist Party to the Trotskyites. See Rubio, "Coping with Political Change," 29.

103. Smith, "Political Dimensions of the Peso Crisis," 43.

104. Domínguez, "The Transformation of Mexico's Electoral and Party System, 1988-1997 . . . ," 5.

105. Frieden, "The Politics of Exchange Rate," 92.

106. Smith, "Political Dimensions of the Peso Crisis," 34; Frieden, "The Politics of Exchange Rate," 91.

107. Weintraub, *Financial Decision-Making in Mexico: To Bet a Nation*, 82, 92.

108. Frieden, "The Politics of Exchange Rate," 91.

109. Smith, "Political Dimensions of the Peso Crisis," 34.

110. Ibid., p.34.

111. Smith, "Political Dimensions of the Peso Crisis," 44; Frieden, "The Politics of Exchange Rate," 91.

112. Weintraub, *Financial Decision-Making in Mexico: To Bet a Nation*, 26.

113. Frieden, "The Politics of Exchange Rate," 91.

114. Smith and Bartley, "Mexico: A Chronology of Financial, Economic, and Political Events," 316.

115. Edwards, "Bad Luck or Bad Policies? An Economic Analysis of the Crisis," 115.

116. Dresser, "Falling From the Tightrope: The Political Economy of the Mexican Crisis," 67.

117. One of the banks that the government attempted to strengthen was Banca Cremi, which was then the fourth largest bank of Mexico. Edwards, "Bad Luck or Bad

Policies? An Economic Analysis of the Crisis," 115.

118. Neither of them was available for interview with Weintraub, *Financial Decision-Making in Mexico: To Bet a Nation,* 84

119. Weintraub, *Financial Decision-Making in Mexico: To Bet a Nation,* 83.

120. Ibid., p.93.

121. Edwards, "Bad Luck or Bad Policies? An Economic Analysis of the Crisis," 115.

122. Loser and Williams, "The Mexican Crisis and Its Aftermath: An IMF Perspective," 262.

123. Bartley, "The Peso Folklórico: Dancing Away From Monetary Stability," 151.

124. See Schulz and Williams, "Crisis of Transformation: The Struggle for the Soul of Mexico," 19-21; Smith, "Political Dimensions of the Peso Crisis," 34-35. They were implicating violence and disorder in the country, and bribing the Mexican authorities. According to Smith (1997), they could spend as much as $500 million per year on bribery out of an about $7 billion estimated annual profit. This was more than twice the total budget of the attorney general's office. Smith, "Political Dimensions of the Peso Crisis," 35.

125. Schulz and Williams, "Crisis of Transformation: The Struggle for the Soul of Mexico," 19-21; Smith, "Political Dimensions of the Peso Crisis," 35-36. The assassination in particular involved two prominent families in the Mexican political system. Carlos Salinas de Gortari and his older brother Raúl, and José Francisco Ruíz Massieu and his younger brother, Mario. Later, Raúl Salinas de Gortari was arrested in connection with the assassination on February 28, 1995, and there were rumors that Carlos Salinas must have been involved and obstructed the investigation. In an attempt to clear his reputation, Carlos Salinas went on a hunger strike between March 2 and 4, 1995. He ended his hunger strike after the Zedillo government issued a mollifying statement on March 3. A few days later he left Mexico for the U.S. It is argued that Zedillo or the government officials asked Salinas to leave the country. On March 1, 1995, the Deputy Attorney General, Pablo Chapa Bezanilla, accused Mario Ruíz Massieu of obstructing justice during the investigation of his brother's investigation. Later, Mario Ruíz Massieu was arrested at a Newark, New Jersey airport, for falsely reporting possession of $8,000 while he was actually carrying $40,000. Afterward it was disclosed that he had some $10 million in various U.S. bank accounts. Mexican authorities charged him for having intimidated witnesses and falsifying evidence during his investigation of his brother's death. It was speculated that he was trying to protect Raúl Salinas, who was accused of assassinating José Francisco Ruíz Massieu for personal animosity. On June 22, a U.S. judge rejected the Mexican government's request for extradition of Mario Ruíz Massieu . . . See Smith and Bartley, "Mexico: A Chronology of Financial, Economic, and Political Events," 318; Schulz and Williams, "Crisis of Transformation: The Struggle for the Soul of Mexico," 26-27; Dan La Botz, *Democracy in Mexico: Peasant Rebellion and Political Reform* (Boston, MA: South End Press, 1995), 229-230; *The New York Times,* March 2, 1995, D1.

126. Edwards, "Bad Luck or Bad Policies? An Economic Analysis of the Crisis," 116.

127. Weintraub, *Financial Decision-Making in Mexico: To Bet a Nation,* 97; Donald E. Schulz, "Through a Glass Darkly: On the Challenges and Enigmas of Mexico's Future," in *Mexico Faces the 21st Century* (Westport, CT: Greenwood Press, 1995), 8.194; *The Washington Post,* February 13, 1995, A01.

128. Weintraub, *Financial Decision-Making in Mexico: To Bet a Nation,* 93; Ed-

wards, "Bad Luck or Bad Policies? An Economic Analysis of the Crisis," 116.

129. President Salinas, President-elect Zedillo, Pedro Aspe (the Secretary of Treasury/Finance), Jaime Serra Puche (then the Foreign Trade Ministry), Arsenio Farell (an elder statesman whose judgement was respected by most of the key players), Miguel Mancera (the governor of the Bank of Mexico, and Luis Tellez (who was to become Zedillo's chief of staff) participated in the fateful November 20 meeting. See Weintraub, *Financial Decision-Making in Mexico: To Bet a Nation,* 98.

130. Ibid., 98.

131. Smith, "Political Dimensions of the Peso Crisis," 44.

132. Smith, "Political Dimensions of the Peso Crisis," 39, 42, 43; Schulz, "Through a Glass Darkly: On the Challenges and Enigmas of Mexico's Future,"193; Schulz and Williams, "Crisis of Transformation: The Struggle for the Soul of Mexico," 22, 26; Smith and Bartley, "Mexico: A Chronology of Financial, Economic, and Political Events," 317; Ramírez de la O, "The Mexican Peso Crisis and Recession of 1994-1995 . . . ," 13; Weintraub, *Financial Decision-Making in Mexico: To Bet a Nation,* 69.

133. See Smith, "Political Dimensions of the Peso Crisis," 39-40.

134. Dresser, "Falling From the Tightrope: The Political Economy of the Mexican Crisis," 68.

135. Weintraub, *Financial Decision-Making in Mexico: To Bet a Nation,* 85.

136. Smith, "Political Dimensions of the Peso Crisis," 39.

137. Weintraub, *Financial Decision-Making in Mexico: To Bet a Nation,* 85- 87. Also see Smith, "Political Dimensions of the Peso Crisis," 44; and Ramírez de la O, "The Mexican Peso Crisis and Recession of 1994-1995 . . . ," 13.

138. Weintraub, *Financial Decision-Making in Mexico: To Bet a Nation,* 85.

139. Dresser, "Falling From the Tightrope: The Political Economy of the Mexican Crisis," 67, 68.

140. Weintraub, *Financial Decision-Making in Mexico: To Bet a Nation,* 87.

141. Smith, "Political Dimensions of the Peso Crisis," 44, 45. Reappointment of the finance minister for the second term had historical precedent as well. Antonio Ortiz Mena served two successive terms at this post from 1958 to 1970.

142. Schulz and Williams, "Crisis of Transformation: The Struggle for the Soul of Mexico," 22.

143. Weintraub, *Financial Decision-Making in Mexico: To Bet a Nation,* 101.

144. Ibid., p.101. Also see Ramirez de la O (1996), p.23.

145. Ibid., p.100.

146. Weintraub, *Financial Decision-Making in Mexico: To Bet a Nation,* 101, 102.

147. Heath, *Mexico and the Sexenio Curse . . . ,* 44-45; Ramírez de la O, "The Mexican Peso Crisis and Recession of 1994-1995 . . . ," 24; Weintraub, *Financial Decision-Making in Mexico: To Bet a Nation,* 102; Schulz and Williams, "Crisis of Transformation: The Struggle for the Soul of Mexico," 22; Meier, *The International Environment of Business . . . ,* 210.

148. *The Washington Post,* February 13, 1995.

149. See Burki, "A Fate Foretold: The World Bank and the Mexican Crisis," 248-253; *The Washington Post,* February 13, 1995, A01.

150. Weintraub, *Financial Decision-Making in Mexico: To Bet a Nation,* 3.

151. Weintraub, *Financial Decision-Making in Mexico: To Bet a Nation,* 8.

152. Ibid., p.3, 13.

153. Ibid., p.3,4, 18.

154. Edwards, "Bad Luck or Bad Policies? An Economic Analysis of the Crisis,"

117.

155. Weintraub, *Financial Decision-Making in Mexico: To Bet a Nation,* 102; Weintraub, "Mexico's Foreign Economic Policy: From Admiration to Disappointment," 5. Also see Schulz, "Through a Glass Darkly: On the Challenges and Enigmas of Mexico's Future," 194, and Smith and Bartley, "Mexico: A Chronology of Financial, Economic, and Political Events," 317.

156. From the afternoon of Monday, December 19, to the early morning of Tuesday, December 20, 1994.

157. Weintraub, *Financial Decision-Making in Mexico: To Bet a Nation,* 103, 104.

158. Bartley, "The Peso Folklórico: Dancing Away From Monetary Stability,"152; Weintraub, *Financial Decision-Making in Mexico: To Bet a Nation,* 104, 168.

159. See Heath, *Mexico and the Sexenio Curse . . . ,* 45.

160. Ramírez de la O, "The Mexican Peso Crisis and Recession of 1994-1995 . . . ," 17; Quiroga, "Mexico: Crises and the Domestic Politics of Sustained Liberalization," 181; Weintraub, "Mexico's Foreign Economic Policy: From Admiration to Disappointment," 51; The World Bank, "Mexican Exchange Rate Crisis: A Difficult Week," 1995. Mexican Economic Crisis Homepage, http://www.worldbank.org/wbi/edimp/mex/excri.html (accessed December 4, 2000), 1 of 2.

161. The countries were viewed as having the same general characteristics that afflicted Mexico; namely, low saving rates, large current account deficits, weak banking systems, and significant volumes of short-term debts. Arner, "The Mexican Peso Crisis: Implications for the Regulation of Financial Markets,".9.

162. Botz, *Democracy in Mexico: Peasant Rebellion and Political Reform* , 229-230. Also see *The Baltimore Sun,* December 23, 1994, 12A; *Pittsburgh Post-Gazette,* December 24, 1994, p.A1; *The Atlanta Journal and Constitution,* December 24, 1994, D1; *The Phoenix Gazette,* "Editorial Opinion," December 26, 1994, B18.

163. Weintraub, *Financial Decision-Making in Mexico: To Bet a Nation,* 139.

164. Weintraub, *Financial Decision-Making in Mexico: To Bet a Nation,* 106.

165. Quiroga, "Mexico: Crises and the Domestic Politics of Sustained Liberalization," 191.

166. Gómez, "Crisis and Economic Change in Mexico," 50.

167. Ibid.

168. Serra defended himself, as "he was appearing on radio programs constantly on the morning of December 20 because his first obligation was to inform the Mexican people." He also claimed that he returned the phone calls after he completed his radio interviews. Weintraub, *Financial Decision-Making in Mexico: To Bet a Nation,* 107.

169. Lustig (1998), p.168. Also see Ramirez de la O (1996), p.11; Weintraub, *Financial Decision-Making in Mexico: To Bet a Nation,* 107.

170. Ibid., 108.

171. The World Bank, "Mexican Exchange Rate Crisis: A Difficult Week," 2 of 2; Smith and Bartley, "Mexico: A Chronology of Financial, Economic, and Political Events,".317; Quiroga, "Mexico: Crises and the Domestic Politics of Sustained Liberalization,"181.

172. He is a Stanford-educated economist, who was serving as the communications and transport secretary before he was assigned to his new post. The resignation of Serra was the first big cabinet shake-up of Zedillo's presidency. *The Guardian,* December 30, 1994, 12.

173. Smith and Bartley, "Mexico: A Chronology of Financial, Economic, and Political Events," 318; Quiroga, "Mexico: Crises and the Domestic Politics of Sustained

Liberalization," 181; Smith, "Political Dimensions of the Peso Crisis," 32; Weintraub, *Financial Decision-Making in Mexico: To Bet a Nation,* 107.

174. Weintraub, *Financial Decision-Making in Mexico: To Bet a Nation,* 120-130.

175. Naím, "Mexico's Larger Story," 295.

176. Quitoga (2001), p.179.

177. Naím, "Mexico's Larger Story,".296; Dresser, "Falling From the Tightrope: The Political Economy of the Mexican Crisis," 55.

178. Gómez, "Crisis and Economic Change in Mexico," 50-52.

179. On January 3, 1995, the Labor Ministry released an 11 page Spanish version of the plan on the same day, but the policies and specifics were different from those in a press bulletin released in English a few hours later. Heath, *Mexico and the Sexenio Curse . . . ,* 46.

180. Loser and Williams, "The Mexican Crisis and Its Aftermath: An IMF Perspective," 263, 264; Gómez, "Crisis and Economic Change in Mexico," 50-52; Heath, *Mexico and the Sexenio Curse . . . ,* 46; Ramírez de la O, "The Mexican Peso Crisis and Recession of 1994-1995 . . . ," 24; *Wall Street Journal,* January 5, 1995, A14; *The Houston Chronicle,* January 6, 1995, 16.

181. Weintraub, *Financial Decision-Making in Mexico: To Bet a Nation,* 129; Loser and Williams, "The Mexican Crisis and Its Aftermath: An IMF Perspective," 263.

182. See *The New York Times,* December 29, 1994, D18.

183. Riordan Roett, "The Mexican Devaluation and the U.S. Response: Potomac Politics, 1995-Style," in *The Mexican Peso Crisis: International Perspectives* (Boulder and London: Lynne Rienner Publishers, 1996), 34.

184. One half of $9 billion coming form the Treasury Department's Exchange Stabilization Fund, and the other half from the Federal Reserve System.

185. $17 billion are held by foreigners and $11 billion by Mexicans. *The Houston Chronicle,* January 6, 1995, 16.

186. Schulz, "Through a Glass Darkly: On the Challenges and Enigmas of Mexico's Future," 194; Weintraub, "Mexico's Foreign Economic Policy: From Admiration to Disappointment," 52-53; Smith and Bartley, "Mexico: A Chronology of Financial, Economic, and Political Events," 318; Heath, *Mexico and the Sexenio Curse . . . ,* 46; Loser and Williams, "The Mexican Crisis and Its Aftermath: An IMF Perspective," 263, 264; Ramírez de la O, "The Mexican Peso Crisis and Recession of 1994-1995 . . . ," 24.

187. Roett, "The Mexican Devaluation and the U.S. Response: Potomac Politics, 1995-Style," 35-36.

188. New loans guaranteed by the U.S. could last as long as ten years, a time period that would allow Mexico to reschedule its external debt to a longer maturity profile. In essence the U.S. was acting as a co-signer for Mexico's long-term debt, and in turn the U.S. was going to receive "insurance" fees for its guarantees. Meier, *The International Environment of Business . . . ,* 212.

189. Meier, *The International Environment of Business . . . ,* 212; Roett, "The Mexican Devaluation and the U.S. Response: Potomac Politics, 1995-Style," 360; Ngaire Woods, "International Financial Institutions and the Mexican Crisis," in *The Post-NAFTA Political Economy: Mexico and the Western Hemisphere* (University Park, PA: The Pennsylvania State University Press,1998), 151; *Los Angeles Times,* January 14, 1995, B7. The opposition in Congress wanted to impose political conditions such as privatization of PEMEX, and breaking relations with Cuba. Meier, *The International Environment of Business . . . ,* 211.

190. Susan Kaufman Purcell, "The New U.S.-Mexican Relationship," In *Mexico Under Zedillo* (Boulder and London: Lynne Rienner Publishers, 1998), 110, 111.

191. Weintraub, *Financial Decision-Making in Mexico: To Bet a Nation,* 118.

192. Smith and Bartley, "Mexico: A Chronology of Financial, Economic, and Political Events," 319.

193. *The New York Times,* January 10, 1995, D1; *The Daily Telegraph,* January 11, 1995, 31; *Journal of Commerce,* February 23, 1995, 1A.

194. *The Washington Post,* January 1, 1995, A29; *The Houston Chronicle,* January 5, 1995, A18; *The New York Times,* January 9, 1995, A5.

195. It was the largest multilateral economic assistance package in IMF history. Following the Mexican financial crisis, world leaders agreed to double the emergency fund of the IMF in order to increase the official lending power of the IMF. Arner, "The Mexican Peso Crisis: Implications for the Regulation of Financial Markets,"17.

196. Arner, "The Mexican Peso Crisis: Implications for the Regulation of Financial Markets," 9, 10; Weintraub, "Mexico's Foreign Economic Policy: From Admiration to Disappointment," 52-53; Smith and Bartley, "Mexico: A Chronology of Financial, Economic, and Political Events," 318; *The Washington Post,* February 05, 1995, C02.

197. Latin American countries gave $1 billion in short-term swaps of dollars for pesos, and commercial banks provided $3 billion in new loans. *The San Diego Union-Tribune,* February 26, 1995, G4.

198. *Journal of Commerce,* January 30, 1995, 2A; *Journal of Commerce,* March 7, 1995, 1A. Woods, "International Financial Institutions and the Mexican Crisis," 150.

199. Purcell, "The New U.S.-Mexican Relationship," 101, 110.

200. Woods, "International Financial Institutions and the Mexican Crisis," 150.

201. Meier, *The International Environment of Business . . . ,* 213; Woods, "International Financial Institutions and the Mexican Crisis," 153, 154; *USA Today,* February 22, 1995, A1; Weintraub, *Financial Decision-Making in Mexico: To Bet a Nation,* 151.

202. Meier, *The International Environment of Business . . . ,* 213.

203. Heath, *Mexico and the Sexenio Curse . . . ,* 46, 51, 52; Smith and Bartley, "Mexico: A Chronology of Financial, Economic, and Political Events," 319; Loser and Williams, "The Mexican Crisis and Its Aftermath: An IMF Perspective," 264.

204. *The Phoenix Gazette,* March 10, 1995, A10; Also see Weintraub, *Financial Decision-Making in Mexico: To Bet a Nation,* 147.

205. Quiroga, "Mexico: Crises and the Domestic Politics of Sustained Liberalization," 197.

206. Pastor Jr., "Pesos, Policies, and Predictions . . . ," 131.

207. Ibid., p.138.

208. Dresser, "Falling From the Tightrope: The Political Economy of the Mexican Crisis," 69, 70.

209. Quiroga, "Mexico: Crises and the Domestic Politics of Sustained Liberalization," 189; Rubio, "Coping with Political Change," 8.

210. Quiroga, "Mexico: Crises and the Domestic Politics of Sustained Liberalization," 189, 196; Rubio, "Coping with Political Change," 8.

211. "The big financial groups managed 93 percent of the capital of the banks in Mexico and 76 percent of the total capital in the entire financial system of the country." Only two of 15 authorized financial groups—Banamex-Accival, owned by Hernandez and Harp Helu, and Bacomer, owned by Garza Laguera—controlled 67 percent of the financial activity within Mexico in 1992. This situation led to "what one Mexican businessman calls a 'pyramid structure' of power," allowing those at the top of the pyramid to

influence the policy outcomes more than any other group. Remonda Bensabat Kleinberg, "Economic Liberalization and Inequality in Mexico: Prospects for Democracy," in *Economic Liberalization, Democratization and Civil Society in the Developing World* (London: Macmillan Press Ltd & New York: St. Martin's Press, Inc., 2000), 227-228.

212. Quiroga, "Mexico: Crises and the Domestic Politics of Sustained Liberalization," 191, 197; Kleinberg, "Economic Liberalization and Inequality in Mexico: Prospects for Democracy," 230-232.

213. Quiroga, "Mexico: Crises and the Domestic Politics of Sustained Liberalization," 191.

214. Ibid., 196.

215. Weintraub, "Mexico's Foreign Economic Policy: From Admiration to Disappointment," 52-53.

216. Quiroga, "Mexico: Crises and the Domestic Politics of Sustained Liberalization," 1984.

217. Smith and Bartley, "Mexico: A Chronology of Financial, Economic, and Political Events," 319; *The Houston Chronicle*, April 22, 1995, 1; *Financial Times*, June 15, 1995, 22; *Wall Street Journal*, July 11, 1995, A2; *The Washington Post*, July 12, 1995, F03; *Business Week*, July 17, 1995, 46; *Los Angeles Times*, October 6, 1995, D12; Bradford De Long, Christopher De Long, & Sherman Robinson , *Foreign Affairs* (May /June 1996), 8.

218. The Mexican GDP's contraction in 1995 was partly due to Zedillo's insistence on paying the external debt and his belief that "a crash program, not gradual changes were essential to achieve the turnaround." Weintraub, *Financial Decision-Making in Mexico: To Bet a Nation,* 148.

219. Smith and Bartley, "Mexico: A Chronology of Financial, Economic, and Political Events," 319; Weintraub, *Financial Decision-Making in Mexico: To Bet a Nation,* 148, 153; Domínguez, "The Transformation of Mexico's Electoral and Party System, 1988-1997 . . . ," 7; Otero, "Neoliberal Reform and Politics in Mexico: An Overview," 8, 9; Heath, *Mexico and the Sexenio Curse . . . ,* 53-54; *Business and Industry*, April 1996, 3.

220. Quiroga, "Mexico: Crises and the Domestic Politics of Sustained Liberalization," 181; Heath, *Mexico and the Sexenio Curse . . . ,* 153.

221. In December 1998, the FOBAPROA was replaced by a relatively more independent Institute for Bank Savings Protection (Instituto de Protección al Ahorro Bancario or IPAB). Quiroga, "Mexico: Crises and the Domestic Politics of Sustained Liberalization," 184.

222. Ibid., 184.

223. *The Economist*, April 12, 1997, S18; *Financial Times*, April 2, 1998, 36.

224. Heath, *Mexico and the Sexenio Curse . . . ,* 53-54; Loser and Williams, "The Mexican Crisis and Its Aftermath: An IMF Perspective," 267; Domínguez, "The Transformation of Mexico's Electoral and Party System, 1988-1997 . . . ," 7; Bartley, "The Peso Folklórico: Dancing Away From Monetary Stability," 158; *Los Angeles Times*, January 16, 1997, A1.

225. Dresser, "Falling From the Tightrope: The Political Economy of the Mexican Crisis," 71.

226. Trejo and Jones, "Political Dilemmas of Welfare Reform: Poverty and Inequality in Mexico," 68.

227. June 2, 1996, 4A.

228. Kleinberg, "Economic Liberalization and Inequality in Mexico: Prospects for

Democracy," 219.

229. Ibid., 219-220.

230. Smith, "Political Dimensions of the Peso Crisis," 45, 46; Dresser, "Falling From the Tightrope: The Political Economy of the Mexican Crisis," 72; Weintraub, *Financial Decision-Making in Mexico: To Bet a Nation,* 158.

231. Gómez, "Crisis and Economic Change in Mexico," 38.

232. Quiroga, "Mexico: Crises and the Domestic Politics of Sustained Liberalization," 190, 196.

233. Dresser, "Falling From the Tightrope: The Political Economy of the Mexican Crisis," 69, 76.

234. Heath, *Mexico and the Sexenio Curse . . . ,* 54; Smith and Bartley, "Mexico: A Chronology of Financial, Economic, and Political Events," 319; Kleinberg, "Economic Liberalization and Inequality in Mexico: Prospects for Democracy," 237; Quiroga, "Mexico: Crises and the Domestic Politics of Sustained Liberalization," 196.

CHAPTER V: THE SHORTCOMINGS OF THE ECONOMIC EXPLANATIONS: THE MALAYSIAN CASE

This and the next chapters examine the Malaysian case within the context of the Asian financial crisis. This chapter questions the shortcomings of the economic explanations in predicting and explaining the Asian financial crisis and the Malaysian government's policy behavior. It also critically surveys *ex-post* economic explanations of the Asian financial crisis and their conception of the Malaysian government's behavior to demonstrate their insufficient incorporation of non-economic impacts into their analyses. The next chapter will identify, trace, and assess the impact of various non-economic factors in order to evidence the argument of this chapter.

The chapter starts with some background information about the Asian financial crisis and the Malaysian economic developments (in comparison with some other regional countries) prior to the crisis. Then, it questions why the Asian financial crisis was not predicted and prevented and critically reviews the ex-post explanations of the crisis. In the meantime, Malaysia's macroeconomic conditions before and during the Asian financial crisis of 1997-1998 (comparatively with some other Asian countries) are explored in light of crisis models and the relevant literature.

ECONOMIC DEVELOPMENTS PRIOR TO THE ASIAN FINANCIAL CRISIS

With the exception of Japan, many countries in Southeast Asia achieved their rapid economic growth and transformation during the last couple of decades. Following the 1969 riots, the Malaysian government adopted a New Economic Policy (NEP) to address the ethnic concerns raised by the riots and to bring equality between Malays and other ethnic groups in 1974.[1] The NEP was a unique policy, which can be seen as a system of social and economic affirmative action. The NEP aimed at increasing *bumiputera* ownership in the commercial and industrial sectors to 30 percent, and reducing Chinese and Indian ownership to just 40 percent as well as foreign control to 30 percent by 1990.[2] It also set goals of eradicating poverty and spreading education. By the end of the 1980s, some of the NEP's objectives were partially achieved. Poverty was reduced 15 percent in Malaysia overall and 49 percent in peninsular Malaysia. Although *bumiputera* were still predominantly occupied with agriculture, their ownership of businesses increased and a significant Malay middle class emerged.[3]

During the 1980s and 1990s, Mahathir's government too followed the objectives of the NEP that were set in 1974. In the early 1990s, the National Development Policy, NDP, which was a reformulated version of the NEP, was introduced. The NDP's objectives were first outlined by Mahathir when he presented his "Vision 2020" plan, which aimed at achieving a "fully developed country status" for Malaysia by the year 2020, in February 1991.[4] In fact, Mahathir was able to transform Malaysia from a relatively poor country to a newly industrializing country by the mid-1990s.[5] Malaysia has been one of the most rapidly developing countries in Southeast Asia during the years preceding the Asian financial crisis. Malaysian income per capita growth has been amongst the highest in the world over the last twenty-five years. In the mid-1980s, Malaysia experienced a banking crisis and a subsequent economic recession, which started with the collapse of the Bumiputra Malaysia Finance (BMF), a subsidiary of Bank Bumiputra that operated in Hong Kong, with losses of about $1 billion in 1983. Following the banking crisis between 1985 and 1988, Malaysia's growth rate averaged nearly 8 percent from the late 1980s to the 1997-1998 Asian financial crisis.[6]

During the 1970s and early 1980s, Malaysia's economic development model was based on the Import Substituting Industrialization (ISI) strategy. The ISI was not very successful, partially due to a relatively small population base, which prevented many industries from operating efficient economies of scale. Policies that mainly focused on the provision of education, health care, and basic amenities such as water and electricity brought more substantial outcomes, which provided Malaysia with a well-educated labor force in the 1980s and 1990s. By the mid-1980s, a major reversal took place in the Malaysian industrialization policy by adoption of the export-oriented industrialization strategy.[7] Since then, Malaysia has been following this East Asian development model, i.e. an export-oriented strategy influenced by social, political, and economic particularities of the country, and similar to other regional countries in terms of the government intervention into markets.[8]

Starting from the mid-1980s, Mahathir, reflecting the worldwide trend, promoted privatization in Malaysia. The Malaysian government's deregulation and privatization initiatives attracted foreign direct investments, especially from East Asian Tigers. The contribution of FDI to the overall economy reached high levels in the early 1990s. FDI together with privatization and economic liberalization encouraged domestic private investments and contributed substantially to the export growth and foreign debt repayment of the country. Thus, international debt has never become a pressing problem in Malaysia.[9]

The Asian financial crisis started in Thailand on July 2, 1997, when the Bank of Thailand announced that it would no longer defend the peg system. The baht had been fluctuating and market participants had been concerned about devaluation of the baht since the Bank restricted loans to property and stocks in late March 1997.[10] Following the Bank of Thailand's declaration of a consolidation plan of 16 cash-strapped finance companies, market participants became even more worried of devaluation of the baht. On June 30, Thai Prime Minister Chavalit Yongchaiyudh, in order to calm the markets, assured the nation in a television address that the baht would not be devalued. However, two days later the Bank's announcement of the free float of the baht came. Shocked money dealers around the globe dumped the baht, and the same day the baht lost nearly 15% of its value in the markets. It triggered speculators around the world to attack the other ASEAN currencies.[11] By December 1997, the crisis engulfed the Philippines, Malaysia, Indonesia and Korea.

Thus, the crisis started in Thailand and quickly spread to some of the regional countries, including Malaysia. The Philippine peso was the first to come under serious attack, and other regional currencies, including the Indonesian rupiah, the Malaysian ringgit, and the Korean won, followed the peso. These attacks forced these countries to devalue their currencies, and the devaluation of the currencies triggered a disastrous financial crisis, the implications of which were felt around the globe, particularly in Japan. It surprised everyone and drew people's attention to the weaknesses of this "miraculous growth." The East Asian model was seen as a "miraculous" economic development model, which other developing countries could emulate. Paul Krugman pronounced the Asian miracle a "myth," based on "low total factor productivity growth", in 1994.[12] However, no one expected a financial crisis, including Krugman.

Initially, the crisis was thought to be short and temporary. It was blamed on the maintenance of the fixed exchange rate system and greedy foreign speculators.[13] Later, different economists pointed to different economic weaknesses such as large current account deficits, overvalued currencies with fixed exchange rate systems, corrupt, mismanaged and weak banking systems, real estate speculations, "crony capitalism," as well as the shortcomings of international capital markets and speculative attacks. The crisis prompted the largest bailout in history. Despite the large rescue packages and policy changes, currency values continued to fall throughout 1997, and a severe recession followed.[14]

Soon after the attacks on the Philippine peso, the currency crisis reached Malaysia. Before the crisis the Malaysian ringgit was pegged to the dollar between a 2.36 to 2.51 band of exchange rate. As the speculative pressure intensified in the course of the crisis, the Malaysian Central Bank, Bank Negara Malaysia (BNM), attempted to defend the ringgit until July 14, 1997. However, as its ability to defend the currency was reduced due to reserves loses and intense speculations, the Bank gave way to market forces by abandoning the defense of the ringgit on that day. By January 7, 1998, market forces depreciated the ringgit 50% down to 4.88 ringgit equaling 1 dollar. After some signs of stability during February and March 1998, the fluctuations of the exchange rate continued to deteriorate with wide swings until it was fixed again at the 3.80 level in September 1998. The stock market collapse was even more drastic with an over 65% fall, on average of the all ordinaries index of the Kuala Lumpur Stock Exchange (KLSE) between July 1997 and mid-January 1998. This meant that almost $225 billion of share values melted down. The stock market did not recover until the Malaysian government introduced capital controls in early September 1998. As a result of market crashes and massive capital outflows, non-performing loans in the banking system began to increase and deepened the crisis.[15] What went wrong? Was the Asian financial crisis predictable given these countries' macroeconomic indicators (presented in Appendix D)?

MACROECONOMIC INDICATORS OF MALAYSIA AND OTHER REGIONAL COUNTRIES: WHY WASN'T THE ASIAN FINANCIAL CRISIS PREDICTED AND WHY WAS MALAYSIA AFFECTED?

In fact, fundamental macroeconomic indicators that analysts should look at according to the crisis models seemed sound across the region. For example, government budget deficits, which were at the center of the economic crisis in Latin America in the 1980s, were not there. In fact, as the crisis was approaching, the central government's budget balance was recording regular surpluses in each country, including Malaysia. In addition, domestic saving and investment rates were high throughout the region, which implied that the robust growth would continue even if foreign capital flows slowed down. On the negative side, current account deficits were very high in Thailand and Malaysia in the 1990s, but considerably lower in Indonesia and Korea. In Malaysia, the CA deficit as a percentage of GDP declined to -4.89 in 1996 from -8.43 in 1995. Capital inflows exceeded the CA deficits and foreign exchange reserves grew across the region. Moreover, world market conditions did not negatively affect these countries, since the world interest rates were unusually low, and repaying foreign obligations were not burdensome.[16] Massive capital inflows to the region in the 1990s were stimulated by changes in the domestic conditions of these countries as well as world markets.[17] For example, capital inflows to Malaysia increased from 0.5% of GDP over the 1986-1990 period to 9.6 percent over the 1990-1996 period. In Thailand, capital inflows reached 10.3 percent of GDP over the 1990-1996 period. In turn, high capital inflows led to a real appreciation of the exchange rate, which in turn caused an expansion of non-tradable sectors as opposed to tradable sectors, and high capital inflows brought new pressures on the underdeveloped financial system. These factors together contributed to the increase of financial risk, according to Radelet and Sachs (2000).[18]

According to some, Thailand acted as a wake-up call for international investors to reassess credit worthiness of the Asian borrowers, and the countries affected by the crisis were vulnerable to external shocks and contagion, since the health of their economies depended on foreign capital inflows.[19] They argue that Malaysia was also vulnerable to the crisis due to similar economic weaknesses. In the late 1980s and early 1990s, most domestic and international macroeconomic indicators were positive in Malaysia. Following the 1985 mild recession, the Malaysian government lifted restrictions on both portfolio and FDI investments, liberalized the labor markets, and brought about tax relief. These liberal economic measures promoted higher investment and growth in Malaysia afterwards. In fact, Malaysia achieved large current account surpluses and an increase in domestic savings during 1987 and 1988. Capital inflows increased sharply into Malaysia starting in 1989, and the positive balance in the finance account of $1.5 billion (2.4 percent of GDP) reached $14.4 billion (22.5% of GDP) in 1993. In addition, the greater percentage of the capital flows was long-term and only one third of the total was short-term in 1992-1993.[20] The FDI averaged 6.9% of GDP from 1990-1995. However, starting from the early 1990s, Malaysia had large and erratic current account deficits: a small surplus of CA in 1989 left its place to a CA deficit of 8.69 percent of GDP in 1991. It fell in 1992, but increased again to 6.24% in 1994 and reached -8.43% in 1995. Nonetheless, it fell back to -4.85% in 1996 before the crises.

Although there were several signs of growing financial vulnerability throughout the region in 1996 and early 1997, such as growing current account deficits (high especially in Thailand), overvalued exchange rates, and slowing export growth, they did not suggest any radical departure from the macroeconomic fundamentals, and were generally ignored.[21] At the onset of the crisis, Malaysia's currency became overvalued and the current account deficit was still high, even though it fell in 1996 from the 1995 level. This appreciation of the currency constrained authorities from defending the ringgit. In addition, in Malaysia, the economy was overheated and the health of the financial system was deteriorated. Malaysia had one of the highest domestic debt to GDP ratios in the world prior to the crisis. About 90 percent of corporate debts were owed to domestic banks. A significant portion of this debt was invested in real estate and the stock market, indicating that in a crisis situation, loan holders would lose the value of their assets significantly, and could not pay their debts. The domestic debt situation was exacerbated by an average increase of 30 percent in the extension of new loans, especially by the smaller, second-tier banks, to private businesses.[22] Moreover, analysts estimate that about ten families controlled one fourth of the market capitalization in Malaysia, and a few conglomerates dominantly controlled most of the financial institutions and corporations through interlocking ownership. As Toyoda (2001) indicates, many analysts asserted that this fact was at the heart of Malaysia's vulnerabilities.[23]

On the positive side, there was not much build-up in the short-term foreign debt of Malaysia. In addition, foreign capital inflows to Malaysia, in contrast to Thailand and Indonesia, over the past ten years have been mainly FDI, rather than short-term private sector borrowings and portfolio investments. During the period of 1990-1995, net FDI averaged 6.9 percent of GDP, whereas portfolio investment was −1.0 percent of GDP on average during the same period. As it may be seen in Appendix D, all of the other crisis-hit countries had much higher portfolio investments relative to FDI. Moreover, Malaysia's foreign currency sovereign credit rating was A+, in the same league as Hong Kong. According to the Bank of International Settlement, BIS, the country's short-term debt stood at $16.27 billion and reserves were at $26.59 in late 1996 and early 1997.[24]

As we have seen, these macroeconomic indicators showed some negative trends, but also positive trends across the region, particularly in Malaysia. It was hard to predict that a crisis would halt capital inflows into these countries and deteriorate their economic prosperity. Although some observers did see some signs of the possibility of a crisis, most market participants and analysts were surprised. "All signs point to a very recent and dramatic shift in expectations," according to Radelet and Sachs (2000).[25] Capital inflows remained strong through 1996, even until mid-1997 in most cases, and risk premiums attached to loans to Asian markets did not increase. Credit-rating agencies and investment banks did not provide any indication of risk in the lead-up to the crisis. The IMF's periodic *World Economic Outlook* and country assessments "gave very little indication of a sense of macroeconomic risk to the Asian region" in regard to the market forecasts. Falling stock prices were the only indication of growing concern among market participants in the months preceding the crisis.[26]

One reason why the Asian financial crisis was not predicted is that fundamental macroeconomic indicators that analysts should look at according to the crisis models did not seem to be unsustainable throughout the region. Those macroeconomic imbalances were not large enough to warrant a crisis of the magnitude that has been seen in Asia, according to Radelet and Sachs (2000).[27] Economic vulnerabilities do not lead to a crisis under every condition, and economic vulnerability cannot adequately explain the development of the Asian financial crisis as well. For example, Malaysia recorded current account deficits above the "critical level" of 5 percent in three of the seven years preceding the crisis, and it declined in 1996 from its 1995 level. The Philippines had a similar pattern in regard to current account deficits. Thailand had notably high (around 8 percent) CA deficits, but it did not lead to a crisis during the early years of the decade. In Indonesia and Korea, the CA deficits were below 5 percent in all years.[28]

As mentioned, for some economists, the devaluation of Thai baht played a trigger role in transforming the Malaysian and the other four countries' economic vulnerabilities into a financial disaster. It was a "wake-up call" for fund managers and for speculative attacks around the globe. Panicked investors dumped the assets of these countries. Malaysia and other countries that were considered to be in the same club succumbed to these speculative attacks. Certainly, the collapse of the Thai baht was contagious, and these countries had some economic weaknesses. However, the economic weaknesses and the Thai "trigger" do not adequately explain the occurrence of the financial crisis and the regional governments' responses to it. Sources of economic weaknesses are not purely economic but also political, legal/institutional, and societal. The current and future political parameters along with economic ones affect investors' perception of countries. For example, a political regime that is not committed to sound economic policies, a likelihood of a current regime being replaced in the future, and a large degree of polarization between the opposing political forces increase the uncertainty about the future of an economy. Lack of political and economic freedom implies that some gains from investment might be expropriated by or lost to the government. Such negative political factors decrease investors' incentives to invest or increase their incentives to withdraw their investments out of such countries.[29]

Was the crisis not predicted because of the weaknesses of the crisis models in assessing the macroeconomic conditions of these countries? Some economists, thinking this way, proposed new crisis models based on another set of economic/financial indicators to explain the Asian financial crisis as well as the Mexican peso crisis. However, when we look closely at how the crisis actually unfolded, we can observe that various non-economic factors affected the development of the crisis along with these countries' economic indicators. Similar to the Mexican case, external and domestic-political, societal, and institutional/legal factors impacted the expectations of market participants, and thus economic variables, and the Malaysian government's behavior.

As the next chapter will show, external and domestic political, institutional, and societal factors played as important roles as the economic weaknesses of these countries in bringing the Asian financial crisis. Political and policy uncertainties negatively affected market expectations in the region, as the next chapter illustrates. Political uncertainty due to potential changes in the governments of Indonesia,[30] Korea, Thailand, and the Philippines, preceded the crisis and increased the vulnerability of these countries. The pre-crisis developments such as the failures of finance companies in Thailand, the bank closures in Indonesia, and troubles of the corporate sector in Korea were not only results of economic factors. They were also outcomes of the previous policies made by politically motivated policy-makers and the legal/institutional framework of these countries. In addition, the implications of these events were not limited to economics, but also were societal and political.[31]

The crisis emerged and evolved within the external and domestic political, societal, and legal contexts, as well as the economic context. Policy responses of the regional governments to the crisis were also shaped within these contexts under multiple influences. It seems that crisis models and other economic explanations that base their analyses only on the economic variables explain neither the causes of financial crises nor government behaviors during a financial crisis adequately. In order to increase our understanding in terms of how financial crises develop and how governments shape their policy responses, we have to incorporate the impact of non-economic factors on the market participants' behaviors and therefore on macroeconomic variables as well as on governments' policy behaviors into our analysis. After a brief review of *ex post* explanations of the Asian financial crisis in the next section, the upcoming chapter attempts to demonstrate how multiple non-economic factors impacted the development of the Asian financial crisis and the Malaysian government's policy response.

EX-POST EXPLANATIONS OF THE ASIAN FINANCIAL CRISIS AND WHY MALAYSIA WAS AFFECTED

Literature on the Asian financial crisis is quite large and this section only summarizes basic explanatory arguments offered by this literature. It is possible to divide the explanations of the Asian financial crisis into two categories. The explanations in the first category see the origins of the crisis in the fundamental macroeconomic deficiencies in the affected countries, such as current account deficits, overvaluation of their currencies, and over-investing in poor projects stemming from pervasive moral hazard problems in domestic financial institutions. In addition, according to these explanations, the Asian financial crisis reflected structural and policy distortions in the countries hit by the crisis, even though the crisis may have been exacerbated by overreaction and herding behavior of market players. From this perspective the crisis was inevitable, and was going to happen sooner or later. Explanations in the second category bring to our attention sudden shifts in market expectations and confidence as the key generators of initial financial turmoil, the crisis's development, and regional contagion. According to these explanations, although there was some deterioration in the macroeconomic performance of some countries, macroeconomic fundamentals are not responsible for the extent and depth of the crisis. Rather, the crisis was started by a panic on the part of domestic and international investors and somewhat worsened by the faulty policy response of the IMF and the international financial community. The crisis was avoidable, according to this perspective, if there were not financial panic and "bank runs" against otherwise viable economies.[32] Nonetheless, both sides agree that the liquidity mismatch was one of the main factors that made the crisis possible or inevitable.[33] In the following paragraphs some examples of these explanations from both sides are presented. In the meantime, how far these explanations consider non-economic influences in the development of the Asian financial crisis and what the stands of these explanations are in terms of government behavior are questioned.

Corsetti, Pesenti, and Roubini (1998) explain the Asian financial crisis in regard to these countries' deteriorating macroeconomic fundamentals and policy and political mistakes of the governments. They argue that underlying problems in the macroeconomic fundamentals were the root causes of the crises. Goldstein (1999) similarly locates the origins of the crisis in financial sector weaknesses, current account deficits, and contagion affects. According to her, Thailand acted as a wake-up call for international investors to reassess creditworthiness of the Asian borrowers.[34]

Corsetti, Pesenti, and Roubini's (1998) explanation of the crisis builds on a few interrelated propositions/arguments, and integrates the first category explanations offered by the literature. First of all, moral hazard problems were common across the region due to close links between private and public institutions and regulatory agencies, explicit and implicit public guarantees to private projects, occasional direct subsidization, policies that directed credit to favored firms and industries, and widespread business sector networks of personal and political favoritism. In this context, not only did the corporate sector overlook the costs and risks of production plans and strategies, but leading national banks also borrowed excessively from abroad and lent excessively at home. International banks also neglected the standards for sound risk assessment when lending to the region's domestic intermediaries. Financial market liberalizations and deregulations in the region reinforced this trend. As a result, the financial institutions had many problems, ranging from low capital adequacy ratios to non-market criteria of credit allocation.[35] Moral hazard arguments quite explicitly point to political and societal factors as contributing to the deterioration of macroeconomic factors.

Secondly, current account imbalances in the region were sizable, even though not all countries' CA deficits exceeded 5% of GDP, which most economists consider as a threshold. Malaysia and Thailand had larger and the most persistent current account imbalances for about a decade. In 1996, Thailand had a -8.10 percent current account deficit. The CA deficits of Malaysia (-4.89), Korea (-4.75), and the Philippines (-4.77) were close to the threshold, whereas Indonesia had a -3.37 percent CA deficit. Corsetti, Pesenti, and Roubini (1998) believe that these countries' current account deficits played a significant role in the dynamics of the crisis, since the countries with smaller CA deficits or actual surpluses, i.e. China, Hong Kong, Singapore, and Taiwan, did not suffer comparable currency depreciations.[36] If a country is running a current account deficit and accumulating foreign debt relative to its GDP, then solvency[37] requires the country to run trade surpluses at some point in the future. They believe that "a path of current account deficits and foreign debt accumulation is sustainable when the reversal in the trade balance consistent with solvency can be expected to materialize without a sharp change in current policies and/or an external crisis."[38] They believe that it was not sustainable in the countries that were most affected by the crisis. However, these countries had larger or similar CA deficits before 1996. For example, in 1991 Malaysia had a -8.69 percent deficit and Thailand had a -7.71 percent deficit. Thailand's CA deficits were over 5% throughout the 1990s until after the crisis. Why were the large CA deficits sustainable before, and not sustainable in 1997? The answer that Corsetti, Pesenti, and Roubini (1998) provide is not satisfactory.

Thirdly, they argue that Asian countries were characterized by very high rates of investment throughout the 1990s, but efficiency of investments was already falling in the years prior to the 1997 crisis. The fast output growth in the region was less due to total factor productivity (TFP) growth and more due to growth in the availability of inputs, i.e. increasing rates of investment and labor participation. In addition, data on stock market prices suggest that these countries had speculative over-investments in land and real estate.[39] Although most of the governments of these countries had either fiscal surpluses or small deficits during the years preceding the crisis, excessive credit growth in the banking system led to a large stock of non-performing loans and the eventual collapse of several financial institutions. The deteriorating conditions of the financial institutions represented an implicit fiscal liability for these governments, since the restructuring of the financial sector posed a severe burden on the fiscal balances of the affected countries later. Injections of liquidity into the banking system created inflationary pressures, which were explicit in Indonesia and masked by tight price controls in Malaysia.[40] Moreover, "with the important exception of Korea, all the currencies that crashed in 1997 had experienced a real appreciation."[41] The overvaluation of the currency was correlated with a worsening of the current account. As a result, current account deficits were not sustainable according to these macroeconomic fundamentals as well.[42] Furthermore, in some countries, in particular Korea and Thailand, only a small fraction of their current account deficits was financed with long-term FDI.[43] These arguments explicitly or implicitly point to policy mistakes that these governments made. Then the question is what caused governments to make these kinds of policy mistakes?

They also point to the structure of incentives under which not only the corporate but also the banking and financial sectors operated in the region. Along with moral hazard problems in the region, poorly supervised and regulated banking and financial systems led to over-lending. In addition, many loans were of low quality, as they were financing investments of dubious profitability or speculative purchases of existing financial assets. According to their estimates, the pre-crisis share of non-performing loans as a proportion of total lending was 13% in Thailand, 13% in Indonesia, 8% in Korea, 10% in Malaysia, 14% in the Philippines and 4% in Singapore.[44] While over-lending was one problem in the region, the mismatch between foreign liabilities and foreign assets of Asian banks and non-bank firms was another problem. Domestic banks borrowed heavily from foreign banks but lent mostly to domestic investors in domestic currencies. The high ratio of foreign liabilities to foreign assets became a serious financial problem when these countries' currencies collapsed.[45] Chang and Velasco (1998a, 1998b) also assert that the crises primarily reflected a liquidity mismatch between the assets and liability sides on the balance sheet of the corporate sector. Liabilities in dollars were backed by assets in domestic currency in some cases.[46]

External conditions were not very favorable for these countries as well, according to Corsetti, Pesenti, and Roubini (1998). The long period of stagnation within the Japanese economy led to a significant slowdown of export growth for its Asian trading partners and the increasing weight of China in total exports from the region enhanced the competitive pressures in many Asian countries. Moreover, the international financial community was not convinced that the governments of these countries were committed to sound macroeconomic policies, due to policy and political uncertainties in the region, such as unstable governments in Thailand, elections and political tension in Indonesia, and Malaysian PM Mahathir's blame of speculators. Markets reacted to these political and policy uncertainties throughout the crisis.[47] Here they refer to the political factors directly as they contributed to the development of the crisis. How these political factors contributed to the emergence of the crisis should be studied more closely.

In the second category, Radelet and Sachs (2000) find explanations that emphasize the inevitability of the crisis due to deep flaws in macroeconomic imbalances, policy mistakes, and crony capitalism. Macroeconomic imbalances, weak financial institutions, widespread corruption, and inadequate regulations contributed to the vulnerability of these countries. These weaknesses needed to be corrected. However, despite these weaknesses, these countries were attracting huge capital inflows, and their economies were growing. They find the explanations that view the huge capital inflows as a result of explicit and implicit guarantees, which ensured the investors despite the weaknesses and flaws in the fundamentals, inadequate. According to them, these explanations do not explain that much of the lending went to private firms that did not enjoy these guarantees.[48]

They argue that the Asian financial crisis was caused by several interlinked phenomena, the most important of which was "rapid reversal of private capital inflows into Asia."[49] A sustained period of a large increase in cross-border loans to five countries (Indonesia, Korea, Malaysia, the Philippines, and Thailand) was followed by a sudden drop in bank lending in 1997. According to the estimates of the Institute of International Finance in its January 1998 report, net private inflows to the five countries dropped from $93 billion in 1996 to minus 12.1 billion in 1997, a swing of $105 billion, $77 billion of which came from commercial bank lending. The swing in bank loans between 1996 and the second half of 1997 was 9.5 percent of a combined GDP of these five countries. Although these countries had some emerging market weaknesses, in particular, growing short-term debt, a reversal of this magnitude in such a short time period cannot be attributed to economic fundamentals, according to them.[50] Large withdrawals of foreign funds triggered a chain reaction and caused financial panic, which was responsible for the Asian financial crisis to a large extent. The emerging market vulnerabilities combined with a series of policy missteps and accidents were the proximate causes of the withdrawals.[51] Radelet and Sachs (2000) also recognize the impact of political factors in the form of policy missteps and accidents as proximate causes of the crisis along with macroeconomic vulnerabilities that were widespread in the emerging market economies. In order to understand the impact of these political factors, their sources or causes and impacts need to be evaluated within each country's domestic-political, societal and legal settings. Similar policy missteps do not create similar outcomes in every context.

According to them, the sudden withdrawals caused dramatic exchange rate depreciations as the central banks failed to defend the pegs. As a result, domestic interest rates soared and tightened domestic credit conditions. All of these together caused a rapid rise in non-performing loans in the banking sector, especially as real estate projects went bankrupt. In addition, the depreciation led to a sudden loss of bank capital to the extent that they were net dollar borrowers. The

IMF programs up until the end of 1997 added to the contractionary force of the financial crisis and to the panic.[52] Radelet and Sachs, (2000), as in the Diamond-Dybvig (1983) model of a bank run, argue that the financial panic was an adverse equilibrium outcome of multiple equilibria in the financial markets. Short-term creditors suddenly withdrew their loans from otherwise solvent borrowers. According to them, the crisis could have been avoided with moderate adjustments and appropriate policy changes.[53]

Berg (1999) agrees with the panic aspect of the Asian financial crisis. However, according to him, affected countries had a high ratio of short-term external debt to GDP. When foreign creditors became convinced that other creditors would not roll over their claims, there were not enough reserves to cover the maturing obligations. Thus panic became self-fulfilling. The solution to the panic was to provide liquidity and reassure investors that they could safely maintain their investments.[54] However, unlike Radelet and Sachs (2000), Berg (1999) thinks "weak and deteriorating fundamentals and violent reactions in capital markets were both important."[55] Thailand and Korea showed the most severe deteriorating fundamentals, particularly over investment in certain areas, and the vulnerability of the banking and financial systems to negative changes. Domestic financial systems were less vulnerable in Indonesia, Malaysia, and the Philippines than those of Thailand and Korea, but they differed among themselves. According to Berg (1999), Thailand and Korea were more vulnerable than Indonesia, Malaysia and the Philippines in terms of deteriorating macroeconomic conditions. In addition, several countries, particularly, Korea, Indonesia, Thailand, and to some extent the Philippines, had external vulnerability in the form of high levels of short-term external debt relative to reserves. Malaysia had the least external vulnerability.[56] Therefore, these countries were defenseless against capital flights, and the weak banking systems made fighting against the capital flight with higher interest rates costly. In this macroeconomic environment the speculative attacks became self-fulfilling. Changes in the external environment were not favorable for these countries as well. Some external factors reduced these countries' export growth; the ongoing banking and financial problems in Japan reduced the capital flows from Japan to other Asian countries.[57]

With the exception of Malaysia, four of the five afflicted economies accepted the IMF's bailout packages and used its programs. The programs included fiscal contraction, bank closures, the enforcement of the capital-adequacy standards, tight monetary policy, and repayment of foreign debt obligations backed by the IMF "bailout funds." Along with austerity measures, some structural reforms on non-financial sectors such as reduction of tariffs, opening of sectors to foreign investment, and reducing monopoly powers, were also included.[58] Financial sector and structural reform measures changed from one country to another, but the closure of insolvent financial institutions was a key feature of programs in Thailand, Korea, and Indonesia. Other structural reforms were complementary to financial sector policies. Macroeconomic, monetary and fiscal adjustments followed the structural reforms. Countries that adapted the

IMF programs maintained open finance accounts and floated their exchange rates.[59] None of these programs were implemented in their original forms and new letters of intent were signed with Thailand, Korea, and Indonesia a few weeks after the signature of the original programs. The programs did not bring an immediate restoration of confidence and economic relief as well. Bank closures in Thailand and Indonesia added to the sense of financial panic, output fell all over the afflicted countries and credit ratings collapsed in each country after the agreements were in place.[60]

As we have seen, although these particular explanations of the Asian financial crisis refer to some external and domestic political and societal factors, they do not consider their impacts adequately and incorporate all the relevant political, societal, legal, and external factors into their analyses. In addition, their reference to government behavior is rather limited, except in regards to the policy mistakes of governments of the regional countries, and some policy prescriptions that they offer. As the next chapter will demonstrate, multiple non-economic factors intermixed with economic variables in bringing the crisis and in shaping these governments' policy responses. Non-economic factors played as significant roles as the economic ones.

The Malaysian government not only rejected the IMF bailout package and its policy advice, but also imposed only a few austerity measures, lowered its interest rates, and brought capital controls to avoid further attacks on its currency, contradicting the IMF programs.[61] The policy response of the Malaysian government was shaped by its Prime Minister within the Malaysian political system. How can we explain the differences in the response policies of these countries? How can we explain the Malaysian government's policy response? We cannot answer these questions with the differences in the economic indicators of these countries, although they might have played some role. It seems that each country's policy responses were shaped within an interaction process among domestic and external actors, and within each country's political, societal and legal contexts. Chapter VI presents an account of non-economic influences both on the development of the Asian financial crisis and on the Malaysian government's response policies to the crisis.

NOTES

1. Milne and Mauzy, *Malaysian Politics under Mahathir*, 21.
2. Schlossstein, *Asia's New Little Dragons . . .*, 228.
3. Gomez and Jomo K.S., *Malaysia's Political Economy: Politics, Patronage and Profits* (1997), 166.
4. Gomez and Jomo K.S., *Malaysia's Political Economy: Politics, Patronage and Profits* (1997), 169; Milne and Mauzy, *Malaysian Politics under Mahathir*, 72.
5. Malaysia's agricultural population fell from 65.2 percent to 33.5 percent, the Malay middle class rose from 13 percent to 28 percent of the population, and the working class tripled from 7.8 percent between 1970 and 1993. Robert E. B. Lucas and Donald

Verry, *Restructuring the Malaysian Economy: Development and Human Resources* (New York: St. Martin's Press, Inc., 1999), 1.

6. The ratio of non-performing loans to total lending reached 35 percent in 1987 during the banking crisis, but it fell to a reasonable level of 3.6 percent by the Asian financial crisis, during which it increased again. See Rasiah, "Class, Ethnicity and Economic Development in Malaysia," 121; Milne and Mauzy, *Malaysian Politics under Mahathir*, 63, 68-70; A. Maria Toyoda, "Malaysia: Ethnic Cleavages and Controlled Liberalization," in *The Political Economy of International Financial Crisis: Interest Groups, Ideologies, and Institution* (New York and Oxford: Rowman & Littlefield Publishers, Inc., 2001), 104; Lucas and Verry, *Restructuring the Malaysian Economy . . .* , 1.

7. Pillay, "The Malaysian Model . . . ," 207, 208.

8. Supian Ali and Mohammad Anuar Adnan, "Microeconomic Approaches to Socioeconomic Development in the Third World," in *Alternative Perspectives in Third World Development: The Case of Malaysia* (New York: St. Martin's Press, Inc., 1996), 63-69. Economic development strategies of the regional countries have not been homogeneous, as each nation developed its own policies. Therefore, there is no established and agreed definition of the East Asian development model, as noted by most commentators. Nonetheless, there are commonalties, such as a state-guided economy and a high level of unity among technocrats, politicians, and managers of the big conglomerates, which describe the general characteristics of the East Asian development model. Malaysian Prime Minister Mahathir Mohamad, Shintaro Ishihara (the Japanese Diet member), Eisuke Sakakibara (the former Japanese vice minister of finance), and Lee Kuan Yew (the former Prime Minister of Singapore) have been the most prominent proponents of the Japanese/East Asian development model. Frank-Jürgen Richter, "Economic Development and Crisis in East Asia," in *the East Asian Development Model: Economic Growth, Institutional Failure and the Aftermath of the Crisis* (The U.K.: Macmillan Press, Ltd. and the U.S.: St. Martin's Press, Llc., 2000), 3-5.

9. Gomez and Jomo K.S., *Malaysia's Political Economy: Politics, Patronage and Profits* (1997), 4; Lucas and Verry, *Restructuring the Malaysian Economy . . .* , 311, 312.

10. Thailand had first signs of the Crisis in March 1997. On March 28, 1997, Thailand's government restricted loans to property and stocks to head off a crisis. On May 14-15, Thailand's bath came under a massive attack by speculators prompted by Thailand's slowing economy and political instability, which we will discuss several paragraphs later. See Nouriel Roubini, *Chronology of the Asian Currency Crises and its Global Contagion*, 1997-1998, Professor Nouriel Roubini's web page at New York University, http://www.stern.nyu.edu/~nroubini/asia/AsiaChronology1.html (accessed October 12, 1999).

11. Henderson, *Asia Falling: Making Sense of the Asian Crisis and Its Aftermath*, 109, Crash '97, p.8.

12. Paul R. Krugman, "The Myth of Asia's Miracle," *Foreign Affairs* 73 (November/ December 1994), 62-78.

13. Karl D. Jackson, "Introduction: The Roots of the Crisis," *Asian Contagion: The Causes and Consequences of a Financial Crisis* (Boulder, CO: Westview Press, 1999), 3.

14. Steven Radelet and Jeffrey Sachs, "The Onset of the East Asian Financial Crisis," in *Currency Crises* (Chicago and London: The University of Chicago Press, 2000), 105; Jackson, "Introduction: The Roots of the Crisis," 10.

15. Prema-chandra Athukorala, "Swimming against the Tide: Crisis Management in Malaysia," *ASEAN Economic Bulletin* 15, No.3 (December 1998), 282. Also see Roubini, *Chronology of the Asian Currency Crises and its Global Contagion*.

16. Radelet and Sachs, "The Onset of the East Asian Financial Crisis," 123-124.

17. The factors that stimulated the capital flows to the region in the 1990s include: continuous high economic growth, wide-ranging financial deregulations accompanied by inadequate supervisions, pegged exchange rates and therefore the predictability it brought for investors, and government incentives that encouraged foreign borrowing. See Radelet and Sachs, "The Onset of the East Asian Financial Crisis," 116.

18. Radelet and Sachs, "The Onset of the East Asian Financial Crisis," 116-118.

19. See Morris Goldstein, *The Asian Financial Crisis: Causes, Cures, and Systemic Implications* (Washington, DC: Institute for International Economics, 1998), 7-22; and Henderson, *Asia Falling: Making Sense of the Asian Crisis and Its Aftermath*, 27-28 for example.

20. Sachs, Tornell, and Velasco, *Financial Crises in Emerging Markets: The Lessons From 1995*, 29, 30.

21. Radelet and Sachs, "The Onset of the East Asian Financial Crisis," 124- 133.

22. Malaysia restructured its banking system following the banking crisis of 1985-1988 and non-performing loans fell to 3.6 percent in 1997 from a crisis peak of 35 percent in 1987. However, with the onset of the Asian financial crisis, non-performing loans increased sharply again in the second half of 1997. See Toyoda, "Malaysia: Ethnic Cleavages and Controlled Liberalization," 104.

23. Ibid., 104-105.

24. Athukorala, "Swimming against the Tide: Crisis Management in Malaysia," 282, 283; Lucas and Verry, *Restructuring the Malaysian Economy . . .* , 311; *Business Times*, February 16, 1998, 4.

25. Radelet and Sachs, "The Onset of the East Asian Financial Crisis," 119.

26. Ibid., pp.118-123.

27. Ibid., pp.123-124.

28. Athukorala, *Crisis and Recovery in Malaysia*, .57.

29. Giancarlo Corsetti, Paolo Pesenti, and Nouriel Roubini, What Caused the Asian Currency and Financial Crisis? (Part I: A Macroeconomic Overview, Part II: The Policy Debate), Revised Draft of September 1998, http://www.stern.nyu.edu/globalmacro (accessed July 13, 2001), 23; Yi Feng, "Political Foundations of Economic Management: an Interpretation of Economic Development and Economic Crisis in East Asia," in *the East Asian Development Model: Economic Growth, Institutional Failure, and the Aftermath of the Crisis* (The U.K.: Macmillan Press Ltd. & the U.S.: St. Martin's Press, Llc., 2000), 71-96, 77.

30. In Indonesia, although the elections were scheduled for mid-March 1998, there was no chance that the president would change through elections. However, President Suharto's weakening health and the absence of a clear successor along with growing discomfort with the economic role played by Suharto's family were the causes of political uncertainty in Indonesia. After the onset of the crisis, governments changed in Korea and Thailand, and presidential elections were held in the Philippines (May 1998) and Indonesia (March 1998). See Radelet and Sachs, "The Onset of the East Asian Financial Crisis," 135-136.

31. See Radelet and Sachs, "The Onset of the East Asian Financial Crisis," 135, 136, for the events that took place in the regional countries during late 1996 and early 1997, preceding the crisis.

32. Andrew Berg, "The Asia Crisis: Causes, Policy Responses, and Outcomes," *IMF Working Paper* WP/99/138 (October 1999), 3-5; Corsetti, Pesenti, and Roubini, What Caused the Asian Currency and Financial Crisis?, 1,4.

33. Jeanne, *Currency Crises: A Perspective on Recent Theoretical Developments*, 38.

34. Goldstein, *The Asian Financial Crisis: Causes, Cures, and Systemic Implications*, 7.

35. Corsetti, Pesenti, and Roubini, What Caused the Asian Currency and Financial Crisis?, 2,3,4.

36. Ibid., pp.6-7.

37. According to Corsetti, Pesenti, and Roubini (1998), the standard theoretical criterion for assessing current account imbalances is the notion of solvency. "A country is solvent to the extent that the discounted value of the expected stock of its foreign debt in the infinitely distant future is non-positive. . . . A popular 'test' of solvency in practical terms is a non-increasing foreign debt to GDP ratio." Corsetti, Pesenti, and Roubini, What Caused the Asian Currency and Financial Crisis?, 8.

38. Ibid., 10.

39. Corsetti, Pesenti, and Roubini, What Caused the Asian Currency and Financial Crisis?, 12-16.

40. Ibid., 18-19.

41. Ibid., 20.

42. Ibid., 21.

43. The FDI financed about 10% of Korea's CA deficits and about 16% of Thailand's CA deficits by 1996. Other countries received much more FDIs. These percentages were especially high for Indonesia, above 60%, and for Malaysia, above 90%, in the early 1990s. In the Philippines, FDI covered on average 45% of the current account deficit. Nonetheless, the growth of foreign reserves between 1990 and 1996 was quite remarkable for all the countries, according to Corsetti, Pesenti, and Roubini, What Caused the Asian Currency and Financial Crisis?, 37, 38.

44. Corsetti, Pesenti, and Roubini, What Caused the Asian Currency and Financial Crisis?, 24-25, 28.

45. Ibid., 34-35.

46. Jeanne, *Currency Crises: A Perspective on Recent Theoretical Developments*, 38.

47. Corsetti, Pesenti, and Roubini, What Caused the Asian Currency and Financial Crisis?, 22, 23.

48. Radelet and Sachs, "The Onset of the East Asian Financial Crisis," 149-150.

49. Ibid., p.111.

50. Ibid., pp.111-112.

51. Radelet and Sachs, "The Onset of the East Asian Financial Crisis," 136.

52. The IMF programs called for immediate banks closures, quick restoration of minimum capital adequacy standards, tight domestic credit, high interest rates on central banks' discount facilities, fiscal contraction, and non-financial sector structural changes. See Radelet and Sachs, "The Onset of the East Asian Financial Crisis," 111-116, 149.

53. Ibid., 149-150.

54. Berg, "The Asia Crisis: Causes, Policy Responses, and Outcomes," 3-5.

55. Ibid., p.46.

56. Ibid., p.18. According to Berg (1999) there was little dependence on foreign capital, particularly, short term flows due to strict controls on short-term borrowing, net foreign exchange positions of banks, and off-balance-sheet-activities in Malaysia. Berg, "The Asia Crisis: Causes, Policy Responses, and Outcomes," 52.

57. Ibid, 9, 14, 17.

58. Radelet and Sachs, "The Onset of the East Asian Financial Crisis," 140, 141.
59. Berg, "The Asia Crisis: Causes, Policy Responses, and Outcomes," 19-26.
60. Radelet and Sachs, "The Onset of the East Asian Financial Crisis," 141-142.
61. Toyoda, "Malaysia: Ethnic Cleavages and Controlled Liberalization," 91-92.

CHAPTER VI: THE IMPACT OF NON-ECONOMIC FACTORS: THE MALAYSIAN CASE

This chapter identifies, traces, and assesses the impact of non-economic factors on the development of the Asian financial crisis and on the Malaysian government's response policies to the crisis within Malaysia's external and domestic-political, societal, and institutional/legal contexts. It evidences the arguments proposed in the previous chapter and demonstrates the significance of non-economic factors in bringing the crisis and in shaping the Malaysian government's policy response. In order to illustrate the interplay of a number of complex political, societal, and institutional factors with economic factors, it traces how the initial conditions translated into successive situations in a near-chronological order with references to Malaysian history, culture, and external and domestic contexts.

1997: THE DEVELOPMENT OF THE CRISIS AND MALAYSIA'S INITIAL REACTIONS

The Asian financial crisis started in Thailand on July 2, 1997, and engulfed the Philippines, Malaysia, Indonesia and Korea in several weeks. The crisis came as a surprise. By January 7, 1998, market forces depreciated the Malaysian ringgit 50%. The stock market fell over 65% on average of the all ordinaries index of the Kuala Lumpur Stock Exchange (KLSE) between July 1997 and mid-January 1998.[1] Mahathir's first reaction was to blame speculators and "unnecessary" currency trading as the causes of the crisis in the region.[2] Economists pointed to overvaluation of the real exchange rate, chronic current account imbalances, rapid build-up of mobile capital in relation to the level of international reserves, a worsened savings-investment gap, and soaring indebtedness. The economy was overheated and the health of the financial system was deteriorated. Domestic loan advances as a proportion of GDP rose beyond sustainable levels by the mid-1990s.[3] The argument of this book is that a combination and interaction of economic and non-economic factors led these countries to their crises.

The Impacts of Non-Economic Factors in the Region

The impacts of institutional contexts and moral hazard problems in the regional countries. Lingle (2000) asserts that the Asian financial crisis "reflected a general failure of governance. In effect, the turmoil resulted from systematic politicization of domestic financial markets."[4] The political and societal contexts of these countries created moral hazard problems in the region. As Shin (2000) upholds, "politico-economic institutions significantly affect the performance of an economic system."[5] Institutions, as systems of rules, laws, regulations, norms, and customs not only provide stability and a degree of predictability, but also provide incentives and constraints for economic actors, who try to maximize their interests.[6] Close links between private and public institutions, widespread business sector networking of personal and political favoritism and a long tradition of implicit or explicit public guarantees to private projects existed in these countries. In such a business environment with inadequate supervision and regulations, the production plans and strategies of the corporate sector had overlooked the costs and risks of their investments before the crisis. Explicit and implicit government guarantees created an impression that the return on investment was somewhat "insured." The governments, under the pressure of political goals and ambitions to achieve high growth rates, sometimes directly subsidized or directed credit to favored firms and industries. Directed credit programs to specific industries prevented the development of a micro-credit analysis structure in the banking industry, and led to the failure of official supervision.[7]

As Bisignano (1999) puts it, "the weaknesses in financial transparency, corporate governance, and prudential regulation and supervision in a high-growth environment led to excessive credit creation, an asset price boom, and large foreign currency exposure."[8] Large foreign capital inflows, mediated by the domestic banking system in these countries, were partly a result of explicit and implicit government guarantees. Poorly supervised and regulated banking systems, by mediating large amounts of short-term capital between the foreign creditors and their domestic clients, took on risks that they could not properly manage. Excessive lending for highly risky projects escalated in many of these countries, including Malaysia, in 1996 and early 1997. As a result of their over-borrowing and over-lending syndromes they became very fragile before the onset of the crisis.[9] Non-transparent lending practices and corruption made the fragile situation worse.[10]

Political and economic institutions that were once thought to promote economic growth in these countries became incompatible with the demands of the international marketplace and started to be counterproductive. In addition, the East Asian political culture that was based on consensus and communality rather than diversity and individuality did not fit into the modern market economy very well, according to Lingle (2000). The search for political harmony brought limitations on free speech and manipulation of information flows in order to control or shape public opinion. In such an environment, entrepreneurial creativity and innovation were constrained.[11] Lingle (2000) asserts:

> The simple explanation for the decline of East Asia's 'miracle' economies lies in the incompatibility of their political and commercial institutions with an increasingly efficient global capital market. While these arrangements worked under other conditions, they did not allow for a ready response to the external competitive shocks that visited their shores. . . .Governments characterized by strict and inflexible hierarchical rule will inadvertently hinder high rates of economic growth by stunting innovation. In the context of global mega-competition, such a politically self-serving approach is fatally flawed.[12]

Keeping the preceding general observations in mind, let us give some specific examples of non-economic influences on the development of the crisis and on behaviors of the governments. Then, the rest of the chapter will focus on the Malaysian case. The five most seriously affected economies by the crisis were those of Thailand, Indonesia, Malaysia, the Philippines, and Korea. Before we focus on the Malaysian case, several examples of significant political, societal, and legal factors that affected the development of the crisis in the other four countries are presented.

The impacts of credibility of governmental authorities, unstable coalition governments and the political system in Thailand. The Asian financial crisis started in Thailand. The macroeconomic conditions of Thailand appeared to be very shaky by the end of 1996, due to the decline of GDP growth, an increased current account deficit (up to 8.5% of GDP), decreased exports, and a large amount of short-term foreign indebtedness. Financial conditions of corporate firms and finance companies were extremely fragile, due to the fact that they had heavily borrowed from abroad to finance speculative booms in real estate and equity investments. The accumulation of foreign loans by the domestic finance institutions were a result of moral hazard and government bailout guarantees among others. During this fragile economic condition, the governmental officials were backing troubled financial institutions, and these public interventions in turn were implying a very large injection of liquidity in the economic system.[13]

As a result of deteriorating financial and economic conditions, both domestic and foreign investors lost their confidence in the sustainability of Thailand's balance of payment and their concerns about a consequent depreciation of the Thai baht grew. Also of crucial significance in the loss of investors' confidence was that the authorities in Thailand did not seem to be able and willing to frame and implement "the right mix of policies" in order to correct the deteriorating situation and absorb temporary shocks. For example, the baht was overvalued and the authorities were too late to take corrective steps. The policy of keeping the exchange rate fixed to the U.S. dollar made the currency overvalued and Thai exports non-competitive in the world markets. Neither did the Bank of

Thailand intervene in the currency markets to reduce the overvaluation of the baht, nor did the government change its fixed exchange rate policy before 1997. The late change of policy in the exchange rate on July 2, 1997 triggered a financial disaster, similar to Mexico's December 20, 1994 devaluation. Also, Thailand experienced a property boom, as people borrowed excessively from Thailand's finance companies in order to buy properties, cars, and other durable consumer goods prior to the crisis. These finance companies were making easy money by borrowing from abroad, lending domestically, or by selling stocks and bonds to international investors. In the meantime, trade and current account deficits grew and non-performing loans reached about one third of Thailand's GDP in the spring of 1997. In fact, Thai financial institutions gave early warning signs of the problems in the mid-1990s.[14] The sickness of a large majority of financial firms was largely due to lack of effective supervision by the monetary authorities. Yet, the government did not take any step to improve regulations and supervision of these finance companies in order to correct the situation. Nor did the government attempt to curb over-expansion of bank credit through an increase in interest rates or other monetary fiscal devices. As a result, nearly two thirds of finance companies, all of which borrowed large amounts from international markets, came to the edge of bankruptcy prior to the start of the crisis.[15]

The Thai government's inability to address these and similar issues in a timely manner shook investors' confidence in the policymakers. The political situation was one of the important factors that discouraged local and foreign investors, if it was not the major one. Here, it is not our focus to analyze Thailand's political system. However, it is necessary to indicate that the political structure and the dynamics of the coalition government in Thailand had a powerful negative influence over the economic policy environment. Such an influence allowed serious economic problems to accumulate, and set the stage for the currency crisis and the rapid outflow of capital. Since July 1995, a coalition government led by Banharn Silpa-archa of the Chart Thai Party was in power. About a year later the government collapsed amidst corruption scandals. However, another unstable government was established in 1996. The New Aspiration Party led by General Chavalit Yongchaiyudh emerged as the largest party from the 1996 elections with 125 seats in the 393-member House of Representatives, and established a coalition government. The closest one was the Democrat Party with 123 seats. Business had hoped for the Democrats to win. The Stock Exchange of Thailand (SET) fell by 5.8% on news of the 1996 election result. General Chavalit's government brought neither confidence nor stability. It survived until after the crisis, but only in 1997 was the Thai cabinet reshuffled a few times.[16] As Thailand further sank into economic difficulties in 1997, the government was criticized for its immobilization, indecisiveness, and corruption. Nonetheless, these were not new, but applied to the previous governments, led by Banharn Silapa-archa, Chuan Leekpai, and Chatichai Choonhavan, as well. All of these governments rested on very shaky multiparty coalition arrangements, and were afflicted with serious and ongoing corruption scandals, and did not make progress in the way of major economic reform. Chavalit's government inherited accumulated economic problems.[17] According to MacIntyre (1999):

> The indecisiveness of political leadership in Thailand was a function of the fragmentation of the party system and the tendency toward weak coalition governments. With parliamentary majorities composed of approximately six parties, each with its own internal weaknesses, cabinet instability was a chronic problem. Party leaders were always vulnerable to defections by factions and individuals within their own parties who could find better prospects for advancement in another party. And the Prime Minister, as leader of the governing coalition, was always vulnerable to policy blackmail by coalition partners threatening to defect in pursuit of better deals in another alliance configuration. This was the key political dynamic of coalition government in Thailand.[18]

As a result, the Thai government was unable to act to correct the situation in a timely manner. Thailand's combination of a parliamentary structure with multiple weak parties caused policymaking to be indecisive, as it allowed the existence of numerous veto players within the government. Therefore, any sorts of major policy initiatives were extremely difficult to undertake. Even after the crisis broke, the Thai government was unable to respond to the situation in a timely or effective manner, until later times.[19]

The impacts of the authoritarian regime, corruption, and problem of political succession associated with the president's health in Indonesia. The Indonesian economy was also vulnerable, even though some of its economic indicators were in better shape than those of Thailand. For example, inflation was moderate, and the current account deficit to GDP ratio was much less than that of Thailand. On the negative side, there was excessive lending to the property sector in Indonesia as well. Indonesia's banking sector was the region's most politicized and the weakest, to an extent that funds could be channeled to friends of the Suharto regime. Credits were not allocated based on the economic merits of business projects. Non-performing loans to regime cronies accounted for much of the total private debt. A list of bad debtors that was leaked in 1994 revealed that Suharto's children and their associates were high on the list of privileged borrowers. Internal corruption was tolerated within the Indonesian banking system. For example, loan supervisors were usually bribed about 10-15 percent of a loan up front as a kickback.[20] Indonesia was the "most corrupt country in Asia" according to a private Hong Kong survey of expatriate businessmen in March 1997. Thus, the Indonesian economic environment was polluted with bribery, corruption, and kickbacks. The country's regulatory framework was weak and many regulations were applied arbitrarily. It was possible to get "exemption" from a government regulation by bribing. Sometimes, government regulations targeted prices, which were supposed to be determined by the market. These kinds of weaknesses, all of which have political, institutional and societal sources and implications, made the Indonesian economy vulnerable to shocks. The Indonesian government's initiatives to address the economic problems were received with serious doubts prior to the crisis. For example, the government initiated an effort to improve the efficiency and competitiveness of the export sector. But, in February 1996, the heavily indebted Asri Petroleum group, established by a group of prominent local businessmen, including Suharto's son Bambang Trihatmodjo, received the most significant tariff support. Suharto's government initiated a National Automobile Program, which aimed at exempting qualified "pioneer" firms from the sales tax and tariffs on imported components, but "the only firm to qualify was Suharto's youngest son Hutomo (Tommy)'s Mandala Putra. The company made an agreement with the Korean firm Kia, but it was yet to produce a single car."[21]

"If the basic problem in Thailand was that the institutional framework produced hopelessly divided and thus indecisive government (of all coalition complexions), in Indonesia the problem was that the institutional framework imposed no constraints on executive action—thus opening the way for erratic policy behavior," MacIntyre (1999) asserts.[22] Besides President Suharto, no other institution or political actor was either able to veto the president's policy initiatives and their implementation, or initiate alternative policies. In the middle of 1996, massive anti-government demonstrations took place in Jakarta. However, foreign capital did not leave the country that time. President Suharto's government was still in power and firmly in control, but the big question was the political succession of the president. The Indonesian presidential election was scheduled to be held in March 1998. In the meantime, there was repeated bad news about the health of President Suharto. It was not clear who was going to replace Suharto and whether policy reversals would take place.[23] The unfettered power of the presidency made things seem like everything was dependent on Suharto. Therefore, uncertainty about after-Suharto governments and policies was highly destructive for investor confidence. This political situation also delayed the recovery of Indonesia from the crisis as compared to that of Thailand and Korea, which all received the IMF-sponsored bailout packages.[24] Thus, in Indonesia as well, political factors played as significant a role as economic ones in bringing the Asian financial crisis into Indonesia, and during the policy response and recovery periods.

The impacts of statements of the presidential candidate, government-chaebol relations (domestic interest groups), and moral hazard problems in South Korea. Korea's economic indicators also were not as bad as those of Thailand, even though the CA deficit rose from 1.5% of GDP in 1994 to 4.8% of GDP in 1996. The growing CA deficit was associated with an unprecedented accumulation of short-term foreign debt and declining export growth.[25] Nonetheless, in Korea too, there were multiple non-economic factors that affected the government's economic policies, investors' confidence in the government, and the economic indicators themselves. For example, then presidential candidate and later president Kim Dae Jung sent contradictory signals to the markets in 1997 and scared investors about policy reversal. There was a threat of labor strife.[26] A more significant example of these non-economic influences was the government-*chaebol* relations in South Korea. "A *chaebol* is a group of large companies operating in diverse and mostly unrelated industries, usually under the ownership and control of a single family," as Shin (2000) defines it.[27] These *chaebols*, along with South Korea's political and economic institutions, served as the main engines of rapid economic growth until the mid-1980s. However, they and their intricate relations with the government became a hindrance for the economy's adaptation to the new conditions as time passed. During the heydays of economic development, these corporations enjoyed various favors such as special financing and import and export subsidies. Over time, they became large conglomerates with highly diversified business activities and a monopoly in the market. The government continued to support them strongly at the cost of small and medium sized firms. By 1997, a small number of *chaebols* had dominated the economic landscape in South Korea. About 30 of the largest *chaebols* accounted for more than 70 percent of GDP.[28] Woo-Cumings (1999) argues that:

> The financial crisis in Korea was born of an inability to resolve the long-standing and widely recognized dilemma of its developmentalism. Twenty years of 'financial liberalization' notwithstanding, the Korean state was unable to sever the Gordian knot between the state and the banking sector on the one hand and the hugely leveraged corporate sector on the other. This was because the state was hamstrung between a highly effective bureaucracy that sought to regulate the corporate sector and a political ruling group that, relying on the financial support of big business, ended up circumventing the best efforts of the bureaucrats.[29]

This situation created moral hazard problems in Korea. These corporations, encouraged by implicit and explicit government guarantees, were heavily indebted. Corruption and moral hazard problems also made these conglomerates take risks beyond the levels that they could manage. For example, Hanbo Steel, a company in the Hanbo Group and the country's 14th largest *chaebol*, defaulted on its loans in January 1997. Afterwards, it was revealed that it had massive debt of $6 billion or sixteen times its own capital. This led to a scandal. Later it was uncovered that bribery on a colossal scale, involving bankers, civil servants, and members of the government took place. The scandal forced then President Kim Young Sam to apologize on television for the collapse of Hanbo in February 1997.[30] The Asian financial crisis forced more *chaebols* to default on their debts. The Korean government struggled to settle these conglomerates' debts for several years after the crisis.[31] In the end, the government brought a web of credit controls and loan ceilings in order to prevent such situations again. Yet, "it took a massive banking and corporate crisis and the institution of a democratic regime to break this logjam," as Woo-Cumings (1999) puts it.[32]

The impacts of weak governments and weak bureaucracy in the Philippines. The Philippines' macroeconomic conditions were more solid as compared to the other countries, but it also had large CA deficits, and its currency was appreciated in real terms. The Philippines as well had a lending boom to the

private sector, which fueled investment in risky projects and speculative investments in the property sector.[33] Nonetheless, the Philippines was not as deeply
affected by the crisis as the other four countries were. The reason was not that
the Philippines had better economic and political foundations, but that it did not
achieve towering economic growth in the past years to fall down, while
neighboring high-growth economies found themselves toppling from the peaks
of their economic growth. Despite this fact, the Philippines could not avoid the
impact of the crisis due to weak economic fundamentals as well as a lack of
stable political and institutional foundations for economic growth. The Ramos
administration achieved economic reforms toward further liberalization in the
1990s, but much remained to be done. The economic liberalization was not
associated with political and institutional reforms. The country's weak governments and bureaucracy were incapable of providing even the basic foundation
for a market-oriented economic growth, such as supplying electricity and providing even-handed regulation and supervision of the financial system. The
government with its weak performance has been vulnerable to the plunder of
oligarchic groups.[34]

All of these examples show that non-economic factors played as significant roles as economic factors in creating the conditions that led to the crisis. In
fact, economic and non-economic factors intermixed to the extent that they
cannot be clearly separated. The unstable coalition governments in Thailand, the
uncertainty about the succession of Suharto in Indonesia, the intricate relations
between government and *chaebols* in South Korea, and weak government and
bureaucracy in the Philippines, are only several examples of non-economic
factors that impacted the origination and consequences of the crisis. These factors severely impacted economic indicators, affected the behavior of these governments before and after the crisis, and sent wrong signals to markets. All of
these in turn determined the perception of investors and caused the outflow of
domestic and foreign capital from these countries. In addition, external actors
and developments as well as contagion played significant roles in the spread of
the crisis. For example, the international interventions, in particular the IMF
recommendation of immediate suspensions or closures of some financial institutions, further sent negative signals to the creditors, according to Radelet and
Sachs (2000). Since many creditors treated the region as a whole, withdrawal of
foreign funds created a chain reaction, quickly developed into a financial panic,
and spread into the regional countries with similar economic conditions.[35] The
rest of this chapter explores the impact of non-economic factors within the Malaysian domestic and external contexts.

The Impacts of Non-Economic Factors in Malaysia

The impacts of Mahathirism and the semi-authoritarian regime in Malaysia. PM
Mahathir's political and economic development ideology is often referred to as
Mahathirism, about which more information is provided in Appendix B. Since
he came to power in 1981, Mahathir has been an economic modernizer and "an

ideologue of the state-sponsored constructive protection."[36] He announced the "Look East Policy" (to catch up with the West) in 1981. The "Look East Policy" aimed at emulating Japanese and South Korean models, known as the East Asian model, and intensification of relations with these countries for the purpose of transferring technologies and learning business skills. Mahathir proposed to adopt especially two features of the Japanese development model: (1) creating large companies similar to Japanese large trading companies and (2) becoming "Malaysia incorporated" as a state like its Japanese counterpart, in order to encourage and support businesses, in particular Malay businessmen.[37] Mahathir had a vision of transforming Malaysia into a newly industrialized country, NIC, under genuine *bumiputera* capitalist entrepreneurship. According to him, the best examples of Malays are the ones who have come up from the 'old' Malay backgrounds to join the highest ranks of the *bumiputera* commercial and industrial community.[38] During the early 1990s, Mahathir promoted his "Vision 2020" plan. The plan's main goal was to achieve a "fully developed country" status for Malaysia by the year 2020, mainly by accelerating industrialization, growth, and modernization.[39]

As the crisis was approaching, the Malaysian government was financing mega-projects, such as the massive Bakun hydro-electric project, partly with short-term debts. Mahathir was advocating his new development objectives under the slogan of "Vision 2020" that aimed at propelling his country into the ranks of the developed world in the next two decades. The country's new airport and the soaring Petronas Towers were almost finished before the crisis. His latest, and maybe greatest project, was the Multimedia Super Corridor (MSC) with lower trade barriers. It was a comprehensive project that aimed at moving Malaysia into an information-based economy, and it is conceived as the final phase of the country's industrialization program. Malaysia's aim of entering the league of developed nations by 2020 seemed feasible until the Asian financial crisis halted it.[40] Critics were worried that these projects were over-burdening the country and the economy was overheating, prior to the crisis. Mahathir's government dismissed these criticisms by arguing that Malaysia's growth of the Consumer Price Index (CPI) (the inflation) was low.[41] Also, Mahathir blocked any effort of slowing these projects down by other members of the government. In 1996, investments accounted for 43 percent of GDP in Malaysia, the highest in the region. The investment surge was not only actualizing the goals of Mahathir's vision 2020, but was also compensating for the deteriorating economic growth prior to the crisis.[42] However, the economic returns of these grandiose industrial projects were not immediate, and the investment surge was feeding the current account deficits by increasing demand for imports. In the meantime, Malaysia's exports were slowed down due to the real appreciation of the ringgit, lowered productivity rates because of higher real wages, and export competition by China and other low-cost countries.[43]

The impacts of patron-client relations (domestic interest groups), historic ethnic concerns, the semi-authoritarian political system and political leadership. By the onset of the Asian financial crisis, Malaysia had one of the healthier banking systems in the region.[44] Despite the experience of the 1984-1985 crisis, however, Malaysia's banking system extended domestic credit extensively and overland in property markets with direct or indirect encouragement of the Malaysian government. Many companies continued to borrow excessively until after the crisis started. The growth rate of bank credit to the private sector (in nominal terms) rose from 8 percent during 1985-1989 to 120 percent in 1994 and then to over 160 percent by mid-1997 when the financial crisis began. By the end of 1997, total domestic loans stood at around 170 percent of GDP. The Malaysian banking system had a massive accumulation of outstanding domestic credits, with heavy exposure to the property sector (real estate and stock market) in the lead up to the crisis. High loan exposure fuelled asset prices. Once the asset prices started to dive during the financial crisis, Malaysian banks were left with bad loans, which became the source of major financial difficulties.[45]

The Malaysian government encouraged such expansion of domestic credit with direct or indirect government guarantees and/or through direct credit allocation to favored companies, in particular those with close ties with the UMNO. Direct government influence on bank lending had a long history, dating back to the initiation of the NEP in 1974 and continued with Mahathir's NDP in the 1990s. One of the major goals of both the NEP and the NDP was to restructure business ownership in favor of *bumiputera* companies, and the credit allocation was one of the tools in achieving this goal. However, the state-sponsored NEP and NDP policies have increasingly blurred the lines between the state, markets, and the dominant party UMNO. Dominated by the UMNO leader Mahathir, the Malaysian government's influence grew out of proportion and turned out to be a major source of macroeconomic instability and financial fragility under his "big push" towards the year 2020.[46]

The executive dominance of power has had significant consequences for how the economic policies were made and how they were implemented, as the policies initiated by the NEP, privatization, and later by the NDP as well as their implementation have demonstrated. Along with the Prime Minister, the Minister of Finance and the Minister of Trade and Industry, who are appointed by the Prime Minister, have been the main determiners of economic policies.[47] Mahathir and his coalition partners had been trying to achieve many political and economic goals through the deliberate creation and allocation of rents in order to secure legitimacy and support for the government as well as to encourage investment and industrialization. Arbitrary executive power enabled the political elite, in particular the leading members of the UMNO hierarchy, to secure government-created rents for themselves and/or to allocate to those with close political connections in return for their economic and political support. Access to rents had become increasingly contingent on political access and influence. As a result, rent-seeking activities increased and served the politically well-connected businessmen the most. Political patronage and rent-seeking activities led to inefficient resource allocation, as they encouraged businesses to make huge profits without facing market competition.[48] They created a new business class during the implementation of the NEP and privatization, and the NDP and public enterprises became increasingly politicized as a means for transferring re-sources to the *bumiputera*. The political patronage and rent seeking activities mostly benefited the well-connected *bumiputera* corporations, but Chinese and Indian businesses, which had connections with the UMNO's coalition partners (the MCA and the MIC) or directly with the UMNO, also got their share to a lesser extent. Most of the corporations had ties with the UMNO through its main investment arms, the biggest ones being the Fleet Group Sdn Bhd and Hatibudi Nominees Sdn Bhd. Some others, such as Magnum and Multi-Purpose Holdings Bhd (MPHB) were associated with the MCA, and still others with the MIC. Overtime, the political ambitions of senior UMNO leaders, in particular that of Mahathir, further expanded political patronage, and consolidated the mutual dependence of the "new business class" and the political elite.[49] This had a sig-nificant impact on the policy behavior of Malaysia as we shall see in the upcom-ing paragraphs.

The BNM had a historical reputation among the central banks of newly in-dependent countries in the British Commonwealth for its strict pursuance of conservative monetary policy and banking regulations. However, in the context of a credit boom that had government backing at the highest political level, the role of BNM naturally diminished to that of a passive observer of an impending crisis. As a result, the BNM was not very effective in checking the growing fragility of the financial sector. From 1992 onward, the BNM implemented some restrictive measures such as bringing administrative controls on consumer lending for cars and houses, tightening reserve requirements on Malaysian banks, and raising interest rates. As it was revealed later, the BNM also warned the Prime Minister's office about the potential economic problems ahead during the years preceding the crisis.[50] However, Mahathir's office did not act upon the BNM's recommendations. Most of the BNM measures were not backed by the fiscal side and were dismantled as result of the influence of well-connected business lobbies. The BNM eventually was allowed to increase the interest rates substantially in 1995 and 1996, but these increases did not have a significant effect on credit flows in the context of a massive asset price boom.[51] Any further action was not taken at that time. Eventually, the BNM introduced some more restrictions on lending to the property sector and stock market investments on March 28, 1997,[52] as a result of the Malaysian government's growing concerns about the upcoming financial crisis, as the market disturbances in Thailand oc-curred. But, it was a late action. The BNM intervention caused foreign investors, led by U.S. fund managers, to sell their stocks in the KLCI stock exchange, which was heavily weighted toward property and financial shares. Thus the KLCI index dropped 6.6% on March 28, and reached a level that was 17.2% lower than the peak of February 25. In May, as the speculative attacks on the Thai bath took hold, the KLCI index fell to the lowest level in 16 months.[53]

The impacts of policy mistakes. According to Toyoda (2001), the Malay-sian government made a mistake by maintaining a strong ringgit. Instead, the government should have pursued more competitive exchange rates to encourage exports.[54] The real appreciation of the ringgit[55] encouraged huge foreign capital inflows, which served to finance the current account deficits, as well as bank borrowing, as elsewhere in the Southeast Asian region. Some of these capital inflows came in the form of short-term portfolio capital, and created opportunities for speculative investments.[56]

MALAYSIA FACING THE CRISIS

Policy Struggle in the Malaysian Government

Although the Malaysian government's concerns about an emergence of a crisis started as early as March 1997, as the markets were becoming volatile in Thailand, the Asian financial crisis arrived in Malaysia in the second week of July. Following the heavy speculations on the Thai baht on July 2, 1997, speculative pressures on the ringgit mounted as well. The BNM was forced to start a series of aggressive interventions in the foreign exchange market by selling dollars to prevent the ringgit from falling. It spent 10% of its reserves in one week defending the ringgit. But, the interventions were only briefly successful, and the bank's ability to defend the ringgit was substantially reduced in the second week of July 1997. At the end, the BNM gave up defending the ringgit on July 14 by letting the ringgit exchange rate be determined by market forces. However, the Kuala Lumpur Stock Exchange (KLSE) responded to the free float of the ringgit with a sharp decline. It fell down to the 1000 level for the first time since 1996,[57] and the ringgit hit a 38-month low of 2.6530 to the dollar on July 24.

The impacts of Mahathir's rhetoric (as a reflection of his political and economic ideology as well as political interests) and the government's miscalculated policy trials. Mahathir launched a bitter attack on "rogue speculators" on July 26, and blamed George Soros as the man responsible for the attack on the ringgit.[58] As the crisis deepened in Malaysia, Mahathir continued to blame speculators in a state of shock, anger, and denial. He blamed foreign fund managers as being "racist" because they were selling the Malaysian shares. Greedy currency speculators were ignoring Malaysia's sound economic fundamentals, according to Mahathir. A "Jewish conspiracy" was at work against the country, and the West was gloating over the crisis, as it was jealous of Asian prospects. However, the ringgit and stock prices continued to fall as Mahathir attacked his perceived enemies.[59] In the meantime, the IMF offered $1.1 billion to the Philippines in July, and approved a $16.7 billion bailout package, which later reached $17.2 billion with Brunei's contribution to Thailand in early August 1997. The Indonesian rupiah came under severe pressure as well in early August.[60] On August 18, Standard & Poor's Ratings lowered the Malaysian outlook from positive to stable.[61]

As the stock market continued to crash in Malaysia, the government imposed restrictions on the short selling of 100 blue-chip stocks of the KLSE index on Thursday, August 28. Additional rules, such as the requirement of a physical share of certificates from sellers, were introduced in order to discourage the sale of stocks. The Malaysian government's decisions (direct interventions) for the stock market operation were even more damaging to investors' confidence than Mahathir's rhetoric. They caused one of the largest falls in Malaysian stock market history, which forced the government to take its decisions back on Friday. However, they were the early signs of restrictions on stock market trading for foreign investors that led them to get out of it at the first opportunity. Following the government interventions in the stock market, the U.S. Securities Exchange Commission declared that Malaysia was a controlled market and obliged U.S. pension funds to withdraw their investment interests in the country.[62]

On September 3, Mahathir announced a vaguely defined 60-billion ringgit ($20 billion) state fund that would be used to buy shares from locals at a premium and from foreigners at market prices. Mahathir also threatened those helping foreign dealers in their short selling of the Malaysian stocks with punitive measures, including arrest. Later, it became clear that the Employees Provident Fund (EPF) was going to be used for the purchases of shares. It was an attempt to prop up share prices by buying stocks from Malaysian shareholders—but not foreigners—above prevailing market prices. Ironically, the government's plan of share purchases was seen as an opportunity to get rid of Malaysian shares by both local and foreign shareholders. It was also seen as an attempt to save selected Malaysians, or 'cronies,' from a disaster. As a result, the government's policy attempt also backfired and triggered a massive sell-off of stocks in KLSE, which undermined sentiment on other regional stock markets as well. Mahathir's *ad hoc* measures were only having reverse effects. They never became institutionalized and some government officials even denied their existence.[63]

The impacts of psychological factors (shock, denial, wishful thinking) and Mahathir's rhetorical and policy responses to the crisis. Mahathir was reluctant to accept any of the Malaysian economic weaknesses, and therefore the government was delaying to produce sound policies to address the real situation. Nonetheless, government officials of other regional countries were inclined to see the market turbulence that was unleashed by the Thai devaluation in the region as temporary. According to the *Financial Times*, this view was shared by a number of influential western officials as well.[64] In the meantime, the Malaysian government threatened to use repressive measures against domestic commentators making unfavorable reports about the Malaysian economy. Press freedom was already constrained in Malaysia, but the political leadership increased their repressive measures further during the crisis period. These measures as well had a reverse effect on the markets, as they strengthened the impression that the government had much to hide from public scrutiny.[65]

The decline of the stock market and the ringgit continued throughout September. In September, Mahathir started giving the signs of restrictions on currency trading. He initially suggested that currency trading be limited to trade finance. Later, on September 8 and on September 20, before the IMF and the World Bank delegation at the meeting in Hong Kong, Mahathir called for outlawing currency manipulations. In his interview with the *South China Morning Post*, on September 20, he said that Malaysia would limit currency trading to only financing trade. Mahathir seemed to be threatening a unilateral ban on foreign exchange purchases unrelated to imports and exports. Although it did not happen and such ideas were not supported by the regional governments, if supported by his cabinet colleagues, Mahathir's remarks continued to undermine investors' confidence and further exacerbated the situation by panicking investors. As a result, the Malaysian stocks declined further and the ringgit continued to fall to the level of 3.13 to the dollar.[66] As Gomez and Jomo K.S. notes: "the ringgit probably fell much further than might otherwise have been the case, as a result of international market reaction to Mahathir's rhetorical and policy responses to the unfolding crisis."[67] The Deputy Prime Minister and Finance Minister Anwar Ibrahim tried to calm the situation by announcing the Malaysian government's commitment to the open market and financial liberalization and no government plans to change the currency-trading regime in Malaysia. In September, Anwar also pushed the Malaysian government to introduce measures that would cut down government spending on big projects, and ease the regulations on investors' selling their shares. As a result, the government announced the postponement of the grandiose infrastructure projects, including the Bakun Dam and the proposed new international airport, which amounted to about $10 billion of investment commitments.[68] In September, Standard & Poors cut the Malaysian outlook again, from stable to negative, due to the reluctance of the Malaysian authorities to curb credit growth and the deteriorating asset quality of Malaysian banks.[69]

The impacts of denial and the political and economic ambitions of Mahathir (Mahathirism). In the meantime, the IMF conveyed its policy prescriptions to the Malaysian government. Although the IMF recognized the effects of the regional contagion for the crisis in Malaysia, it blamed sustained and rapid growth in money supply and credit expansion along with some other structural weaknesses of Malaysia's economy. It suggested austerity measures and a cut in public spending on some of the country's multibillion-dollar projects. It advised Mahathir's government not to bailout the weak corporations, but to let the market decide about them. The IMF suggestions also included improvements in corporate management, fiscal transparency, and avoidance of government guarantees. It suggested that the Malaysian government further liberalize markets for the entry of foreign investment in key sectors of the economy.[70] Although Anwar's limited interventions were a step forward toward the IMF-prescribed policies, Mahathir was reluctant to accept any IMF suggestion from the beginning. He was determined to protect his mega-projects as well as the interests of UMNO-connected businesses, which were associated with these projects. He denounced external calls as an attempt to undermine Malaysian growth, and criticized the IMF intervention in Thailand as unhelpful.[71]

The impacts of Mahathir's rhetorical and policy stance, domestic political interests, and Anwar's contrary policy measures. According to Hilley (2001), as the crisis was deepening, the broad business community was in expectation of a more comprehensive set of confidence-building measures taken by Anwar.[72] However, Mahathir had a different agenda. On October 1, he repeated his call for a tighter control or total ban of foreign currency trading which caused the rinngit to fall to the 3.40 level against the dollar. On October 17, the Malaysian government announced "a belt-tightening budget" for the year 1998. The budget postponed large-scale projects, cut government spending by about 2 percent, and envisioned increased fiscal surplus in 1998. But markets were unimpressed by the budget and skeptical about the government's economic forecast, notably the projected GDP growth rate of 7%. The budget contained some austerity measures, but they were accompanied by incentives to assist lagging sectors of the economy. It order to reduce the current account deficit, it increased duties on a range of capital and consumer goods imports, brought 10-15% range tax incentives for high performing exporters, and started a "buy Malaysia" campaign. It also reduced corporate tax from 30 percent to 28 percent. The measures were seemingly "tough," but they were also designed to maintain the support of domestic businesses. The government failed to come up with a coherent program of reforms in order to deal with the crisis. In sum, market participants did not find the budget realistic, and Anwar's reassuring messages did not change their perception.[73]

Throughout October, Mahathir continued to blame foreign speculators for being responsible for the market turbulence and the consequent economic instability that Malaysia was experiencing. In a meeting of fifteen developing nations in Kuala Lumpur, Mahathir warned attendees against lowering trade barriers to the West and thus making themselves unnecessarily vulnerable. Mahathir's continued rhetoric was damaging Malaysia's credibility and cast doubts about Malaysia's commitment to open market practices. Some argued that Mahathir's blame of speculators and anti-western rhetoric was aimed at a domestic audience rather than an international one. Nonetheless, they were well received by many in Indonesia, Thailand, and even in the Philippines, as well as many segments of Malaysian society. The majority of Malaysians, not only *bumiputra* but also the Indians and Chinese communities, were backing Mahathir's rhetorical stance. On October 27, 1997, around 2000 members of the Indian community burned an effigy of George Soros.[74] David I. Hitchcock (1998) surveyed different groups, including Malaysian scholars, in the countries that were affected by the crisis. Malaysian scholars pointed to a "fear that major economies will push liberalization at too fast a pace" in Malaysia in order to destroy some aspects of the Malaysian economy and to make sure the West stays ahead. Another fear in Malaysia was that more rapid economic liberalization would damage small and medium-sized industries.[75] In general, one's ideas or beliefs about the causes of the crisis shape his/her policy stance. For Malaysians, besides having the fear of Western conspiracy and believing in Mahathir's rhetoric, there seemed to be no realistic alternative view and explanation of the crisis within the Malaysian political context that had been dominated by the UMNO and its leader Mahathir.

While Mahathir continued his blame of speculators and criticism of the IMF, twelve Asian finance ministers (including that of Malaysia) had a meeting with representatives from the U.S. and Canada and delegates from the IMF, the World Bank, and the Asian Development Bank in Manila on November 19.

After the meeting they issued a statement that proposed to enhance the IMF's role in identifying possible financial crises. On November 25, the Asia Pacific Economic Cooperation, (APEC) ended its annual summit with a call for greater trade freedom and a common front against the economic turmoil that was developing. At this meeting, Mahathir's criticism of the IMF was opposed by then Mexican President Ernesto Zedillo. In the meantime, the crisis spread to South Korea in early November 1997.[76]

The impact of policy struggles between Mahathir and Anwar within the government, and the UMNO and its clients (domestic interest groups). As the markets continued to deteriorate in Malaysia, Mahathir's command of the economy was shaken. By December 1997, his continuance in the office started to be questioned.[77] In 1997, Anwar was seen as Mahathir's heir. When Mahathir left for a two-month vacation, from which he returned just before the Asian financial crisis started, he left Anwar behind as the acting Prime Minister and acting president of the UMNO. This was highly significant since Mahathir had never left a deputy in charge for such an extended period. Seemingly, Anwar was loyal to Mahathir and Mahathir trusted him. Most analysts agreed that Anwar did not make any major decision without consulting Mahathir during that time.[78] During the crisis, however, the Deputy Prime Minister and Finance Minister Anwar, unlike Mahathir, was inclined to deal with the crisis by cutting down expenditures and bringing austerity measures, similar to the IMF recommendations. He pushed the Malaysian government toward his policy direction whenever he had the chance. Anwar was forced to take further "post-budget measures," as the capital flight and the ringgit's slide continued. On December 5, 1997, Anwar was able to push the Cabinet in his direction of policy, while Mahathir was attending an air show and Maritime exhibition on his beloved resort island of Langkawi. During that cabinet meeting, Anwar presented reports (position papers) back to 1995 that disclosed the warnings of the Finance Ministry and the BNM of impending economic problems due to the overheating economy and multibillion dollar projects that would overburden the country. They challenged Mahathir's blame of foreign speculators as the cause of the crisis, and implicitly accepted that policy mistakes were made. These position papers revealed that there were differences over the course of economic policy between the BNM and the Finance Ministry on the one hand, and the Prime Minister's department on the other hand.[79]

The Malaysian cabinet, which Anwar chaired, decided to reduce government expenditures drastically by 18 percent, restrict bank credits, and defer all proposed mega-projects. It took measures that aimed at reducing the country's current account deficit to the level of 3 percent of GDP, and revised the earlier growth projection downward from 7% to 4-5 percent, recognizing the market's reservations over the government's budget forecasts in October. According to the cabinet decision, the Malaysian government would also try to shore up foreign-exchange reserves, which declined to $24 billion from $27 billion in 1996. These measures were akin to what the IMF would have liked to see and were received well outside Malaysia. Bill Clinton sent a message of "support" for continued investment in Malaysia and the World Bank president James Wolfensohn expressed confidence in Malysia's recovery efforts in early February 1998, following the previous visit and positive assessment of the IMF managing director Michel Camdessus. However, international investors showed cautious optimism.[80]

Although Anwar's "revised budget" was well received outside Malaysia and markets initially reacted favorably to the revised measures, it was not favored by Mahathir orthe UMNO and its clients since the privileges of UMNO business clients would negatively be affected. Anwar's "austerity measures" would reduce investment and consumption spending and therefore the domestic sales of Malaysian companies. Many of these companies, which were already weakened by declined stock and property values, would possibly face bankruptcy due to their heavy debts and unavailability of additional capital. An increase of non-performing private corporate debt, without a safety net of a bailout, would endanger the Malaysian banks' financial health. In addition, the cabinet decisions would rebuke Mahathir's rhetoric, slash public spending and halt the big projects championed by him. Therefore, heavily indebted UMNO-linked businesses would not only face these challenges, but also lose their source of enrichment, if the big projects associated by Mahathir's Vision 2020 were halted. As a result, the enforcement of the decided measures would have been quite difficult. In fact, Anwar's "austerity" measures disclosed the growing tensions between Anwar and his Bank Negara allies on the one hand, and Mahathir and his associates within the UMNO on the other. Although Mahathir appeared to accept the cabinet decisions and gave his consent at the beginning, it was a temporary approval until he later retook control of the economy in his and his friend Daim's hands.[81]

The IMF-style austerity measures were initially well received by the markets, but it did not last. This was probably because there seemed not to be enough political support and commitment behind these measures, and they were already too late to correct the economic situation and restore market confidence. Despite the austerity measures, the ringgit continued to slip, reaching the 3.83-3.88 range against the dollar by the end of December. Although the BNM tried to stop the decline of the ringgit, it reached the 4.05 level on January 5, 1998. Both currency and stock markets continued to decline throughout January. On December 22, Moody's customer service lowered the credit ratings of Malaysia along with those of Indonesia, South Korea, and Thailand. Later, Moody's downgraded four Malaysian banks, which included Public Bank Bhd and Sime Bank Bhd on January 29, 1998, and cut Malaysia's sovereign foreign currency ratings outlook to negative on February 6, 1998. In the meantime, the Bank of International Settlement, BIS, released new figures that showed that Malaysia's short-term debt was at 56 percent of total borrowings from overseas, higher than an earlier estimate of 30 percent.[82]

Mahathir Taking Control of Response Policymaking

The impacts of policy struggle within the Malaysian government, patron-client relations, "money politics" and associated historical experiences. As the downward spiral of the economy continued, not only Mahathir's but also Anwar's image as an able finance minister was being tarnished.[83] In January 1998, Mahathir established a National Economic Action Council (NEAC) chaired by him, and comprised of Cabinet Ministers and leaders from private commerce and industrial sectors. The declared objective of the council was to restore investor confidence, particularly foreign investors, and to take measures to prevent any economic recession. As the split between Mahathir and Anwar was growing, Mahathir brought back his loyal and trusted man Daim Zainuddin as the executive director of the newly created NEAC. Daim served as a finance minister before Anwar, and he was the man who managed the UMNO's "money politics" as Mahathir's loyal man. Soon after, speculations started about the real intentions behind the creation of the NEAC. There was a cynical speculation that it was created to bailout troubled tycoons linked to the ruling party, especially those who were linked to Mahathir and Daim. Anwar also had his friends in the business elite. It seemed that Daim was brought back in order to bailout favored corporate figures and former protégés. The creation of the NEAC and Daim's return also created a perception that the economic policymaking was taken over by Mahathir and Daim and away from Anwar, who had more credibility in the eyes of market participants and was more liked by the international financial community. Daim's return caused ambiguity in terms of who was really in charge of the economic policy making and about what to expect from early to mid-1998. All these speculations and ambiguities worsened the economic situation further. As expected, much of the crisis management centered around the NEAC in the following weeks. Anwar's "austerity measures" and the BNM's policy initiatives, in order to calm the situation, lost their credibility further.[84]

The UMNO business activities started with the aims of providing finance for the UMNO in order for it to become independent from Chinese contributions, of creating a fund to finance a UMNO headquarters building, and of gaining control over the media. These activities had been conducted through a small number of company managers whose market operations provided finance for the UMNO. Fleet Holdings was the UMNO's first significant business venture, which came under the control of Mahathir's friend and then the Finance Minister Daim Zainuddin. It bought the Kuala Lumpur edition of the Singapore-based Straits Times, renaming it New Straits Times. Over time, it extended its business activities into many different industries including that of television, manufacturing, mining, and property. At one point, control of Fleet Holdings slipped into the hands of parties who were not close to Daim and Mahathir. A company with the name of Renong was created to take over Fleet Holdings. Renong was supposed to be a purely private company, but it was only designed that way to insulate the UMNO's business activities from public view. It was controlled by

Daim's proxies, principally Halim Saad and others such as Wan Azmi. Daim often awarded Renong and its associated companies state contracts.[85] These business activities of the UMNO have been under the control of only a few at the apex of the party hierarchy.[86] They were hidden not only from the public but also from most of the UMNO members.

In the mid-1980s, the controversy around the financial disaster involved then Finance Minister Daim, with an accusation of misuse of government funds and manipulation of the stock market.[87] Relations between politics and businesses had become increasingly more complex over time. Competition and factionalism within the UMNO created various patron-client relationships and structures within the party, and increased the cost of rising up through the party hierarchy. Over time, the UMNO was deeply affected by "money politics." For example, the competition for the UMNO deputy presidency between Deputy Prime Minister Musa Hitam and Finance Minister Tengku Razaleigh Hamzah in 1981 and 1984 involved a lot of "money politics" and patronage to secure the support. In 1987, Razaleigh allied himself with Musa and challenged Mahathir for the UMNO presidency. Since the stakes were so high, Mahathir depended heavily on Daim and his clients to avoid being toppled. As it became widespread, "money politics" gradually started to be referred to as "lobbying", or more blatantly as "vote buying." Although the privatization probably reduced the "money politics" in the 1990s, "funds are increasingly being raised through the stock market by manipulating the trading and prices of politically controlled corporations" in order to finance increasingly expensive political campaigns.[88]

Nonetheless, privatization created a whole new patronage network, as the UMNO-connected businesses got the biggest shares, during the late 1980s and the 1990s. For example, the North-South Highway project, which was the largest public works contract to date, was awarded to United Engineers Malaysia (UEM) by the decision of the UMNO leadership in 1984, even though the UEM was inexperienced in the field, insolvent, and was not quoting the lowest tender. The UEM's top personnel were linked to Fleet Holdings. Tan Sri Halim Saad, one of Fleet's directors, was also appointed director of UEM. He was one of the "proxies" who were visible as directors, but informally acted for the UMNO and managed holdings to advance the party's business interests. The North-South Highway privatization evidenced some of the links between privatization contracts and the UMNO's corporate operations. During the awarding of the Highway to the UEM, open tendering was not enforced. Public outcry and complaints about it caused a court injunction that halted the construction, but only temporarily. Nonetheless, the public protest and the subsequent court decisions secured better terms in regards to public interest, as the government loans to the UEM were reduced, and the period of toll collection from the highway decreased from thirty years to twenty-five years. After the UMNO gained the control of UEM, the company was awarded a number of other privatized government contracts as well.[89] Another example of the privatization scams was the awarding of the construction of Bakun hydro-electric dam in Sarawak to a consortium in which UMNO-linked businesses had the biggest share. One of those businesses was Ekran, which was a key player in the consortium that was building the dam.[90] There are multiple other such examples.[91] By the early 1990s, the most influential and wealthy Malaysian businessmen were also those who were most closely associated with the Prime Minister Mahathir and Daim Zainuddin.[92]

After the creation of the NEAC and Daim's return as the executive director, Anwar gradually lost his position and influence in the Malaysian government's policymaking process in 1998. Temporarily, Daim worked with Anwar cooperatively until he took over the management of the economy as well as until he checked some of Mahathir's less conventional economic ideas. In late June 1998, Daim was appointed as the Minister with Special Functions, operating from the Prime Minister's Department. Subsequently, he became the Finance Minister in late 1998, taking over Anwar's position.[93] As he took control over the economy, Daim reversed Anwar's contractionary monetary and fiscal policies that were introduced in late 1997 in an ad hoc manner rather than as part of a crisis management package, and supported Mahathir's expansionist policies.[94] The following paragraphs further explore the process of policy reversal.

The impacts of Mahathir's policy trials, moral hazard problems, non-performing loans and the troubled banking system. In February, Mahathir went to three Southeast Asian capitals to propose his new idea of reducing dependence on the American dollar by trading goods in regional currencies. Although he got informal support from Manila and Bangkok, Indonesia declared that it would implement a currency-board system that would effectively peg the rupiah to the U.S. dollar. He also proposed setting up an Asian fund in order to rescue the region from the crisis without relying on the IMF. However, Mahathir's attempts did not bring concrete action from the regional countries.[95] In the meantime, Malaysia's statistics department explained that Malaysia recorded a RM400 million ($96 million) trade surplus in 1997, as a result of the weakened ringgit, which made Malaysia more competitive in exports.[96] However, the Malaysian banking system got into trouble.

Malaysia's foreign borrowings were modest as compared with those of the other countries in the region, but its domestic debt to GDP ratio was the highest in the region. It reached 160 percent of GDP at the end of 1997. Such a large amount of debt became the source of trouble for the banking system during the Asian financial crisis. According to BNM data, the proportion of non-performing assets increased from about 2% in July to 3.6% percent in December 1997 and then to 11.8% in July 1998. But independent estimates indicated that it reached the 25-30 percent range by mid-1998. The burden of non-performing loans was exacerbated by an outflow of RM32 billion from the domestic banking system because of withdrawals and capital flight during the period from May 1997 to June 1998.[97] On the positive side, although Malaysia's domestic debt was extremely high, its foreign exposure was limited. As a result, Malaysia's external debt did not inflate much when its currency fell sharply. Malaysia's banking system was not as plagued with foreign debt, as was the case in the other countries that were affected by the crisis.[98]

In early March 1998, the Bank Negara reported that four of Malaysia's largest financial institutions, including the prestigious Sime Darby Bhd's banking unit and the state-run Bank Bumiputra Malaysia Bhd, were in need of fresh capital injections, due to non-performing loans. Sime Darby Bhd's banking unit, one of the country's top 10 banks, declared a loss of RM1.8 billion and was in need of about RM1.2 billion. The country's second largest bank needed assistance of at least RM750 million to stay afloat. The huge losses of these banks evidenced the abuse of financial institutions in Malaysia.[99] Here, one example of such abuse is explored. Sime Darby Bhd was owned by the Rashid Hussain Bhd (RHB) Group, which was headed by Rashid Hussain who allegedly had close ties to Mahathir, Daim and Anwar. Sime Darby Bhd bought Sime Bank from Datuk Keramat Holdings Bhd in 1996. Within one decade, Rashid Hussain had gained control of a significant segment of Malaysia's financial sector, and RHB became one of the few financial giants in Malaysia. As mentioned in Chapter V, the domination of the banking sector by a few conglomerates and the interlocked ownership of financial institutions and corporations had been one significant weakness of the Malaysian banking system. Before the RHD group's takeover, major shareholders of Sime Bank had included the UMNO cooperative, KUB (M) Bhd with a 30 percent stake. Also, there had been numerous allegations about financial impropriety of the Sime Bank. The sale of Sime Bank to the RHB Group was widely seen as a bailout for the UMNO cooperative, with Sime Darby absorbing Sime Bank's losses. Sime Darby would probably handle those losses if the crisis did not occur. The crisis worsened the situation and therefore for the first time in its history, the Sime Darby declared a huge loss of over one billion RM, most of which was attributed to Sime Bank, at the end of 1997.[100]

Toward the end of March 1997, the BNM announced that the country's 34 finance companies would merge into eight, without scheduling any deadline. This news shattered the markets, in particular the KLSE stock market.[101] RHB groups sought a merger between its two banks, RHB Bank Bhd and Sime Darby's Sime Bank Bhd unit from the BNM, and Anwar as the Finance Minister gave his confirmation to the merger on April 23, 1998.[102] As the scale of collapse and indebtedness grew in the banking sector, the government established three special agencies. Pengurusan Danaharta Nasional Berhard, or briefly Danaharta was set up in May to acquire and manage non-performing loans from banks. Danamodal Nasional Berhard, briefly referred to as Danamodal was established with the purpose of recapitalizing troubled financial institutions in July. Also, a Corporate Debt Restructuring Committee (CDRC, a joint public and private sector steering committee) was established in order to facilitate the restructuring of corporate debts through an out-of-court settlement between debtors and creditors in August. These three institutions together provided a systematic institutional framework in addressing the banking sector's problems during the crisis. In the meantime, the BNM continued to cushion the banking sector by maintaining lower interest rates[103] and by injecting liquidity into the system through printing money.[104] In September 1998, Bank Bumiputra was bailed out with a capital injection of RM 1.1 billion (RM400 million in equity plus RM700 million worth of irredeemable cumulative preference shares). In addition, the government took over 65 percent of Bank Bumiputra's non-performing loans. Bank Bumiputra had been bailed out two more times in 1984 and 1989.[105] By August 1999, Danaharta took over most of the non-performing loans in the banking system.[106] In July 1998, the projected re-capitalization of the banking system during 1998 and 1999 was expected to cost a total of RM16 billion.[107] "Moral hazard" problems would probably accompany this generous takeover of the non-performing loans.

During early 1998, bad news started to build up as the corporations announced their losses and economic activities slowed down. Despite restrictions on the press, authorities were no longer able to shield the deteriorated economic situation from people. Anwar started to talk about a possibility of accepting a World Bank loan during late March 1998, although the Malaysian government had not wanted any international assistance before. Around this time, Daim, as the head of the NEAC, was preparing his economic policy recommendations.[108]

The impacts of patron-client relations, cronyism, and "money politics." As time passed, Mahathir increasingly took control of the crisis management in 1998. In the meantime, two of the controversial rescue/bailout operations took place. One was the indirect bailout of Renong Bhd, which had close connections with the UMNO. Halim Saad's United Engineers Malaysia (UEM), also an UMNO connected business, took a huge short-term loan in order to acquire 32.6 percent shares of Renong Bhd at an inflated price of RM2.34 billion. The UEM owned the cash-rich North South Highway toll-operator PLUS, and did not need a loan to buy the shares. Investors, deeply suspicious of the circumstances surrounding the UEM deal, dumped both Renong and UEM stocks. The shares of these companies lost almost half of their values and the KSLE index slipped 17%. Anwar suspended the deal due to its shocking effect, but it was revived again in January 1998.[109] The second controversial rescue operation was the Malaysian International Shipping Corporation's decision to buy the shipping arm of Korsortium Perkapalan (KPB), 51 percent of which was owned by Mahathir's son, Mr. Mirzan Mahathir.[110] The KPB's shipping assets were sold to Petronas, the Malaysian state oil company.[111] These deals showed that favored large companies and indebted tycoons were going to be bailed out. In April, while Anwar was in New York assuring fund managers that Malaysia was making serious efforts to address problems in its economy and that the worst had passed, Mahathir was preparing the country for more rescue operations. Mahathir defended a controversial plan to restructure Malaysian Airlines that would essentially help major shareholder Tajudin Ramli settle his personal debt. Then, the Malaysian government under Mahathir's leadership reversed its decision of retracting the RM2.2 billion funding of the monorail project in the capital, and decided to extend RM300 million in soft loans to the original benefactors of the project, which included well-connected tycoon Vincent Tan. The government officials also announced that they were considering helping other struggling businessmen too. Most of the early bailout deals involved ethnic-Malay companies close to the UMNO or PM Mahathir.[112] Some of the bailout money was allegedly taken from the Employees Provident Fund, EPF, without consulting the contributors.[113] The government lent to three state-sponsored companies and projects from the EPF: 1 billion ringgit to the capital's new international airport, 2 billion ringgit to Khazanah Nasional, the government's investment arm, and 710 million to Perwaja Trenggamu, a debt-laden steel maker.[114]

In April 1998, Standard & Poors lowered its rating of Malaysia's currency and in early May 1998 cut the country's outlook from stable to negative.[115] In April, the IMF also called on Malaysia again not to bailout corporations, to tighten monetary policy, and to improve corporate governance and fiscal transparency.[116] Mahathir responded to the IMF calls against bailout: "it depends how you interpret bailout . . . if a company is badly managed and we go in [and] use public money, it is wrong. When they devalue the ringgit and depress the value of shares, any company may collapse." Mahathir argued that the Malaysian bailouts were just like the U.S. government's aid to Chrysler to save it from bankruptcy when it lost half of its share capital and the U.S. dollar was depressed. Mahathir also rejected IMF calls on Malaysia to further tighten its monetary policies on the grounds that "we have already tightened so much that businesses are screaming because they can't breathe . . . . How much more tighter do they want it to be?"[117] It was also revealed during U.S. Treasury Secretary Robert E. Rubin's visit to Malaysia that Malaysian business executives supported Mahathir's policies, arguing that adapting a tight monetary policy would force even sound companies into bankruptcy.[118] In the meantime, Mahathir continued to repeat his rhetoric that Malaysia would continue to limit adverse foreign influences on the national economy, such as manipulative control over the currency.

In May 1998, the Malaysian government established a special body to help cash-strapped private companies. Securing funds for companies in trouble was considered vital to national interests. In the meantime, companies were advised to merge and/or takeover. According to the Mid-term Review of the Seventh Malaysia Plan (1996-2000), bumiputera businesses and/or state-aided entrepreneurs were affected by the crisis and subsequent recession the most. Later, this created a new debate about better ways of promoting entrepreneurship among the Malays and of accomplishing the unfinished goals of the NEP and the NDP.[119] In 1998, the issue was to find ways to rescue/support financially broke bumiputera-controlled businesses. One way to promote this objective was to allow Chinese capital greater access to struggling bumiputera businesses in order to save and rebuild them. This was one of the most politically sensitive issues in terms of the protection of bumiputera businesses' privileges that the Malaysian government had been promoting for decades. At the end, the Malaysian government relaxed the existing rules and allowed non-bumiputera-owned companies to assume the liabilities of bumiputera businesses by relaxing existing rules in some cases.[120]

The impacts of policy struggle within the Malaysian government and the UMNO and Mahathir's dominance in the Malaysian government. In mid-1998 Malaysia's deteriorated economic and financial situation was not getting any better yet. The Malaysian stock market had been declining, although temporary rises were recorded, and it reached the 518.00 level on June 1 from the over 1100 level before the crisis.[121] During the first quarter of 1998, annualized real GDP contracted by 1.8 percent as a result of weakened domestic demand and a decline in exports to East Asian countries. Thus, Malaysia had a negative GDP growth for the first time in thirteen years. Output of the manufacturing sector declined by 5 percent during the first five months of 1998. In the same period, Malaysian exports in U.S. dollar terms declined also by 10.3 percent due to the decline of imports in ASEAN countries and Japan. The CA deficit was recovering in Malaysia mostly due to sharp drops in Malaysian imports.[122] The deteriorated economic and financial situation tarnished Anwar's prestige and the reputation of his tight monetary and fiscal policies. Tight monetary policies caused a fast deceleration in lending, and Malaysian businesses increasingly complained about the high interest rates during the first half of 1998. Anwar was for interest rates being determined by market forces. In his view, they were high because of high offshore ringgit deposit rates, mostly in Singapore. However, the business sector's cries moved Mahathir to complain publicly that "the banks were throttling Malaysia's economy." Mahathir started to push for looser fiscal and monetary policies. Fiscal policy increasingly became expansionary, as the proposed cuts in government expenditure were restored and a number of large projects were reactivated. In July, a politically weakened Anwar reversed his course and agreed with a stimulus package that boosted government spending by 20%. Moreover, the government announced a fiscal stimulus package of RM7 billion as development expenditure for projects meeting certain criteria, such as those that would increase exports and substitutes imports, and established an additional Infrastructure Fund worth RM5 billion. The increase in the budget deficit as a result of increased public spending was going to be financed with the domestic sale of bonds.[123] In parallel, the BNM relaxed its monetary policy and injected liquidity into the financial system in order to relax banks, as we mentioned earlier. About RM30 billion was injected into the banking system, due to the BNM's reduction of the statuary reserve requirement for banks from 13.5 percent in February 1997 to 4 percent by September 1998.[124]

As these expansionary fiscal and monetary policies were fully reversing Anwar's economic policy approach, the international news media often speculated about the rift between Anwar, on the one hand, and Daim and Mahathir on the other hand. The differences in policy approach within the government were not only preventing the government from tackling the crisis decisively, but also reducing the effectiveness of whatever policy measures were taken due to perceived political risk.[125] According to Financial Times (May 1, 1998), conflicting statements from the Malaysian government, poor company performances and bankruptcies, and bailouts of allegedly well connected companies diminished hopes that the Malaysian government was concretely dealing with the consequences of the crisis and pushed share prices further down.[126] Key business journals, such as the Economist, Asiaweek, Far Eastern Economic Review, Newsweek, and Time, often criticized Mahathir's rhetoric and policy approach, and backed reforms that the IMF and international capital would have liked to see.[127] Mahathir, on the other hand, kept complaining about international media which was "tarnishing Malaysia's image by broadcasting a distorted view of the country's political and economic conditions."[128] However, it seems that Mahathir had not ruled out the IMF option completely. The Washington Post (July 18, 1998) reports from Mahathir that Malaysia might "have to bow to the IMF" if the economic problems were not solved soon.[129]

Although Malaysian businesses, including the Chinese Chamber of Commerce, publicly showed solidarity for Mahathir, their more quietly spoken feeling, especially that of the Chinese business class, was that Mahathir's acerbic interventions were contributing to the deep and fast slide, according to Hilley (2001).[130] The crisis created some backlash against Mahathir's choice of economic policies. In June 1998, in the crucial annual UMNO delegates' conference, Mahathir's policies were criticized by a number of party officials, such as Zahid Hamidi, who were seen as Anwar's allies. The criticisms focused on problems associated with corruption, cronyism, and nepotism. The anti-Suharto movement in Indonesia successfully used these types of criticisms, but they were not going to succeed in Malaysia. They only made the rift between Mahathir and Anwar appear to be irreconcilable. On June 20, Mahathir released a list of Anwar's allies, including Zahid, as beneficiaries of government programs. In July, two pro-Anwar newspaper editors were forced to resign.[131] At the end, Mahathir prevailed, and Anwar and his allies were gone. The opposition parties, the PAS and the DAP (Democratic Action Party), blamed Mahathir for the economic crisis, cronyism, bailouts, and other social and economic problems. However, the opposition as well could not rally big crowds behind them partly due to the Malaysian media's limited coverage.[132]

The impacts of policy struggle, political calculations, Mahathir's and his associates' dominance of the economic policy, and patron-client relations (domestic interest groups). On July 24 Daim Zainuddin was appointed as the Minister of Special Functions in order to curb Anwar's power. One day later, he revealed a National Economic Recovery Plan (NERP). The package included a new RM1.5 billion fund for small-firm lending in addition to RM7 billion and RM5 billion infrastructure funds.[133] "By and large, NERP took the form of a policy blueprint rather than a concrete action plan for managing the crisis. It made a case, in broader terms, for easing of fiscal and monetary policies and expediting reforms to revitalize the financial sector, but failed to come up with a concrete program of action for restoring macroeconomic stability and investor confidence," according to Athukorala (2001).[134] In the meantime, Moody's downgraded the country's sovereign credit rating three notches more, which made international capital more expensive for Malaysia. As a result, the Malaysian government postponed a $2 billion bond offering to the foreign markets, which had been intended to be on sale in August 1998. The Malaysian government needed about $13 billion to strengthen its banking system and to revive the economy, which shrank by 6.8 percent in the second quarter of 1998, as compared with the same quarter in 1997. As the prospect of finding foreign capital was weakened, the Malaysian government turned to domestic sources such as the money in Malaysia's Consolidation Fund, the Employees Fund, and state company Petronas which had billions of ringgit at its disposal.[135] In addition, the Malaysian government sought $1 billion to $2 billion in loans from Japan in August 1998.[136]

Toward the end of August 1998, Deputy Prime Minister Anwar, once assumed to be Mahathir's chosen successor, was losing his strong position in the government and in the UMNO. His bold calls for political and economic reforms were being halted, his supporters, such as the governor of the Bank Negara, were forced to resign from their jobs during late August, and a rumor of his resignation was already spreading.[137] In the meantime, the loosened fiscal and monetary policies began to put pressure on the exchange rate. Mahathir revived his 1997 theme that the ringgit had to be protected from speculators. Free from any opposition to his policies, he introduced capital control measures on September 1, 1998, and fixed the ringgit at 3.80 against the dollar in early September. The capital controls were technically aimed at curbing capital flight and ending speculation against Malaysia's currency, and closed Malaysia off to international financial markets to a certain extent. The ringgit outside the country would become worthless after September 30, 1998, and foreign portfolio investments would earn no returns unless they remained in the country for at least a year.[138]

The capital controls denied domestic credit to foreign banks and brokers. Most transfers required administrative approval, except foreign direct investment. They eliminated offshore ringgit transactions and required that profits made from the sale of securities had to be deposited for one year in ringgit accounts, without being converted.[139] Athukorala (2001) notes: "this policy choice was expected to provide the Malaysian authorities with breathing space to engineer the recovery through monetary expansion and fiscal pump priming, while affecting needed banking and corporate sector reforms without being subject to vagaries of market sentiment."[140] It was an important policy experiment as compared to the IMF neo-liberal policy orthodoxy. There was some confusion about the rules of the capital controls and how long they were going to be applied. The BNM promised periodic review of the capital control rules, but Mahathir declared that "they would remain until the international financial system was reformed to eliminate currency speculators."[141] In the later months, Mahathir brought further restrictions to foreign investors, despite reservations by Daim.[142]

A day after making his economic gamble, Mahathir dismissed Anwar from the government and the UMNO. Two weeks later Anwar was arrested at his home and later charged with 10 counts of corruption and sexual misconduct. This halted Anwar's calls for economic and political reforms.[143] Until the time he was arrested, Anwar organized large political rallies, calling for reform and an end to corruption, cronyism and nepotism.[144]

Anwar asserted himself as the strategist of Malaysia's recovery plans until he lost his strong position during the first half of 1998. He and his supporters within government proposed economic reforms akin to IMF style policies. They also had a political reform agenda as a necessary corollary to economic re-forms.[145] Apparently Anwar's approach to economic management played a significant role in putting him in conflict with Mahathir. The New York Times reports that, during the second day of his trial, "Anwar said he and his boss, Prime Minister Mahathir Mohamad, had major differences about how to respond to the 'financial convulsion engulfing the region' . . .as tensions grew, the police began an aggressive investigation into his personal life."[146] According to Milne & Mauzy (1999), the division of opinion between Anwar and Mahathir was exacerbated by disagreement about the time when Mahathir should hand over power to his supposed successor, Anwar. Mahathir had been anxious about Indonesia since the fall of President Suharto in May 1998, and his discomfort grew when Anwar began calling for change, and his supporters demanded re-formasi (reform), which was the rally cry of Suharto's opponents. Apparently, Suharto's recent forced resignation in Indonesia activated Mahathir to avoid a similar fate.[147]

According to Hilley (2001), Mahathir and his allies were not only afraid of Anwar's influence within the party, but also of his firsthand knowledge of cor-ruption within the cabinet and corporate circles. Hilley (2001) notes:

> While it was, seemingly, more prudent to keep Anwar on the inside, given what he now knew about internal corruption and nepotism, it was the emerg-ing policy differences over crisis management and the implications of an IMF scenario vis-à-vis bailouts that may have tipped the balance, prompting Mahathir to use the sodomy allegations and corruption charges as part of a strategy to contain him.[148]

In addition, Anwar and his allies could have used their power and what they knew in order to force Mahathir to resign, if their economic and political reform agenda appealed to people and gained mass public support. By pushing Anwar decisively out of the political scene, Mahathir also dismissed the biggest poten-tial challenge to himself. Thus, the Asian financial crisis and subsequent devel-opments created a political crisis in Malaysia as well, even though it was a much milder one as compared to that of Indonesia.

In the background, the Malaysian corporate elite was also afraid of An-war's economic and political reforms agenda, since any practical show of trans-parency and shakeout would mean a denial of bailouts to them. They also feared that he would give "big names" to the Anti-Corruption Agency (ACA) of Ma-laysia, according to Hilley (2001).[149] Anwar was ambivalent in regards to bail-outs, while the other government officials openly declared helping the troubled businessmen. He did not seem to be supportive of rescue packages for Renong and Mahathir's son Mirzan. When Anwar forwarded compensation around RM700 million to Bakun hydro-power constructor, Ting Pek Khiing's Ekran Bhd, due to a temporary halt of construction during the crisis, he claimed that it was no bailout.[150] Anwar also had his own cronies within the UMNO machine. "Business elites linked to Anwar were also now caught up in a complex scenario of financial bailouts and judgements over whom to back," Hilley (2001) notes.[151] In addition, Anwar went along with the government decisions that were initiated by Mahathir or Daim and reversed earlier tight fiscal and monetary policies toward mid-1998. He did not seem terribly against capital controls, and was dogmatically committed to full capital account convertibility. Malaysia had temporary capital controls in early 1995, when Anwar was in charge.[152]

On October 23, Mahathir presented an expansionary budget for 1999, which opened the way for new spending in construction, housing, and information technology (including his Multimedia Super Corridor), and deferred personal income tax collection for a year. After the imposition of currency controls in early September, the Malaysian government was left with the choice of looking for domestic sources to fund the country's economic recovery. It was said that Malaysia needed 31 billion ringgit to cover bad debts to save only the troubled banking industry. Later, Daim announced that RM60 billion was needed for the recovery plan that he prepared. As mentioned earlier, the Malaysian government turned to domestic sources, in particular state provident and retirement funds such as Malaysia's Consolidation Fund and Employees Provident Fund, along with borrowing some loans from Japan, the Asian Development Bank, and the World Bank. Domestic sale of government bonds was another way of raising capital. The BNM also injected liquidity by lowering statutory reserve requirements down to 2%. In addition, Mahathir used the cash-rich state company Petronas for some bailout operations.[153]

On October 29, 1998, Mr. C. Rajandram, the chairman of the committee established to mediate between creditors, announced that Malaysia's government was going to help about 20 ailing companies with restructuring their more than RM6 billion in debt.[154] *Danaharta*, Malaysia's asset-management company established during the crisis, bought RM 8.1 billion of non-performing loans from the banking system by the end of 1998. The company also explained that it was managing RM11.6 billion non-performing loans for Sime Bank and Sime International Bank.[155] About a year later, the BNM announced the government's plan to combine Malaysia's 58 financial institutions (21 commercial banks, 12 merchant banks and 25 finance companies) into six financial groups (later modified to ten). These institutions were instructed to sign merger agreements by the end of September 1999, and mergers were expected to take place in April 2000.[156] "Interestingly, the proposed financial restructuring only reinforced the corporatist links between party and business, for the terms of amalgamation depend not on their bottom lines but on their ties to politically favored UMNO patrons," according to Jones (2000).[157]

Mahathir started to boast of his "heterodox" economic policies as early as November 1998, pointing to a jump in foreign exchange reserves and a steadier stock market, as well as increased sales of cars and homes, which were bolstered by an aggressive government home-ownership campaign. Foreign direct investment had not been adversely affected as well. As it will be reviewed further in the next section, the Malaysian economy rebounded strongly in the second quarter of 1999. As the economy recovered, so did Mahathir's prestige. At the end, *Mahathirism* survived both the domestic and external challenges.[158]

Further Questioning Mahathir's Dealing with the Crisis

The intermixing of economic and non-economic factors—political calculations, sensitivity to ethnic disturbances, Mahathirism, strong executive power and weak opposition, and the supportive political culture. What caused Mahathir to come up with these sets of policy measures, rather than an IMF-style policy response? Were the causes of Mahathir's policy responses political or economic? Unlike the other crisis-hit countries, Mahathir formed his own "unorthodox" policies and imposed capital controls as the Malaysian response instead of following IMF instructed neoliberal policy prescriptions. He bailed out troubled companies with public sources. The crisis in Malaysia, in contrast to other Asian countries, did not lead to further financial openness or institutional reforms or regime change. Prime Minister Mahathir's response was defiant and isolationist, even though the Malaysian financial crisis of 1984-1985 pushed Mahathir in the direction of liberalization and privatization.[159] What caused a contrasting response this time? There were economic and political reasons.

One obvious reason why Mahathir's government did not seek an IMF-sponsored rescue package was that the country was not desperately in need of a rescue package because it had little foreign debt exposure of its banking system when the crisis arrived. The other four countries, in particular Indonesia, Korea, and Thailand, had huge short-term external debts. From the mid-1980s to the crisis, there had been a steady trend toward financial liberalization in Malaysia, and Malaysia had succeeded with a great deal of capital inflows. But, unlike the other crisis-affected economies, a greater proportion of Malaysia's external liabilities consisted of equity rather than debt. The capital flows to the other crisis-affected economies were in the form of short-term bank loans into their more bank-based financial systems. Malaysia received international capital either in the form of FDI, or as short-term volatile portfolio capital, mainly into its stock market, which escaped when the crisis started. As compared to the other countries, the Malaysian banks had not been allowed to borrow heavily from abroad and lend domestically. However, as mentioned earlier, Malaysia had one of the highest domestic debt to GDP ratios. Much of this debt was private rather than public, and long-term rather than short-term. As a result, the Malaysian corporations were not faced with currency and term mismatching when the ringgit was largely depreciated. But they became very sensitive to domestic interest rate increases, as they complained throughout the crisis. It was in fact difficult for the Malaysian government to use interest rate increases as a policy tool to support the depreciating exchange rate due to continued capital outflows.[160]

Another economic reason that affected the policy course in Malaysia was the economic collapse in the first half of 1998. By mid-1998, the economy was in a deep recession. The exchange rate and stock markets were not stabilized.

This created doubts about the merits of Anwar's policies that were akin to the IMF suggestions. The situation prompted a serious rethinking, and the stage was set for a radical policy change.[161] Mahathir took advantage of the situation to reverse the economic policies according to his political calculations and economic ideology.

Technically, Mahathir could have chosen the neoliberal economic policies prescribed by the IMF, and this choice with the IMF's backing would also have stabilized markets, as in Korea and Thailand. Instead, Mahathir resorted to capital controls with fixed exchange rates in order to protect his economic policies from the vagaries of market sentiments by insulating the domestic financial markets from short-term financial flows.[162] According to Mahathir: "Although in the initial stages Malaysia found it necessary to follow the advice of the IMF, [it] had to abandon the IMF prescription because things actually got worse faster. [The leadership] noticed that the IMF approach of high interest rates and tight liquidity, far from reviving confidence, led to a severe contraction of the real economy and an overhang of debts."[163] However, "the real issue was that entering an IMF program was not politically acceptable to the Malaysian leadership," Athukorala (2001) notes.[164]

The economic effectiveness of Mahathir's policies is discussed in the next section. The Malaysian leadership's political calculations behind Mahathir's rhetorical statements and his actions should be considered further. Among these political calculations was the Malaysian leadership's sensitivity to potential ethnic disturbances. The Malaysian government's economic policies had been very sensitive to ethnic considerations since the 1969 riots, which were thought to be a result of Malays' economic grievances that had not been sufficiently addressed. The NEP and NDP as well as Mahathir's economic development ideology were targeted to address this situation. You may see Appendix B for details. In Malaysia, ethnic considerations still dominate the political culture over an "interest-based" politics that is non-communal and non-ethnic in nature.[165] The Malaysian government had to watch out for its economic policies' potential negative effects on the sociopolitical stability of the country, which was achieved through the NEP and the NDP's "affirmative action" policies. Tight fiscal and monetary policies that were prescribed by the IMF would impoverish the already poor rural and urban Malays, at least in the short run. In turn, a delay in the economic recovery would turn these impoverished, mostly bumiputera groups into enemies of heavily subsidized urban business networks with Chinese and foreign components, and of liberalization. The Malaysian government's policy choices in the form of expansionary fiscal and monetary policies along with capital controls reflected the leadership's sensitivity to the need to maintain national stability and unity, as they observed the ethnic, political, and economic instability that engulfed Indonesia.[166] It is hard to know to what extent these ethnic considerations played a role in Mahathir's choice.

Beyond possible ethnic considerations, Mahathir's policy choice served him well politically. Capital controls and state-directed fiscal and monetary policy subsidies were designed to protect the business elite networks around the

UMNO. Besides preserving the UMNO's business networks, Mahathir's policies served to shore up the UMNO's mass support and to prevent the mass anger/disturbance being transformed into mass political support for the Malaysian opposition. As Toyoda (2001) puts it, Mahathir's policies served him "as a means to steal the thunder of the opposition."[167]

Although the crisis provided the Malaysian opposition with new opportunity to gain the support of the mass public, it has been weak and constrained (as Appendix B informs in more detail). The BN has never been defeated in national elections until now. It always has had more money to spend than the opposition and more patronage to dispense. Opposition in the parliament has been weak due to the fact that the BN has always been the majority. This situation has enabled the BN leaders to manipulate national issues and problems to maintain and/or increase their power. Individuals, political organizations, and other civic institutions have not been protected from arbitrary state power, and there have not been enough opportunities for independent political opinion making.[168] Economic growth led to the emergence of interethnic middle-classes, which pressured toward more participatory democracy and governmental accountability in the 1980s. However, this was reversed in the 1990s with the consolidation of BN rule and of the executive power over civil society. Mahathir achieved further centralization of power in the executive arm of the government through the repeated amendments in the Federal constitution.[169]

The government apparatus and the UMNO, dominated by its leader, have been efficient organizations to ensure Mahathir's popularity, to renew his mandate through general elections, and to sustain his power.[170] Munro-Kua (1996) characterizes the Malaysian system as "authoritarian populist," due to the fact that Mahathir has expanded his executive power extensively, constrained all kinds of intermediate institutions including opposition parties, and has still been able to rally popular support behind him and renew his mandate.[171] In addition, Malaysian political culture has been permissive toward the authoritarianism exercised by Mahathir. Although there has not been a common civic culture, some minimum consensus on a stable and effective government has existed among Malaysian ethnic communities. According to Means (1991):

> large segments of the public and many leaders seem to assume that the answers to nearly all political and social problems ultimately rest with the Prime Minister armed with extraordinary powers at the apex of the political system. There appears to be a common popular assumption that order and social harmony ultimately depend on unconditional defense given by citizens to a political hierarchy capped by a powerful, benevolent, and usually awesome leader.[172]

The Malay middle class, which grew during the Mahathir era, has not cared about political liberalization, as long as they lived comfortably and people were happy. The state-controlled media along with government-designed mass mobilization campaigns have reinforced this disposition.[173] As a result, Mahathir's policies were well received by the *bumiputera* urban middle class, as many of them conceive the UMNO and the state as protectors of their political and economic interests, as Gomez (1999) notes.[174] In addition, the UMNO's non-Malay coalition partners did not object to Mahathir's policies. Their main concern has been to deliver public works and services to their non-Malay constituents to ensure electoral success and maintenance of the status quo. The political culture that was promoted by Mahathir and the BN parties did not teach the Malay society, especially non-Malays, popular participation and public debate over important issues. Instead, the political culture during Mahathir's era has been that of developmentalism, emphasizing economic development, delivery of goods and services, and a state governed by the BN, which was the status quo. A considerable number of non-Malays, especially those who had benefited from the projects and services rendered, have been supportive of the BN parties and the status quo.[175]

The timing of the imposition of the capital controls raised questions about the real intention behind it. The capital controls were imposed on September 1, 1998 and one day later Anwar was dismissed from the government and the UMNO. Perkings and Woo (2000) recognize that capital controls isolated the country from market pressures and enabled the government to undertake expansionary fiscal and monetary policies without significantly worsening the balance of payments. But another significant, maybe the primary reason, for the imposition of the capital controls was to enable Mahathir to oust Anwar without causing further market disturbances and capital outflow, according to Perkins and Woo (2000). They argue that foremost among the significant factors that shaped the Malaysian government's policy response to the crisis was the political struggle and difference of opinion between Anwar and Mahathir. Mahathir had foreseen that violent street demonstrations would take place following Anwar's expulsion. If the capital controls had not been placed, already nervous investors would have further withdrawn their funds from Malaysia and the ringgit and Kuala Lumpur stock market would have gone into a free fall in the same manner of the Indonesian rupiah and the Jakarta stock market in May 1998, just before Suharto was forced to leave office. Such a free fall would have weakened Mahathir politically and his grip on the UMNO, as the economic situation further deteriorated and many more powerful business groups associated with the UMNO went bankrupt. In order to prevent all of these, Mahathir imposed the capital controls one-day before the firing of Anwar. As the anticipated demonstrations by Anwar supporters became less frequent over time, the capital controls were reduced, Perkins and Woo (2000) argue.[176]

Recovery from the Crisis and the Continuation of "Mahathirism"

Economic, societal, political, and institutional implications of the crisis and Mahathir's policy response. The Malaysian economic growth resumed again in the second quarter of 1999, with 4.1 percent growth, following the country's worst economic contraction by 7.4 percent in 1998. Malaysia's economy recorded 5.8% growth in 1999, and 8.6% growth in 2000. The country's exports surged due to the undervalued ringgit, and its trade surplus increased. As a result, Malaysia had current account surpluses of 16% of the GDP in 1999 and of 9.6% in 2000. Malaysian reserves rose up to $28 billion by mid-1999 from $19 billion in September 1998, when the capital controls were introduced. After one year from the imposition of the capital controls—even though foreign capital was allowed to be withdrawn after a one-year stay—large capital flight did not occur, contrary to some speculations. One year later, only $78 million left the country in September 1999. By that time the capital controls were already eased. The relatively little outflow of capital was partly because volatile foreign capital had already gone before the imposition of the capital controls.[177] By mid-1999 Malaysia returned to the debt market by issuing government bonds.[178] Restructuring of the Malaysian banking system was still debated in 2000, due to complaints from Chinese bankers that the earlier plans favored indigenous Malays.[179]

How did the Malaysian economy do as compared to the economies of other crisis-affected Asian countries? A research paper by Ethan Kaplan and Dani Rodrik argues that, as compared to IMF programs, Malaysian policies produced faster economic recovery, smaller declines in employment and real wages, and a more rapid comeback in the stock market. But it suggests that Malaysia's economic recovery might not be due to the capital controls, since Korea and Thailand recovered in parallel.[180] The role of capital controls in the Malaysian economic comeback is still being discussed. Analysts who think that the capital controls played a significant role in the economic recovery point out that the economic decline stopped and the stock market slide turned around in Malaysia soon after the imposition of the capital controls. Analysts, who oppose this, argue that such reversals have been more pronounced in the rest of the region. Even though the role of capital controls in Malaysia's economic recovery seems ambiguous, they, at least, had not caused the recovery in Malaysia to be slower than that in the other crisis countries. Malaysia had its own economic strengths, which might have contributed to its economy's revival. The 1998 economic collapse was less deep in Malaysia than in Thailand and Indonesia and pre-crisis problems in Malaysia were less serious than in the other countries. Malaysia had high saving rates, budget surpluses, flexible labor markets and low taxation. As a result, the Malaysian economy had a relatively faster recovery, and by mid-2000 the economy was back to the pre-crisis output level.[181]

The capital controls did not backfire "as the proponents of economic globalization at the International Monetary Fund and U.S. Treasury had not-so-secretly hoped."[182] As indicated earlier, Mahathir's policy choice received criticism and skepticism by many economists and senior officials of the IMF, the World Bank and the U.S. Only Paul Krugman intellectually backed the capital control policy, arguing that temporary foreign exchange controls might be successful under certain conditions. The longer the capital controls lasted, the more the economy would be distorted from the market forces.[183] While domestic-political considerations played a significant role in Mahathir's decision to impose the capital controls, as the Malaysian economy revived, more Western economists recognized that a policy of capital control might help smaller economies to protect themselves from increasingly larger speculative flows, as Robert A. Litan, a Brookings Institution analyst, notes.[184] By the year 2000, both the World Bank and the IMF have also accepted that capital controls may be appropriate in certain circumstances. Thus, capital controls gained a measure of international legitimacy in economics debates.[185] Rubin in *The State* newspaper commented that: "Malaysia's successful policy response has been an assault to the conventional policy prescriptions of the Washington consensus . . . [which] holds that global prosperity can only be achieved through open markets, open capital flows and open trade policies."[186]

Non-economic implications of the crisis and the subsequent developments. Nonetheless, Mahathir's popularity was shaken at home during the crisis, and it further deteriorated with Anwar's dismissal. Despite the dual economic and political crises, Malaysia did not face ethnic conflagration as it had occurred in neighboring Indonesia. Opposition parties, the Chinese-based Democratic Action Party (DAP), the Malay-based Party Islam (Parti Islam SeMalaysia—PAS), and Anwar's *refomasia* movement posed growing challenges to Mahahir. The economic downturn during the crisis has given the best chance to opposition parties in 1999. However, due to their internal fighting and factionalism, they could not organize a coordinated action. In addition, they were constrained by limited coverage in the media. The opposition parties had been covered in the front pages of the Malaysian national newspapers mostly for their feuds in the party, but not much for their criticism of the government.[187]

Mahathir, of course, took full advantage of the economic turnaround as his prestige recovered and the elections were approaching. He presented himself as the defender of Malay and Malaysian interests. Internationally, he was the defender of "the national interests against interfering Western democrats, Jewish speculators and IMF economic colonialism." Then U.S. Vice President Gore's support for Anwar and his *reformasia* movement at the APEC meeting in Kuala Lumpur in November 1998 ironically helped Mahathir's domestic appeal. He portrayed Anwar and the opposition as foreign collaborators. The incoherence of the opposition also helped Mahathir in his domestic appeal.[188] Mahathir continued to claim that the root cause of the Asian financial crisis was currency trading and not domestic economic and/or political weaknesses or mistakes.[189] In an UMNO meeting in June 1999, Mahathir blamed foreign enemies, especially "foreign colonialists and their puppets in Malaysia . . .[who] were out to weaken [the] country."[190] In defense of his policy, he proclaimed "no one . . .wants to return to the fixed exchange rates. But if anarchy is abhorred . . .there is no reason why we should not abhor anarchy in the world financial system. A certain degree of uncertainty is fine, but an absolutely uncertain financial world is no good for anyone, except of course for those who deliberately create uncertainty."[191]

Mahathir bought himself some time through different tactics in order to regain popular support. In early January 1999, Mahathir appointed Datuk Seri

Abdullah Ahmad Badawi as his new Deputy Prime Minister and Home Minister while maintaining Daim Zainuddin as the Finance Minister. In June 1999, he dissolved the parliament and decided to go to early elections on November 29, 1999, in order to refresh his political mandate to rule. He tried to pump up the economy as the elections approached, as he was faced with stronger opposition this time.[192] While Anwar was on trial, his *reformasia* movement subsequently launched a multiethnic party, the Justice Party (or Parti keADILan), under his wife's leadership, in order to contest the November 1999 general elections. Later, the Justice Party, together with the DAP and the PAS, formed a new multiethnic opposition coalition called Barisan Alternatif (BA), or the Alternative Front, in order to compete against the UMNO's coalition of Barisan Nasional (BN), or the National Front. "Moreso than any other previous multiethnic opposition effort, the BA has picked up considerable grassroots support across the various ethnic groups," Loh Kok Wah (2001) notes.[193]

Nonetheless, the BN once again won more than two-thirds of the parliamentary seats, winning 148 seats in the 193-seat parliament. The UMNO won 71 seats out of the BN's 148 seats. Before, the UMNO had had 94 seats out of 162 BN seats in the then 192-seat parliament. The election results revealed a significant drop in UMNO votes and opposition within the *bumiputera* community to Mahathir's continued leadership. Except for Sabah, UMNO parliamentary candidates received their all-time low of votes in the election. Anwar's trial and his imprisonment in April 1999 wounded some of Mahathir's Malay supporters and created division among Malays. The PAS was the UMNO's chief competitor for Malay votes, and emerged as the main opposition party. It was for a long time isolated in northeastern peninsular Malaysia, but in this election, it won control of one more state government and obtained strong support in Mahathir's home state, Kedah.[194]

General elections have been conducted under unfair conditions in Malaysia. The BN parties have been able to utilize government facilities and mass media in order to promote their campaign. There have always been some allegations of election fraud, such as getting into the register of voters and having a biased election commission. In addition, lack of transparency, the loss of judicial integrity, and erosion of the rule of law further weakened the opposition stance.[195] Under these conditions, Mahathir survived through the Asian financial crisis, almost unscathed. Business groups wanted Mahathir's victory, but after the elections they were concerned that "the loss of Malay support may lead the government to put political revival before economics."[196]

Thomas L. Friedman in *The New York Times* commented: "capital controls can never be a long-term solution for an export-oriented economy such as Malaysia's. They are instituted to buy time to stabilize an economy. . . . Economically, Malaysia has used the time pretty well. Politically, it has gone backward."[197]

As indicated earlier, the other four crisis-affected countries accepted the IMF's bailout packages and used its programs. However, these programs were not implemented in their original forms and new letters of intent were signed with Thailand, Korea, and Indonesia a few weeks later than the signature of original programs, mostly due to political factors. It is another discussion as to whether the initial IMF plans were appropriate. But, as Corsetti, Pesenti, and Roubini (1998) write:

> It is clear the governments failed to enforce even the most sensible components of such plans. In Indonesia, a corrupt and authoritarian regime effectively ignored most of its agreed-upon commitments until the severe deterioration of macro-conditions led to a full-fledged collapse and the free fall of the rupiah. The currency board 'saga' following the second IMF plan and the continued resistance of the Indonesian governments to macro and structural reforms were important elements of the financial demise experienced by Indonesia. For the case of Korea, there were serious doubts about the implementation of the first IMF plan, given the coming elections in December and the broad policy uncertainty associated with that event. In Thailand, it was only with a new government truly committed to economic reforms that the value of the baht stabilized, and even appreciated relative to the lows reached in December.[198]

CONCLUSIONS

The examination of the Malaysian case in these last two chapters also demonstrated the inadequacy of crisis models and explanations. As we have seen, an interplay of various non-economic factors with economic ones led to the Asian financial crises and shaped the Malaysian government's policy responses within a process that took place within Malaysia's domestic and regional contexts. The sequence of non-economic developments along with economic ones transformed the initial economic/ financial conditions into the crisis situation and impacted policy outcomes within the Malaysian context.

Thus, the examination of the Malaysian case also demonstrated that explanations of financial crises and governmental responses must consider domestic political, societal/cultural, and legal factors, as well as external links and influences in assessing the causes of financial crises and explaining governmental responses to crises. The next chapter will comparatively discuss the findings of the previous chapters and this one, and offer an analytical framework in order to consider both economic and non-economic factors.

NOTES

1.Athukorala, "Swimming against the Tide: Crisis Management in Malaysia,".282; Jackson, "Introduction: The Roots of the Crisis," 3. Also see Roubini, *Chronology of the Asian Currency Crises and its Global Contagion.*
2. Dan Biers, ed., *Crash of '97: How the Financial Crisis is Reshaping Asia.*, Far Eastern Economic Review, 1997, 11.
3. See Athukorala, *Crisis and Recovery in Malaysia,* .58, 59; *Financial Times* (Special Report-Asia in Crisis), January 13, 1998, p.08.

4. Christopher Lingle, "The Institutional Basis of Asia's Economic Crisis," in *the East Asian Development Model: Economic Growth, Institutional Failure and the Aftermath of the Crisis* (The U.K.: Macmillan Press Ltd. & the U.S.: St. Martin's Press, Llc., 2000), 53.

5. Dongyoub Shin, "Dual Sources of the South Korean Economic Crisis: Institutional and Organizational Failures and the Structural Transformation of the Economy, " in *the East Asian Development Model: Economic Growth, Institutional Failure and the Aftermath of the Crisis* (The U.K.: Macmillan Press Ltd. and the U.S.: St. Martin's Press, Llc., 2000), 170.

6. Ibid., p.170.

7. Corsetti, Pesenti, and Roubini, What Caused the Asian Currency and Financial Crisis?, 2,3; Joseph R. Bisignano, "Precarious Credit Equilibria: Reflections on the Asian Financial Crisis," in *the Asian Financial Crisis: Origins, Implications, and Solutio* (Boston and London: Kluwer Academic Publishers, 1999), 75, 77.

8. Ibid., 101.

9. Ibid., 75, 101; Corsetti, Pesenti, and Roubini, What Caused the Asian Currency and Financial Crisis?, 24-25, 28.

10. See Shang-Jin Wei and Sara E. Sievers, "The Cost of Crony Capitalism," in *the Asian Financial Crisis: Lessons for a Resilient Asia* (London & Cambridge, MA: 2000), 91, for more information about corruption in these countries.

11. Lingle, "The Institutional Basis of Asia's Economic Crisis," 53, 68, 69.

12. Ibid., 68, 69.

13. Corsetti, Pesenti, and Roubini, What Caused the Asian Currency and Financial Crisis?, Part II, 1, 5.

14. For example, the government took control of the Bangkok Bank of Commerce (BBC) in mid-1996, due to its lending of around $3 billion in non-performing loans. It was later revealed that the beneficiaries of these loans included several government ministers and well connected businesspersons. Leo Gough, *Asia Meltdown: The End of the Miracle?* (Oxford, the U.K.: Capstone Publishing Limited, 1998), 112.

15. Mihir Ra Rakshit, *The East Asian Currency Crisis* (New York and Oxford: Oxford University Press, 2002), 63-64, 67, 86; Gough, *Asia Meltdown . . .* , 34, 110,111.

16. Gough, *Asia Meltdown . . .* , 32.

17. Andrew MacIntyre, "Political Institutions and the Economic Crisis in Thailand and Indonesia," in *the Politics of the Asian Economic Crisis* (Ithaca and London: Cornell University Press, 1999), 146-147.

18. Ibid., 147.

19. Ibid.," 148-153; Gough, *Asia Meltdown . . .* , 34;

20. Hilton L. Root, "Suharto's Tax on Indonesia's Future," in *the East Asian Development Model: Economic Growth, Institutional Failure and the Aftermath of the Crisis* (The U.K.: Macmillan Press Ltd, and the U.S.: St. Martin's Press, Llc., 2000), 235.

21. Corsetti, Pesenti, and Roubini, What Caused the Asian Currency and Financial Crisis?, Part II, 2; Feng, "Political Foundations of Economic Management . . . ," 87.

22. MacIntyre, "Political Institutions and the Economic Crisis in Thailand and Indonesia," 155.

23. Gough, *Asia Meltdown . . .* , 114.

24. MacIntyre, "Political Institutions and the Economic Crisis in Thailand and Indonesia," 154-155, 161.

25. Corsetti, Pesenti, and Roubini, What Caused the Asian Currency and Financial Crisis?, Part II, 4.

26. Ibid., Part I, 23.

27. Shin, "Dual Sources of the South Korean Economic Crisis . . . ," 174.

28. Ibid., 174, 195.

29. Meredith Woo-Cumings, "The State, Democracy, and the Reform of the Corporate Sector in Korea," in *the Politics of the Asian Economic Crisis* (Ithaca & London: Cornell University Press, 1999), 116.

30. Gough, *Asia Meltdown . . .* , 112.

31. Shin, "Dual Sources of the South Korean Economic Crisis . . . ," 195, 196.

32. Woo-Cumings, "The State, Democracy, and the Reform of the Corporate Sector in Korea," 117.

33. Corsetti, Pesenti, and Roubini, What Caused the Asian Currency and Financial Crisis?, part II, 4.

34. Paul Hutchcroft, "Neither Dynamo nor Domino: Reforms and Crises in the Philippine Political Economy," in *the Politics of the Asian Economic Crisis* (Ithaca and London: Cornell University Press, 1999), 164, 181.

35. Radelet and Sachs, "The Onset of the East Asian Financial Crisis," 133-136.

36. Teik, *Paradoxes of Mahathirism: An Intellectual Biograph of Mahathir Mohamad*, 9.

37. Means, *Malaysian Politics: The Second Generation*, 92-93; Milne and Mauzy, *Malaysian Politics under Mahathir*, ix, 55.

38. Jomo K.S., *Growth and Structural Change in the Malaysian Economy*, 201; Teik, *Paradoxes of Mahathirism: An Intellectual Biograph of Mahathir Mohamad*, 337-338.

39. Gomez and Jomo K.S., *Malaysia's Political Economy: Politics, Patronage and Profits* (1997), 169; Milne and Mauzy, *Malaysian Politics under Mahathir*, 72.

40. Athukorala, "Swimming against the Tide: Crisis Management in Malaysia," 281; Biers, ed., *Crash of'97*, 11; *Far Eastern Economic Review*, April 16, 1998, 50-53, 76.

41. As some analysts point out, the CPI was not truly reflecting the "real" prices in Malaysia, since the government had "effective price controls on items that were heavily weighted in the CPI basket." Therefore, overheating was reflected by the deterioration of the trade balance rather than the CPI growth rates in Malaysia. Corsetti, Pesenti, and Roubini, What Caused the Asian Currency and Financial Crisis?, Part II, 3-4.

42. For several years before the crisis, Malaysia had a chronic shortage of labor, which caused wages to increase at a rate higher than the productivity rate. High real wages, combined with the real appreciation of the ringgit, reduced Malaysia's export competitiveness in the international markets, in which China and other lower-cost countries brought new challenges. *Financial Times* (Special Report: Asia In Crisis), January 13, 1998, 08.

43. Ibid.,

44. Following the 1984-1985 financial crisis, the Malaysian government brought new measures and regulations. From the late 1980s to mid-1997 Malaysian banks had a period of recovery and restructuring. As a result, the ratio of non-performing loans to total lending fell from a crisis peak of 35 percent in 1987 to a respectable 3.6 percent in 1997. The process of recovery was aided by rapid economic growth. Toyoda, "Malaysia: Ethnic Cleavages and Controlled Liberalization," 104-108.

45. Toyoda, "Malaysia: Ethnic Cleavages and Controlled Liberalization," 104-108; Athukorala, *Crisis and Recovery in Malaysia*, 47-49; *Financial Times* (Special Report: Asia In Crisis), January 13, 1998, 08.

46. Toyoda, "Malaysia: Ethnic Cleavages and Controlled Liberalization," 97; Athukorala, *Crisis and Recovery in Malaysia,* .52.

47. Milne and Mauzy, *Malaysian Politics under Mahathir,* 75.

48. Gomez and Jomo K.S., *Malaysia's Political Economy: Politics, Patronage and Profits* (1997), x-xi, 4-6.

49. Ibid., 7, 9, 129; Toyoda, "Malaysia: Ethnic Cleavages and Controlled Liberalization," 97.

50. As it is presented in the next section, then Deputy Prime Minister and Finance Minister Anwar Ibrahim held a cabinet meeting and announced an IMF-style crisis management package on December 5, 1997. The policy dialogue in that meeting was revealed that both the Finance Minister and the Central Bank had warned of potential economic problems ahead. The warnings included an overheated economy, mega-projects that strained the country's resources, and unproductive Malaysian investment abroad. Athukorala, *Crisis and Recovery in Malaysia,* .52. The original source: *Far Eastern Economic Review,* December 18, 1997, 14-15.

51. For example, the prime lending rate rose from 7.4 percent in April 1995 to 9.25 percent by the end of 1996. Despite this increase in the interest rates, the Kuala Lumpur Stock Exchange Composite Index credit increased by 26 percent during this period, and total bank lending increased by 26 percent in 1996, compared to 21 percent in the previous year. Athukorala, *Crisis and Recovery in Malaysia,* 51-52; Corsetti, Pesenti, and Roubini, What Caused the Asian Currency and Financial Crisis?, Part II, 3-4; Kok Fay Chin and Jomo K.S., "Financial Liberalization and System Vulnerability," in *Malaysian Eclipse: Economic Crisis and Recovery* (London and New York: Zed Books Ltd., 2001), 110.

52. See Athukorala, *Crisis and Recovery in Malaysia,* 51-52; Toyoda, "Malaysia: Ethnic Cleavages and Controlled Liberalization," 105; Roubini, *Chronology of the Asian Currency Crises and its Global Contagion.*

53. Corsetti, Pesenti, and Roubini, What Caused the Asian Currency and Financial Crisis?, Part II, 7-8.

54. Toyoda, "Malaysia: Ethnic Cleavages and Controlled Liberalization," 107.

55. The Malaysian economic development from the late 1980s to early 1990s was helped by the significant depreciation of the ringgit against the U.S. dollar. Since the ringget was pegged to the U.S. dollar, as the U.S. dollar appreciated against the yen from mid-1995 to the crisis, the ringgit was also appreciated. Many agree that the ringgit was overvalued according to purchasing power parity in 1995. Chin and Jomo K.S., "Financial Liberalization and System Vulnerability," 108-109.

56. Ibid., 109-110.

57. Athukorala, "Swimming against the Tide: Crisis Management in Malaysia," 282; Henderson, *Asia Falling: Making Sense of the Asian Crisis and Its Aftermath,* 121.

58. Roubini, *Chronology of the Asian Currency Crises and its Global Contagion.*

59. *Financial Times* (Special Report: Asia in Crisis), January 13, 1998, 08.

60. Roubini, *Chronology of the Asian Currency Crises and its Global Contagion.*

61. Henderson, *Asia Falling: Making Sense of the Asian Crisis and Its Aftermath,* 123.

62. Athukorala, *Crisis and Recovery in Malaysia,* 64; John Hilley, *Malaysia: Mahathirism, Hegemony and the New Opposition* (London and New York: Zed Books, 2001), 66; Biers, ed., *Crash of '97,* 54.

63. Athukorala, *Crisis and Recovery in Malaysia,* .64; Hilley, *Malaysia: Mahathirism, Hegemony and the New Opposition,* 66; Biers, ed., *Crash of '97,* 54.

64. *Financial Times* (Special Report: Asia In Crisis), January 13, 1998, 08.

65. Jomo K.S., "From Currency Crisis to Recession," in *Malaysian Eclipse: Economic Crisis and Recovery* (London & New York: Zed Books Ltd., 2001a), 15; Toyoda, "Malaysia: Ethnic Cleavages and Controlled Liberalization," 103.

66. Jomo K.S., "From Currency Crisis to Recession," 14; Biers, ed., *Crash of'97,*14, 54; Henderson, *Asia Falling: Making Sense of the Asian Crisis and Its Aftermath,* xii; Roubini, *Chronology of the Asian Currency Crises and its Global Contagion.*

67. Gomez and Jomo K.S., *Malaysia's Political Economy . . .* , 189.

68. Milne and Mauzy, *Malaysian Politics under Mahathir,* 76; Hilley, *Malaysia: Mahathirism, Hegemony and the New Opposition,* 66; Athukorala, *Crisis and Recovery in Malaysia,* .65.

69. Henderson, *Asia Falling: Making Sense of the Asian Crisis and Its Aftermath,* 124.

70. *The Straits Times,* April 30, 1998, Internet; Biers, ed., *Crash of'97,* .57.

71. Hilley, *Malaysia: Mahathirism, Hegemony and the New Opposition,* 66, 67.

72. Ibid., p.69.

73. Hilley, *Malaysia: Mahathirism, Hegemony and the New Opposition,* 70, 71; Pillay, "The Malaysian Model . . . ," 220; Athukorala, *Crisis and Recovery in Malaysia,* .65; Jomo K.S., "From Currency Crisis to Recession," 15. In the meantime, Vietnam and Taiwan experienced relatively slight devaluations, and repercussions of the Asian Financial crisis were felt in Latin American countries, in particular Brazil's and Argentina's stock markets, as well. Also, the IMF and the Indonesian government reached an agreement on a $23 billion multilateral financial package, which was increased to about $40 billion in later months. See Roubini, *Chronology of the Asian Currency Crises and its Global Contagion.*

74. Henderson, *Asia Falling: Making Sense of the Asian Crisis and Its Aftermath,* 153-157; Biers, ed., *Crash of'97,* 238; Hilley, *Malaysia: Mahathirism, Hegemony and the New Opposition,* 68.

75. David I. Hitchcock, "Internal Problems in East Asia," *The Washington Quarterly* 21, No.2 (Spring 1998), 123.

76. By November 20, South Korea's government officials had realized that they could not find domestic resources to solve the crisis situtation and sought an IMF-sponsored multilateral rescue package, as the Thai and Indonesian governments did. The South Korean government and the IMF reached an initial agreement on the conditions of the highest IMF led multilateral rescue package of $57 billion in early December, 1997. See Roubini, *Chronology of the Asian Currency Crises and its Global Contagion*; *The San Francisco Chronicle* (January 8, 1998), p. A1.

77. Milne and Mauzy, *Malaysian Politics under Mahathir,* 75, 76.

78. Mahathir left for a two-month holiday in early May and returned on July 12, 1997 to Kuala Lumpur. He spent most of his time in Europe. During his stay in Europe, he engaged in government business in order to promote foreign investment, particularly for the Multimedia Super Corridor. See Mark L. Clifford and Pete Engardio, *Meltdown: Asia's Boom, Bust, and Beyond* (Paramus, NJ: Prentice Hall Press, 2000), 196, 203; James Chin, "Malaysia in 1998: Mahathir's Annus Horribilis," in *Asian Survey* 38, No.2 (February 1998), 184; Milne and Mauzy, *Malaysian Politics under Mahathir,* 151.

79. See Athukorala, *Crisis and Recovery in Malaysia,* 52, 66. (Original source: "Malaysia: Hit the Brake," *Far Eastern Economic Review,* December 18, 1997, 14-15). Also see Hilley, *Malaysia: Mahathirism, Hegemony and the New Opposition,* 71.

80. Hilley, *Malaysia: Mahathirism, Hegemony and the New Opposition,* 72, 74;

Jomo K.S., "From Currency Crisis to Recession," 16.

81. Hilley, *Malaysia: Mahathirism, Hegemony and the New Opposition*, 72; Toyoda, "Malaysia: Ethnic Cleavages and Controlled Liberalization," 105; *Business Week* (via Lexis-Nexis), November 9, 1999; Roubini, *Chronology of the Asian Currency Crises and its Global Contagion.*

82. Roubini, *Chronology of the Asian Currency Crises and its Global Contagion*; Henderson, *Asia Falling: Making Sense of the Asian Crisis and Its Aftermath*, 308, 309.

83. Pillay, "The Malaysian Model . . . ," 223.

84. Hilley, *Malaysia: Mahathirism, Hegemony and the New Opposition*, 104; *Business Week* (via Lexis-Nexis), November 9, 1999; *The Star*, January 23, 1998, Internet. *Far Eastern Economic Review*, February19, 1998, 15; Roubini, *Chronology of the Asian Currency Crises and its Global Contagion.*

85. Milne and Mauzy, *Malaysian Politics under Mahathir*, 60-62.

86. According to Milne and Mauzy, *Malaysian Politics under Mahathir*, 60, "it is probable that 99 percent of UMNO members knew nothing about it."

87. Milne and Mauzy, *Malaysian Politics under Mahathir*, 68-70.

88. Gomez and Jomo K.S., *Malaysia's Political Economy: Politics, Patronage and Profits* (1997), 123-124.

89. Milne and Mauzy, *Malaysian Politics under Mahathir*, 59-60; Gomez and Jomo K.S., *Malaysia's Political Economy* . . . , 97.

90. Milne and Mauzy, *Malaysian Politics under Mahathir*, 59, 67, 175.

91. Other examples include the granting of the license for a privatized broadcasting channel TV3. UMNO's Fleet Holdings Group and the MIC's Maika Holding emerged as the major share holders. This action brought the entire major broadcasting media and press in Malaysia under UMNO control. Well-connected Chinese businesses, such as the MCA's principal investment arm Multi Purpose Holdings (MPH), got their shares from the privatization as well. Some Chinese tycoons established direct links with the UMNO. 70% of Sports Toto was awarded to such Chinese business owned by Vincent Tan Chee Yioun. Also RM6 billion worth of a national sewage disposal project was awarded to Indah Water Konsortium Sdn Bhd, led by Vincent Tan's the Berjaya Group Bhd. Company, without tender in early 1993. For more examples and for detailed accounts of their links with the UMNO see Gomez and Jomo K.S., *Malaysia's Political Economy . . .*, 91-98; and Hilley, *Malaysia: Mahathirism, Hegemony and the New Opposition*,.63.

92. Gomez and Jomo K.S., *Malaysia's Political Economy: Politics, Patronage and Profits* (1997), 177.

93. Jomo K.S., "From Currency Crisis to Recession," 15-16.

94. Milne and Mauzy, *Malaysian Politics under Mahathir*, 176; Also see *Financial Times* (Special Report: Asia In Crisis), January 13, 1998, 08.

95. *Far Eastern Economic Review*, February 19, 1998, 25.

96. *Financial Times*, February 9, 1998, 02.

97. Toyoda, "Malaysia: Ethnic Cleavages and Controlled Liberalization," 104; Gomez and Jomo K.S., *Malaysia's Political Economy* . . . , 193; Greg (1999), p.48; Athukorala, "Swimming against the Tide: Crisis Management in Malaysia," 282; *Financial Times*, August 22, 1998.

98. *Asian Business*, June 1998, p.25.

99. Gomez and Jomo K.S., *Malaysia's Political Economy . . .* , 193; Roubini, *Chronology of the Asian Currency Crises and its Global Contagion.*

100. Gomez and Jomo K.S., *Malaysia's Political Economy . . .*,193-194.

101. *Asian Business*, June 1998, p.25.

102Roubini, *Chronology of the Asian Currency Crises and its Global Contagion.*

103. In February 1998, the BNM reduced the statutory reserve requirement from 13.5 percent to 10 percent, and to 8 percent in July 1998. The BNM justified these reductions as necessary steps to 'avoid a recession-deflation spiral' as the non-performing loans in the banking system were building up with rapid contraction in economic activity and corporate failures. In August it reduced the three-month inter-bank intervention rate from 11 to 9.5 percent. Athukorala, *Crisis and Recovery in Malaysia,* 66.

104. Athukorala, *Crisis and Recovery in Malaysia,* .66-67; Hilley, *Malaysia: Mahathirism, Hegemony and the New Opposition,* 104; Pillay, "The Malaysian Model . . . ," 224.

105. Gomez and Jomo K.S., *Malaysia's Political Economy . . .* , 193; Roubini, *Chronology of the Asian Currency Crises and its Global Contagion.*

106. Pillay, "The Malaysian Model . . . ," 224.

107. *New Straits Times* (Malaysia), July 14, 1998, 12.

108. *Financial Times,* March 24, 1998, 09.

109. Gomez and Jomo K.S., *Malaysia's Political Economy . . .* , 195; Hilley, *Malaysia: Mahathirism, Hegemony and the New Opposition,* 68, 69; Greg Felker, "Malaysia in 1998: A Cornered Tiger Bares Its Claws," in *Asian Suvery* 39, No.1 (January/February1999), 49.

110. *The Straits Times,* "Region Business News," May 7, 1998, Internet.

111. Milne and Mauzy, *Malaysian Politics under Mahathir,* 60-62.

112. *Far Eastern Economic Review,* May 21, 1998; *Far Eastern Economic Review,* April 30, 1998, 62; *New Straits Times* (Malaysia), April 17, 1998, 17.

113. Milne and Mauzy, *Malaysian Politics under Mahathir,* 60-62. The EPF held 129 billion ringgit ($34 billion) on behalf of workers. *Far Eastern Economic Review,* April 30, 1998, 60.

114. *Far Eastern Economic Review,* April 30, 1998, 60.

115. *Business Week* (Number: 3576), May 4, 1998, 58.

116. The IMF also suggested that using higher interest rates would counter any renewed pressure on the ringgit's value and control credit growth and inflation. According to the IMF, rapid and sustained growth in money supply and credit was worsening the crisis in Malaysia. See *The Straits Times,* "Regional News," April 30, 1998, 30.

117. *The Straits Times,* "Regional News," April 30, 1998, 30. For the IMF calls see Roubini, *Chronology of the Asian Currency Crises and its Global Contagion,* April 30, 1998.

118. In early July 1998, U.S. Treasury Secretary Robert E. Rubin visited the regional countries in order to backup the international bailout packages. During his trip he also visited Malaysia and met with business executives. *The Washington Post,* July 02, 1998, E01.

119. *Far Eastern Economic Review,* May 6, 1999, 50.

120. Milne and Mauzy, *Malaysian Politics under Mahathir,* 175; Hilley, *Malaysia: Mahathirism, Hegemony and the New Opposition,* 104.

121. Roubini, *Chronology of the Asian Currency Crises and its Global Contagion,* June 1, 1998.

122. *New Straits Times,* July 14, 1998, 12.

123. Felker, "Malaysia in 1998: A Cornered Tiger Bares Its Claws," 50; *New Straits Times* (Malaysia), July 14, 1998, 12.

124. Pillay, "The Malaysian Model . . . ," 223; Athukorala, *Crisis and Recovery in Malaysia,* .66.

125. Ibid.

126. *Financial Times*, May 1, 1998, 15.

127. Hilley, *Malaysia: Mahathirism, Hegemony and the New Opposition*, 69.

128. Felker, "Malaysia in 1998: A Cornered Tiger Bares Its Claws," 52.

129. *The Washington Post*, July 18, 1998, A08.

130. Hilley, *Malaysia: Mahathirism, Hegemony and the New Opposition*, 69.

131. Pillay, "The Malaysian Model . . . ," 222-223; *Far Eastern Economic Review*, September 17, 1998, 13.

132. *The Straits Times*, May 16, 1998, Internet; *Far Eastern Economic Review*, June 18, 1998, 21.

133. Felker, "Malaysia in 1998: A Cornered Tiger Bares Its Claws," 50; *Far Eastern Economic Review*, September 17, 1998, 13.

134. Athukorala, *Crisis and Recovery in Malaysia*, 66.

135. *Far Eastern Review* (August 6, 1998), p.72; *Financial Times*, August 28, 1998, 05

136. *Business Times* (Malaysia), August 20, 1998, 18.

137. *Far Eastern Economic Review*, August 27, 1998; *Far Eastern Economic Review*, September 17, 1998, 13.

138. Milne and Mauzy, *Malaysian Politics under Mahathir*, 177; Pillay, "The Malaysian Model . . . ," 223; Toyoda, "Malaysia: Ethnic Cleavages and Controlled Liberalization," 106. The ringgit would become worthless outside Malaysia because it would not be brought back into Malaysia in whatever form. Since the ringgit is legal tender only in Malaysia, not being able to bring the ringgit back into Malaysia makes it useless.

139. Toyoda, "Malaysia: Ethnic Cleavages and Controlled Liberalization," 106. According to *New Straits Times* (Malaysia), September 2, 1998, 23, which reflects official government views, the aim of capital controls was to regain monetary independence and insulate the Malaysian economy from the risks and vulnerabilities of external developments. They were taken in order to limit the contagion effects of external developments, to stabilize the domestic economy, and to ensure stability in domestic prices and the ringgit exchange rate. They brought rules constraining the transaction of withdrawal of ringgit from external accounts (except for the purchase of ringgit assets), and transfer of funds between external accounts. All purchases and sales of ringgit financial assets had to be made through authorized depository institutions. All settlements of exports and imports were required to be in foreign currency. Travelers were allowed to import or export a maximum of RM1,000 per person starting from October 1, 1998. Resident travelers were allowed to export only up to a maximum of RM10,000 in equivalent foreign currency. Non-resident travelers were allowed to export foreign currency up to the amount of foreign exchange they brought into Malaysia.

140. Athukorala, *Crisis and Recovery in Malaysia*, 81.

141. Felker, "Malaysia in 1998: A Cornered Tiger Bares Its Claws," 50.

142. *Far Eastern Economic Review*, November 12, 1998, 74.

143. *Far Eastern Economic Review*, September 17, 1998, 10, 11; *Far Eastern Economic Review*, October 1, 1998, 18.

144. Jason Abbott, "A Foul Smelling Affair," *The World Today* 55, no.7 (1999), 22-23.

145. Jones, "What Mahathir Has Wrought," 110.

146. *The New York Times*, February 10, 1999, A.9, 1.

147. Milne and Mauzy, *Malaysian Politics under Mahathir*, 177; *The Straits Times*, February 14, 2000, Internet.

148. Hilley, *Malaysia: Mahathirism, Hegemony and the New Opposition*, 76, 77.

149. Ibid., p.76.

150. The Malaysian government agreed to stop the 13.6-billion-ringgit Bakun Dam project following Anwar's December economic measures. Ting Pek Khiing's Ekran Bhd, the construction company which the contract to build the dam was awarded, asked for several hundred million ringgit in compensation. Ting also objected to the indefinite delay in dam construction. At the end, the Malaysian government compensated Ting with an amount around RM700 million. Gomez and Jomo K.S., *Malaysia's Political Economy* . . . , 194. Mahathir resumed the dam project again, later. See *Far Eastern Economic Review*, March 5, 1998, 28; *Far Eastern Economic Review*, June 18, 1998; *Far Eastern Economic Review*, May 21, 1998; *Business Week* (Number: 3596), September 21, 1998, 30.

151. Hilley, *Malaysia: Mahathirism, Hegemony and the New Opposition*, 75-76.

152. Jomo K.S., "From Currency Crisis to Recession," 44.

153. Felker, "Malaysia in 1998: A Cornered Tiger Bares Its Claws," 50-51; *Far Eastern Economic Review*, August 6, 1998, 72; *Financial Times*, August 28, 1998, 05. Petronas had always been a highly profitable petroleum company, and known for going to the aid of ailing companies and Mahathir's ambitious projects. During the crisis, Petronas bought debt-burdened shipping assets controlled by Mahathir's eldest son and was preparing to buy control of the national carmaker, Proton. Mahathir also pressured Petronas to take over the ailing national carrier, Malaysia Airlines. Although Petronas' financial and managerial resources ultimately belonged to the public, the Malaysian parliament had not been able to scrutinize its dealings, since Petronas reported directly to Mahathir's office and its accounts were not put before parliament. *Far Eastern Economic Review*, August 12, 1999, 10.

154. *The Strait Times* (Interactive-October 29, 1998).

155. *South China Morning Post*, March 17, 1999, 6.

156. *Far Eastern Economic Review*, September 9, 1999, 10.

157. Jones, "What Mahathir Has Wrought," 111.

158. Felker, "Malaysia in 1998: A Cornered Tiger Bares Its Claws," 50-51. Mahathir also denied the patron-client relations in Malaysia, arguing that the leadership "believes in cooperating with the private sector simply because the revenue of the Government comes largely from corporate taxes. Twenty-eight percent of the profits of the private sector belong to the government. In helping the private sector to make profits we are actually helping ourselves, the government." See Dato' Seri Dr. Mahathir Bin Mohamad, "Currency Controls the Best Way Out," *New Straits Times* (Malaysia), October 17, 1998, 10.

159. Toyoda, "Malaysia: Ethnic Cleavages and Controlled Liberalization," 102.

160. Jomo K.S., "Capital Flows," in *Malaysian Eclipse: Economic Crisis and Recovery* (London and New York: Zed Books Ltd., 2001b), 170; Athukorala, *Crisis and Recovery in Malaysia*, 71.

161. Athukorala, *Crisis and Recovery in Malaysia*, 71.

162. Athukorala, *Crisis and Recovery in Malaysia*, 73-74.

163 Dato' Seri Dr. Mahathir Bin Mohamad, His Talk at the Plenary Session of the Tenth United Nations Conference on Trade and Development (UNCTAD X), Bangkok, Thailand, on February 12, 2000, www.smpke.jpm.my/UcapWebNew/PMMain. . . . (accessed March 1, 2000).

164. Athukorala, *Crisis and Recovery in Malaysia*, 74-75.

165. Shamsul A.B., "The Redefinition of Politics and the Transformation of Malaysian Pluralism," in *the Politics of Multiculturalism: Pluralism and Citizenship in Malaysia, Singapore, and Indonesia* (Honolulu: University of Hawai'i Press, 2001), 225.

166. Athukorala, *Crisis and Recovery in Malaysia*, 74-75; Toyoda, "Malaysia: Ethnic Cleavages and Controlled Liberalization," 103. Mahathir declared that they were "in the process of redistributing wealth between the different communities in order to eliminate racial jealousies. [They would] continue to do this with apology to no one." See Mohamad, "Currency Controls the Best Way Out,"10.

167. Toyoda, "Malaysia: Ethnic Cleavages and Controlled Liberalization," 103.

168. Gomez and Jomo K.S., *Malaysia's Political Economy: Politics, Patronage and Profits* (1997), 2; Milne and Mauzy, *Malaysian Politics under Mahathir*, 2,3.

169. See Schlossstein, *Asia's New Little Dragons . . .*, 6; Wah and Kahn, "Introduction: Fragmented Vision,".4; Kok-Wah Loh, "State-Societal Relations in a Rapidly Growing Economy: the Case of Malaysia, 1970-1997," 84-85.

170. Milne and Mauzy, *Malaysian Politics under Mahathir*, 63, 181; Rasiah, "Class, Ethnicity and Economic Development in Malaysia," 141, 182; Lucas and Verry, *Restructuring the Malaysian Economy . . .*, 312.

171. Anne Munro-Kua, *Authoritarian Populism in Malaysia* (London: Macmillan Press Ltd., New York: St. Martin's Press, Inc., 1996), 3,8,9; Gomez and Jomo K.S., *Malaysia's Political Economy: Politics, Patronage and Profits* (1997), 2.

172. Means, *Malaysian Politics: The Second Generation*, 290-291.

173. Jones, "What Mahathir Has Wrought," 108.

174. Gomez and Jomo K.S ., *Malaysia's Political Economy . . . .*, 140.

175. Frances Loh Kok Wah, "Where Has (Ethnic) Politics Gone? The Case of the BN Non-Malay Politicians and Political Parties," in *Singapore and the Politics of Multiculturalism: Pluralism and Citizenship in Malaysia Indonesia* (Honolulu: University of Hawai'i Press, 2001), 201-202.

176. Dwight Heald Perkins and Wing Thye Woo, "Malaysia: Adjusting to Deep Integration with the World Economy," in *the Asian Financial Crisis: Lessons for a Resilient Asia* (London and Cambridge, MA: The MIT Press, 2000), 227-255), 230-231, 242-243. On February 15, 1999, the government decided to tax only the profits of foreign capital that entered after this date, if it left after less than one year, while it taxed the repatriation principal of the funds that had entered before that date. Thus, the government exempted new capital flows from exchange controls. On September 21, 1999, the government brought a flat tax rate of 10 percent on repatriated profits, and exempted repatriated principal from tax and legal impediments. Perkins and Woo, "Malaysia: Adjusting to Deep Integration with the World Economy," 243.

177. William D. Coplin and Michael K. O'Leary, eds., *Country Forecast*, Vol.XXXII (East Syracuse, NY: The PRS Group, LLC, April 2001); *The Observer*, September 12, 1999, 5; *Global Intelligence Update*, September 22, 1999, Internet; *The Straits Times*, May 26, 1999, Internet. According to Perkins and Woo (2000), less than US$350 million flowed out between mid-February and the end of September 1999. Perkins and Woo, "Malaysia: Adjusting to Deep Integration with the World Economy," 243.

178. *Financial Times*, May 10, 1999, 17, 28.

179. The BNM finally announced on February 14, 2000 that the nation's 54 banks, brokerages, and financial institutions have picked up their partners and would merge into 10 banking groups by the yearend. The debt-restructuring program had also been slow and problematic in Malaysia. The country's biggest debtor was the Renong Group, which is linked to Daim, and the UMNO, with 5 percent of Malaysia's outstanding debt. *Busi-*

ness Week (Number: 3672), March 13, 2000, 140, E6.

180. Ethan Kaplan and Dani Rodrik, "Did the Malaysian Capital Controls Work?" *NBER Working Paper* No. W8142 (February 2001).

181. Milne and Mauzy, *Malaysian Politics under Mahathir,* 176; Athukorala, *Crisis and Recovery in Malaysia,* 66; Jomo K.S., "Capital Controls," in *Malaysian Eclipse: Economic Crisis and Recovery* (London and New York: Zed Books Ltd., 2001c), 213.

182. *The Washington Post,* November 21, 1998, G01.

183. Milne and Mauzy, *Malaysian Politics under Mahathir,* 178; *South China Morning Post,* September 7, 1998, 8.

184. *Los Angeles Times,* September 16, 1998, S3.

185. *The Observer,* September 12, 1999, 5; Athukorala, *Crisis and Recovery in Malaysia,* 76.

186. Trudy Rubin, "Western Way not Always Right," *The State* (SC), September 30, 1999, A15.

187. *Far Eastern Economic Review,* December 10, 1998, 18; *Far Eastern Economic Review,* June 18, 1998, 21; Loh Kok Wah, "Where Has (Ethnic) Politics Gone? . . . ," 183.

188. Jones, "What Mahathir Has Wrought," 111.

189. See *FT Asia Intelligence Wire* (Bernama the Malaysian National News Agency), November 2, 1998. An IMF report on hedge funds, released in April 1998, claims that currency speculators were not major participants and thus not responsible for the Asian financial crisis. Barry Eichengreen, who is one of the authors of the report, indicated that only a few hedge funds took modest positions on the Malaysian ringgit and many hedge funds incurred losses from the ringgit's depreciation. He also noted that "the initial pressure on the ringgit appears to have emanated from institutional investors closing out long equity positions, reflecting their concern that the stock market was overvalued, rather than a buildup of speculative short positions reflecting concerns about the sustainability of the external debt and the state of the banking system." See *FT Asia Intelligence Wire* (Bernama the Malaysian National News Agency), April 17, 1998.

190. *The Economist* (via Lexis-Nexis), June 26, 1999.

191. Biers, ed., *Crash of '97,* 75.

192. Perkins and Woo, "Malaysia: Adjusting to Deep Integration with the World Economy," 227; *The Washington Post,* November 21, 1998, G01; *The Star Online,* January 9, 1999, http://www.TheStar.com.my/current/09pg1.html (accessed on January 9, 1999).

193. Loh Kok Wah, "Where Has (Ethnic) Politics Gone? . . . ," 183.

194. Perkins and Woo, "Malaysia: Adjusting to Deep Integration with the World Economy," 227, 230; *The Guardian,* November 29, 1999, 19; *Financial Times,* October 6, 2000, 18; *Far Eastern Economic Review,* January 21, 1999; *Star Online,* December 20, 1999. http://www.TheStar.com.my/online/newsreport (accessed December 20, 2000).

195. Loh Kok Wah, "Where Has (Ethnic) Politics Gone? . . . ," 201-202.

196 *Far Eastern Economic Review,* December 9, 1999, 14.

197. Thomas L. Friedman, "Shakespeare Does Malaysia," *The New York Times,* August 24, 1999, A15.

198. Corsetti, Pesenti, and Roubini, What Caused the Asian Currency and Financial Crisis?, Part I, 23,24.

CHAPTER VII: FINANCIAL CRISES, NON-ECONOMIC FACTORS, AND GOVERNMENTAL RESPONSES

> In nearly every economic crisis, the root cause is political, not economic.
>
> Lee Kuam Yew[1]

As indicated earlier, this book revolves around two large questions of how financial crises develop and how governmental policies come about. Examination of the cases has shown that non-economic factors can play as significant a role as economic ones in bringing financial crises and in shaping governmental policy responses, and that economic crisis models and explanations based on economic indicators are insufficient for addressing these questions. The interplay of economic and non-economic, and domestic and external factors brought the Mexican peso crisis of 1994-1995 and the Asian financial crisis of 1997-1998, and shaped the Mexican and Malaysian governments' policy responses. The interplay took place within these countries' domestic and external contexts and led to these outcomes through an interaction process, as the sequence of economic and non-economic developments translated the initial conditions into subsequent situations.

This chapter first critically reviews the recent economic literature that proposes new explanations to the questions of how financial crises develop and how governments behave. Then, it offers an alternative explanatory framework, inspired by the findings of the previous chapters as well as the relevant literature from political science, international studies and political economy. It speculates as to how things might be related in terms of the interplay and intermixing of economic and non-economic factors as causes of financial crises and governmental policy responses. The chapter also discusses the nature of cause and effect relations that lead to financial crises and shape governmental responses within domestic and external contexts of countries.

THE SHORTCOMINGS OF THE RECENT ECONOMIC LITERATURE ON FINANCIAL CRISES

According to some economists, the Mexican peso crisis and the Asian financial crises do not seem to fit with the logic of either first or second generation crisis models, which were explored in Chapter II. Economic crisis literature that came after the Mexican peso crisis and the Asian financial crisis emphasized different economic variables as significant. Therefore, they proposed new models, what Paul Krugman calls "third-generation models," due to the shortcomings of the first and second-generation crisis models. *Ex post* explanations of the Mexican peso crisis and the Asian financial crisis, which are reviewed in Chapters III and V, in fact, reflect the logic of the third generation crisis models. The following paragraphs summarize the recent economic literature on financial crises.

According to some, the second-generation crisis models did not predict sharp growth slowdowns or a recession after a financial crisis and assumed that governments gain more freedom to follow expansionary policies following a devaluation. However, both the Mexican Peso crisis and the Asian financial crisis were followed by severe recessions. In addition, the earlier crisis models sufficiently take into consideration the causes and consequences of large capital inflows and outflows. Capital inflows, in particular portfolio or short-term capital, can come to a sudden stop due to loss of confidence or external factors such as an increase in interest rates in industrialized countries. Such large capital movements can make countries vulnerable to a crisis, even if the country's macroeconomic conditions are sound, due to their multiple impacts in the financial markets. Three variants of third generation models emerged in the late 1990s. One version blames moral-hazard-driven investments as the root cause of a crisis, since these kinds of investments cause an excessive buildup of external debt and then a collapse. This version originated from the work of McKinnon and Pill (1996) and was developed and applied to the Asian financial crises by Corsetti, Pesenti, and Roubini (1998) as we have already seen in Chapter V. They emphasized the role of explicit and implicit loan guarantees in generating excessive risky investments. Capital inflows into an economy with an unregulated banking sector with deposit insurance and moral hazard problems lead to over-borrowing or over-lending cycles, which cause consumption booms, and possibly booms in the stock and real estate markets. They also lead to exaggerated current account deficits, a real exchange rate appreciation, a loss of competitiveness, and a slowdown in growth. In turn, these developments make investors worried about the possibility of default on foreign loans. When investors lose their confidence and start pulling their capital out of the country, investments that are dependent on capital inflows collapse and lead to a macroeconomic setback.[2]

The second version of the third generation crisis models is built around the open-economy version of the Diamond—Dybvig (1983) bank-run model. According to this version, a financial panic develops when short-term creditors suddenly withdraw their loans from solvent borrowers due to loss of confidence or when some kind of balance sheet-driven financial contraction occurs. This kind of financial panic is an adverse equilibrium outcome in the case of multiple equilibria in the financial markets. Each creditor withdraws capital from the banks or borrowers, thinking that other creditors are also fleeing. The panic leads to a self-fulfilling financial collapse.[3] The third version of these models emphasizes the balance-sheet implications of a currency depreciation. For example, Krugman's (1999) balance-sheet view of the crises, somewhat similar to Chang-Velasco's bank-run models, explains crises in terms of a flight of capital from an economy with fundamental weaknesses. This flight from such an economy first leads to a currency depreciation and in turn causes huge imbalances in companies' balance-sheets and reduces their net worth due to depreciation of the currency. Companies with lots of foreign-currency-denominated debt are the most vulnerable to these kinds of financial collapse. According to all versions of the third generation crisis models, crises are seen as bad things as they lead to a sharp contraction of economic activity and a recession. According to these third generation models, something out of many possibilities— including the causes of speculative attacks proposed by the second-generation crisis models, but not limited to them—could cause a sudden large currency depreciation. In turn, the depreciation severely damages balance sheets and leads the economy into the crisis equilibrium.[4]

However, the "third-generation" crisis models also fail to consider the impacts of non-economic factors sufficiently. Would the same macroeconomic weaknesses, identified by third generation models as causes of financial crises, such as sudden reversals of capital inflows, currency depreciation, and balance sheet imbalances, generate a financial collapse in the same way in every country? Would they not be affected by political, societal, and legal factors, and would governments and market participants react to them in the same ways? It is hard to answer yes to these questions. As we have seen from the examination of the Mexican and the Malaysian cases, non-economic factors played as significant roles as economic factors, by affecting investors' confidence, by impacting these governments' policy behaviors, and by indirectly impacting macroeconomic indicators, in generating their crises. Multiple non-economic factors also greatly affected how governments handled their crises. The predictive and explanatory power of the crisis models is deeply reduced by expected and unexpected non-economic developments occurring within different political and societal contexts.

Some of the crisis literature that came after the Mexican Peso crisis and the Asian financial crisis refer to political and institutional factors along with economic ones as important contributors to financial crises, but they do so in rather limited ways. Calvo (2000) argues that "sovereignty and nonexplicit government policy rules may go a long way toward generating financial vulnerability and multiple equilibriums. Sovereignty induces 'country risk,' and the latter prompts the government—explicitly or implicitly—to favor short-term debt and deposits."[5] In addition, Calvo (2000) asserts that ". . .together with sovereignty, large capital inflows magnify the financial vulnerability caused by short-term debt and deposits."[6] Wei (2000) demonstrates a relationship between crony capitalism and self-fulfilling expectations. According to him, corruption may increase a country's chance of running into a financial crisis by weakening domestic financial supervision and producing deteriorated balance sheets for banks and firms. But also "corruption in a capital importing country tends to tilt the composition of its capital inflows away from foreign direct investment and towards foreign bank loans. . . [in turn] a capital inflow structure that is relatively low in FDI is associated with a greater propensity of a future currency crisis," as the Frankel and Rose (1996) study also showed.[7]

The other empirical researches find not necessarily contradictory but somewhat incompatible results. For example, Frankel and Rose (1996) in their empirical treatment of "a panel of annual data for over 100 developing countries from 1971 through 1992" find that "[currency] crashes tend to occur when FDI inflows dry up, when reserves are low, when domestic credit growth is high, when northern interest rates rise, and when the real exchange rate shows overvaluation. They also tend to be associated with sharp recessions; though the causal linkages are very unclear . . . neither current account nor government budget deficits appear to play an important role in a typical crash." [8] On the other hand, Eichengreen, Rose, and Wyplosz (1995), using a quarterly panel of data from 1959 through 1993 for twenty OECD countries, find that political instability, budget and current account deficits, and fast growth of money and prices precede devaluation.[9] Milesi-Ferretti and Razin (2000) in their survey of 105 low and middle income countries conclude, "Currency crises are more likely to occur when reserves are low, real exchange rates are appreciated, and external conditions are unfavorable, [i.e.] high interest rates and low growth in industrial countries. Growth tends to decline the year of the crisis and to recover. . . ."[10] Sachs, Tornell, and Velasco (1996a), from their comparison of 20 emerging markets, find that a high real exchange rate appreciation, a recent lending boom, and low reserves are the macroeconomic fundamentals that make countries more vulnerable to suffer a financial crisis than others. They argue that high current account deficits, excessive capital inflows, and loose fiscal policies are not among the most significant variables according to their survey.[11]

Kaminsky (1999) denies the claims that the Mexican Peso crisis and the 1997 Asian crises were unforeseeable and new kinds of crises. Based on the empirical regularities observed in the 102 financial crises in 20 countries from 1970-1995, he offers four different composite leading indicators in order to assess the distress level, i.e. the degree of fragility of the economy. The indicators he chose to observe in his empirical study are basically the same macroeconomic indicators that the crisis literature has identified before him. He combines the information provided by all the indicators "to assess the likelihood of an upcoming crisis" in four ways.[12] According to his conclusion, both the Mexican Peso crisis and the Asian financial crisis were predictable, and maybe preventable, since "these economies were far from healthy, with clear signs of distress surfacing as early as eighteen months [in the case of the Asian Financial crisis] before the currency collapse."[13] However, as we have seen from our cases, political, societal and institutional factors affected the behaviors of market participants and governments, and indirectly macroeconomic variables. Therefore, it is hard to argue that his measurement of the distress level will give the same or similar outcomes in different contexts, without assessing the impact of non-economic variables.

The incompatible results of empirical studies also show that these studies do not consider the idiosyncrasies caused by political, societal, and legal events and situations in different countries. Although these studies find some patterns from large data sets, the contextual influences are not integrated into their analyses. In addition, it is hard to assume that the data sets and the financial crises these studies use are the same. As Eichengreen, Rose, and Wyplosz (1995) indicate, "in contrast to the panoply of theoretical models made available by the economics profession, evidence on the empirical importance of the factors on which theorists focus is partial and conflicting in the case of economic variables and essentially nonexistent in the case of political factors."[14] Radelet and Sachs (2000, 107) identify five types of financial crises,[15] which could be intertwined in any particular historical episode, in terms of their key features. Diagnosis, underlying mechanisms, prediction, prevention, and recovery policies differ significantly among these five types of crises, according to them. The probability of the anticipation of a crisis by market participants and analysts is also different according to the crisis types. Not all types are destructive for real economic activity, and what governments should do differs according to each crisis type.[16] These complexities considered together with the contextual influences further complicate prediction and explanation of financial crises, what governments should do, or what they actually do. Another issue is that the global context of a financial crisis is constantly changing due to growing globalization and interdependence. These changes in the global context affect the causes and the occurrence of a financial crisis and contagion. Even the external non-economic, in particular political, events/developments could have a role in the occurrence of a currency crisis.

In sum, the third generation models and the recent crisis literature have made new contributions for understanding and explaining financial crises. However, they also do not illuminate us in terms of how non-economic factors stemming from different external and domestic, political, societal, and legal contexts might impact the development of financial crises as well as governmental policy responses during a crisis. Economic studies that consider the impacts of some political factors in their analyses, such as Corsetti and Roubini's (1997) consideration of "the trade-off between rules and discretion in fiscal policy in the presence of politically motivated fiscal deficits," and Alesina, Roubini, and Cohen's (1997) consideration of the impacts of political cycles on the macroeconomy are positive contributions to the literature. However, they are rather limited in showing the multiplicity of non-economic factors as well as their impacts and interplay with economic factors, and they are not directly helpful for explicating the impacts of non-economic factors during financial crises.

Economic variables are outcomes of market participants' behaviors, which are determined by both economic and non-economic factors as well as governmental policy behaviors, and governments act differently under different political, societal and legal contexts. Drazen (2000) asserts that all devaluation decisions are political in their nature. Political circumstances and processes influence the preferences and behavior of policymakers, and in the end, politics shapes government behavior and response policies to financial crises under the influence of various economic and non-economic factors.

AN ANALYTICAL FRAMEWORK FOR EXPLAINING THE IMPACTS OF NON-ECONOMIC FACTORS

As the recent economic literature also demonstrates, many economists acknowledge the impacts of some political, societal, and institutional influences, but they fail to integrate them into their financial crisis explanations or models sufficiently, partly because economics and political science/international studies are separate disciplines. Lack of consideration of the full impact of non-economic factors on financial crises and governmental response policies leads to poor understanding, inadequate explanations and poor forecasts. In order to better understand causes and consequences of financial crises as well as government behavior, we need to bridge political science, international relations, and political economy literature with economic explanations and analyses. There is a need for systematic studies that illuminate how economic and non-economic factors intermix or interrelate with one another in bringing financial crises and in determining governmental response policies. This section offers an analytical framework in order to contribute to the crisis literature in this direction.

Analytical Framework

In light of the findings of the previous chapters as well as the relevant literature, we can speculate as to how economic and non-economic factors are interrelated in bringing financial crises and in shaping governmental policy responses. It seems that non-economic factors affect the development of financial crises mainly through two channels, i.e. by affecting governments' policymaking processes and policy makers' behaviors, and by affecting market participants' economic or financial decisions and behaviors. These non-economic impacts on governments' policy behaviors and market participants' decisions and actions, in turn, affect economic/financial indicators positively or negatively. This is, of course, not a one-way effect. Economic indicators can also directly or indirectly affect various political, societal, and institutional non-economic factors along with affecting the decisions and behaviors of governments and market participants.

Economic and non-economic factors that impact development of financial crises and governmental policy responses exist within the domestic and external contexts of countries. The examination of the cases pointed to various types of non-economic factors stemming from these contexts. We might group them as follows: *Domestic Context:* (1) Societal context, events, developments and domestic interest groups; (2) Political system, intermediate institutions and associations; (3) State structure, institutional and legal frameworks; (4) the nature of ruling/executive power and problems associated with it; (5) ideological and psychological factors associated with economic policymakers, and political ambitions and interests of political leadership. Economic policies can potentially be affected by all of these kinds of non-economic factors along with being affected by the economic conditions and variables themselves. All of these non-economic factors are embedded in one another, and they are parts and constituents of the domestic context. *External context:* (1) External economic and non-economic developments in other countries, pressures and influences of external actors, such as interest groups, other governments, and monetary/financial institutions; (2) Global economic/financial developments and their impacts on governments and international markets. Impacts of the first group of external factors may change according to a country's location and its particular relations with these actors. However, the impacts of global financial and economic developments affect every country's external environment more or less in the same way, and every country that is exposed to these influences is affected in similar ways. The chart on the next page summarizes the possible relationship between economic and these various non-economic factors in bringing financial crises and in shaping governmental policy responses.

Examining the Analytical Framework I: The Findings of the Case Studies and the Relevant Literature

As demonstrated in the earlier chapters and the previous section, most of the economic explanations solely emphasize deteriorated economic and financial indicators and market participants' interaction with them as the causes of financial crises, and ignore or downplay the impacts of non-economic factors. Economists are concerned with which deteriorating economic/financial indicators cause investors to withdraw their funds and lead to a speculative attack, investors' panic, and eventually a financial crisis. They are not much concerned with which non-economic developments and events also lead to changes in investors' market behaviors. On the chart above, the emphasis of economic crisis models and explanations could be summarized as the relationships/interactions shown with the dashed line arrows. In addition, economists mostly point to economic indicators and a country's overall economic conditions along with some external economic/financial developments as the reasons behind economic policies. They either ignore or do not sufficiently consider the relationships indicated by the solid line arrows on the chart. Their assumed, prescribed, or predicted government behaviors are usually simplistic. However, as the examination of the cases has illustrated, neither the development of the crises nor the Mexican and Malaysian governments'

Figure 7.1. The Impact of Non-Economic Factors on the Development of Financial Crises and Governmental Responses

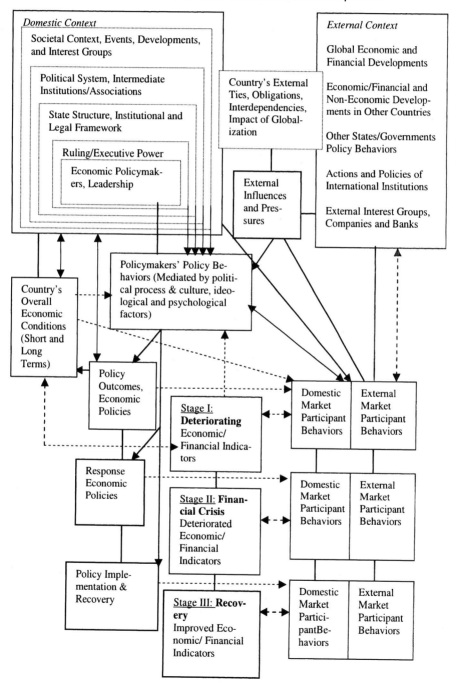

behaviors could be explained purely with the logic of economics. Although macroeconomic variables might be useful for predicting which countries are vulnerable, they are not that useful for predicting and explaining the actual occurrence and timing of financial crises, which have been the focuses of much of the theoretical literature. Eichengreen, Rose, and Wyplosz (1995) indicate that "while some attacks are plausibly motivated by imbalances in fundamentals, others are not. . . ."[17] On the one hand, macroeconomic fundamentals may deteriorate slowly and make a currency crisis likely, and on the other hand, non-economic factors intermixed with economic weaknesses may cause a self-fulfilling attack. It is incorrect to make empirical generalizations solely based on macroeconomic variables. As Espinosa and Russell (1996) assert, economics is not a science that offers "a single, generally accepted explanation for most major economic issues or events."[18] There is no single set of variables and no stable set of relationships on which crisis forecasting can be based. Although crisis models and explanations identify the kinds of variables that make countries vulnerable and reduce governments' ability to defend a peg, "the domestic [and external] considerations that governments weigh when contemplating a costly defense of the currency vary across time and country."[19]

Thus, economists do address the question of how financial crises develop; however, their consideration of non-economic factors is not sufficient. Although the literature on financial crises is abundant, studies that consider the impacts of non-economic factors on the development of financial crises and on governmental response policies are few and limited in scope. There are only a few studies that are closely related to the questions of this inquiry. Several articles by Leblang and Bernhard (2000 and 2002), and by Leblang (2002a and 2002b) attempt to demonstrate relationships between exchange-rate expectations in market actors and several political factors, such as cabinet duration and partisanship, democratic political processes (elections, cabinet formation, and cabinet dissolutions), and expected change in political leadership in a particular country in different sets of sample countries. Also, Leblang (May 2001) and Chang (2002) investigate the interaction between governments and markets during financial crises. Although these studies are useful for demonstrating the impacts of various political factors on market participants' behaviors across countries, they are limited in terms of considering the multiplicity of non-economic factors, such as societal and institutional factors, expected and unexpected developments, and political factors. Each country has different external and domestic contexts to a certain extent, and the characteristics of each country's society, institutions and leadership differ from one another. These differences could potentially affect how various political factors, or non-economic factors in a larger sense, may impact market participants' behavior and governmental policy behavior in each country. Leblang and Bernhard (2000) also assert, "Market actors incorporate information from a variety of sources into their expectations."[20] However, these sources could be quite different in regards to each different country during different time periods.

Gourevitch's (1986) book, *Politics in Hard Times,* is closely related to the question of how governments respond to financial crises. It compares the policy responses of the United States, the United Kingdom, Germany, France, and Sweden to three financial/economic crises—the long deflation at the end of the nineteenth century from 1873 to 1896, the Great Depression of the 1930s, and the wide gyrations of the 1970s and 1980s. Gourevitch examines domestic political procedures and pressures that led to the policy responses in each of his case countries in terms of "how alliances among societal actors form, crumble and reform in each crisis period."[21] Nonetheless, his study is limited to Western democratic and industrialized countries, and his emphasis is on domestic factors with limited consideration of external factors. Additional relevant works include the Horowitz & Heo (2001) edited book, *The Political Economy of International Financial Crises: Interest Groups, Ideologies, and Institutions,* which "focuses on political explanations of economic policies and institutional changes."[22] It argues that continuity and change in economic policy and political institutions cannot be adequately explained "by looking at internal economic structures and the associated patterns of concentrated, highly organized interest group cleavages, and at political institutions that mediate such interest group pressures. . . .Pivotal roles are often played by more dispersed, weakly organized interest groups and by political leadership."[23] As indicated earlier, Sidney Weintraub (2000) studies the decision-making process of the Mexican government during the peso crisis, but his inquiry does not go beyond an account of the decision-making process.

In addition to these studies, there is a large body of political science/comparative politics, political economy, and international studies literature that could be helpful in explicating impacts of some domestic and external non-economic factors on political processes, governmental behaviors, policy outcomes, and market participants' behaviors. For example, the Haggard, Lee, and Maxfield (1993) edited volume, *The Politics of Finance in Developing Countries,* shows that differences in domestic political/structural settings led to different policy preferences concerning credit allocation in eight developing countries. Also, various political economy literatures, such as Gilpin (2000; 2001), Milner and Keohane (1996), and Frieden (1991) address different aspects of the interrelations between economics and politics. Frieden (1994; 1998) examines the politics of exchange rate. Moreover, Olson's and Kähkönen's (2000) edited book deals with "the intellectual advances that are broadening economics and integrating the social sciences." Olson (2000) investigates institutional bases for economic performance and Sabatier's (1999) edited book brings together political process theories/explanations. These studies in cooperation with economic studies could be utilized in assessing the impacts of non-economic factors both on the development of financial crises and on governmental policies.

The upcoming section will discuss the nature of the causal mechanism that leads to financial crises and governmental policy responses. This section reviews and compares various non-economic factors that affected the developments in the Mexican and the Malaysian cases in the order of the aforementioned categories, which are shown on the framework, and discusses to what extent the framework and findings of cases are compatible with the relevant literature. As it discusses and compares the findings of the case studies, it refers to the relevant literature, in particular to Gourevitch's (1986) work. In doing so, this section further explicates how the non-economic factors are related to economic factors on the analytical framework.

The impacts of societal context, events, developments, and domestic interest groups

As Chapter IV and VI have demonstrated, various political science and political economy literature referred to the impacts of societal events and developments on the Mexican and Malaysian governments' policy behaviors as well as on the market participants' behaviors during these countries' financial crises. One outstanding example of such developments was the Zapatista uprising in Chiapas (in Mexico), which was an outcome of multiple societal, political, and economic factors, in particular poverty and income inequality, distributive impacts of Salinas' neoliberal economic policies, the implementation of NAFTA as an extension of such policies, and the Mexican authoritarian political system. The uprising affected the development of the peso crisis and the Mexican government's behavior in several ways. It affected the market participants' behavior and their perception of Mexico negatively throughout the peso crisis. The resumption of armed conflict between rebels and the military on December 18, 1994 triggered further capital flights that forced the Mexican government to take the devaluation decision, which led to the peso crisis. The uprising also distracted President Salinas and limited his focus on deteriorating economic/financial conditions. Thus, it affected the Mexican government's policy priorities and policy outcomes.

In addition, societal characteristics such as historical and cultural/ideological factors affected the developments both in Mexico and Malaysia and mediated the impacts of the non-economic factors discussed later. Mexico's historical inheritance, political culture, and its "defensive type of nationalism" generated and allowed a strong and defensive type of leadership that did not accommodate policy debate outside a small number of people in Mexico and policy suggestions from abroad, as discussed in Chapter IV. Malaysia's political culture, which favored a strong leader and strong government, enabled Mahathir to manipulate the public's perception of the crisis and popularize his policy preferences and action. Malaysian society has been permissive and responsive to Mahathir's rhetoric, populism, and policy choices. Although Mahathir's popularity was somewhat shaken by the dispute with Anwar, Mahathir was able to rally public support behind his policy choice.

In Malaysia, there was not a particular societal event that occurred during the Asian financial crisis. Nonetheless, ethnic divisions and past experiences, particularly the ethnic riots of 1969, concerned the Malaysian government for decades as well as during the crisis. Although ethnic division and the Malaysian political leadership's consideration of it did not have any significant effect on how the Asian financial crisis developed in Malaysia, they have profoundly affected the Malaysian government's economic policies. The NEP and the NDP were designed as "affirmative action" economic programs that aimed at promoting the *bumiputera*'s economic wellbeing along with carrying out other goals. The ethnic considerations and these economic programs shaped Malaysia's political economy and, in turn, affected how the Malaysian government or Prime Minister Mahathir responded to the Asian financial crisis. As some argue, the ethnic considerations also played a role in Mahathir's rejection of IMF-style economic policies.

The relevant literature usually refers to the impacts of societal events and developments as they occur. Nonetheless, many political economy works systematically refer to the impacts of societal groups or domestic interest groups on governments' economic policies. Gourevitch (1986) refers to political economy literature that explains governmental policies based on domestic interest groups as *production profile explanations.* These explanations see governmental policy choices as reflections of major interest groups and economic actors, whose interests are mediated by intermediate institutions and state structures. The interests and policy preferences of these societal actors are shaped by their economic situations in the international and domestic economy. Governmental decision-making reflects the demands, struggles, and compromises of these interest groups at particular times concerning policy alternatives.[24] The works of Jeffry Frieden are good examples of this explanatory approach. Frieden, in his 1991 article, suggests that the interests of various interest groups shape the politics of national policymaking concerning international capital mobility by determining the support coalitions or the oppositions to certain policies. Frieden (1997) argues that policymakers choose politically sustainable policies and respond to general and/or specific political pressures by their constituencies, whether they are the voters, powerful interest groups, or a cabal of military rulers and their supporters. Frieden's (1998) analysis of the politics of the Euro, and Frieden and Rogowski's book chapter in the Milner and Keohane (1996) edited book *Internationalization and Domestic Politics*, also reflect a similar analytical approach. Some other examples of this explanatory approach could be Hefeker's (1997) book, *Interest Groups and Monetary Integration: The Political Economy of Exchange Rate Regimes*, and Verdier's (1998) article on domestic responses to capital market internationalization under the Gold Standard period of 1870-1914.

In fact, various interest groups in Mexico had access to the Mexican political and policy-making processes via formal representation or informal connections. During the elections, the Mexican political leadership was concerned with the potential impact of its economic policies over different segments of society, from which the political leadership expected to get its votes. Nonetheless, it seems that the Mexican big businesses, in particular outwardly oriented sectors, impacted the Mexican government's economic policies the most during the 1990s and during the peso crisis. The weak banking system that constrained the

Mexican government's policy options was an outcome of the relationship between the ruling party PRI and the big businesses along with some other economic policies. The Mexican political leadership did not listen to the advice of the World Bank officials to take measures to strengthen the banking system in order not to sever its relationship with the big businesses.

In Malaysia, among various domestic interest groups, selected business groups from all three ethnic groups, in particular those that had close links with the UMNO, have been most favored by the Malaysian government's economic policies. Intricate relations between Malaysian businesses and the government have created patron-client relations and rent-seeking activities, as the chapter has described. Mahathir's response policy to the crisis was a continuation of the patron-client relations embedded in the Malaysian political economy. As mentioned earlier, Mahathir's government bailed out troubled companies, especially the ones which had links to the UMNO and Mahathir, instead of allowing their destiny to be determined under free market conditions. The crisis, to a large extent, occurred in Malaysia's private sectors, but private companies were bailed out with public sector money.

The impacts of the political system and intermediate associations/institutions

As Gourevitch (1986) describes, the literature that emphasize the impact of intermediate association on governmental policy outcomes stress the role of a vast network of associations, such as political parties and unions, which are designed to represent societal actors and to mediate between politicians and societal actors, that is, between government and society. Although this explanatory approach recognizes the considerable power of interest groups and economic actors, it argues that intermediate associations play the major role in shaping policies.[25] The different roles of intermediate associations in different countries and their comparison across the countries have been widely considered topics of comparative politics. One example of this approach from the political economy literature could be Walsh's (2000) book, which compares British, French and Italian response policies to the economic challenges since the 1970s. Walsh applies two different explanations of domestic political influences on economic policies, namely the explanation of a policy as an outcome of political struggle between groups, and the explanation of policy responses that resulted from mediation of the domestic political economy institutions. He applies these explanations across British, French and Italian response policies for their economic challenges since the 1970s. He concludes that the "institutional explanation does a better job" than the explanations that define economic policy as the outcome of a political struggle among interest groups. In contrast, Katzenstein in his 1978 book, which compares the foreign economic policies of five industrial countries, the U.S., Britain, Japan, W. Germany, Italy and the "French State", argues that parties and elections are often less important than interest groups in the formulation and implementation of a foreign economic policy.

Nevertheless, it seems that intermediate associations play more significant roles in democratic political systems than in authoritarian or semi-authoritarian political systems. In democracies, economic policies are directly subject to the voting and lobbying pressures from various interest groups and to intermediate associations that articulate and mediate their demands and pressures. In the semi-authoritarian political systems of Mexico and Malaysia, however, independent and effective intermediate associations did not exist, other than ruling parties and state institutions. Independent political parties were weak and various associations of interest groups have been either linked to the ruling party and the state structure, or were suppressed. As Chapter IV demonstrated, the Mexican semi-authoritarian political system consisted of a one-party rule and corporatist structure through which various interest groups were linked to executive power formally or informally. Similar to Mexico's one partly rule, which lasted until the year 2000, the coalition of three ethnic parties, the BN, has been in power in Malaysia since the country's independence. Horowitz and Heo (2001) assert that "authoritarian regimes are more likely to exclude some important interest groups from the political process while privileging others."[26] In Malaysia, as well, while the UMNO-linked businesses were privileged, various other societal interest groups were manipulated by the ruling coalition within the Malaysian semi-authoritarian political system. Independent interest groups and associations and the opposition parties have been weak. The Malaysian semi-authoritarian political system, which is dominated by the executive power, similar to that of Mexico during the peso crisis, only allowed interest representation via the ruling coalition, in particular the UMNO, as explained earlier. The Malaysian political system enabled Prime Minister Mahathir to manipulate the development of the Asian financial crisis, at least in Malaysia, and eventually shape the government's response policies.

Gourevitch's (1986) study suggests that financial crises create a challenge to the old policies and support coalitions, provide opposition groups and/or alternative policies with new opportunities, and through the political process new policy approaches and coalitions are formed.[27] However, within the Malaysian and the Mexican semi-authoritarian political systems, opposition groups to the old policies and their support coalitions were too weak to create a credible alternative policy that could get public support. The ruling parties and political leaderships in these countries were able to survive through the crisis and maintain their pre-crisis economic policies with minor revisions as well as their support coalitions. Although the financial crises in these countries created a policy debate and a certain degree of controversy, they were of a far lesser extent when compared to those in the democratic countries that Gourevitch (1986) studied.

The impacts of state structure and the institutional and legal framework

Within the semi-authoritarian political systems of Mexico and Malaysia, mainly the state structures and its institutional/legal framework mediated the demands and pressures of societal interest groups, rather than independent intermediate associations. Literature that emphasizes the importance of state structure stress the structure of the state, its rules, formal institutions, and bureaucracies, through which societal forces and representative associations must act, as Gourevitch (1986) describes. The state and its institutions exert a huge influence in both mediating and defining interests and intermediate associations.[28] Comparative politics literature along with some political economy literature often refers to state structure and its impacts on policy outcomes.

As Horowitz and Heo (2001) assert, "political institutions determined the extent to which the government is formally and informally accountable to economic interest groups, as well as the specific manner in which economic policies are chosen and implemented."[29] In authoritarian regimes, political institutions may limit or enhance influences of particular interests groups, depending on their importance for cultivating mass legitimacy and their links to the ruling party and political leadership. As Horowitz and Heo (2001) point out, state structure and its institutions could restrict or amplify the influence of various groups and offer political leadership different means of choosing and implementing policies.[30]

The *pacto* mechanism in Mexico reflected Mexico's corporatist way of running the country, periodically brought together a limited number of people, and provided major interest groups, in particular big businesses and bankers, with a platform to affect the government's economic policies. The most significant of such effects during the peso crisis was the 15% devaluation decision of the Mexican government, which was taken under the influence of Mexican bankers. In addition, the *pacto* mechanism constrained the policy flexibility of the Mexican government throughout the peso crisis.

The PRI's dominance over the state institutions and the corporatist structure not only privileged certain groups but also led to top-down hierarchical decision making, corruption, and secrecy, all of which in turn affected the Mexican government's policy behavior, the behavior of market participants, and indirectly economic indicators. They affected the BOM's monetary policies, even though it was officially independent since 1993. The one party rule and the PRI's stronghold in Congress enabled the Mexican government to take "tough" or unpopular measures in response to the crisis.

In addition, the 1994 presidential election, which for the first time endangered one-party rule, intensified the political concerns of the political leadership and led them to prioritize political calculations over economic concerns. As a result, the Mexican government followed expansionary fiscal and monetary policies through the mediation of the Mexican development banks and through expansion of credit, which were incompatible with maintaining the fixed exchange rate and low inflation rate. The political leadership was especially resistant to a devaluation decision prior to the election, since depreciation of the peso would hurt important electoral groups as well as the weakened banking system due to expansionary credit policies. In addition, the political leadership's focus on the PRI's election victory led to the mobilization of economic policy institutions and officials for that purpose and to ignorance of the deteriorating economic indicators.

Similar to the PRI's dominance over the Mexican state structure, the UMNO and its leaders have dominated the government, state structure and political system in Malaysia. Interest groups were linked to the executive elite through patron-client relations via the mediation of state structures. The weak parliament, dependent judiciary, bureaucracy, and press, as well as weak opposition parties and the opposition within the UMNO could not impose strong checks and balances to Mahathir's way of dealing with the crisis and prevent his purge of Anwar. Mahathir and his associates' dominance over the state structure and economic policies generated "money politics" and past experiences and memories of it impacted investors' confidence of the Malaysian government. Under such conditions, an IMF-style policy approach or Anwar's policy approach could not become a serious policy challenge to that of Mahathir within the Malaysian political and institutional context, as Chapter VI demonstrated. The institutional contexts of Malaysia and regional countries affected by the Asian financial crisis privileged particular interest groups and created moral hazard problems, which led to the increase of non-performing loans and a troubled banking system.

Gourevitch (1986), based on his analyses of political processes in the five Western democratic countries, asserts that economic conditions are almost always mediated through mechanisms of representation such as political parties, interest group associations, organizations of state structure such as electoral laws, a balance between the legislative and executive branches, and bureaucratic institutions.[31] However, obviously this mediation has been much more different in both Mexico and Malaysia than it was in the countries he examined. In both Mexico and Malaysia, the roles of political parties (other than the ruling parties) and interest group associations were insignificant as compared to the organizations of state structure, which were dominated by executive power. The legislature and bureaucracy did not have strong impacts in the policymaking process and policy outcomes as compared to the political leadership. Halperin's (1974) *Bureaucratic Politics*, and Allison's (1971 and 1999) *Essence of Decision*, show the huge impacts of bureaucratic politics and organizational routines on the U.S. political process, policy outcomes and implementation. Their arguments seem more applicable to democratic countries than to authoritarian or semi-authoritarian countries. These differences between Gourevitch's (1986) case countries and the Mexican and Malaysian cases suggest that the mediations are different between democratic and authoritarian countries.

The nature of ruling/executive power and problems associated with it

The nature of ruling power and problems within the ruling party affected the policymaking process and policy behaviors of both the Mexican and the Malaysian governments. The strong leadership restricted the size of the group that made key decisions, and information was kept exclusively within this small group. Literature on the impact of cognitive factors in decision-making, and Janis' (1982) *Groupthink* show how dysfunctional group decisions can be. The almost unlimited power of the Mexican presidency made the small number of decision-makers arrogant in the sense that "we know the best, and there really is no need to have open, national debates on economic policy."[32] Neither the public nor the Congress was informed sufficiently about the economic trends. There was a deliberate secrecy. They persisted in pursuing failing policies, and did not realize their "wishful thinking." As a result, political calculations dominated the economic ones during the fateful year of 1994, and the Salinas government resisted taking "necessary" adjustment measures when the external conditions severely turned against Mexico in mid-1994.[33]

In addition, Mexico witnessed the political assassinations and the internal quarrels in the ruling party, the PRI. The assassination of the presidential candidate Colosio in March 1994 was a major shock to the Mexican markets, and led to a drastic reduction in investors' confidence in Mexico and the Mexican government. It marked the beginning of turbulent developments in the Mexican markets. Internal quarrels within the PRI throughout 1994 distracted President Salinas and indirectly affected the Mexican government's policies and priorities. The second major political killing, the assassination of Ruíz Massieu in September 1994, further shook the already volatile markets.

Moreover, the presidential transitions in Mexico had been worrisome for investors, especially for those who knew Mexican history. It increased devaluation expectations of market participants. In addition, Zedillo's exclusion of Aspe from the cabinet further reduced investors' confidence in the Mexican government, since market trust was tied to Aspe himself rather than the government. Zedillo's cabinet was not well received. Short and superficial briefings of the outgoing cabinet secretaries for the new ones did not make new cabinet members fully aware of the fragile financial/economic conditions. The new Secretary of Finance, Serra, and the old one, Aspe, were personal rivals. Serra was inexperienced in his new post and he was not well informed about the economic situation by Aspe. Serra prioritized preparing the new budget rather than taking preemptive measures in order to halt the deteriorating financial situation. Moreover, the new Zedillo administration made policy mistakes due to their inexperience. The 15% devaluation was not accompanied with a comprehensive policy package that contained complementary fiscal and monetary measures. The government did not seem realistic about the situation, and its policy approach was not well received by the markets. The devaluation decision further destroyed the reputation of the Zedillo administration. The Mexican government was not prepared to deal with volatile, huge global capital inflows and outflows. After the crisis, the government's Emergency Economic Plan was insufficient for persuading the markets and addressing the real situation.

Malaysia did not have political assassinations during the crisis, but economic policy differences between Mahathir and his deputy Anwar along with each one's different political ambitions created friction and policy struggles within the UMNO and the Malaysian government. Different policy approaches and policy friction between Anwar and Mahathir affected both the development of the crisis in Malaysia and the government's policy behaviors until Mahathir eventually dominated the economic policymaking process and ousted Anwar from his position. As a result, policy quarrels within the ruling parties were somewhat similar in Mexico and Malaysia. However, the political interaction processes that brought the policy outcomes were different in these countries in many ways, and probably these differences along with other ideological and psychological differences between the leaderships of these countries led to different policy outcomes.

Ideological and psychological factors associated with economic policymakers and the political ambitions and interests of the political leadership

Some literature emphasizes the economic ideology or policy approaches of policymakers as significant for the policy outcomes. As Gourevitch's (1986) "economic ideology explanation" points out, the economics models and theories that are in the minds of policymakers as well as policymakers' values and perceptions impact their understanding of financial/economic developments andcrisis situations, guiding their policy behaviors. These ideological and psychological factors also affect societal actors' evaluations of their own positions in regards to certain governmental policy behaviors. How actors define, understand, and analyze the financial/economic situations determine their policy prescriptions and choices.[34] In political economy literature, the Gramscian approach also points to the impact of a knowledge-based consensus of "epistemic communities" on economic policy choices.[35]

In both the Mexican and the Malaysian cases, economic ideologies or policy approaches of policy makers along with psychological factors and political interests/ambitions of political leadership played significant roles within decision making processes, which affected policy behaviors of these governments and the development of the crises in these countries. It seems that these factors mediated between other non-economic factors and policy outcomes.

For example, Aspe and Mancera's preference of the symbolic single-digit inflation at the cost of lower economic growth made them resistant to a devaluation decision that would sour inflation. The political leadership, in particular Salinas and the PRI's presidential candidates (Colosio and Zedillo) probably were more concerned with lower economic growth or recession in the 1994 election year, and did not want higher interest rates that would help maintain the exchange rate. In addition, the Mexican political elite's commitment to the neoliberal economic ideology had played a significant role in shaping the Mexican government's policy response to the peso crisis.

In addition, psychological/perceptual factors such as "wishful thinking," misperception and miscalculations also affected the Mexican officials. Under the influence of various non-economic factors, the Mexican officials misperceived the emergency of the economic situation and downplayed the deteriorating economic indicators, in particular the current account deficit and the overvaluation of the peso. For example, after the assassination of Colosio they thought that the situation was temporary, due to their wishful thinking rather than a careful assessment of the economic situation. They also neglected the negative impacts of external developments, in particular the increases in the U.S. interest rate on the capital flows in and out of Mexico. Psychological factors also affected market participants' perceptions of Mexico and their confidence in the Mexican government. Since the maintenance of the exchange rate was a symbol of overall policy credibility, the Mexican government was constrained by this psychological factor as well. The popular image of Zedillo's cabinet as being inexperienced and incapable affected the credibility of the new government.

Moreover, President Salinas' personal political ambitions and concerns, in terms of leaving office with a good reputation and his candidacy for directorship of the WTO, made him resist a devaluation decision even after the 1994 election. His ambitions along with multiple distractions—the Zapatista rebellion, the internal quarrels within the PRI, emotional issues concerning his marriage and the murder of Ruíz Massieu (who had been married to his sister), resignation of his close advisor—changed his priorities and daily routines, reduced his consultations with his economic advisers, and led him to not see or to downplay the emergency of the economic situation.

Ideological and psychological factors as well as political calculations and ambitions also significantly impacted the developments in Malaysia. In particular, Mahathir and his economic and political ideology, *Mahathirism*, profoundly affected how the Asian financial crisis developed in Malaysia and how the Malaysian government eventually responded to the crisis. Mahathir's beliefs in strong government, an East Asian developmentalist economic policy approach, anti-Western ideology, and promotion of *bumiputera* businessmen, combined with his political pragmatism and leadership style resonated in his pre-crisis economic policies and his rhetorical stance and policy choices during the crisis.

His ideological and political goals were behind his ambitious big projects that overheated the economy prior to the crisis. Direct or indirect government influence on the banking system led to domestic loan expansion and a credit boom. In turn, over-lending weakened the Malaysian banking system. Mahathir also constrained the "independent" BNM's monetary policy. Under the influence of Mahathir's office, the BNM was late to bring credit restrictions for property and equity purchases. When the BNM brought credit restrictions for property and stock investments, the government did not support these restrictions with fiscal policies. Moreover, Mahathir ignored the warnings and recommendations of the BNM and the Malaysian Finance Ministry about the overheated economy.

From the beginning of the crisis Mahathir blamed speculators, especially mentioning U.S. fund manager George Soros, and the West for having conspired the Asian financial crisis, and criticized the IMF. His rhetorical stance that blamed foreigners and his policy signals of restrictions on currency trading exacerbated the deteriorating situation in the Malaysian markets by panicking investors. He did not seem to be realistically dealing with the crisis, but was seen as being in a state of shock, anger and denial. In September 1997, Mahathir's government attempted to intervene directly in the Kuala Lumpur stock market, but the attempt backfired and reduced investors' confidence in the Malaysian government. Mahathir's policy stance was ideologically and politically motivated, rather than economically motivated. Ideologically, he distrusted foreign speculators, the West, and the IMF. Politically, by blaming foreigners he was able to mislead the Malaysian public, hide his government's policy mistakes prior to the crisis, and rally public support around his policy choices and actions. The Deputy Prime Minister Anwar's austerity measures were not acceptable for Mahathir, the UMNO and the UMNO clients. While Anwar was promoting IMF-style economic austerity measures, Mahathir continued his rhetoric that blamed speculators and the West for the crisis as well as criticized the IMF, and he pushed for *ad hoc* policy actions that fit his political goals and protected UMNO's clients. Neither taking an IMF-sponsored bailout package nor following its policy instructions was politically acceptable to Mahathir. If IMF-style policies were followed, Mahathir's big projects were going to be halted with the cuts in government spending, and UMNO's support coalition would be weakened. In addition, having the IMF as the rescuer of the Malaysian economy would have been an important rebuke to Mahathir's anti-IMF rhetoric and to *Mahathirism* in general. Different policy approaches of Mahathir and Anwar led to conflicting statements from the Malaysian government that further reduced investors' confidence in the government's dealing with the crisis and contributed to the depth of the crisis in Malaysia. Anwar acted according to his economic policy ideology and/or policy approach as well as his political calculations and ambitions, which were not fully compatible with those of Mahathir. Mahathir took policy actions according to his and the UMNO's political needs. Mahathir's policy choice became the Malaysian government's policy in a political process within the Malaysian context.

Having not been dependent on foreign loans like Thailand, Indonesia and Korea, the Malaysian government under Mahathir's leadership was able to muddle through without the IMF rescue package or without needing any drastic reforms to attract foreign capital. Instead, Mahathir established the National Economic Action Council, brought his loyal friend Daim Zainuddin back as its executive director, and bailed out mostly the UMNO-linked businesses. He dismissed his deputy Anwar, who seemingly had a different policy stance, and imposed capital controls one day before Anwar's dismissal. In the end, Mahathir's rhetoric and policy choices served him well politically and provided him with another election victory in 1999.

External factors and pressures and influences of external actors

Unlike the Malaysian government, the governments of Thailand, Indonesia and South Korea chose to take the IMF loan packages and followed its policy prescriptions with revisions and changes during the implementation process. There were probably various economic and non-economic factors that shaped these governments' policy choices, but they were also constrained by the huge amounts of short-term debt their banking and private sectors had. The external ties and obligations of these countries, in particular their need for external loans, significantly pressured those governments. In today's economic and financial affairs, depending on a country's external ties, obligations, commitments, interdependencies, various external (global and regional) developments, and events, state and non-state actors could have strong influences and exert pressures on governments' policy behaviors as well as impact market participants' behaviors. We can divide external pressures and influences on one country into two types. One type of external influence is somewhat specific to that country, due to its special links, obligations to the outside world, its location and specific relations with neighboring states. The other type of external pressure is exerted by global financial, economic, and political developments that impact the global financial and economic markets and the countries involved. Both types of external influences arguably impacted the developments in Mexico and Malaysia.

Increased U.S.-Mexico relations not only led to the NAFTA agreement, but also increased sensitivities of both sides to each country's domestic developments. For example, the NAFTA opposition in the U.S., in particular in the U.S. Congress, worried the Mexican officials and restrained them from making a devaluation decision during 1993 and 1994. The peso crisis was not only a concern for the Mexican officials, but it involved the Clinton administration closely in the process of addressing the crisis situation in Mexico. The peso crisis and the Clinton administration's rescue package initiatives led to new debates between the pros and cons of NAFTA in the U.S. and affected how the IMF and U.S.-sponsored rescue package and attached policy conditions for Mexico were shaped. The Zedillo administration, with the push of the U.S. and the IMF, took the necessary economic measures after the crisis.

Not only did the U.S. and the IMF affect the Mexican government's policy behavior, but also private foreign interest groups affected both the development of the crisis and the Mexican government's policy behavior during the crisis. The most significant example of such effects is the Weston Forum's pressures on the Mexican government to take economic policy measures that would benefit the Forum members. As Naím (1997) asserts, "foreign mutual funds mattered as much as the most powerful domestic institutions in determining Mexican economic policy. After the devaluation, again, investment decisions made in the world's financial centers and political decisions made in Washington and other capitals determined the nature of the crisis, its ramifications, and the response to it as much as or more than did any action by the Mexican government."[36]

In the Malaysian government's policy behavior, external interest groups played insignificant roles as compared to its domestic interest groups and other non-economic factors. However, Malaysia's location and similarities with other regional countries made the Asian financial crisis easily spread into Malaysia. The Asian financial crisis started outside Malaysia, in Thailand, and quickly spread to the other ASEAN countries with similar characteristics, at least according to investors' perceptions. Two types of regional non-economic factors impacted the development of the Asian financial crisis: non-economic factors that were specific to each of the crisis-affected countries, and non-economic factors that were widespread in the region, which included Malaysia as well. For example, moral-hazard problems, inadequate regulations and supervisions, and close links between government and business or private and public enterprises led to personal and political favoritism, patronage and rent-seeking activities, and implicit and explicit government guarantees that created an impression that investments were almost insured. Thus, these regional non-economic factors produced expansion of credit/loans for risky and unproductive investments, in particular to property and stock markets, and resulted in a fragile banking system mostly due to this excessive lending. Non-economic factors that were specific to each country affected mostly the developments in that country where they existed, but their effects reached beyond one country's borders via contagion. Thus, unstable and weak coalition governments, the political/parliamentary structure that was conducive for such governments in Thailand, uncertainty about the succession of Suharto in Indonesia, the intricate relations between government and *chaebol*(s) in South Korea, and weak government and bureaucracy in the Philippines all contributed to the development and spread of the Asian financial crisis. The non-economic factors that were specific to Malaysia further contributed to the development of the Asian financial crisis in Malaysia.

The impacts of global economic/financial and political contexts

During the last three decades, international capital stimulated by technological innovations, economic trends, and government policies has increasingly become mobile, and the size of international financial flows has grown to hundreds of billions of dollars a day. Financial crises of the 1990s made many analysts think that large and volatile international capital flows severely impacted the development of these crises, and constrained governments' policy options in a world of rapidly expanding international trade and financial flows. Hilley (2001) asserts that "the volatile fluctuations within the financial markets across the region by mid-1997 offered a stark illustration of how external forces could critically undermine domestic policy."[37]

During the postwar period, new economic policies, international economic cooperation and eight rounds of multilateral trade negotiations under the GATT, which led to the establishment of the WTO, decreased trade barriers considerably. Since the 1970s, removal of capital controls by leading economies and consequent freedom of capital movement, stimulated by novel technologies in transportation, computers and telecommunication, not only reduced the costs of international trading and investment, but also have greatly increased global financial flows. The end of the Cold War provided the necessary political conditions for increased integration of national capital markets and the creation of a global financial system. For example, the daily turnover of currency exchanges increased from $15 billion in 1973 to $1.2 trillion in 1995. In parallel, the equity and bond markets also grew and became more global.[38] In the meantime, as Naím (1997) points out, the power and significance of private international actors, as compared to international monetary institutions, has increased tremendously. "Between 1990 and 1994, the World Bank disbursed $84 billion to all developing countries. In the same period, private investors poured a net $660 billion into these countries."[39] These trends certainly impacted international and domestic economies. On the one hand, it became easier for capital-poor developing countries to borrow from international markets; on the other hand, national and international economies became more sensitive to volatile capital flows.[40] "In particular, the increased importance of speculative, short-term investments by financiers such as George Soros, by "hedge funds" in emerging markets, and by international banks has significantly increased the vulnerability of the international financial system and the world economy more generally; speculative funds amount to hundreds of billions of dollars."[41] Mahathir blamed such volatile and speculative international capital throughout the Asian financial crisis and justified his capital controls policy on this ground.[42] "In the past, the main international actors in the unfolding of a country's economic collapse were international commercial banks, the IMF, and the World Bank. Now, the priority of the finance minister of any country is to persuade money managers and other private institutional actors not to take their money out—and for good reasons," Naím asserts.[43] "Many economists and public officials believe that these short-term, speculative flows increasingly threaten the stability of the global economy and should therefore be regulated."[44]

Given these developments in the global financial markets, some analysts worried that these immense capital flows could easily overwhelm national economies, as they did the Italian and British economies in 1992 and many other economies in the late 1990s.[45] Susan Strange's several works (1986, 1996, 1998) and Peterson (1995) strongly argue that states' control over markets has increasingly diminished and that international capital mobility has transformed the world into one in which states have surrendered, "or retreated" to markets.[46] Similarly, Michie and Smith's (1999) edited book, *Global Instability: The Political Economy of World Economic Governance*, argues that national governments are increasingly at the mercy of global markets. Toussaint (1999) claims that the deregulation of capital markets implemented by the governments of main economic powers created a tyranny of the financial markets over the weaker developing countries. Some believed that the 1994-1995 Mexican peso crisis and the 1997-1998 Asian financial crisis were also mainly the result of these volatile global capital movements and speculative attacks.

Hilley (2001) disputes with the claims that the Asian financial crisis was due to homegrown causes such as Asian crony capitalism and argues that "the circumstances within which the cycle comes to a crisis point was also being determined by the increasingly complex gyrations of speculative capital and non-productive accumulation."[47] According to Winters (1999), the crises of the

1990s were "the results not only of government policies, but specifically of their interactions in an international environment dominated by private controllers of capital who are willing and able to relocate massive resources away from perceived danger in a very short time frame—though not necessarily willing to bring them back as quickly as they withdrew them."[48] Naím (1997) asserts that there is nothing new with imprudent economic policies leading to painful economic and social consequences. "What is new and was dramatically illustrated by the Mexican crisis is how unforgiving the international financial system has become to unsound economic policies and how quickly, how deeply, and how far the shock waves of a crash can be felt. This has more to do with the profound transformations of the international financial system in the past two decades than with Mexico's policy mistakes"[49]

Nonetheless, the impact of the global financial system on the national economies as well as on government policies is disputed. Gilpin (2001) rejects the idea that "economic and technological forces have eclipsed the nation-state and are creating a global world economy in which political boundaries and national governments are no longer important."[50] According to him, "although globalization had become the defining feature of the international economy at the beginning of the twenty-first century, the extent and significance of economic globalization have been greatly exaggerated and misunderstood in both public and professional discussions; globalization in fact is not nearly as extensive nor as sweeping in its consequences (negative or positive) as many contemporary observers believe. This is still a world where national policies and domestic economies are the principal determinants of economic affairs."[51] Frieden (1991) argues that "intentional capital mobility restricts but does not eliminate the possibility for national economic policies."[52] He adds that national governments have to be careful about their regulations if they do not want foreign capital to flow out or foreign capital to come in, due to globalization and integration of the capital markets. Milner and Keohane (1996) suggest that increased capital mobility has become a "structural characteristic of the international system, similar to anarchy."[53]

Of course, the discussion of globalization is not limited to global capital mobility and their impacts on the development of financial crises and governmental responses. A wide range of literature identifies various impacts of globalization, regional and global integration, interdependence, international institutions and regimes, and transnational relations on policy-making processes and governmental policy outcomes, in particular economic/financial policies.[54] It seems that how each country is affected by various external forces depends on its external links and interdependencies. Interdependence is a mutual dependence which "is translated into policymaking most directly when certain policies which a government might otherwise follow become prohibitively costly."[55] It applies to social and political as well as economic relations.

The examination of the Mexican and Malaysian cases pointed to the influence of global financial flows and sudden withdrawal of volatile capital, but their impacts were different across the Asian countries and the cases due to each country's different degrees of sensitivity and vulnerability,[56] and are mixed with various domestic and external, and economic and non-economic factors discussed earlier. A mixture or combination of domestic and external, and economic and non-economic factors brought the Mexican peso crisis and the Asian financial crises and also shaped the Mexican and Malaysian governments' policy behaviors. The examination of the cases and the relevant literature suggest that the kinds of economic and non-economic factors involved in the process and the extent that each factor exerted influence varies across countries and time.

Nonetheless, global financial developments in particular and globalization in general have changed the external context of the countries. As Milner and Keohane (1996) point out, "we can no longer understand politics within countries . . . without comprehending the nature of the linkages between national economics and the world economy, and changes in such linkages."[57] In the Milner and Keohane (1996) edited volume, *Internationalization and Domestic Politics*, authors Frieden and Rogowski and Garrett and Lange, and Frieden (1991) offer frameworks that guide how internationalization affects domestic economic preferences and therefore domestic politics. Such literature could be utilized in understanding the impact of external links and interdependencies on domestic political processes and policy outcomes.

Along with economic and financial globalization, global political context could affect governments' economic policies. Mancur Olson (1993) argues that the political and security interests of states play the central role in the creation of international economy, even though private economic interests, especially those of powerful business groups, also obviously play an important role.[58] In fact, for realists in IR theory, security and political interests of states are at the top of their foreign policy agenda, and their foreign economic relations serve this agenda. The United States' efforts to rebuild Western European economies and forge a powerful anti-Soviet alliance through the Marshall Plan, and subsequent economic aids to U.S. allies at the beginning of the Cold War, support this argument. "In effect, the United States used its political, economic, and other resources to create an open world economy embracing its political allies and much of the Third World."[59] One of Gourevitch's (1986) "explanatory approaches" for explaining governments' economic policy behaviors is the international system approach, which "stresses the impact of war, security issues, military procurement, and other elements of the state system in shaping economic policy."[60] His explanatory approach refers to Kenneth Waltz (1979)'s "third image," i.e. that the international system has a strong influence on behaviors that comprise the domestic system. However, impacts of external factors on governmental policies, especially in regards to economic and financial issues, are not limited to that of the international system. In addition, the impact of the international system on the policy choices of countries is much more complex than realist and neo-realist explanations, as Jervis (1997) expounds.[61]

As Gilpin (2001) asserts, "the ways in which the world economy functions are determined by both markets and the policies of nation-states, especially those of powerful states; markets and economic forces alone cannot account for the structure and functioning of the global economy. The interactions of the political ambitions and rivalries of states, including their cooperative efforts, create the framework of political relations within which markets and economic forces operate."[62] Nonetheless, "with the end of the Cold War, military interests have tended to become less influential."[63] International economic ideologies also affect the policy makers in each country, as discussed earlier. According to Horowitz and Heo (2001), "in the 1980s and 1990s, the international trends have been toward increasing economic openness, as well as toward increasing ideological confidence in the superior performance of more open economies."[64]

Examining the Analytical Framework II: Cause and Effect Relations within Contexts

The preceding discussion is helpful in terms of what kinds of non-economic factors might play important roles along with economic ones when searching for answers to the questions of how financial crises develop and how governments shape their response policies. The analytical framework outlined the possible interrelationship of economic and non-economic factors. Although the framework can guide us in terms what kinds of non-economic factors interplay with economic factors and possible directions of causality, it is not clear about the dynamics of cause and effect relations among multiple non-economic and economic factors and their interplay. This section further clarifies the nature and dynamics of the causal mechanism and discusses what caused the differences between the cases.

Contexts and Dynamics of the Causal Mechanism in the Framework

Given the previous discussion, let us think about how a financial crisis might develop from stage one on the framework to stage two and stage three and how a government might behave during these periods. We can speculate about the structural and dynamic elements of the framework, and what leads to immediate decision making and governmental behaviors.

Structural and dynamic elements of the framework. Some elements of the domestic and external contexts are structural and they maintain a certain degree of stability and continuity, and some elements are dynamic and change within the interaction process as they progress. For example, within a domestic context, certain country characteristics, such as the political system and its components, state structure, its institutions and legal framework, ruling party, its position and various relationships within the political system, and ideological and political characteristics of political leadership, are "structural" elements with a certain degree of continuity. On the other hand, societal events and developments, economic developments, economic policy makers' policy behaviors as well as market participants' behaviors within the interaction process are dynamic elements of the framework which could change as quickly as things develop. Similarly, a country's external locations, external ties and relationships, and global financial environment has a certain degree of stability as things develop from stage one to stage two and three on the framework. However, external political and economic developments, policy behaviors of external actors and external market participants' behaviors are more dynamic.

Nonetheless, all of the structural and dynamic elements are interconnected within the domestic and external contexts of countries. They affect the development of financial crises from stage one to stage two and three by affecting governmental decision makers' policy behaviors and market participants' behaviors within an interaction process and their behaviors deteriorate or improve the economic indicators. Market participants behave according to their perceived or actual interests and in order to protect their interests from perceived or actual risks that economic and non-economic, particularly political developments, might bring. Governmental policymakers are influenced by various domestic and external and economic and non-economic pressures, as well as the political, institutional and societal contexts in which they operate. Impacts of all of these pressures and influences on policy outcomes are mediated by political processes, ideological and psychological factors associated with policymakers as well as policymakers' perceived or actual political ambitions and interests.

An interaction process among societal, institutional, and political actors, as well as market participants and various external actors—which are all at different degrees and in different ways affected by the structural and dynamic elements of domestic and external contexts—moves the interaction process from stage one to stage two and three. Within this interaction process, we cannot explain the actors' behaviors only with their preferences and power, but we need to consider how they are positioned within a country's domestic and external environments. Within an environment in which various structural and dynamic elements are interconnected, actors' behaviors and their relationships with each other are strongly influenced by interactions at other places and at earlier periods of time. Depending on the density of interconnectedness, a change in one element could constrain, require, or prohibit other elements in a context and affect how actors are positioned within. Therefore, we cannot understand outcomes by adding together various elements of domestic and external contexts and actors' relations since in an interconnected environment a change could create a wide range of effects and cause unintended results. Interconnectedness also could make many effects indirect and delayed. Moreover, actors' relations are often not bilaterally determined, but determined by each one's relations with others in such an interconnected environment. Moreover, the effect of one action or factor may depend on what other factors are present, and what kinds of relations they have among them.[65]

Since the effect of one variable may depend on the state of other variables, the result of an action cannot be predicted without looking at the process of interactions. Understanding the role of one element or action in bringing financial crises and shaping governmental policy responses requires us to understand the interaction process in order of the sequence of events, developments, and behaviors. Policymakers' behaviors as well as market participants' behaviors are determined interactively. Actions of actors change the environment in which they operate, and identical but later actions may not produce the same results. An actor's behavior may yield different results in a different time and place, not necessarily due to changes in the actor's motivations and behaviors, but because of changes in the contexts as well as in the behaviors of other interacting actors.[66] As a result, the impact of a non-economic factor, governmental policy, or an actor's behavior depends on other developments, events, policies and behaviors of other actors involved in the interaction process.

Conjectural Causation within Domestic and External Contexts

The preceding discussion suggests that, to a certain extent, cause and effect relations in each country or in each different context is conjectural, i.e. causal patterns vary according to contexts and they need to be figured out separately in each context. Of course, this is not to deny similarities along with differences across the cases. It might be possible to observe similar political or non-economic factors across similar cases, as Leblang and Bernhard's several works did. However, it is hard to know whether Mexico's economic and non-economic developments would lead to a crisis in different domestic and external contexts other than those of Mexico. To what extent would other governments behave the way that the Mexican government behaved during the peso crisis? We can ask similar questions in regards to the Malaysian case as well. In order to uncover cause and effect relations we need to trace the interaction process within contexts/environments, in which various initial conditions transform into financial crises and governmental policy outcomes.

In tracing the dynamic interaction process, we need to consider its domestic and external contexts/environment with their structural and dynamic elements, the attributes of actors involved in the interaction process as well as their positions and relationships within these contexts. Considering Sprouts' (1965) "ecological triad" we need to take into account actors, their environment and their relationship with their environments. The interaction process transforms the initial conditions into the next and following situations during the development of a financial crisis, the menu available to actors at each stage of the process changes and the actors adapt to these changes. Multiple non-economic factors as parts and constituents of these contexts interplay with economic factors and affect actors' behaviors as well as their relationships with the elements of contexts. Who the actors are in the process, what their attributes and capabilities are, the characteristics of political, societal, institutional as well as external contexts in which they interact, and how they are positioned and linked to domestic and international contexts do matter in the development of financial crises and making of governmental policy responses. Therefore, different interaction processes involving different actors, different contexts, and different behaviors may lead to different outcomes across time and countries.

Understanding the Differences between the Cases and across Countries

What caused the differences between the cases? Why was the Mexican government's policy response not possible in Malaysia, and the Malaysian government's policy behavior not possible in Mexico and in other countries that were affected by the Asian financial crisis? Of course differences between the economic variables of Mexico and those of Malaysia and between the Mexican peso crisis and the Asian financial crisis might partially account for the differences between these two cases.[67] However, as the previous chapters have argued and evidenced, we cannot explain all of the differences between the cases with economic variables. This section argues that the following non-economic differences among countries also generate different interaction processes that involve different non-economic and economic factors in bringing financial crises and shaping governmental response policies. (1) Non-economic factors involved in the interaction process could vary across countries as they varied between Mexico and Malaysia. (2) Domestic and external contexts of countries in which non-economic factors interact with economic factors are different in each country to a certain extent. Domestic and external contexts of each country are shaped by historical developments surrounding a country and are somewhat unique to each country. Therefore, it is hard to isolate non-economic factors and their interplay with economic ones from their contexts as well as their historical roots. (3) The degree to which non-economic factors affect economic developments and the way they intermix could differ from one country to another. (4) Each country's sensitivity and vulnerability to external events, developments, and pressures are different due to their different degrees of linkages, obligations and interdependencies. Such differences could lead to differences in the development of financial crises and governmental policy outcomes, as they did across the Mexican and Malaysian cases.

The uprising in Chiapas, the political assassinations, Mexico's political and legal institutions, and the political ambitions of political leaders emerged and interacted with economic factors within the Mexican context. Non-economic political, societal/cultural, and legal/institutional factors along with economic factors and multiple external factors consciously or unconsciously led to actions taken or not taken by the Mexican decision-makers and impacted market participants' behaviors. The impacts of external factors, such as the sharp rise in U.S. interest rates and the decisions of external actors as a reaction to the developments in Mexico or developments outside Mexico, converged with the impacts of domestic factors. In Malaysia, the UMNO, the ethnic division, the coalition of three ethnic parties, the BN *(Barisan Nasional), Mahathirism* and other non-economic factors are all products and parts of Malaysian political, societal and institutional/legal contexts and they impacted the developments in Malaysia the way they did within these contexts.

Domestic versus external factors. Domestic factors played the most significant roles in bringing the Mexican peso crisis and a mix of domestic and external factors played the most significant roles in bringing the Asian financial crisis into Malaysia. However, the Mexican government was more responsive to external pressures when shaping its policies than the Malaysian government was. It seems that domestic factors played the most significant roles in shaping the Malaysian government's response policies, whereas external factors played the most significant roles in shaping the Mexican government's response policies. The answer to the questions of how and why each country's policymakers chose the response policies they did lies in the differences between the two countries in terms of (1) non-economic and economic factors involved in the interaction process within each country's domestic and external contexts; (2) how each government managed the political balancing of domestic versus external concerns, influences, and pressures. Also such differences between Malaysia and the regional crisis-affected countries led to a distinctly different policy response in Malaysia from the responses of Malaysia's regional neighbors, for example, Indonesia and Thailand.

Governments' responsiveness to domestic versus external influences / pressures changes according to contextual differences of policymaking and the different degrees of perceptual and actual imperatives decision-makers have when shaping response policies due to different types of domestic and external ties/linkages. Mexico responded to its crisis in a regional and international environment with which it had much stronger ties than those of Malaysia. Malaysian external dependencies, obligations, commitments, and demands of external actors were not consequential enough to politically constrain PM Mahathir's policy choice. Therefore, Malaysian PM Mahathir prioritized accommodating the demands of Malaysia's domestic constituents, whereas the Mexican government responded first to demands of external actors, in particular the U.S. government and the IMF. In the Malaysian case, it seems that Mahathir's political interests as well as ideological standing had the largest impact on the Malaysian government's policy behavior within the Malaysian contexts. Foreign opposition to Mahathir's policies was, in fact, useful for him in stimulating internal support for his policies.

The literature that heavily emphasizes the impact of external factors on national economic and financial policies ignores domestic factors and the fact that decision-makers have to consider both domestic and external factors when choosing a policy. Some analysts from international studies and foreign policy fields stress that governments are influenced by both domestic and external influences in shaping their policies, and they balance contradictory internal versus external pressures. For example, Putnam's (1988) article, "Diplomacy and Domestic Politics: The Logic of Two Level Games," points to the fact that governments have to consider domestic contexts when they are negotiating and reaching agreements with the outside world, and vice versa. Moreover, the IR literatures, pioneered by the works of Rosenau and Keohane & Nye, stress the impacts of intensifying internal-external or transnational linkages on the domestic and foreign policies of countries. There is also political economy literature, such as Nelson (1990) and Josselin (1997), that underlines impacts of both domestic and external, and economic and non-economic factors on governments' economic policies. These literatures could be utilized for understanding and explaining the political balancing of external versus domestic influences in different countries.

Concluding Highlights

Economic crisis models and explanations based on economic indicators are inadequate in explaining how financial crises develop and how governments respond to financial crises. Their inadequacies are largely due to their ignorance or downplay of the impacts of non-economic factors on the development of financial crises and governmental policy behaviors. Economic indicators are interdependent with various market participants' behaviors. Market participants' behaviors, however, are not only determined by economic factors, but also strongly affected by a plethora of expected and unexpected non-economic factors stemming from the domestic-political, societal and institutional, as well as external, contexts of countries. As Gilpin (2001) expounds, "markets are embedded in larger sociopolitical systems. . . ."[68] Without adequately taking the impacts of various non-economic factors into account, we cannot fully understand and explain either the development of financial crises or the governmental responses to them. In addition, economic policies that do not take the social, institutional, and political as well as external contexts of a country into account are likely to fail to generate the desired results. As Stiglitz (2002) rightly argues, the IMF's similar economic policy recommendations to every country based on the "Washington Consensus" policies often failed to give desired results due to their ignorance of the different social, institutional, and political contexts of different countries.

In order to explain how financial crises develop and how governmental policies are shaped, one needs to understand the various incentives and interests of market participants and governmental policymakers and the impacts of multiple non-economic factors along with economic trends. The incentives and interests of various market participants are pretty clear. They would like to make profits and protect their interests from the actual and perceptual, expected and potential risks. However, their economic/financial decisions are as much affected by non-economic factors and actual or potential governmental policy behaviors as by economic and financial developments. If market participants perceive risks to their economic/financial interests due to non-economic developments and factors, their actions could deteriorate otherwise sustainable economic indicators and lead to self-fulfilling financial crises. Causes of governmental actors' immediate policy behaviors are not that clear cut. Governmental actors have multiple agendas, and they would like to achieve multiple goals. In Tsebelis' (1990) terminology, they play "nested games," or a whole network of games. "What appears suboptimal from the perspective of only one game is in fact optimal when the whole network of games is considered."[69] Their immediate behavior depends on which "game" they prioritize (or each political actor prioritizes), and which goal they would like to achieve the most. Therefore, it is important to know the political interests and ambitions of political actors and the political, institutional, and societal contexts in which they act. In other words, we need to know which "games" each political actor is involved in, what goal each actor prioritizes, and what opportunities and constraints an actor is surrounded with, in order to understand the immediate policy behaviors of each political actor as well as the subsequent governmental responses to financial crises. Without understanding the political motives of governmental actors, we cannot answer the question that Naím (1997) asked: "How can such smart guys make such dumb mistakes?" in reference to the Mexican policymakers during the peso crisis.

Political leaders or governmental actors do not necessarily behave according to economic logic during a financial crisis, but follow a political logic, which might or might not be compatible with economic logic. Every government or political leadership, to varying degrees, tries to stay in power and maintain its support coalition. Therefore, governments struggle to survive and retain their power during financial crises as well, and they behave with political logic rather than economic logic. If possible, they choose economic/financial policies that would best serve their political interests, in order to stay in power and maintain their support coalition. However, this does not mean that they can always choose the policies that best serve their interests, even though the Malaysian PM Mahathir was able to do so, and the Mexican leadership did follow such policies, at least until the peso crisis occurred. Financial crises could narrow the policy options available to policymakers, and may even force governments to choose policies that are not compatible with their political interests, as for example the Indonesian government's experience during the Asian financial crisis of 1997-1998.

Governmental policy responses to financial crises are the results of an interaction process in which multiple actors and various non-economic and economic, external and domestic factors are involved. Even though a country's political leadership may try to choose economic/financial policies that would best serve its political interests, they may not succeed in doing so. The interaction process involves various domestic and external actors, events, and developments, and transforms initial conditions to the next and consequent situations within a country's domestic and external contexts, and the behaviors of governmental actors and market participants are determined within this interaction process. The sequence of events and developments are as important as what was involved in the interaction process in determining various actors' behaviors. Policymakers under the influences and pressures of multiple actors, and various economic and non-economic, domestic and external factors may end up choosing policies that are not compatible with their political interests. In addition, every government is to varying degrees subjected to pressures both by domestic economic and non-economic factors and actors, and by external factors and actors. By implication, governments whose countries are broadly and deeply linked externally, and are "vulnerable" and "sensitive" to these linkages, are likely to get themselves into domestic political trouble when trying to manage their financial crises and international interdependencies. On the contrary, governments that are relatively less "vulnerable" and "sensitive" to external linkages will have an easier going domestically as they try to manage pressures and shocks from the outside world.

How financial crises develop and how governments behave could vary across time and country due to differences among countries in terms of their domestic and external contexts as well as due to the economic and non-economic factors involved in the interaction process. As Gourevitch (1986) argues as well, the relationships among the various actors and factors are not constant; they change with changes in circumstances and time periods.[70] Therefore, it is hard to make across-time and country generalizations, even though some common patterns might be observed. As mentioned earlier, although there are a few studies that investigate the impacts of non-economic factors on market expectations and on governmental policies, there is still much that needs to be done. This inquiry has approached the topic broadly and the analytical framework it offers is comprehensive. It could serve not only to enhance our understanding of financial crises and governmental policy responses, but also may be utilized to guide further research and bridge economics literature with larger social science literatures.

It seems that political leaderships in semi-authoritarian regimes, such as those of Mexico and Malaysia, can control the policymaking agenda and process, and can impose their policy choices, unless the crisis situation dictates different policies due to the country's external dependencies and obligations, or external pressures and influences overwhelm their domestic political agendas. As argued, a political leadership's immediate policy behavior depends on which "game" they prioritize and what goal it wants to achieve. It is most likely that policymakers will try to choose policy options that satisfy their supporters and are compatible with their political interests. In authoritarian or semi-authoritarian countries, political leaders have a better chance of choosing such policies than those in democratic countries. In authoritarian countries, the leadership controls the state structure and dominates the political agenda and policymaking process, and the intermediate associations and opposition groups are usually weak. In such countries, political leadership with the support of selective interest groups can overcome any opposition and dictate its policy choices. If there is a split in political leadership, as was the case in Malaysia during the Asian financial crisis between Prime Minister Mahathir and the Deputy Prime Minister Anwar, the stronger actor usually wins, unless the interaction process, which involves expected and unexpected developments and various domestic and external actors, dictates something different. In these countries, since the intermediate associations and opposition is weak, they cannot challenge old policies, policymakers and their support coalition, as Gourevitch's (1986) research concludes for the democratic Western countries. As a result, not only differences between the external ties, obligations, and dependencies of countries, but also differences between political systems of countries could strongly affect how governments shape their response policies and respond to financial crises.

NOTES

1. Then Singapore's Senior Minister, from his October 1997 address to leading American businessmen at the Fortune 500 Forum in Boston. Quoted in Jeffrey A. Winters, "The Determinant of Financial Crisis in Asia," in *the Politics of the Asian Economic Crisis* (Ithaca & London: Cornell University Press, 1999), 87, and Winters quoted from Chowhury and Paul (1997).

2. Kaminsky, "Currency and Banking Crises: The Early Warnings of Distress," 6, 7; Krugman, "Introduction," 4.

3. Krugman, *Crises: The Next Generation?*, 8; Radelet and Sachs, "The Onset of the East Asian Financial Crisis," 108; also see R. Chang and A. Velasco, *Financial Fragility and the Exchange Rate Regime*, Working Paper (New York: New York University, C. V. Starr School of Business, 1998a), and R. Chang and A. Velasco, *Financial Crises in Emerging Markets: A Canonical Model*, Working Paper (New York: New York University, C. V. Starr School of Business, 1998b) for more information.

4. Kaminsky, "Currency and Banking Crises: The Early Warnings of Distress," 7; Krugman, *Crises: The Next Generation?*, 8, 14; Krugman,"Introduction," 5.

5. Calvo, "Balance of Payments Crises in Emerging Markets . . . .," 2.

6. Ibid., 72.

7. Shang-Jin Wei, *Negative Alchemy? Corruption and Composition of Capital Flows,* Technical Papers No.165 (Paris: OECD Development Center, October 2000), 26.

8. Jeffrey A. Frankel and Andrew K. Rose, "Currency Crashes in Emerging Markets: An Empirical Treatment," *Journal of International Economics* 41 (1996), 351, 364.

9. Eichengreen, Rose, and Wyplosz, "Exchange Market Mayhem: The Antecedents and Aftermath of Speculative Attacks," 1.

10. Gian Maria Milesi-Ferretti and Assaf Razin, "Current Account Reversals and Currency Crises: Empirical Regularities," in *Currency Crises* (Chicago & London: The University of Chicago Press, 2000), 318.

11. Sachs, Tornell, and Velasco, *Financial Crises in Emerging Markets: The Lessons From 1995,* 1.

12. Kaminsky, "Currency and Banking Crises: The Early Warnings of Distress," 4, 21.

13. Ibid., p. 4.

14. Eichengreen, Rose, and Wyplosz, "Exchange Market Mayhem: The Antecedents and Aftermath of Speculative Attacks," 23.

15. These types are: (1) macroeconomic policy-induced crisis, in the line of Krugman's 1979 model, or first generation models: A balance of payment crisis arises when domestic credit expansion is inconsistent with the pegged exchange rate. (2) Financial panic, following the Diamond-Dybvig (1983) model of a bank run: A panic is an adverse equilibrium outcome in the case of multiple equilibria in the financial markets, "in which short-term creditors suddenly withdraw their loans from a solvent borrower." (108). (3) Bubble collapse, modeled by Blanchard and Watson (1982): A stochastic financial bubble that occurred due to speculators' purchase of a financial asset at a price above its basic value with an expectation of a subsequent capital gain; grows for a while and then collapses, not totally unexpectedly. (4) A moral hazard crisis, following Akerlof and Romer (1994), occurs when banks borrow funds excessively on the basis of implicit or explicit public guarantees of bank liabilities. (5) Sachs' (1995) disorderly workout, which "occurs when an illiquid or insolvent borrower provokes a creditor grab race and a forced

liquidation even though the borrower is worth more as an ongoing enterprise. . . . occurs especially when markets operate without the benefit of creditor coordination via bankruptcy law." See Radelet and Sachs, "The Onset of the East Asian Financial Crisis," 109.

16. In the case of a macroeconomic policy-induced crisis, governments should reorient their macroeconomic policies, make adjustments and go to budgetary reduction. In the case of financial panic, governments need a lender of last resort, whereas in the case of bubble-collapse, governments should not do anything that would delay the bursting of the bubble, to not to cause a deeper crisis later. In the case of a moral hazard crisis, governments should stop state guarantees, which prolong the misallocation of resources. In the case of a disorderly workout, governments should provide a framework for an orderly workout. See Radelet and Sachs, "The Onset of the East Asian Financial Crisis," 109-110.

17. Eichengreen, Rose, and Wyplosz, "Exchange Market Mayhem: The Antecedents and Aftermath of Speculative Attacks," 51.

18. Espinosa and Russell, "The Mexican Economic Crisis: Alternative Views," 21.

19. Barry Eichengreen and Andrew K. Rose, "The Empirics of Currecny and Banking Crises," Andrew K. Rose's web page, http://www.haas.berkeley.edu/~arose/RecRes.html (acccessed August 12, 2001), 12.

20. Lebhard and Bernhard (2000), p.320.

21. Peter Gourevitch, *Politics in Hard Times: Comparative Responses to International Economic Crisis* (Ithaca and London: Cornell University Press, 1986), 10.

22. Shale Horowitz and Uk Heo, eds., *The Political Economy of International Financial Crisis: Interest Groups, Ideologies, and Institutions* (New York & Oxford: Rowman & Littlefield Publishers, Inc., 2001), 4.

23. Ibid., p. 5.

24. Gourevitch, *Politics in Hard Times . . .* , 55.

25. See Ibid., 60.

26. Horowitz and Heo, eds., *The Political Economy of International Financial Crisis,* 7.

27. Gourevitch, *Politics in Hard Times . . .* , 19-20, 21, 221-29.

28. Ibid., 61.

29. Horowitz and Heo, eds., *The Political Economy of International Financial Crisis,* 7.

30. Ibid., p.15.

31. Gourevitch, *Politics in Hard Times . . .* , 21, 221-229.

32. Weintraub, *Financial Decision-Making in Mexico: To Bet a Nation,* 168.

33. Weintraub, *Financial Decision-Making in Mexico: To Bet a Nation,* 162, 167-170; Edwards, "Bad Luck or Bad Policies? An Economic Analysis of the Crisis," 97.

34. See Gourevitch, *Politics in Hard Times . . .* , 62.

35. See Dombrowski, "Haute Finance and High Theory: Recent Scholarship on Global Financial Relations,"18 for a brief review of this kind of literature.

36. Naím, "Mexico's Larger Story," 296.

37. Hilley, *Malaysia: Mahathirism, Hegemony and the New Opposition,* 65.

38. Robert Gilpin, *Global Political Economy: Understanding the International Economic Order* (Princeton and Oxford: Princeton University Press, 2001), 21, 261.

39. Naím, "Mexico's Larger Story," 304.

40. Gilpin, *Global Political Economy: Understanding the International Economic Order,* 261.

41. Ibid., 263.

42. Mohamad, "Currency Controls the Best Way Out," 10. Contrary to Mahathir's rhetoric, Barry Eichengreen argued in a report prepared for the IMF that "while hedge funds are large in absolute terms, they are dwarfed by other institutional investors (banks, pension funds, and mutual funds), some of whom engage in the same activities as hedge funds. . . . Hedge funds did have large positions against the Thai baht in mid-1997, but so did other investors, and most hedge funds were relatively late to take those positions. . . ." See *FT Asia Intelligence Wire* (Bernama the Malaysian National News Agency), April 17, 1998.

43. Naím, "Mexico's Larger Story," 304.

44. Gilpin, *Global Political Economy: Understanding the International Economic Order*, 263.

45. Ibid., 36.

46. See Dombrowski, "Haute Finance and High Theory: Recent Scholarship on Global Financial Relations," for a review of similar arguments.

47. Hilley, *Malaysia: Mahathirism, Hegemony and the New Opposition*, 73.

48. Winters, "The Determinant of Financial Crisis in Asia," 88.

49. Naím, "Mexico's Larger Story," 303.

50. Gilpin, *Global Political Economy: Understanding the International Economic Order*, 21.

51. Ibid., 3.

52. Jeffry A. Frieden, "Invested Interests: The Politics of National Economic Policies in a World of Global Finance," *International Organization* 45, Issue 5 (August 1991), 426.

53. Milne and Mauzy, *Malaysian Politics under Mahathir*, 257.

54. See Dombrowski, "Haute Finance and High Theory: Recent Scholarship on Global Financial Relations," 5-22 for a broader review of literature in regards to global financial affairs.

55. Robert O. Keohane and Joseph S. Nye, "Transnational Relations and World Politics: An Introduction," *International Organization* XXV, No. 3 (Summer 1971), 335.

56. Concepts of sensitivity and vulnerability are important for understanding the impacts of interdependence on governments or various actors. Sensitivity refers to the "degree of responsiveness within a policy framework—how quickly do changes in one country bring costly changes in another, and how great are the costly effects? . . . Sensitivity interdependence created by interactions within a framework of policies [which are assumed to remain] unchanged [due to] the difficulty in formulating new policies within a short time [or] a commitment to a certain pattern of domestic and international rules." The vulnerability dimension of interdependence is about "the relative availability and costliness of the alternative that various actors face. . . . [It] can be defined as an actor's liability to suffer costs imposed by external events even after policies have been altered. Since it is usually difficult to change policies quickly, immediate effects of external changes generally reflect sensitivity dependence. Vulnerability dependence can be measured by the costliness of making effective adjustments to a changed environment over a period of time." Robert O. Keohane and Joseph S. Nye, *Power and Interdependence.* 2nd ed. (New York and London: Harper Collins Publishers, 1989), 12-13.

57. Milne and Mauzy, *Malaysian Politics under Mahathir*, 3.

58. Gilpin, *Global Political Economy: Understanding the International Economic Order*, 42.

59. Ibid., p.43.

60. Gourevitch, *Politics in Hard Times . . . ,* 63.

61. See Robert Jervis, *System Effects: Complexity in Political and Social Life* (Princeton: Princeton University Press, 1997).

62. Gilpin, *Global Political Economy: Understanding the International Economic Order*, 23.

63. Horowitz and Heo, eds., *The Political Economy of International Financial Crisis*, 7-8.

64. Ibid., p. 8.

65. These ideas are inspired by Jervis, *System Effects: Complexity in Political and Social Life*. You may see pp. 5-9, 17, 23, 26, 32-35 in his book for similar arguments. Although Jervis arguments apply to the interaction process that this section discusses, a country's domestic and external contexts, in which the interaction takes place, may not be characterized as systems since they are not only composed of units, but also characteristics, events, and developments.

66. See Jervis, *System Effects: Complexity in Political and Social Life*, 40, 55, 73, 77, 91 for similar arguments.

67. The Mexican and the Malaysian government responded to a different financial crisis, with different policy tools and outcomes. As Buiter, Corsetti, and Pesenti (1998) puts it, the Mexican Peso Crisis of 1994-1995 and the Asian Financial Crisis of 1997-98 are different in their dynamics and underlying causes, yet are alike in terms of their rapid and "contagious" developments. See Willem H. Buiter, Gancarlo M. Corsetti, and Paolo A. Pesenti, *Interpreting the ERM Crisis: Country-Specific and Systemic Issues* (Princeton, N.J.: International Finance Section, Dept. of Economics, Princeton University, 1998), 53. Similarly, Bhalla (2001) argues that the Mexican Peso crisis and the Asian financial crises were similar in terms of their immediate economic triggers, which included sizeable current account deficits, overvalued exchange rates, deficiencies in rescheduling short-term debts, speculative attacks and capital flight. The underlying economic causes of these crises differed, however. Capital flows led to a consumption surge in Mexico, whereas they went to property investments, causing a bubble in property prices. Asian countries, in particular Malaysia, had huge internal debts along with external debts, and only 21.6 percent of Mexico's debt was internal. In the aftermath of the peso crisis, some self-correcting mechanisms operated, such as a 40 percent upsurge in its exports after the devaluation. In the aftermath of the Asian financial crisis no export surge occurred, according to Bhalla (2001). See A.S. Bhalla, *Market or Government Failures? An Asian Perspective* (New York, NY: Palgrave, 2001), 69-73. Underlying non-economic causes of these crises and the Mexican and Malaysian governments' policy responses also had similarities and differences.

68. Gilpin, *Global Political Economy: Understanding the International Economic Order*, 3.

69. George Tsebelis, *Nested Games: Rational Choice in Comparative Politics* (Berkeley, Los Angeles, Oxford: University of California Press, 1990), 7.

70. Gourevitch, *Politics in Hard Times . . .* , 66.

APPENDIX A: MEXICO'S HISTORICAL BACKGROUND

Until its independence in 1821, Mexico was a Spanish colony that provided the Crown of Spain with gold, silver and other valuable resources. Before the Spanish colonization that took place between 1519 and 1521, Mexican territory was inhabited by numerous Indian civilizations, two of which were the Maya and Aztec civilizations. Throughout the centuries, the proportion of the Indian population who identified themselves as Indian has been reduced, due to attrition, intermarriage[1] and Spain's cultural penetration into Indian communities.[2] In New Spain (Mexico), the process of "racial mixing," *mestizaje,* was not only ethnic but also intensely cultural. It was somewhat unique to Mexico. According to historian Enrique Krauze,[3] fundamental characteristics of Mexican culture and its basic religious, ethical and intellectual values were formed with a mixture of Spanish and Indian elements and as a multicultural Mexican mosaic of customs and traditions. Mexican society, maybe due to its cultural mixture as well as the strong impact of the Roman Catholic Church,[4] had been resistant to the political and intellectual currents of the European Enlightenment.[5]

Mexico won its independence in 1821 through the War of Independence (1810-1821). Although Mexico's independence symbolized the Mexican people's freedom from foreign domination, the establishment of a Mexican empire in 1822 protected colonial era privileges of the Spanish elite, military and clergy, rather than promoting indigenous peoples' rights. For the first fifty years of its independence, Mexican society lived through economic stagnation and political displacement. Industrial infrastructure was insignificant, and politics were not stable. Forty-five administrations came and went in this period.[6] Mexican independence was recognized by European states as well as the United States, but its sovereignty was frequently violated. Mexico lost over half of its territory to the United States through the United States annexation of Texas in 1845 and the Mexican-American War of 1846-1848.[7] Mexico's territorial losses and its increasing economic dependence on the U.S. economy through the nineteenth and twentieth centuries generated a Mexican nationalism with an anti-American tone.[8]

Although Mexico experienced a somewhat decentralized form of government during this first fifty year period, authoritarian qualities inherited from the colonial period eventually were to dominate Mexican politics.[9] Mexican history marked another period with Porfirio Díaz's dictatorship, known as *Porfiriato* (1875-1911). On the positive side, Díaz's dictatorship brought order and stability to Mexico. During his rule, considerable industrial development was achieved based on the export of primary commodities largely in the hands of foreign firms. However, the majority of the population did not benefit much from this economic development, and they were excluded from political participation. The foreign firms and about 250 elite families, who had access to the presidential office, controlled nearly 80 percent of the national territory, and they, along with the dictator and his family, were the beneficiaries of the economic growth. This "unfair" political and economic system generated a series of grievances among workers and peasants, and incited the "first great social revolution of the twentieth century" in 1910.[10] The revolution had multiple actors with different goals. Francisco Madero represented the political reformers and social conservatives. Emiliano Zapata led a peasant army demanding agrarian reform, and Pancho Villa led an army of jobless workers, small landowners, and people who were seeking steady employment. Venustiano Carranza and Alvaro Obregón were constitutionalist. As a result, the revolution was followed by a civil war, which lasted until 1919. By the end of the revolutionary decade, Zapata and Villa, who represented the most popular demands, were assassinated.[11]

Nonetheless, the revolution and the subsequent civil war gave birth to the contemporary Mexican state. A "progressive constitution" was formulated in 1917, replacing the constitution of 1857.[12] The early 1920s witnessed political assassinations, a Catholic counterrevolution, and animosity from foreign firms and their governments. Most of these challenges and political instabilities were resolved in 1929 with the leadership of Plutarco Elías Calles (1929-1934), who created a new political body, the National Revolutionary Party, PNR,[13] which later became the PMR,[14] and was the precursor of today's Institutional Revolutionary Party, PRI.[15] Calles was able to bring competing interests under the PNR and to establish a set of formalized rules to govern the political game. The PNR was pragmatically designed to play the role of a broker among different segments of the revolutionary elite and to constrain the nature of opposing demands. These initial legal, institutional, and political developments have shaped Mexican political life up until today. The political system has been based on massive concentration of power in the presidency with a prohibition of reelection for presidents. Presidents through the bureaucratic apparatus have had dominance over both the state and the party, and the state-party network has dominated the society.[16]

During the period of Porfirio Diaz (1876-1911), economic policies, which were made by Diaz himself and a small circle of technocratic advisers, benefited the small number of elite families and foreign firms the most. The Mexican revolution represented a coalition of interest groups and produced an ideology that held the government responsible for social justice. Influenced by the revolutionary ideology, Mexico's political economy evolved toward a corporatist system of interest representation. Under the corporatist system, individuals and societal interest groups have been expected to relate themselves to the state through an institutionalized structure that is recognized by the state. The ruling political party, the PRI, has had three sectors. One sector represented peasants, another sector represented labor, and the third sector contained professional organizations of government employees, small merchants, and private landowners.[17] The peasants and the working classes started to be represented in the PRI and the state during the *sexenio*—six years of presidency—of Lázaro Cárdenas (1934-1940). According to Centeno (1997), the inclusion of the peasants and the working classes into this corporatist apparatus was not necessarily to assure the interests of lower classes, but to prevent any independent challenge to the regime. Nonetheless, an agrarian reform was achieved; a system of communal landholdings, known as *ejidos*, was created, labor rights were improved, and the oil industry was nationalized during Cárdenas' *sexenio*. Later, Cárdenas' successors, Manuel Ávila Camacho (1940-1946) and Miguel Alemán (1946-1952) informally institutionalized an implicit alliance between state and private capital as well.[18] According to Camp (1999), the Mexican state through its corporatist structure has been controlling and constraining the scope of its citizens' demands on the government, mobilizing electoral support for the ruling party/regime, and distributing jobs and other material rewards to select individuals and groups.[19]

Although under the Mexican corporatist system each interest group has its own representation, in reality, most interest representation had been taking place within the upper level of government bureaucracy, and consequential policies were initiated and shaped within the inner circle of presidential advisers before they were announced to the public. Therefore, the groups formally incorporated in the party structure have not necessarily been the most effective in protecting their interests. Some groups that are not formally represented within the party, in particular businesses, have had a bigger impact than the groups incorporated with the party.[20] Although foreign and domestic entrepreneurs, the military, and the Catholic Church have not been formally represented in the PRI, they have had access to bureaucracy and governmental elite groups at the presidential and cabinet level. Moreover, business communities are organized into several "government-chartered" organizations. For example, they established the Businessmen's Coordinating Council (CCE) to represent the larger business community. In addition, about thirty-eight top businessmen created another organization, the semisecret Mexican Businessmen's Council (CMHN[21]) whose members have frequent access to both cabinet members and the president.[22] Over time, the Mexican corporatist system benefited the interests of the middle classes and the wealthy the most, even though it was supposed to protect the interests of all groups formally associated with the system.

Maxfield (1990) argues that Mexican economic policies from the revolution to the 1982 crisis have been shaped by the struggle between "two competing policy alliances"— on the one side, a coalition, that she calls "the Cardenas coalition," of state-organized labor and peasant groups and the government officials favoring their interests; and on the other side, the "bankers' alliance" of private bankers, large scale traders and industrialists, and public sector monetary authorities. She adds, "the bankers' alliance dominated the government in the 1920s and early 1930s, from the mid-1950s to 1970, and after 1982. Its periods of dominance coincided with years of heavy Mexican reliance on foreign credits."[23]

On paper, Mexico's political system looks like that of the United States. It is a federal and presidential system with three autonomous branches—executive, legislative and judicial. Unlike the system in the United States, however, Mexican presidents have dominated the legislative and judicial branches in Mexico due to their constitutionally and informally recognized powers, at least until the mid-1990s. In fact, Mexico's political system was highly authoritarian with a rigidly hierarchical government and party apparatuses. The PRI dominated both houses of the federal legislature until the mid-1990s. It had been governing unchallenged.[24] Although many opposition parties were established, their activities were highly constrained. Only the National Action Party, PAN[25] was tolerated to a certain extent as an opposition party. It had about 15 percent of votes in presidential elections and rarely won control of a municipality prior to the 1980s.[26]

Nonetheless, the Mexican system has been politically stable from the late 1920s to the early 1990s. Unlike most other Latin American countries, the Mexican state appeared to have solved the problems of succession, governmental autonomy, and achieved mass legitimacy.[27] "The perfect dictatorship,"[28] as Cothran (1994) calls the Mexican regime, owes its stability to the institutionalization of the regime, its effectiveness in achieving economic growth, its adaptability to demands from its society, elite unity, and its willingness to use coercion. Political stability in Mexico provided the country with a macroeconomic context that was conducive for economic growth. Its location next to the U.S. also indirectly supported the Mexican regime by providing economic relief in the form of investment and emigration.[29]

However, the authoritarian, single party-controlled corporatist structure gave privileges to many elements of the party, and corruption was tremendously widespread.[30] There has been a chain of patron-client relations within the corporatist structure of the Mexican political system. Patrons, who have a higher political status, have provided clients, who have a lower political status, with protection, support in clients' political struggles with their rivals, and chances for their upward political or economic mobility. In return, clients have given their loyalty, respect, and some useful services such as voter mobilization and political control. Neither do patrons limit themselves to a certain client, nor do clients invest all their hopes in a single patron. Every new president, as the "supreme patron," had his own clientage structure that replaced that of the previous president.[31] Corruption has been widespread along with the patron-client relations at every level of the governmental pyramid. Strong government intervention, partly stemming from the ISI development strategy between the 1940s to the 1980s, ranging from regulations, subsidies, and licensing, gave bureaucrats a broad base of power in dealing with businesses, which has been conducive to corrupt dealings. The early 1980s witnessed a series of public investigations and scandals centering around once-powerful figures, leaders of national trade unions, state governors, and even former presidents, some of them for their relations with the huge state-owned oil monopoly, PEMEX (Mexican Petroleum).[32] Raúl Salinas, a senior official of CONASUPO,[33] an agency that controlled much food distribution, and the brother of (next) president Carlos Salinas, was charged with illegal enrichment.[34]

In the late 1980s, the political legitimacy of the regime was historically low, mostly due to economic decline and corruption. The support of significant segments of the middle class was lost. The government's limitations in dealing with the earthquake of September 17, 1986, further damaged its prestige. The failures of the government gave rise to grassroots organizational efforts and a number of independent movements. The economic decline and later market-oriented economic reforms made many interest groups question their positions within the corporatist structure and some interest group organizations underwent internal changes. In the meantime, the ruling elite were divided, and the split within the PRI built up a democratic current. The opposition parties grew stronger.[35]

By 1988, the PRI's hegemony was crumbling. The economic decline and declining popular support weakened the party and its corporatist system. As the PRI was not able to meet the demands of corporatist sectors, it lost representatives within its bases, and was plagued by internal fractionalism.[36] As a result, the selection of a presidential candidate was very important for the PRI during the July 6, 1988 presidential elections. After a plethora of disputes and speculations, Carlos Salinas de Gortari, the Minister of Programming and Budget for president de la Madrid's administration, was agreed upon to be the candidate. However, leading labor leaders, in particular Fidel Velázquez of the Mexican Workers Confederation (CTM), disliked him and it seemed that there was little real support for Salinas. The Mexican private sector was mostly happy with his candidacy, but their support partly went to the opposition party, PAN.[37] In the elections, the PRI had its worst performance, and won the elections with barely over 50 percent of the vote. By official count, the PAN's presidential candidate, Clouthier,[38] received 17%, and Cárdenas[39] obtained 32% of the votes cast.[40] The opposition parties objected to the election results, accusing government election officials of massive fraud. The July 6, 1988 elections were a political earthquake in Mexico. On July 7, 1988, Salinas, before television cameras, said that "the era of the virtual one-party system has ended." The PRI's control over the Congress was weakened.[41]

Salinas was inaugurated on December 1, 1988. He was aware of the declining legitimacy of the regime that Mexico had since 1920. He "placed the burden of legitimizing the political system on the institution of the presidency itself."[42] He was "determined to enter the presidency with a bold program for change that would revive the popularity of the regime."[43] He started with the economy. In the early 1990s, Salinas was regarded as the Gorbachev of Mexico as he pushed for reform and change, but his reforms remained within the domain of the Mexican economy and did not include much significant political reform. Until mid-1994, Salinas' neoliberal economic reforms seemed to be very successful and were continuously praised by the media, financial experts, academics and international financial institutions, specifically the IMF and the World Bank.[44] These successes in the economic front erased the misgivings about the legitimacy of Salinas' election in 1988, and provided Salinas and the PRI with an election victory in the nationwide congressional elections in 1991. Although Mexico's economic growth slowed down in 1993 and in 1994, Salinas' popularity was high, and the political stability of the regime no longer seemed fragile until the devaluation of the Mexican peso on December 20, 1994.

NOTES

1. In particular, early Spanish settlers had Indian mistresses and wives due to the initial absence of Spanish women. See Cornelius and Craig, *The Mexican Political System in Transition*, 5, 6.

2. Camp, *Politics in Mexico*, 22; Cornelius and Craig, *The Mexican Political System in Transition*, 5, 6; and George W. Grayson, *A Guide to the 1994 Mexican Presidential Election* (Washington, DC: The Center for Strategic and International Studies, 1994), xi.

3. Enrique Krauze, *Mexico: Biography of Power: A History of Modern Mexico, 1810-1996* (New York and London: Harper Collins Publishers, 1997), xiii.

4. The Catholic Church has been one of the strongest colonial institutions, which continued to influence Mexican society and the State for centuries. See Cornelius and Craig, *The Mexican Political System in Transition*, 5, 6.

5. Krauze, *Mexico: Biography of Power: A History of Modern Mexico, 1810-1996*, xiv.

6. Julie A., Erfani, *The Paradox of the Mexican State: Rereading Sovereignty from Independence to NAFTA* (Boulder, London: Lynne Rienner Publishers, 1995), 2, 3; and Centeno, *Democracy within Reason*, 5.

7. Mexico's territorial losses include Texas, California, Nevada, and Utah, most of New Mexico and Arizona, and part of Colorado and Wyoming. See Centeno, *Democracy within Reason*, 5, 6; Cornelius and Craig, *The Mexican Political System in Transition*, 17, 18.

8. Camp, *Politics in Mexico*, 47.

9. Ibid., p.47.

10. Centeno, *Democracy within Reason*, 6.

11. Centeno, *Democracy within Reason*, 6; Cornelius and Craig, *The Mexican Political System in Transition*, 9.

12. Erfani, *The Paradox of the Mexican State: Rereading Sovereignty from Independence to NAFTA*, 2; Cornelius and Craig, *The Mexican Political System in Transition*, 10.

13. *Partido Nacional Revolucionario.*

14. *Partido de la Mexicana Revolución.*

15. *Partido Revolucionario Institucional.*

16. Centeno, *Democracy within Reason*, 7-8; Morris, *Political Reformism in Mexico: An Overview of Contemporary Mexican Politics*, 17, 18.

17. Cornelius and Craig, *The Mexican Political System in Transition*, 55-56; Camp, *Politics in Mexico*, 129, 139; Pedro Aspe and Paul E. Sigmund, "Introduction," in *The Political Economy of Income Distribution in Mexico* (New York and London: Holmes & Meier Publishers, Inc., 1983), 4,5.

18. Centeno, *Democracy within Reason*, 7, 8.

19. Camp, *Politics in Mexico*,55, 151-152.

20. Ibid.

21. *Censejo Mexicano de Hombres de Negocios.*

22. Cornelius and Craig, *The Mexican Political System in Transition*, 55-56; Camp, *Politics in Mexico*, 139.

23. Sylvia Maxfield, *Governing Capital: International Finance and Mexican Politics* (Ithaca and London: Cornell University Press, 1990), 9.

24. Opposition parties won 240 seats out of the 500 seats for the first time in Mex-

ico's history after the 1988 elections. See Cornelius and Craig, *The Mexican Political System in Transition,* 23-25, 31.

25. The PAN, *Partido Acción Nacion,* is a right party. It was formed as a reaction to the PRI in 1939.

26. Rodríguez and Peter M. Ward, "Introduction: Governments of the Opposition in Mexico," 3-5.

27. Krauze, *Mexico: Biography of Power: A History of Modern Mexico, 1810-1996,* xiv.

28. Cothran (1994) took the phrase from Andrew Reding, "Mexico: The Crumbling of the 'Perfect Dictatorship," *World Policy Journal* 8, No.2 (Spring1991).

29. Cothran, *Political Stability and Democracy in Mexico,* 233.

30. Weintraub, *Financial Decision-Making in Mexico: To Bet a Nation,* 19.

31. Cornelius and Craig, *The Mexican Political System in Transition,* 4.

32. Stephen D. Morris, *Corruption & Politics in Contemporary Mexico* (Tuscaloosa and London: The University of Alabama Press, 1991), 51-52, 54, xvi-xvii.

33. *Compañía Nacional de Subsistencias Populares.*

34. Weintraub, *Financial Decision-Making in Mexico: To Bet a Nation,* 19.

35. Morris, *Political Reformism in Mexico: An Overview of Contemporary Mexican Politics,* 17; Centeno, *Democracy within Reason,* 9,10; Schulz and Williams, "Crisis of Transformation: The Struggle for the Soul of Mexico," 2, 3; Aspe and Sigmund, "Introduction," 3.

36. Dresser, "Falling From the Tightrope: The Political Economy of the Mexican Crisis," 61.

37. Centeno, *Democracy within Reason,* 11-20, 95.

38. The PAN nominated Manuel Clouthier, an entrepreneur, for the 1988 election, who favored less government intervention in the economy than the PRI.

39. In addition to the PRI and PAN's candidates, Cuauhtémoc Cárdenas, a former governor of the state of Michoacá, and son of the Mexico's most well regarded president, Lázaro Cárdenas (1934-40), ran for presidency. He led a left party that favored government intervention in the economy and objected to further liberalization of the economy.

40. Morris, *Political Reformism in Mexico: An Overview of Contemporary Mexican Politics,* 17; Domínguez, "The Transformation of Mexico's Electoral and Party System, 1988-1997 . . . ," 4.

41. Cornelius and Craig, *The Mexican Political System in Transition,* 1,2.

42. Dresser, "Falling From the Tightrope: The Political Economy of the Mexican Crisis," 61.

43. Cothran, *Political Stability and Democracy in Mexico,* 177.

44. Edwards, "Bad Luck or Bad Policies? An Economic Analysis of the Crisis," 99.

APPENDIX B: MALAYSIA'S HISTORICAL BACKGROUND

Malaysia is a relatively new state. It gained its independence from Britain in 1957. Before the British takeover of the Malay Peninsula, Malacca, which is situated on the southern part of today's peninsular Malaysia, was first colonized by the Portuguese in 1511 and taken over by the Dutch in 1641. The British colonization of the Malay Peninsula started in 1771 when the British East Indian Company established a strategic and commercial port on the island of Penang, which is situated in the Malacca Straits, and lasted until the country's independence. In the late 19th century, Malaysia became the world's largest rubber and tin exporter for the British Empire. Until the British colonization, the Malaysian territory consisted of indigenous *bumiputera*[1] (chieldren of the soil), who were occupied with wet-rice cultivation and the seagoing trade. The British brought Tamil laborers (Indians) from southern India to work in the cultivation of rubber tree plantations, and Chinese to mine the tin in Malaysia. By 1900, Chinese made up one third of the total population, and Indians 10 percent of the Malaysian peninsula. Over time the Chinese and some Indians spread their activities into trade and business, while the *bumiputera,* most of whom are Malays, were occupied with agriculture. By the time of the Malaysian independence, the Chinese transformed into a merchant class, settled in Malaysian urban centers and became the majority of city populations and most of the Indians worked in plantation and construction labor, while *bumiputera* stayed in villages. Thus, Malaysia inherited an ethnically divided society with a specific division of labor among the three ethnic groups.[2]

Malaysia's contemporary political system and its institutions were shaped during the period of independence. They evolved to today with some changes. First, the British established a single crown colony called the Malayan Union from an amalgamation of Malay states, including Penang and Malacca, in 1946. Then, following the Second World War Malay leaders formed the United Malay National Organization, i.e. today's UMNO, in order to seek an independent Malaya that would supplant the Malayan Union. The first elections were held in 1955 and the Alliance Party, a coalition of three ethnic parties—UMNO, MCA (today's the Malaysian Chinese Association, established by the Chinese), and MIC (today's the Malaysian Indian Congress, established by the Indians) — won a sound victory. It won 51 of the 52 seats in the self-governing legislative council of pre-independent Malaya. It was this coalition that negotiated Malaya's independence in 1957. The Alliance Party maintained its unity and won the elections held in 1959, 1964 and 1969 as well.[3]

In 1962, Malaya became Malaysia with the cooperation of Singapore, Sarawak, and North Borneo (today's Sabah). Singapore became a separate state in 1965. Today's Malaysia consists of peninsular Malaysia, which includes 11 states and contains about 80 percent of the population, as well as Sabah and Sarawak, which are located on the northern part of the island of Borneo. The current population is about 22 million. 57.8 percent of the total population is *bumiputera* (8.8 of which are non-Malay). Chinese make up 24.9 percent, Indians are 7 percent and others are 3.1 percent of the total. Resident aliens, made up mostly of Indonesian immigrant workers, comprise a significant 7.2 percent of the total population. The Chinese and Indians are also seen as immigrants by many *bumiputera*, although 90 percent of them are actually Malaysian-born and would regard Malaysia as their motherland.[4]

The Malaysian federation faced its first and maybe biggest challenge in 1969 when ethnic riots broke out on May 13, 1969 (three days after the election), as a result of widespread dissatisfaction with the government among the ethnic groups, in particular the Malays. On the one hand, the expanding middle class Malays, with their rising economic expectations, were not happy with the government's accommodative policies toward the Chinese and foreign capital. On the other hand, the Chinese were concerned over increasing government interventions into the economy in the form of regulation and new public enterprises. They wanted to maintain the economic opportunities open to them. As a result of these economic issues along with other ethnic grievances, support for the Alliance declined and ethnic tensions grew in Malaysia in the 1960s. Three minor racial incidents occurred in different areas of Malaysia during the mid-1960s, but the 1969 riots were not expected. Although the riots were limited almost entirely to Kuala Lumpur and its environs, officially 196 people died and 409 people were injured. The ratio of non-Malay deaths was about six to one and most of the victims were Chinese. The riots showed the vulnerability of the Malaysian multi-racial unity that had been believed to prevail, and ended the alliance among the three ethnic parties.[5]

Following the riots, a 'palace coup' by UMNO's Young Turks ousted Prime Minister Tunku Abdul Rahman, declared a state of emergency, and suspended the parliament for the next two years. Then the Deputy Prime Minister, Tun Abdul Razak, took over Abdul Rahman's place. By 1974, the UMNO, under Abdul Razak's leadership, was able to bring its coalition partners the MCA and MIC back in order to establish a coalition called the National Front, *Barisan Nasional* (BN) along with other smaller parties. In 1974, the BN (the former Alliance) came in power again, and has not lost any election so far. The UMNO and its leaders have been playing the major role in the coalition. Tun Abdul Razak, after his death in 1976, was replaced by Tun Hussein Onn. The current Prime Minister, Mahathir Mohamad, succeeded Hussein Onn after his retirement in 1981.[6]

For the last two decades, Malaysia's most powerful political figure has been the Prime Minister and the UMNO leader Mohamad Mahathir.[7] He is a medical doctor by training. He completed his education at the University of Malaya in Singapore, while Singapore was still part of Malaysia (from 1962-1965). He was the first Malaysian political leader who was not educated in England.[8] Over the years, he articulated an anti-British and an anti-Western ideology, which is often referred to as *Mahathirism*. He reflected his ideological look in his books, speeches, and essays. Although *Mahathirism* has contradictions within, it consists of Malay nationalism and an "indigenous" economic modernization,[9] as explicated in his *The Malay Dilemma* in 1972. According to Mahathir, the "Malay dilemma" was:

> the eugenic and climatologically induced Malay propensity to an inbred dependence, fatalism and apathy. The need to address these flaws in the Malay character through state intervention along the lines prescribed by "Dr. UMNO" was of such urgency that dissent from the proposed course of treatment could not be tolerated. . . . [He had] an acute sensitivity to Malay weaknesses and an awareness of a need to strengthen the country in order to catch up with a West whose economic achievement he wishes to emulate, but whose free-market blandishments and democratic rhetoric he considers an insidious attempt to reimpose colonial subjection.[10]

He, as "the foremost Malay nationalist of his generation," has been anxious to create a dynamic Malay identity and "secure the survival of the Malays." His worldview consisted of a distinctively eugenic and social Darwinian flavor that accentuated his Malay nationalism.[11] Since he came to power in 1981, Mahathir has been an economic modernizer and "an ideologue of the state-sponsored constructive protection."[12]

The Malaysian government's economic policies had been sensitive to ethnic considerations prior to the 1969 riots. The government became even more sensitive after the riots, which were thought to be a result of Malays' economic grievances that had not been sufficiently addressed. The non-Malay ethnic groups, in particular the Chinese, had been getting the biggest slice of the Malaysian economic pie, since they lived in cities where they could effectively deal with business and trade. A New Economic Policy (NEP) was adopted to bring equality between Malays and other ethnic groups in 1974.[13] The NEP was a unique policy, which can be seen as a system of social and economic affirmative action. However, the state sponsored NEP policies have increasingly blurred the lines between the state, markets, and the dominant party UMNO.[14] This intricate relationship continued in the 1980s and the 1990s. During the 1980s and the 1990s, Mahathir's government too followed the objectives of the NEP that were set in 1974. In the early 1990s, the National Development Policy, NDP, which was a reformulated version of the NEP, was introduced.[15]

Privatization, starting from the mid-1980s, was also seen as an ideal vehicle for achieving the aims of the NEP along with reducing the financial and administrative burden of the government and improving the efficiency and productivity of public enterprises.[16] The privatization was initially started as a temporary redistribution measure, according to Toyoda (2001). However, as it attracted foreign capital inflows, particularly from Japan, along with its other economic benefits, it gained greater support from both businesses and political leadership.[17] However, privatization was not only used as a tool for the redistributive objectives of the NEP, but also was used, as it was widely observed, for the development and consolidation of politically linked businessmen.[18]

The Malaysian political system was originally modeled on that of the British; however, there is little resemblance between the actual operations of the two political systems.[19] Since its independence, the basic pattern of political mobilization in Malaysia has been based on the alliances of the three ethnic parties, united through inter-elite negotiations, and on "the distribution of patronage to the leaders and supporters of parties within the ruling coalition."[20] Despite regular multi-party elections, democracy has not been practiced as it has been in the Western countries. Since the BN hold the majority in the parliament, government bills had always been successful, while opposition bills had seldom been successful. The opposition did not have the power to block the constitutional amendments, let alone affect the passage of the bills in the parliament.[21] All these have resulted in a constant shift of balance of power within the state toward executive power, whereas the independence and influence of the bureaucracy, the legislature, the judiciary, and the monarchy have declined. Independent press and civil society could not grow stronger. Moreover, although Malaysia was established as a federal system, the powers of the states (constituents) have been rather limited. Rulers of the constituent states have become even powerless over the years.[22]

Over time, democracy not only declined in Malaysia, but also decreased within the UMNO. The more Mahathir became dominant in the UMNO, the more he was able to orchestrate policies single-handedly. Given the Malay conception of power and their unswerving loyalty, the political ideology of contemporary Malaysia is largely reducible to the personality of its leader. Mahathir, as a firm believer in strong government, has been able to increase his executive power tremendously in the Malaysian political and societal context.[23] Malaysian political culture has been permissive toward the authoritarianism exercised by Mahathir. Although there has not been a common civic culture, some minimum consensus on a stable and effective government has existed among Malaysian ethnic communities.[24] When populist avenues failed, physical coercion has also been used as Mahathir's populist regime moved toward authoritarianism over the years. The Malaysian Internal Security Act and the Official Secrets Act during the Mahathir years reduced transparency and allowed for indefinite detention without trial.[25] Nonetheless, Malaysia has been more successful than Indonesia in terms of keeping democratic institutions, even though both countries have similar historical backgrounds.[26]

The factionalism and competition within the UMNO along with economic development caused the emergence of a new class of business interests outside of UMNO patronage networks in the 1990s. They called for greater economic openness, relaxation of Malay-centered ownership regulations, and greater access to foreign and Malay-Chinese capital.[27] Before the Asian financial crisis, while some groups were benefiting from political patronage, some others were increasingly concerned over the influence of political patronage on the business sector, inequitable distribution of wealth, corruption, and other abuses of power.[28]

Although the ethnic split has dominated Malaysian society, other social cleavages have also existed and some of them grew as a result of economic development.[29] Malaysia is also a multi-religious state, but religion has not been a major issue.[30] During the 1980s, the emergence of a working class that also included substantial Malay components for the first time, and the growth of a solid middle class, which consisted of primarily urban Malay and Chinese, created new polarization between rich and poor and new division between urban and rural populations. These new socioeconomic classes partially transcend racial barriers. Economic interests of the middle class contrast with Malay and non-Malay indigenous groups who mostly populate the rural areas. Other polarization has been between East Malaysia (the states of Sabah and Sarawak), and West (Peninsular) Malaysia. Although peninsular Malaysia is geographically the smaller part, it is by far the more populous, as well as, commercially and economically, the most developed one.[31] Nonetheless, politics in Malaysia is still dominated by ethnic considerations. Malaysian ethnically-based political parties maintained and sometimes exacerbated ethnic consciousness and the ethnic politics. The coalition of the three ethnic parties, the BN, remained in power, even though the main opposition party, PAS (Parti Islam SeMalaysia—Islamic Party) also got considerable Malay votes during the recent elections and divided the Malay votes that went to the UMNO.[32]

NOTES

1. The term *bumiputera* does not refer to one ethnic group, but refers to Malays and other indigenous people. In today's Malaysia, the *bumiputera* segment of Malaysian society consists of dominantly Malay Muslims, but also includes those non-Malay ethnic groups in Sarawak and Sabah. Kok-Wah Loh, "State-Societal Relations in a Rapidly Growing Economy: the Case of Malaysia, 1970-1997," 65.

2. Jomo K.S., *Growth and Structural Change in the Malaysian Econom,.2*; Schlossstein, *Asia's New Little Dragons . . .* , 224; Rasiah, "Class, Ethnicity and Economic Development in Malaysia," 123. Also Professor Donald E. Weatherbee's comments and feedback contributed greatly in writing the historical background of Malaysia.

3. Schlossstein, *Asia's New Little Dragons . . .* , 224-28; Pillay, "The Malaysian Model . . . ," 205-206.

4. Pillay, "The Malaysian Model . . . ," 204, 205; Embong,"Pluralism in Post-Colonial Malaysia,"59.

5. Gomez and Jomo K.S., *Malaysia's Political Economy . . .* , 21, 22; Milne and Mauzy, *Malaysian Politics under Mahathir*, 21; Pillay, "The Malaysian Model . . . ," 206.

6. Schlossstein, *Asia's New Little Dragons . . .* , 224-228; Pillay, "The Malaysian Model . . . ," 206.

7. Ibid., p.229.

8. Ibid., pp.248-249.

9. Teik, *Paradoxes of Mahathirism: An Intellectual Biograph of Mahathir Mohamad*, 2, 6-9.

10. David Martin Jones, "What Mahathir Has Wrought," *The National Interest*, Spring 2000, 106.

11. Teik, *Paradoxes of Mahathirism: An Intellectual Biography of Mahathir Mohamad*, 9; Jones, "What Mahathir Has Wrought," 106.

12. Teik, *Paradoxes of Mahathirism: An Intellectual Biography of Mahathir Mohamad*, 9.

13. Milne and Mauzy, *Malaysian Politics under Mahathir*, 21.

14. Toyoda, "Malaysia: Ethnic Cleavages and Controlled Liberalization," 97. In order to achieve the NEP goals, the government established a powerful trusteeship consisting of a small group of political decision-makers along with subordinate officials and public service staff. The trusteeship decided on the Malaysian budget, allocated resources, and exerted control over the resources that were owned by the state or private parties alike. The powerful trusteeship resulted in "a very rapid process of wealth accumulation under the direct control of trustees themselves," and promoted self-enrichment of trustees through rent-seeking activities and distributional coalitions. Ozay Mehmet, *Development in Malaysia: Poverty, Wealth and Trusteeship* (London, Sydney & Dover NH: Croom Helm, 1986), 157.

15. Gomez and Jomo K.S., *Malaysia's Political Economy: Politics, Patronage and Profits* (1997), 169; Milne and Mauzy, *Malaysian Politics under Mahathir*, 72.

16. Milne and Mauzy, *Malaysian Politics under Mahathir*, 56; Uzir Abdul Malik, "Privatization as an Instrument of National Policy and Socio Economic Restructuring," in *Alternative Perspectives in Third-World Development: The Case of Malaysia* (New York: St.Martin's Press, Inc., 1996), 70. By the late 1990s, privatization expanded to many of the activities including airlines, airports, railroads, road construction, shipping, telecommunication, electricity generation, and so on. On average about fifty entities, either at the federal or state level, were being privatized each year by 1995. The ones that were privatized or in the process of being privatized during the crisis years (1997-1998) included the Bakun hydroelectric dam in Sarawak and the Sabah Electricity Board. Milne and Mauzy, *Malaysian Politics under Mahathir*, 57.

17. Toyoda, "Malaysia: Ethnic Cleavages and Controlled Liberalization," 99.

18. Gomez and Jomo K.S., *Malaysia's Political Economy: Politics, Patronage and Profits* (1997), 178.

19. Milne and Mauzy, *Malaysian Politics under Mahathir*, 2, 3.

20. Means, *Malaysian Politics: The Second Generation*, 283.

21. The constitutional amendments require a 2/3 vote of parliament in which opposition has never held 1/3+1.

22. See Schlossstein, *Asia's New Little Dragons . . .* , 6; Wah and Kahn, "Introduction: Fragmented Vision," 4; Kok-Wah Loh, "State-Societal Relations in a Rapidly Growing Economy: the Case of Malaysia, 1970-1997," 84-85; Gomez and Jomo K.S., *Malaysia's Political Economy: Politics, Patronage and Profits* (1997), 121; Milne and Mauzy, *Malaysian Politics under Mahathir*, 1, 2, 3.

23. Jones, "What Mahathir Has Wrought," 105; Milne and Mauzy, *Malaysian Politics under Mahathir*, 159.

24. Means, *Malaysian Politics: The Second Generation*, 290-291.

25. Munro-Kua, *Authoritarian Populism in Malaysia*, 3, 8,9; Gomez and Jomo K.S., *Malaysia's Political Economy: Politics, Patronage and Profits* (1997), 2.

26. Alatas (1997) asserts that this was the case mainly due to three factors. One is the presence of an internally strong state, and second is a high degree of elite cohesion. The third one is the absence of serious armed resistance against the state. (The Malayan Communist Party (MCP) had armed insurgence between 1947 and 1962. But all of its members were Chinese and it never seriously challenged the state. Also, a confrontation with Indonesia occurred between 1964 and 1966, due to Indonesian objections to the creation of Malaysia. It also did not upset the Malaysian political system, as did the ethnic riots in 1969.) Syed Farid Alatas, *Democracy and Authoritarianism in Indonesia and Malaysia: The Rise of the Post Colonial State* (London: Macmillan Press Ltd. &

New York: St. Martin's Press, Inc., 1997), x; and Professor Donald E. Weatherbee's helpful comments.

27. Toyoda, "Malaysia: Ethnic Cleavages and Controlled Liberalization," 99.

28. Gomez and Jomo K.S., *Malaysia's Political Economy: Politics, Patronage and Profits* (1997), 1.

29. Milne and Mauzy, *Malaysian Politics under Mahathir*, 1.

30. E.K. Fisk, "Development in Malaysia," in *The Political Economy of Malaysia* (Kuala Lumpur: Oxford University Press, 1982), 14, 90.

31. Ibid., 9,12; Toyoda, "Malaysia: Ethnic Cleavages and Controlled Liberalization," 96.

32. Gomez and Jomo K.S., *Malaysia's Political Economy: Politics, Patronage and Profits* (1997), 2.

APPENDIX C: MEXICO'S ECONOMIC INDICATORS IN THE LATE 1980S AND 1990S

Fiscal and Monetary Indicators

Year	1987	1988	1989	1990	1991	1992	1993	1994	95/Jan	95/Dec
M1,real growth rate	-11.4	4.2	17.5	23.4	83.8	2.8	9.0	-3.1	-13.0	-29.6
M2, real growth rate	-7.0	-6.2	19.4	12.5	23.9	7.5	5.0	13.3	13.6	-8.8
M1, billions of Mexican pesos	13	21	29	47	106	122	144	145		
M2, billions of Mexican pesos	49	39	88	160	238	295	340	408		
M1/GDP			0.06	0.07	0.13	0.12	0.13	0.12		
M2/GDP			0.25	0.27	0.31	0.32	0.33	0.36		

Sources: M1 and M2 real growth rates are from A-1, M1 and M2 in billions of Mexican Pesos are from A-2a, and M1/GDP and M2/GDP ratios are from A-3a.

Year	1985	1986	1987	1988	1989	1990	1991	1992	1993	1994
Public Sector Financial Balance (includes all the public sector borrowing requirements), % of GDP	-9.6	-16.1	-16	-12.4	-5.6	-3.3	-1.5	0.5	-2.1	-3.9
Primary Balance (Financial Balance less interest paid on public debt), % of GDP	3.9	3.7	5.8	8	8.4	7.6	5.3	5.6	3.6	2.3
Operational Balance (Primary Balance plus the real portion of the interest paid on public debt), % of GDP	-0.8	-2.4	1.8	-3.6	-1.7	1.8	2.9	2.9	2.1	0.5
Central Government Budget Balance, % of GDP				-10.3	-5.0	-2.8	-0.2	1.5	0.3	-0.7

Source: Central Government Budget Balance is from A-4 and the rest is from A-3b.

Year	1988	1989	1990	1991	1992	1993	1994
Gross Public Debt, % of GDP	74.7	66.6	57.5	46.8	36.3	33.7	50.7
External Debt	46.6	39.5	33.4	28.4	23.2	21.7	36.4
Internal Debt	27.9	27.1	24.1	18.4	13.1	12.0	14.3
OECD Countries (avarage), % of GDP	58.0	57.5	58.3	59.9	64.1	68.1	70.6

Source: A-3c

Year	1987	1988	1989	1990	1991	1992	1993	1994	1995
Consumer Price Index (end of period), 1994=100	28.5	43.2	51.7	67.2	79.8	89.3	96.5	103.3	156.9
Annual % Change	159.7	51.7	19.7	29.9	18.8	11.9	8.0	7.1	52.0

Source: A-1

Year	87	88	89	90	91	92	93	94	95	96	97	98
Domestic Credit in Real Terms (deflated by the CPI), billions of Mexican pesos	54	45	56	62	69	76	78	91	71	43	77	74
Credit to Private Sector in Real Terms (deflated by the CPI), billions of Mexican pesos	18	16	28	35	45	63	72	92	63	40	48	49
Real Adjusted Credit to the Private Sector, annual % change					33.3	33.0	17.0	32.1	-20.6	-11.9	n/a	-0.2
Adjusted Credit to the Private Sector, % of GDP					26.3	33.0	37.4	46.7	43.6	35.7	35.5	35.3

Source: A-2a and A-2b

Current Account

Year	1987	1988	1989	1990	1991	1992	1993	1994	94-Q1	94-Q2	94-Q3	94-Q4	95-Q1	95-Q2
Current Account, billions of US$	2.9	-3.8	-6.1	-7.5	-14.9	-24.8	-23.4	-29.5	-6.7	-7.1	-7.7	-7.3	-1.1	0.5

Source: A-5

Year	87	88	89	90	91	92	93	94	95	96	97	98
Current Account Balance 1, % of GDP	2.9	-1.1	-2.6	-2.9	-4.7	-6.7	-5.8	-7.0	-0.6	-0.7	-1.9	-3.8
Current Account Balance 2, % of GDP	2.2	-2.3	-2.9	-3.2	-4.8	-6.8	-6.4	-8.0				
Nominal Exchange Rate, Index 1987=100	100	161	176	200	213	218	220	239	453	536	559	698
Real Exchange Rate, Index 1987=100	100	130	130	138	153	167	178	144	108	133	155	146

Trade Balance, billions of U.S. dollars	9	3.0	0.0	-1.0	-7.0	-16.0	-13.0	-18.5	7.1	6.5	0.6	-6.1
Trade Balance, % of GDP	6.1	1.7	0.0	-0.4	-2.2	-4.4	-3.2	-4.4	2.5	2.0	0.2	-1.5
Exports (current prices), % of GDP	19.5	16.8	16.0	15.8	13.8	12.6	12.4	13.1				
Imports(current prices), % of GDP	13.4	15.3	13.2	16.9	17.0	18.1	16.7	18.9				

Sources: Current Account Balance 2 is from A-5, Exports and Imports data are from A-3e, and the rest is from A-2c.

Finance Account

Year	1987	1988	1989	1990	1991	1992	1993	1994
Foreign Exchange Reserves, billions of US$	8.0	6.0	6.5	10.1	17.9	19.4	25.4	6.3

Source: A-5

Year	87	88	89	90	91	92	93	94	94-Q1	94-Q2	94-Q3	94-Q4	95-Q1	95-Q2
Finance Account, billions of US$	3.8	-2.9	5.1	10.9	22.5	26.7	30.5	11.6	9.9	0.1	4.9	-3.3	2.5	1.2
Public Sector, net	3.6	1.2	-0.7	-0.2	3.0	1.5	7.5	2.5						
Private Sector, net	0.2	-4.1	5.8	11.1	19.5	25.2	23.0	9.1						
Direct Investment Level, end of year gross	1.8	1.7	2.7	2.6	4.8	4.4	4.9	7.9						
Loans to Commercial Banks and Private Sector							12.6		4.8	-0.3	-0.8	0.7	-2.6	-1.5
Loans to Public Sector							1.5		1.3	0.3	0.5	0.3	9.2	4.4
Direct Investment							4.4		1.8	1.6	2.3	2.2	1.0	1.6
Stock Market							10.7		3.5	0.2	0.7	-0.4	0.1	0.1

Money Market (Mexican Treasury Securities)								7.0	1.5	0.0	1.2	-4.7	-4.7	-3.4
Sales of Foreign Assets (minus signs indicate Mexican accumulation of foreign assets)								-3.6	-3.1	-1.8	0.9	-1.5	-0.4	0.0
Errors and Omissions								-3.1	-2.3	-2.4	2.6	0.5	-0.7	1.4
Change in International Reserves								6.1	0.8	-9.4	-0.1	-10.1	0.7	3.1

Source: A-5

Year	1987	1988	1989	1990	1991	1992	1993	1994	1995
Total Foreign Investment, billions of dollar	1.6	3.9	3.5	6.0	17.5	22.4	33.3	19.2	-3.2
Direct Investment	2.6	2.9	3.2	2.6	4.8	4.4	4.4	11.0	7.0
Portfolio Investment	-1.0	1.0	0.4	3.4	12.8	18.0	28.9	8.2	-10.1

Source: A-1

Year	1989	1990	1991	1992	1993	1994	1995
Net External Debt, billions of dollar	94.7	97.4	104.5	109.8	122.3	133.7	159.5
Net Public Sector External Debt, billions of dollars	75.5	70.8	68.0	68.1	69.4	76.9	90.3
Total External Debt, % of GDP	46.1	42.6	40.6	35.7	36.4	38.3	69.1
Net External Debt, % of GDP	45.8	39.8	36.4	33.4	33.8	36.0	64.8

Source: A-1

Balance of Payment, billions of dollar Year	1989	1990	1991	1992	1993	1994	1995
Current Account	-5.8	-7.5	-14.6	-24.4	-23.4	-29.4	-0.7
Finance (Capital) Account	3.2	8.3	24.5	26.4	32.5	14.6	15.1
Errors and Omissions	3.0	2.5	-2.2	-1.0	-3.1	-3.6	-4.9
Change in International Reserves	0.3	3.5	7.4	1.0	6.0	-18.4	9.6

Source: A-1

Gross Domestic Product and Related Indicators

Year	1988	1989	1990	1991	1992	1993	1994	1995	1996
GDP, billion dollars	171.77	208.25	247.06	290.53	334.33	403.20	421.72	286.84	334.79
Per Capita GDP, dollars	2075	2465	2870	3305	3735	4420	4535	3170	3465
Real GDP Growth	1.2	3.3	4.5	3.6	2.8	0.6	3.5	-6.9	5.1

Source: A-4. Real GDP Growth is from A-1.

Year	1985	1986	1987	1988	1989	1990	1991	1992	1993	1994	1995
Stock Market Index, 1982=1	11	47	106	212	419	629	1432	1759	2603	2376	2779

Source: A-1.

Year	1988	1989	1990	1991	1992	1993	1994	1995
Average Real Earnings (per worker), 1987=100	99.5	108.3	111.8	117.2	128.7	135.0	140.0	122.4
Average Productivity (per worker), 1987=100	103.2	107.5	112.1	118.4	126.0	134.7	145.5	148.0
Change in Real Wages, %	-2.1	13.6	3.9	6.4	2.0	-1.1	-0.9	-25.0
Unemployment Rate, %	3.5	2.9	2.7	2.2	2.8	2.4	3.7	4.7

Source: A-1. Change in Real Wages and Unemployment Rate are from A-4.

Interest Rates (3 Months) **Year/Month**	1989 Dec	1990 Dec	1991 Dec	1992 Dec	1993 Dec	1994 Jan	1994 Jan	1995 Mar	1994 Apr	1994 May	1994 Jun
Interest Rates Cetes (1)	40.19	25.84	17.33	17.53	11.71	10.89	9.13	11.97	16.45	16.54	16.49
Tesobonos(1989-1992 rates are for 28 days) (2)	15.07	12	9.06	3.48	5.09	4.67	4.34	7.27	7.25	7.05	6.95
US Interest Rates (3)	8.01	7.91	4.54	3.53	3.08	3.02	3.21	3.52	3.74	4.19	4.18
Interest Rates Differentials (1)-(2)	25.12	13.84	8.27	14.05	6.62	6.22	4.79	4.7	8.7	9.49	9.54
(2)-(3)		7.06	4.09	4.52	-0.05	2.01	1.65	1.13	3.75	4.01	2.86	2.77

Interest Rates (3 Months) **Year/Month**	1994 Jul	1994 Aug	1994 Sep	1994 Oct	94/Nov (1st w)	94/Nov (2nd w)	94/Nov (3rd w)	94/Nov (4th w)	94/Dec (1st w)	94/Dec (2nd w)
Interest Rates Cetes (1)	17.19	13.82	13.1	14.35	14.5	14.18	14.5	14.76	14.58	14.89
Tesobonos(1989-1992 rates are for 28 days) (2)	7.25	7.24	6.79	6.85	6.81	6.82	6.77	7.5	7.58	7.4
US Interest Rates (3)	4.39	4.5	4.64	4.96	5.1	4.24	5.38	5.52	5.65	5.7

Interest Rates Differentials (1)-(2)	9.94	6.58	6.31	7.5	7.69	7.36	7.73	7.26	7	7.49
(2)-(3)	2.86	2.74	2.15	1.89	1.71	1.58	1.39	1.98	1.93	1.7

Interest Rates (3 Months) Year/Month	94/Dec (3rd w)	94/Dec (4th w)	95/Jan (1st w)	95/Jan (2nd w)	95/Jan (3rd w)	95/Jan (4th w)
Interest Rates Cetes (1)	17	31.99	34.99	44.94	39	38
Tesobonos(1989-1992 rates are for 28 days) (2)	8.26	10.49	12.49	19.5	19.75	24.98
US Interest Rates (3)	5.5	5.5	5.55	5.7	5.65	5.75
Interest Rates Differentials (1)-(2)	7.74	21.5	22.5	25.44	19.25	13.02
(2)-(3)	2.76	4.99	6.94	13.8	14.1	19.23

Source: A-3f

Year	1986	1987	1988	1989	1990	1991	1992	1993	1994
Total Investment (current prices), % of GDP	18.5	19.2	20.4	21.3	21.9	22.4	23.3	22.0	23.6
Private Investment	12.9	13.2	14.2	13.3	13.7	14.9	16.6	6.2	16.6
Public Investment	6.5	5.2	5.0	4.8	4.9	4.6	4.2	4.2	4.5
Change in Inventories	-0.9	0.8	1.2	3.2	3.3	2.9	2.5	1.6	2.5
Private Consumption	68.5	65.8	69.4	70.3	70.9	71.8	72.2	71.5	71.0
Government Consumption	9.1	8.8	8.6	8.5	8.4	9.0	10.1	10.8	11.3

Source: A-3e

Year	1987	1988	1989	1990	1991	1992	1993	1994
National Saving in percentages of GDP	21.6	18.2	18.5	18.7	17.6	16.0	14.1	13.7
Private Saving	14.3	18.8	16.1	12.1	10.0	8.7	8.9	9.1
Public Saving	7.3	-0.7	2.4	6.6	7.6	7.3	5.2	4.6

Source: A-5

Banking Sector

Year	1991	1992	1993	1994	1995	1996	1997	1998
Commercial Bank's Non-performing Loans, % of total loans	4.1	5.6	7.4	8.4	7.4	7.3	11.3	11.3

Source: A-2b

Liability of the Banking System, billions of dollars	Dec.89	Dec.90	Dec. 91	Dec.92	Dec. 93	Oct. 94
Domestic Currency	58.42	75.19	101.18	122.47	145.08	166.30
Percentage	55.98	62.97	66.64	69.67	69.89	68.72
Foreign Currency	45.93	44.21	50.66	53.31	62.50	75.70
Percentage	44.02	37.03	33.36	30.33	30.11	31.28

Source: A-3e

Year	1989	1990	1991	1992	1993	1994
Components of Domestic Debt (the end of the year), millions of dollars Total	46476	54808	55459	42820	43662	32170
Cetes	20437	24445	23567	19047	26084	7456
Bondes	21082	21903	18871	11827	5485	1562
Ajustabonos	1221	4859	12696	11642	10849	5371
Tesobonos	75	408	302	296	1237	17780
Others	3661	3193	24	8	7	2

Source: A-3a

Sources

A-1: *Mexican Economy 1996*, Bank of Mexico, http://www.banxico.org.mx /gPubli cac.../mexicaneconomy/mexecon96, accessed February 9, 2002.

A-2a: "The 1994 Mexican Economic Crisis: The Role of Government Expenditure and Relative Prices." Eliot Kalter and Armando Ribas, *IMF Working Paper*, WP/99/160, December 1999, 21.Original data source is the IMF's International Financial Statistics.

A-2b: "The 1994 Mexican Economic Crisis: The Role of Government Expenditure and Relative Prices." Eliot Kalter and Armando Ribas, *IMF Working Paper*, WP/99/160 December 1999, 21. Original sources are Bank of Mexico and National Banking Commission of Mexico.

A-2c: "The 1994 Mexican Economic Crisis: The Role of Government Expenditure and Relative Prices." Eliot Kalter and Armando Ribas. *IMF Working Paper*, WP/99/160 December 1999, 21. Original sources are Bank of Mexico and IMF's World Economic Outlook.

A-3a: *The Collapse of the Mexican Peso: What Have We Learned?* Jeffrey Sachs, Aarón Tornell, and Andrés Velasco, National Bureau of Economic Research, Working Paper No. 5142, June 1995. Original sources are Banco de Mexico and Indicadores Economicos, February 1995.

A-3b: *The Collapse of the Mexican Peso: What Have We Learned?* Jeffrey Sachs, Aarón Tornell, and Andrés Velasco, National Bureau of Economic Research, Working Paper No. 5142, June 1995. Original source is DGPH, Ministry of Finance of Mexico.

A-3c: *The Collapse of the Mexican Peso: What Have We Learned?* Jeffrey Sachs, Aarón Tornell, and Andrés Velasco, National Bureau of Economic Research, Working Paper No. 5142, June 1995. Original sources are Informe Sobre la Situacion Economica, las Finanzas Publicas y la Deuda Publica, SHCP, 1995 and OECD, Economic Outlook, December 1994.

A-3d: *The Collapse of the Mexican Peso: What Have We Learned?* Jeffrey Sachs, Aarón Tornell, and Andrés Velasco, National Bureau of Economic Research, Working Paper No. 5142, June 1995. Original source is IMF's International Financial Statistics.

A-3e: *The Collapse of the Mexican Peso: What Have We Learned?* Jeffrey Sachs, Aarón Tornell, and Andrés Velasco, National Bureau of Economic Research, Working Paper No. 5142, June 1995. Original source is Banco de Mexico.

A-3f: *The Collapse of the Mexican Peso: What Have We Learned?* Jeffrey Sachs, Aarón Tornell, and Andrés Velasco, National Bureau of Economic Research, Working Paper No. 5142, June 1995. Original sources are Banco de Mexico and Survey of Current Business.

A-4: *Country Forecast,* Volume XVII, William D. Coplin and Michael K. O'Leary, eds., East Syracuse, NY: The PRS Group, January 1998, 222.

A-5: "The Balance of Payments and Borrowing Constraints: An Alternative View of the Mexican Crisis." Andrew Atkeson and José-Víctor Ríos-Rull, 1996. *Journal of International Economics* 41, 331-349. Original source is International Monetary Fund.

APPENDIX D: MALAYSIA'S ECONOMIC INDICATORS IN COMPARISON WITH SOME ASIAN COUNTRIES IN THE 1990s

Fiscal and Monetary Indicators

Year/Period	1993	1994	1995	1996	1997	1998	96-Q1	96-Q2	96-Q3	96-Q4
Net Domestic Assets, Twelve-months Rate of Change	10.3	12.8	19.7	23.5	23.3	-13.9	22.7	22.4	22.3	23.5
Domestic Credit	12.2	14.3	27.7	27.4	27.1	-2.3	28.6	29.4	30.1	27.4
Net Claim on Federal Government	0.5	-2.0	-1.5	-0.1	1.7	-3.0	-1.3	-0.7	0.0	-0.1
Claims on Private Sector	12.3	17.3	30.0	27.7	25.5	0.7	30.9	30.6	30.3	27.7
Other items net	-2.2	-0.4	-5.5	-3.4	-4.0	-11.6	-4.5	-5.1	-6.6	-3.4
M1	35.3	16.8	13.2	23.7	8.9	-29.4	19.9	18.4	24.7	23.7
M2	23.0	16.9	20.8	22.8	20.5	-3.4	26.1	22.4	21.2	22.8
Net Foreign Assets, Twelve-months Rate of Change	12.8	3.0	-1.4	0.1	-4.4	12.3	1.7	-1.5	-1.7	0.1

Year/Period	97-Q1	97-Q2	97-Q3	97-Q4	98-Q1
Net Domestic Assets, Twelve-months Rate of Change	21.0	23.0	24.4	23.3	14.8
Domestic Credit	29.1	29.5	26.8	27.1	15.7
Net Claim on Federal Government	-0.1	0.7	-0.5	1.7	-0.1
Claims on Private Sector	29.5	29.0	27.4	25.5	15.5
Other items net	-7.7	-6.6	-3.3	-4.0	-0.8
M1	23.4	20.3	15.1	8.9	-14.5
M2	22.2	22.2	22.1	20.5	11.7
Net Foreign Assets, Twelve-months Rate of Change	-1.1	-1.2	-3.0	-4.4	-1.9

Source: B-1

Year	1990	1991	1992	1993	1994	1995	1996	1997
Central Government's Fiscal Balances, % of GDP Malaysia	-3.10	-2.10	-0.89	0.23	2.44	0.89	0.76	2.52
Korea	-0.68	-1.63	-0.50	0.64	0.32	0.30	0.46	0.25
Indonesia	0.43	0.45	-0.44	0.64	1.03	2.44	1.26	0.00
Philippines	-3.47	-2.10	-1.16	-1.46	1.04	0.57	0.28	0.06
Singapore	10.53	8.58	12.35	15.67	11.93	13.07	14.10	9.52
Thailand	4.59	4.79	2.90	2.13	1.89	2.94	0.97	-0.32

China	-0.79	-1.09	-0.97	-0.85	-1.22	-1.00	-0.82	-0.75
Taiwan	1.85	-2.18	-5.34	-3.88	-1.73	-1.09	-1.34	-1.68

Source: B-2

Year	91-95	1996	1997	1998
Central Government's Public Debt, % of GDP	59	45.8	50.2	54.6

Source: B-3

	Year	1991	1992	1993	1994	1995	1996	1997
Inflation Rate,	Malaysia	4.40	4.69	3.57	3.71	5.28	3.56	2.66
	Korea	9.30	6.22	4.87	6.24	4.41	4.96	4.45
	Indonesia	9.40	7.59	9.60	12.56	8.95	6.64	11.62
	Philippines	18.70	8.93	7.58	9.06	8.11	8.41	5.01
	Singapore	3.40	2.32	2.27	3.05	1.79	1.32	2.00
	Thailand	5.70	4.07	3.36	5.19	5.69	5.85	5.61
	Hong Kong	11.60	9.32	8.52	8.16	8.59	6.30	5.83
	China	3.50	6.30	14.60	24.20	16.90	8.30	2.80
	Taiwan	3.63	4.50	2.87	4.09	3.75	3.01	0.90

Source: B-2

Current Account

	Year	1990	1991	1992	1993	1994	1995	1996	1997	1998
Current Account (BOP Definition), % of GDP,	Malaysia	-2.03	-8.69	-3.74	-4.66	-6.24	-8.43	-4.89	-4.85	12.90
	Korea	-0.69	-2.83	-1.28	0.30	-1.02	-1.86	-4.75	-1.85	12.50
	Indonesia	-2.89	-3.65	-2.17	-1.33	-1.58	-3.18	-3.37	-2.24	4.00
	Philippines	-6.08	-2.28	-1.89	-5.55	-4.60	-2.67	-4.77	-5.23	2.00
	Singapore	8.33	11.29	11.38	7.57	16.12	16.81	15.65	15.37	
	Thailand	-8.50	-7.71	-5.66	-5.08	-5.60	-8.06	-8.10	-1.90	12.40
	China	3.09	3.27	1.33	-1.94	1.26	0.23	0.87	3.24	
	Taiwan	6.82	6.94	4.03	3.16	2.70	2.10	4.05	2.72	

Source: B-2, 1998 data is from B-3.

Year (December)	1990	1991	1992	1993	1994	1995	1996	Mar. 1997	Jun. 1997	Sep. 1997	Dec. 1997
Real Exchange Rate Index, 1990=100	100	99	87	88	86	84	78	72	75	92	108

Source: B-4. Real exchange rate estimated as the ratio (EP)*/P, where P= home country CPI, and (EP)*= foreign country whole sale price index (WPI) expressed in local currency by converting the foreign WPI to the domestic currency. For similar trends in the other crisis-hit Asian countries, see the source.

Year	1990	1991	1992	1993	1994	1995	1996	1997	1998
Trade Balance (BOP Definition), % of GDP	2.10	-3.74	1.39	-0.11	-1.59	-3.75	0.58	4.10	24.90
Korea	-0.81	-3.04	-1.42	0.06	-1.22	-1.63	-4.36	-1.44	12.80
Indonesia	1.68	0.91	1.81	1.48	0.72	-0.76	-1.14	0.22	15.30
Philippines	-5.73	-3.00	-4.27	-8.53	-8.95	-8.80	-9.44	-12.30	0.00
Singapore	6.76	10.62	9.29	8.12	14.87	15.38	13.62	12.55	
Thailand	-7.75	-6.68	-4.70	-4.56	-5.18	-7.09	-6.65	0.14	10.60
China	2.75	2.86	1.03	-1.92	1.39	1.68	2.10	4.41	
Taiwan	4.74	4.39	1.69	1.60	1.66	1.61	3.45	2.35	
Total Exports (BOP basis), In millions of US$						71565.0	76859.0	77389.0	71894.0
Exports, % Change				17.2	22.5	19.0	9.2	5.4	-0.2
Total imports (BOP basis), in millions of US$						71632.0	72850.0	73688.0	54298.0
Imports, % Change				19.1	27.7	23.7	4.9	5.7	-19.4

Source: B-2, B3, and B5.

Finance Account

Year	1993	1994	1995	1996	1997	1998
Finance Account Balance, in billions of US$% of GDP	14.4	2.5	7.6	9.5	2.2	-2.6
Finance Account Balance, % of GDP	22.5	5.2	8.6	9.4	2.2	-3.5
Official Reserves (end of period), billions of US$	28.3	26.6	25.1	27.7	21.7	26.2

Source: B-5

Finance Account (average), % of GDP **Period**	1985-1989	1990-1995	Finance Account (average), % of GDP **Period**	1985-1989	1990-1995
Malaysia, Finance Account	0.5	9.6	Philippines, Finance Account	1.4	5.5
Direct Investment, net	2.4	6.9	Direct Investment, net	1.0	1.1
Portfolio Investment, net	1.0	-1.0	Portfolio Investment, net	0.2	0.3
Other Investment, net	-2.8	3.8	Other Investment, net	0.2	4.0
Korea, Finance Account	-2.5	2.5	Thailand, Finance Account	4.2	10.2
Direct Investment, net	-0.1	-0.3	Direct Investment, net	1.1	1.5
Portfolio Investment, net	0.2	1.9	Portfolio Investment, net	1.2	1.5
Other Investment, net	-2.4	1.0	Other Investment, net	2.0	7.1
Indonesia, Finance Account	3.5	4.1			

Direct Investment, net	0.5	1.2
Portfolio Investment, net	0.0	0.9
Other Investment, net	3.0	2.0

Source: B-7

Year	1990	1991	1992	1993	1994	1995	1996	
Foreign Debt, % of GDP, Malaysia	35.80	35.48	34.51	40.74	40.40	39.31	40.06	
Korea	13.79	13.51	14.34	14.18	14.32	23.80	28.40	
Indonesia	65.89	68.21	68.74	56.44	60.96	61.54	56.74	
Philippines	69.02	71.45	62.29	66.09	62.42	53.21	49.75	
Thailand	32.80	38.38	37.51	34.10	33.31	33.78	50.05	
Short Term Debt, % of Total, Malaysia	12.42	12.14	18.18	26.58	21.13	21.19	27.83	
Korea	30.87	28.19	26.99	25.85	25.47	51.60	50.20	
Indonesia	15.92	18.00	20.52	20.17	18.05	20.87	24.98	
Philippines	14.48	15.24	15.93	14.01	14.29	13.38	19.34	
Thailand	29.63	33.13	35.22	53.01	60.67	72.36	41.41	
Short Term Debt, % of Foreign Reserves, Malaysia	19.54	19.05	21.12	25.51	24.34	30.60	40.98	71.90
Korea	72.13	81.75	69.62	60.31	54.06	171.45	203.23	751.60
Indonesia	149.28	154.62	172.81	159.70	160.36	189.42	176.59	217.10
Philippines	479.11	152.31	119.37	107.68	95.00	82.85	79.45	152.10
Thailand	62.55	71.31	72.34	92.49	99.48	114.21	99.69	129.90
Debt Service as Ratio of Exports, Malaysia	12.60	7.40	9.10	8.40	9.00	7.00	8.20	
Korea	10.80	7.20	7.80	9.40	6.90	7.30	8.80	
Indonesia	33.40	34.30	32.60	33.60	30.70	30.90	36.80	
Philippines	27.00	23.00	24.40	25.60	18.90	16.40	13.70	
Thailand	16.90	13.00	13.80	13.70	13.50	11.60	11.50	

Source: B-2. 1997 data is from B-3.

Year	1994	1995	1996	1997	1998
Total net Capital Flows, millions of US$	1210	7643	9477	2197	-2550
Long-term Capital net	4443	6633	5376	6788	2708
Public net	378	2454	297	1651	545
Private net	4115	4178	5079	5136	2163
Short-term capital net	-3233	1010	4101	-4590	-5258
Commercial Banks	-5070	28	3339	-979	-2677
Non-monetary Financial Institutions	1837	982	762	-3611	-2581

Net Short Term Flows, % of GDP	-4.5	1.1	4.1	-4.6	-7.3
Net Foreign Direct Investment, % of GDP	3.1	3.7	3.5	3.9	2.6

Source: B-5

Balance of Payment

Year	1994	1995	1996	1997	1998	1999
Current Account Balance, billions of US$	-5.6	-8.6	-4.5	-5.6	9.4	12.5
Finance Account Balance, billions of US$	2.5	7.6	9.5	2.2	-2.6	-6.4
Net Errors and Omissions	1.3	-0.6	-2.4	-2.6	-2.4	-1.4
Overall Balance	-1.8	-1.6	2.6	-6	4.5	4.7

Source: B-5

Gross Domestic Product and Related Indicators

Year	1991	1992	1993	1994	1995	1996	1997	1998
GDP, billions of US$	48.14	58.31	64.18	72.50	87.31	100.85	100.20	72.49
Per Capita GDP, US$	2625	3110	3340	3690	4340	4910	4770	3390
GDP Growth Rate	8.48	7.80	8.35	9.24	9.46	8.58	7.81	-6.70
Korea	9.13	5.06	5.75	8.58	8.94	7.10	4.65	-5.80
Indonesia	6.95	6.46	6.50	15.93	8.22	7.98	4.65	-13.70
Philippines	-0.58	0.34	2.12	4.38	4.77	5.76	9.66	-0.50
Singapore	7.27	6.29	10.44	10.05	8.75	7.32	7.55	
Thailand	8.18	8.08	8.38	8.94	8.84	5.52	-0.43	-9.40
Hong Kong	4.97	6.21	6.15	5.51	3.85	5.03	5.29	
China	9.19	14.24	12.09	12.66	10.55	9.54	8.80	
Taiwan	7.55	6.76	6.32	6.54	6.03	5.67	6.81	

Source: GDP and Per Capita GDP data are from B-6. GDP Growth Rate data is from B-2 and 1998 GDP Growth Rate data is from B-3.

Year	1990	1991	1992	1993	1994	1995	1996	1997
Stock Market Prices Index, Malaysia	505.0	556.0	643.0	1275.0	971.0	995.0	1237.0	594.0
Korea	696.0	610.0	678.0	866.0	1027.0	882.0	651.0	376.0
Indonesia	417.0	247.0	274.0	588.0	469.0	513.0	637.0	401.0
Philippines	651.0	1151.0	1256.0	3196.0	2785.0	2594.0	3170.0	1869.0
Thailand	612.0	711.0	893.0	1682.0	1360.0	1280.0	831.0	372.0
Property Sector, Malaysia	113.0	113.0	126.0	369.0	240.0	199.0	294.0	64.0
Indonesia		119.0	66.0	214.0	140.0	112.0	143.0	40.0
Philippines	32.0	34.0	39.0	81.0	80.0	87.0	119.0	59.0

Thailand	74.0	82.0	168.0	367.0	232.0	192.0	99.0	7.0

Source: B-2

Year	1990	1991	1992	1993	1994	1995	1996	1997	1998
Change in Real Wages (%)	2.0	2.2	3.1	3.3	3.5	3.3	8.9	4.0	3.5
Unemployment Rate (%)	7.5	4.3	3.7	3.0	2.9	2.8	2.5	2.5	3.4

Source: B-6

Interest Rates(%), **End of Period**	1993	1994	1995	1996	1997	1998	1999
Treasury Bill Rate (3-month)	5.24	4.50	5.95	6.39	6.76	5.38	2.71
Deposit Rate, Commercial Banks, (12-Months)	6.29	6.15	6.89	7.26	9.33	5.74	3.95

Source: B-1

Year	1990	1991	1992	1993	1994	1995	1996	1997	1998
Saving Rates, % of GDP Malaysia	29.07	23.24	30.06	27.70	33.81	34.65	37.81	39.34	
Korea	35.69	35.71	34.88	34.91	34.60	35.14	33.60	33.06	
Indonesia	31.75	31.10	33.41	28.66	29.52	27.65	27.50	27.98	
Philippines	17.85	17.76	18.16	17.29	20.32	17.16	19.35	18.77	
Singapore	45.32	46.56	48.35	46.17	50.82	51.05	51.33	51.30	
Thailand	32.33	34.83	33.73	34.26	33.89	33.25	33.22	32.64	
Hong Kong	35.85	33.78	33.76	35.67	33.83	31.94	29.95	31.33	
China	37.77	37.84	37.26	41.26	42.04	40.22	39.25	41.15	
Taiwan	30.50	30.26	28.93	28.68	26.99	26.70	25.92	25.43	
Domestic Demand, Annual % Change Malaysia				9.8	13.9	13.6	5.3	7.2	-25.5
Consumption				6.0	9.8	8.9	4.9	4.9	-10.3
Private				4.6	9.8	9.4	6.0	4.7	-12.4
Public				10.7	9.9	7.3	1.4	5.3	-3.5
Investment				16.3	20.3	20.5	5.8	10.2	-44.4
Private				19.1	27.9	25.3	13.4	8.4	-57.8
Public				8.4	-0.6	8.7	1.1	8.6	-10.0
Annual Change in Stocks, % of GDP				0.4	1.1	0.3	-1.8	0.7	0.4

Source: Saving Rates data is from B-2 and the rest is from B-1.

Banking Sector

Year	1990	1991	1992	1993	1994	1995	1996	1997
Bank Lending to Private Sector, % of GDP Malaysia	71.36	75.29	74.72	74.06	74.61	84.80	93.39	106.91
Korea	52.54	52.81	53.34	54.21	56.84	57.04	61.81	69.79

Indonesia	49.67	50.32	49.45	48.90	51.88	53.48	55.42	69.23
Philippines	19.17	17.76	20.44	26.37	29.06	37.52	48.98	56.53
Thailand	64.30	67.70	72.24	80.01	91.00	92.62	101.94	116.33
Bank Lending to Private Sector, % Growth Malaysia		20.58	10.79	10.80	16.04	30.65	25.77	26.96
Korea		20.78	12.55	12.94	20.08	15.45	20.01	21.01
Indonesia		17.82	12.29	25.48	22.97	22.57	21.45	46.42
Philippines		7.33	24.66	40.74	26.52	45.39	48.72	28.79
Thailand		20.45	20.52	24.03	30.26	23.76	14.63	19.80

Source: B-2

Year	1993	1994	1995	1996	1997	1998
Loan/Deposit Ratio, Malaysia						
Commercial Banks	83.5	83.7	88.9	89.3	91.9	92.9
Finance Companies	85.6	87.4	89.7	91.8	96.2	88.6
Merchant Banks			87.9	81.9	87.4	84.3
Non-performing Loans, % of total loans, Malaysia						
Commercial Banks	13.0	6.9	4.9	3.6	4.9	15.0
Finance Companies	14.5	9.9	6.6	4.7	9.2	28.1
Merchant Banks		9.5	7.8	1.7	4.8	32.4
Banking System		7.8	5.5	3.7	6.0	18.9
Public	10.7	9.9	7.3	1.4	5.3	-3.5
Investment	16.3	20.3	20.5	5.8	10.2	-44.4
Private	19.1	27.9	25.3	13.4	8.4	-57.8
Public	8.4	-0.6	8.7	1.1	8.6	-10.0

Source: B-1

Sources

B-1: *Malaysia: Recent Economic Developments.* The International Monetary Fund, IMF Staff Country Report No. 99/85, August 1999; *Malaysia: Statistical Appendix.* The International Monetary Fund, IMF Staff Country Report No.00/130, October 2000; *Malaysia: Selected Issues.* The International Monetary Fund, IMF staff Report No. 98/114, October 1998. Original data is provided by the Malaysian authorities.

B-2: *What Caused the Asian Currency and Financial Crisis?* (Part I: A Macroeconomic Overview), Revised Draft, Giancarlo Corsetti, Paolo Pesenti, and Nouriel Roubini, NBER, September 1998, http://www.stern.nyu.edu/globalmacro, accessed July 15,2001. Original sources include IMF's International Financial Statistics, Economist Intelligence Unit Repots, IMF's World Economic Outlook of December 1997, and Asian Development Bank.

B-3: "The Asia Crisis: Causes, Policy Responses, and Outcomes." Andrew Berg, IMF *Working Paper* WP/99/138, October 1999, 4.

B-4: "The Onset of the East Asian Financial Crisis." Steven Radelet and Jeffrey Sachs, in *Currency Crises*, Paul Krugman ed., Chicago and London: The University of Chicago Press, 2000, 123.

B-5: *Malaysia: Recent Economic Developments*. The International Monetary Fund. IMF Staff Country Report No. 99/85, August 1999; *Malaysia: Statistical Appendix*. The International Monetary Fund, IMF Staff Country Report No.00/130, October 2000. Original data is provided by the Malaysian authorities.

B-6: *Country Forecast*, Volume XIX. William D. Coplin & Michael K. O' Leary, eds., East Syracuse, NY: The PRS Group, LLC, April 2000, 230.

B-7: "The Onset of the East Asian Financial Crisis." Steven Radelet and Jeffrey Sachs, in *Currency Crises*, Paul Krugman ed., Chicago and London: The University of Chicago Press, 2000, 124.

BIBLIOGRAPHY

Books and Articles:

Abbott, Jason. "A Foul Smelling Affair." *The World Today* 55, no.7 (1999): 22-23.

Alatas, Syed Farid. *Democracy and Authoritarianism in Indonesia and Malaysia: The Rise of the Post Colonial State.* London: Macmillan Press Ltd. & New York: St. Martin's Press, Inc., 1997.

Alcocer V., Jorge. "Recent Electoral Reform in Mexico: Prospects for a Real Multiparty Democracy." In *the Challenge of Institutional Reform in Mexico.* Boulder and London: Lynne Rienner Publishers, 1995.

Alesina, Alberto, Nouriel Roubini and Gerald Cohen. *Political Cycles and the Macroeconomy.* Cambridge, MA: MIT Press, 1997.

Ali, Supian, and Mohammad Anuar Adnan. "Microeconomic Approaches to Socioeconomic Development in the Third World." In *Alternative Perspectives in Third World Development: The Case of Malaysia.* New York: St. Martin's Press, Inc., 1996.

Allison, Graham T. *Essence of Decision: Explaining the Cuban Missile Crisis.* Boston: Little Brown, 1971.

Allison, Graham, and Philip Zelikow. *Essence of Decision: Exploring the Cuban Missile Crisis.* New York: Longman, 1999.

Arner, Douglas W. "The Mexican Peso Crisis: Implications for the Regulation of Financial Markets." http://iibf.law.smu.edu/pub/dougla.htm. Accessed December 14, 2000.

Aspe, Pedro and Paul E. Sigmund. "Introduction." In *The Political Economy of Income Distribution in Mexico.* New York and London: Holmes & Meier Publishers, Inc., 1983.

Athukorala, Prema-chandra. *Crisis and Recovery in Malaysia: The Role of Capital Controls.* Cheltenham, UK and Northampton, MA: Edward Elgar, 2001.

_____."Swimming against the Tide: Crisis Management in Malaysia." *ASEAN Economic Bulletin* 15, No.3 (December 1998).

Atkeson, Andrew, and José-Víctor Ríos-Rull. "The Balance of Payments and Borrowing Constraints: An Alternative View of the Mexican Crisis." *Journal of International Economics* 41 (1996): 331-349.

Barry, Tom. *Zapata's Revenge: Free Trade and the Farm Crisis in Mexico.* Boston, Massachusetts: South End Press, 1995.

Bartley, Robert L. "The Peso Folklórico: Dancing Away From Monetary Stability." In *Mexico 1994: Anatomy of an Emerging-Market Crash.* Washington, DC:Carnegie Endowment for International Peace, 1997.

Berg, Andrew. "The Asia Crisis: Causes, Policy Responses, and Outcomes." *IMF Working Paper* WP/99/138 (October 1999).

Bhalla, A.S. *Market or Government Failures? An Asian Perspective.* New York, NY: Palgrave, 2001.

Biers, Dan, ed. *Crash of'97: How the Financial Crisis is Reshaping Asia.* Far Eastern Economic Review, 1997.

Bikhchandani, S., D. Hirshleifer, and I. Welch. "A Theory of Fads, Fashions, Customs, and Cultural Change as Informational Cascades." In *Journal of Political Economy* 100, (1992): 992-1026.

Bisignano, Joseph R. "Precarious Credit Equilibria: Reflections on the Asian Financial Crisis." In *the Asian Financial Crisis: Origins, Implications, and Solutio.* Boston and London: Kluwer Academic Publishers, 1999. 75-113.

Blinder, Alan S. "Eight Steps to New Financial Order." *Foreign Affairs* 78, No. 5 (September /October 1999).

Botz, Dan La. *Democracy in Mexico: Peasant Rebellion and Political Reform.* Boston, MA: South End Press, 1995.

Buiter, Willem H., Gancarlo M. Corsetti and Paolo A. Pesenti. *Interpreting the ERM Crisis: Country-Specific and Systemic Issues.* Princeton, N.J.: International Finance Section, Dept. of Economics, Princeton University, 1998.

Burki, Shahid Javed. "A Fate Foretold: The World Bank and the Mexican Crisis." In *Mexico 1994: Anatomy of an Emerging-Market Crash.* Washington, DC: Carnegie Endowment for International Peace, 1997.

Calvo, Guillermo A. "Balance of Payments Crises in Emerging Markets: Large Capital Inflows and Sovereign Governments." In *Currency Crises.* Chicago and London: The University of Chicago Press, 2000. 71-97.

Calvo, Guillermo A., and Enrique G. Mendoza. "Mexico's Balance-of-payments Crisis: A Chronicle of a Death Foretold." *Journal of International Economics* 41 (1996): 235-264.

Camp, Roderic Ai. *Politics in Mexico: The Decline of Authoritarianism.* 3rd ed. New York and Oxford: Oxford University Press, 1999.

Centeno, Miguel Ángel. *Democracy within Reason: Technocratic Revolution in Mexico.* 2nd ed. University Park, Pennsylvania: The Pennsylvania State University Press, 1997.

Chang, Michele. 2002. "Domestic Politics and Currency Crisis: The European Experience." http://departments.colgate.edu/polisci/papers Accessed November 6, 2002.

Chang, R. and A. Velasco. *Financial Fragility and the Exchange Rate Regime.* Working Paper. New York: New York University, C. V. Starr School of Business, 1998a.

_____. *Financial Crises in Emerging Markets: A Canonical Model.* Working Paper. New York: New York University, C. V. Starr School of Business, 1998b.

Chin, James. "Malaysia in 1998: Mahathir's Annus Horribilis." In *Asian Survey* 38, No.2 (February 1998): 183-189.

Chin, Kok Fay and Jomo K.S.. "Financial Liberalization and System Vulnerability." In *Malaysian Eclipse: Economic Crisis and Recovery.* London and New York: Zed Books Ltd., 2001. 90-133.

Clifford, Mark L. and Pete Engardio. *Meltdown: Asia's Boom, Bust, and Beyond.* Paramus, NJ: Prentice Hall Press, 2000.

Cole, Harold L., and Timothy J. Kehoe. "A Self-fulfilling Model of Mexico's 1994-1995 Debt Crisis." *Journal of International Economics* 41 (1996):309-330.

Collier, David. "The Comparative Politics." In *Political Science: The State of the Discipline II.* Washington, DC: APSA, 1993.

Coplin, William D. and Michael K. O'Leary, eds. *Country Forecast.* Vol.XXXII. East Syracuse, NY: The PRS Group, LLC, April 2001.

Cornelius, Wayne A. and Ann L. Craig. *The Mexican Political System in Transition.* Monograph Series 35. San Diego: University of California, Center for U.S.-Meixcan Studies, 1991.

Corsetti, Giancarlo and Nouriel Roubini. "Politically Motivated Fiscal Deficits: Policy Issues in Closed and Open Economies." *Economics & Politics* (March 1997): 27-55.

Corsetti, Giancarlo, Paolo Pesenti, and Nouriel Roubini. What Caused the Asian Currency and Financial Crisis? (Part I: A Macroeconomic Overview, Part II: The Policy Debate). Revised Draft of September 1998. http://www.stern.nyu.edu/globalmac ro. Accessed July 13, 2001.

Cothran, Dan A. *Political Stability and Democracy in Mexico: The "Perfect Dictatorship"?* London, Westview, Connecticut: Praeger, 1994.

Das, Udaibir S., Plamen Iossifow, Richord Podpiera, and Dmitriy Rozhkov. "Quality of Financial Policies and Financial System Stress." *IMF Working Paper* WP/05/173 (August 2005).

Diamond, Douglas, and Phillip Dybvig. "Bank Runs, Liquidity, and Deposit Insurance." *Journal of Political Economy* 91 (1983): 401-419.

De Long, Bradford, Christopher De Long, and Sherman Robinson. *Foreign Affairs* (May /June 1996): 8.

Dombrowski, Peter. "Haute Finance and High Theory: Recent Scholarship on Global Financial Relations." *Mershon International Studies Review* 42 (1998): 1-28.

Domínguez, Jorge I. "The Transformation of Mexico's Electoral and Party System, 1988-1997: An Introduction." In *Toward Mexico's Democratization: Parties Campaigns, Elections, and Public Opinion.* New York and London: Routledge,1999.

Dornbusch, Rudiger. "Mexico: How to Recover Stability and Growth." In *Stabilization, Debt, and Reform.* Englewood Cliffs, NJ: Prentice-Hall, 1993.

Dornbusch, Rudiger, and Alejandro Werner. "Mexico: Stabilization, Reform, and No Growth." *World Economy Laboratory Working Paper.* Boston, Mass.: Massachusetts Institute of Technology, April 1994. 94-108.

_____. "Mexico: Stabilization, Reform, and No Growth." *Brookings Papers on Economic Activity* 1, (1994): 253-316.

Drazen, Allan. "Political Contagion in Currency Crises." In *Currency Crises.* Chicago and London: The University of Chicago Press, 2000. 47-66.

Dresser, Denise. "Falling From the Tightrope: The Political Economy of the Mexican Crisis." In *Mexico 1994: Anatomy of an Emerging-Market Crash.* Washington, DC: Carnegie Endowment for International Peace, 1997.

Edwards, Sebastian. "Bad Luck or Bad Policies? An Economic Analysis of the Crisis." In *Mexico 1994: Anatomy of an Emerging-Market Crash.* Washington, DC: Carnegie Endowment for International Peace, 1997.

Edwards, Sebastian, and Miguel A. Savastano. "The Mexican Peso in the Aftermath of the 1994 Currency Crisis." In *Currency Crises.* Chicago and London: The University of Chicago Press, 2000. 183-236.

Eichengreen, Barry, and Oliver Jeanne. "Currency Crisis and Unemployment: Sterling in 1931." In *Currency Crises.* Chicago and London: The University of Chicago Press, 2000. 7-43

Eichengreen, Barry, and Andrew K. Rose. *The Empirics of Currecny and Banking Crises.* Andrew K. Rose's web page. http://www.haas.berkeley.edu/~arose/RecRes.htm. Acccessed August 12, 2001.

Eichengreen, Barry and Charles Wyplosz. "The Unstable EMS." *Brookings Papers on Economic Activity* 1 (1993): 51-143.

Eichengreen, Baryy and Richard Portes. "The Anatomy of Financial Crisis." In *Threats to International Financial Stability.* New York & Cambridge: Cambridge University Press, 1987.

Eichengreen, Barry, Andrew K. Rose, and Charles Wyplosz. "Contagious Currency Crises," 1997. Andrew K. Rose's web page. http://www.haas.berkeley.edu/~arose /RecRes.htm. Accessed August 12, 2001.

_____. "Speculative Attacks on Pegged Exchange Rates: An Empirical Exploration with Special Reference to the European Monetary System."In *The New Transatlantic Economy*. New York and Cambridge: Cambridge University Press, 1996a.

_____."Contagious Currency Crises." *NBER Working Paper* No. 5681. Cambridge, Mass.: National Bureau of Economics Research, 1996b.

_____. "Exchange Market Mayhem: The Antecedents and Aftermath of Speculative Attacks." http://www.haas.berkeley.edu/~arose/RecRes.htm. Accessed August 12, 2001. Also available in *Economic Policy* 21 (1995): 249-312.

Embong, Abdul Rahman."Pluralism in Post-Colonial Malaysia." In *the Politics of Multiculturalism: Pluralism and Citizenship in Malaysia, Singapore, and Indonesia*. Honolulu: University of Hawai'i Press, 2001. 59-85.

Erfani, Julie A. *The Paradox of the Mexican State: Rereading Sovereignty from Independence to NAFTA*. Boulder, London: Lynne Rienner Publishers, 1995.

Espinosa, Marco and Steven Russell. "The Mexican Economic Crisis: Alternative Views." Federal Reserve Bank of Atlanta. *Economic Review* (January/February 1996).

Felker, Greg. "Malaysia in 1998: A Cornered Tiger Bares Its Claws." In *Asian Suvery* 39, No.1 (January/February1999): 43-54.

Feng, Yi. "Political Foundations of Economic Management: an Interpretation of Economic Development and Economic Crisis in East Asia." In *the East Asian Development Model: Economic Growth, Institutional Failure, and the Aftermath of the Crisis*. The U.K.: Macmillan Press Ltd. & the U.S.: St. Martin's Press, Llc., 2000.71-96.

Fisk, E.K. "Development in Malaysia." In *The Political Economy of Malaysia*. Kuala Lumpur: Oxford University Press, 1982.

Flood, Robert P. and Peter M. Garber. "Collapsing Exchange Rate Regimes: Some Linear Examples." *Journal of International Economics* 17 (August 1984):1-14.

Flood, Robert P., Peter M. Garber and Charles Kramer. "Collapsing Exchange Rate Regimes: Another Linear Example." *Journal of International Economics* 41 (1996): 223-234.

Frankel, Jeffrey A. and Andrew K. Rose. "Currency Crashes in Emerging Markets: An Empirical Treatment." *Journal of International Economics* 41 (1996): 351-366.

Frieden, Jeffry A. "The Euro: Who Wins? Who Loses?" *Foreign Policy* (Fall 1998): 25-40.

_____. "The Politics of Exchange Rate." In *Mexico 1994: Anatomy of an Emerging-Market Crash*. Washington, DC: Carnegie Endowment for International Peace, 1997.

_____."Invested Interests: The Politics of National Economic Policies in a World of Global Finance." *International Organization* 45, Issue 5 (August 1991).

Frieden, Jeffry A. and Ronald Rogowski. "The Impact of the International Economy on National Politics: An Analytical Overview." In *Internationalization and Domestic Politics*. Cambridge: Cambridge University Press, 1996. 25-47

Friedman, Thomas L. "Shakespeare Does Malaysia." *The New York Times*, August 24, 1999, A15.

Gerlach, Stefan and Frank Smets."Contagious Speculative Attacks." *European Journal of Political Economy* 11 (1994): 5-63.

Gil-Díaz, Francisco. and Agustín. Carstens. "Pride and Prejudice: The Economics Profession and Mexico's Financial Crisis." In *Mexico 1994: Anatomy of an Emerging-Market Crash*. Washinton, DC: Carnegie Endowment for International Peace, 1997.

_____. "One Year of Solitude: Some Pilgrim Tales About Mexico's 1994-95 Crisis." *American Economic Review Papers and Proceedings* 86, No.2 (May 1996):164-169.

Gilpin, Robert. *Global Political Economy: Understanding the International Economic Order.* Princeton and Oxford: Princeton University Press, 2001.

_____. *The Challenge of Global Capitalism: The World Economy in the 21st Century.* Princeton, NJ: Princeton University Press, 2000.

Goldstein, Morris. *The Asian Financial Crisis: Causes, Cures, and Systemic Implications.* Washington, DC: Institute for International Economics, 1998.

Gomez, Edmund Terence, and Jomo K.S. *Malaysia's Political Economy: Politics, Patronage and Profits.* Updated ed. New York & Cambridge: Cambridge University Press, 1999.

_____.*Malaysia's Political Economy: Politics, Patronage and Profits.* New York & Cambridge: Cambridge University Press, 1997.

Gómez, Mauricio A. González. "Crisis and Economic Change in Mexico."In *Mexico Under Zedillo.* Boulder and London: Lynne Rienner Publishers, 1998.

Gough, Leo. *Asia Meltdown: The End of the Miracle?* Oxford, the U.K.: Capstone Publishing Limited,1998.

Gould, David M. "Mexico's Crisis: Looking Back to Assess the Future" In *Changing Structure of Mexico: Political, Social, and Economic Prospects.* New York and London: M.E. Sharpe, 1996.

Gourevitch, Peter. *Politics in Hard Times: Comparative Responses to International Economic Crisis.* Ithaca and London: Cornell University Press, 1986.

Grayson, George W. *A Guide to the 1994 Mexican Presidential Election.* Washington, DC: The Center for Strategic and International Studies, 1994.

Greenspan, Alan. Testimony Before the Committee on Banking, Housing, and Urban Affairs on January 31, 1995. U.S. Congress. Senate. Committee on Banking, Housing, and Urban Affairs. SUDOC: Y4.B22/3:S.HRG.104-164, 1995.

Haggard, Stephen, Chung H. Lee, and Sylvia Maxfield, eds. *The Politics of Finance in Developing Countries.* Ithaca: Cornell University Press, 1993.

Halperin, Morton H., with the assistance of Priscilla Clapp, and Arnold Kanter. *Bureaucratic Politics and Foreign Policy.* Washington, DC: The Brookings Institution, 1974.

Harvey, Neil. *The Chiapas Rebellion: The Struggle for Land and Democracy.* Durham and London: Duke University Press, 1998.

Heath, Jonathan. *Mexico and the Sexenio Curse: Presidential Successions and Economic Crisis in Modern Mexico.* Washington, DC: The CSIS Press, 1999.

Hefeker, Carsten. *Interest Groups and Monetary Integration: The Political Economy of Exchange Rate Regime.* Boulder, CO.: Westview Press, 1997.

Henderson, Callum. *Asia Falling: Making Sense of the Asian Crisis and Its Aftermath.* New York: McGraw Hill, 1998.

Hilley, John. *Malaysia: Mahathirism, Hegemony and the New Opposition.* London and New York: Zed Books, 2001.

Hitchcock, David I. "Internal Problems in East Asia." *The Washington Quarterly* 21, No.2 (Spring 1998):121-134.

Horowitz, Shale and Uk Heo, eds. *The Political Economy of International Financial Crisis: Interest Groups, Ideologies, and Institutions.* New York & Oxford: Rowman & Littlefield Publishers, Inc., 2001.

Hutchcroft, Paul. "Neither Dynamo nor Domino: Reforms and Crises in the Philippine Political Economy." In *the Politics of the Asian Economic Crisis*. Ithaca and London: Cornell University Press, 1999. 163-183.

Jackson, Karl D. "Introduction: The Roots of the Crisis." *Asian Contagion: The Causes and Consequences of a Financial Crisis*. Boulder, CO: Westview Press, 1999.

Janis, Irving Lesler. *Groupthink: Psychological Studies of Policy Decisions and Fiascoes*. 2nd ed. Boston: Houghton Mifflin, 1982.

Jeanne, Olivier. *Currency Crises: A Perspective on Recent Theoretical Developments*. Special Papers in International Economics No. 20. Princeton, NJ: Princeton University Press, Department of Economics, 2000.

Jervis, Robert . *System Effects: Complexity in Political and Social Life,* Princeton: Princeton University Press, 1997.

Jomo K.S. "From Currency Crisis to Recession." In *Malaysian Eclipse: Economic Crisis and Recovery*. London & New York: Zed Books Ltd., 2001a. 1-46

_____. "Capital Flows." In *Malaysian Eclipse: Economic Crisis and Recovery*. London and New York: Zed Books Ltd., 2001b. 134-173.

_____. "Capital Controls." In *Malaysian Eclipse: Economic Crisis and Recovery*. London and New York: Zed Books Ltd., 2001c. 199-215.

_____. *Growth and Structural Change in the Malaysian Economy*. New York: St. Martin's Press, 1990.

Jones, David Martin. "What Mahathir Has Wrought." *The National Interest*, Spring 2000.

Josselin, Daphne. *Money Politics in the New Europe: Britain, France and the Single Financial Market*. Hampshire: Macmillan Press & New York: St. Martin's Press, 1997.

Kalter, Eliot and Armando Ribas. "The 1994 Mexican Economic Crisis: The Role of Government Expenditure and Relative Prices." *IMF Working Paper* WP/99/160 (December 1999).

Kamin, Steven B. and John H. Rogers. "Monetary Policy in the End-game to Exchange-Rate Based Stabilization: the Case of Mexico." *Journal of International Economics* 41 (1996): 285-307.

Kaminsky, Graciela L. "Currency and Banking Crises: The Early Warnings of Distress." *IMF Working Paper* WP/99/178 (December 1999).

Kaminsky, Graciela L. and Carmen M. Reinhart. "Financial Crises in Asia and Latin America: Then and Now." *American Economic Review* 88. No. 2 (1998): 444-448.

Kaplan, Ethan and Dani Rodrik. "Did the Malaysian Capital Controls Work?" *NBER Working Paper* No. W8142 (February 2001).

Katzenstein, Peter. *Between Power and Plenty: Foreign Economic Policies of Advanced Industrial States*. Madison: University of Wisconsin Press, 1978.

Keohane, Robert O., and Joseph S. Nye. *Power and Interdependence*. 2nd ed. New York and London: Harper Collins Publishers, 1989.

_____."Transnational Relations and World Politics: An Introduction." *International Organization* XXV, No. 3 (Summer 1971).

King, Gary, Robert O. Keohane, and Sidney Verba. *Designing Social Inquiry: Scientific Inference in Qualitative Research*. Princeton, NJ: Princeton University Press, 1994.

Kleinberg, Remonda Bensabat. "Economic Liberalization and Inequality in Mexico: Prospects for Democracy." In *Economic Liberalization, Democratization and Civil Society in the Developing World*. London: Macmillan Press Ltd & New York: St. Martin's Press, Inc., 2000.

Kok-Wah Loh, Francis. "State-Societal Relations in a Rapidly Growing Economy: the Case of Malaysia, 1970-1997." In *Economic Liberalization, Democratization and Civil Society in the Developing World.* New York: St. Martin's Press, Inc., 2000. 65-87.

Krauze, Enrique. *Mexico: Biography of Power: A History of Modern Mexico, 1810-1996.* New York and London: Harper Collins Publishers, 1997.

Krugman, Paul R. *Crises: The Next Generation?* Draft, March 2001. http://www.stern. nyu.edu/globalmacro. Accessed July 12, 2001.

_____. "Introduction." in *Currency Crises.* Chicago and London: The University of Chicago Press, 2000.1-6.

_____."Balance Sheets, the Transfer Problem, and Financial Crises." In *International Finance and Financial Crises: Essays in Honor of Robert P. Flood, Jr.* Boston: Kluwer, 1999. 31-44

_____."The Myth of Asia's Miracle." *Foreign Affairs* 73 (November/ December 1994): 62-78.

_____. *Currencies and Crises.* London and Cambridge, Mass.: The MIT Press, 1991.

_____. "A Model of Balance-of-Payments Crisis." *Journal of Money Credit and Banking* 11 (August 1979): 311-335.

Krugman, Paul R. & Maurice, Obstfeld. *International Economics: Theory and Policy.* New York: Addison-Wesley, 2000.

Leblang, David A. "Political Uncertainty and Speculative Attacks." In *Coping with Globalization: Cross-National Patterns in Domestic Governance and Policy Performance.* London: Frank Cass, 2002a.

_____."The Political Economy of Speculative Attacks in the Developing World." *International Studies Quarterly* 46 (2002b):69-91.

_____. "To Defend or to Devalue: The Political Economy of Exchange Rate Policy." May 2001.http://sobek.colorado.edu/~leblang/Research.htm. Accessed November 3, 2002.

Leblang, David A. and William Bernhard. "Domestic Processes and Political Risks: Evidence from Foreign Exchange Markets." *The American Journal of Political Science* 46 (2002):316-333.

_____."The Politics of Speculative Attacks in Industrial Democracies." *International Organization* 54, No.2 (Spring 2000): 291-324.

Lingle, Christopher. "The Institutional Basis of Asia's Economic Crisis." In *the East Asian Development Model: Economic Growth, Institutional Failure and the Aftermath of the Crisis.* The U.K.: Macmillan Press Ltd. & the U.S.: St. Martin's Press, Llc., 2000. 53-70.

Loh Kok Wah, Frances. "Where Has (Ethnic) Politics Gone? The Case of the BN Non-Malay Politicians and Political Parties." In *Singapore and the Politics of Multiculturalism: Pluralism and Citizenship in Malaysia Indonesia.* Honolulu: University of Hawai'i Press, 2001. 183-226.

Looney, Robert E. *Economic Policy Making in Mexico: Factors Underlying the 1982 Crisis.* Durham. NC: Duke University Press, 1985.

Loser, Claudio M. and Ewart S. Williams. "The Mexican Crisis and Its Aftermath: An IMF Perspective." In *Mexico 1994: Anatomy of an Emerging-Market Crash.* Washington, DC: Carnegie Endowment for International Peace, 1997.

Lucas, Robert E. B. and Donald Verry. *Restructuring the Malaysian Economy: Development and Human Resources.* New York: St. Martin's Press, Inc., 1999.

Lusting, Nora. *Mexico: The Remaking of an Economy.* Washington, D.C. Brookings Institution Press, 1992.

MacIntyre, Andrew. "Political Institutions and the Economic Crisis in Thailand and Indonesia." In *the Politics of the Asian Economic Crisis*. Ithaca and London: Cornell University Press, 1999. 143-162.

Malik, Uzir Abdul. "Privatization as an Instrument of National Policy and Socio Economic Restructuring." In *Alternative Perspectives in Third-World Development: The Case of Malaysia*. New York: St.Martin's Press, Inc., 1996.

Masson, Paul. "Gaining and Losing EMS Credibility: The Case of the United Stated Kingdom." *Economic Journal* 105 (1995):571-582.

Maxfield, Sylvia. *Governing Capital: International Finance and Mexican Politics*. Ithaca and London: Cornell University Press, 1990.

McKinnon, R., and H. Pill. "Credible Liberalization and International Capital Flows: The Overborrowing Syndrome." In *Financial Deregulation and Integration in East Asia*. Chicago: University of Chicago Press, 1996.

Means, Gordon P. *Malaysian Politics: The Second Generation*. Singapore: Oxford University Press, 1991.

Mehmet, Ozay. *Development in Malaysia: Poverty, Wealth and Trusteeship*. London, Sydney & Dover NH: Croom Helm, 1986.

Meier, Gerald M. *The International Environment of Business: Competition and Governance in the Global Economy*. New York & Oxford: Oxford University Press, 1998.

Michie, Jonathan and John Grive Smith, eds. *Global Instability: The Political Economy of World Economic Governance*. London and New York: Routledge, 1999.

Milesi-Ferretti, Gian Maria, and Assaf Razin. "Current Account Reversals and Currency Crises: Empirical Regularities." In *Currency Crises*. Chicago & London: The University of Chicago Press, 2000. 285-323.

Milne, R.S. and Diane K. Mauzy. *Malaysian Politics under Mahathir*. London and New York: Routledge, 1999.

Milner, Helen V. and Robert O. Keohane, eds. *Internationalization and Domestic Politics*. Cambridge University Press, 1996.

Mohamad, Dato' Seri Dr. Mahathir Bin. His Talk at the Plenary Session of the Tenth United Nations Conference on Trade and Development (UNCTAD X), Bangkok, Thailand, on February 12, 2000. www.smpke.jpm.my/UcapWebNew/PMMain... Accessed March 1, 2000.

_____."Currency Controls the Best Way Out." *New Straits Times* (Malaysia), October 17, 1998, 10.

Morris, Stephen D. *Political Reformism in Mexico: An Overview of Contemporary Mexican Politics*. Boulder and London: Lynne Rienner Publishers, 1995.

_____. *Corruption & Politics in Contemporary Mexico*. Tuscaloosa and London: The University of Alabama Press, 1991.

Munro-Kua, Anne. *Authoritarian Populism in Malaysia*. London: Macmillan Press Ltd., New York: St. Martin's Press, Inc., 1996.

Naím, Moisés. "Mexico's Larger Story." In *Mexico 1994: Anatomy of an Emerging-Market Crash*. Washington, DC: Carnegie Endowment for International Peace, 1997. Reprinted from *Foreign Policy* 99 (Summer 1995).

Nelson, Joan M. *Economic Crisis and Policy Choice: The Politics of Adjustment in Developing Countries*. Princeton, N.J.: Princeton University Press, 1990.

Obstfeld, Maurice. "Models of Currency Crises with Self-Fulfilling Features." *European Economic Review* 40 (April 1996):1037-1048.

_____. "The Logic of Currency Crises." *NBER Working Paper* No. 4640 (February 1994).

Olson, Mancur. *Power and Prosperity: Outgrowing Communist and Capitalist Dictatorships.* New York: Basic Books, 2000.

_____. Discussion by Mancur Olson on Multilateral and Bilateral Trade Policies. In *New Dimensions in Regional Integration.* Edited by Jaime De Melo and Arvind Panagariya,. New York: Cambridge University Press, 1993.122-127.

_____. *The Logic of Collective Action: Public Goods and the Theory of Groups.* Cambridge, Mass.: Harvard University Press,1971.

Olson, Mancur and Satu Kähkönen, eds. *A Not-so-dismal Science: A Broader View of Economies and Societies.* New York: Oxford University Press, 2000.

Orum, Anthony M., Joe R. Feagin, and Gideon Sjoberg. "Introduction: The Nature of the Case Study." In *A Case for Case Study.* Chapel Hill and London: University of North Carolina Press, 1991.

Otero, Gerardo. "Neoliberal Reform and Politics in Mexico: An Overview" In *Neoliberalism Revisited: Economic Restructuring and Mexico's Political Future.* Westview Press,1996.

Ozkan, F. Gulcin and Alan Sutherland. "A Model of the ERM crisis." *CEPR Discussion Paper* No. 879 (January 1994).

Pastor, Manual, Jr. "Pesos, Policies, and Predictions: Why the Crisis, Why the Surprise, and Why the Recovery?" In *The Post-NAFTA Political Economy: Mexico and the Western Hemisphere.* University Park, PA: The Pennsylvania State University Press, 1998.

Pérez, Al I. "Free Trade with Mexico and U.S. National Security." In *Mexico Faces the 21ˢᵗ Century.* Westport, CT: Greenwood Press, 1995.

Perkins, Dwight Heald and Wing Thye Woo. "Malaysia: Adjusting to Deep Integration with the World Economy." In *the Asian Financial Crisis: Lessons for a Resilient Asia.* London and Cambridge, MA: The MIT Press, 2000. 227-255.

Peterson, Erik R. "Surrendering to Markets." *Washington Quarterly* 18 (1995): 103-115.

Pillay, Subramaniam S. "The Malaysian Model: Governance, Economic Management and the Future of the Development State." In *the East Asian Development Model: Economic Growth, Institutional Failure and the Aftermath of the Crisis.* The U.K.: Macmillan Press Ltd. and the U.S.: St. Martin's Press, Llc., 2000. 203-238.

Pugel, Thomas A. and Peter H. Lindert. *International Economics.* New York: Irwin McGraw-Hill, 2000.

Purcell, Susan Kaufman."The New U.S.-Mexican Relationship." In *Mexico Under Zedillo.* Boulder and London: Lynne Rienner Publishers, 1998.

Putnam, Robert D. "Diplomacy and Domestic Politics: The Logic of Two Level Games." *International Organization* 42, No. 3 (Summer 1988).

Quiroga, Aldo Flores. "Mexico: Crises and the Domestic Politics of Sustained Liberalization." In *The Political Economy of International Financial Crisis: Interest Groups, Ideologies, and Institutions.* New York and Oxford: Rowman & Littlefield Publishers, Inc., 2001. 179-198.

Radelet, Steven and Jeffrey Sachs. "The Onset of the East Asian Financial Crisis," In *Currency Crises.* Chicago and London: The University of Chicago Press, 2000. 105-153.

Ragin, Charles C. *The Comparative Method: Moving Beyond Qualitative and Quantitative Strategies.* Berkeley, Los Angeles, and London: University of California Press, 1987.

Rakshit, Mihir. *The East Asian Currency Crisis.* New York and Oxford: Oxford University Press, 2002.

Ramírez de la O, Rogelio. "The Mexican Peso Crisis and Recession of 1994-1995: Preventable Then, Avoidable in the Future?" In *The Mexican Peso Crisis: International Perspectives*. Boulder and London: Lynne Rienner Publishers, 1996.

Rasiah, Rajah. "Class, Ethnicity and Economic Development in Malaysia." In t*he Political Economy of the South-East Asia: An Introduction*. Melbourne: Oxford University Press, 1997.

Reding, Andrew. "Mexico: The Crumbling of the 'Perfect Dictatorship." *World Policy Journal* 8, No.2 (Spring1991).

Richter, Frank-Jürgen. "Economic Development and Crisis in East Asia." In *the East Asian Development Model: Economic Growth, Institutional Failure and the Aftermath of the Crisis*. The U.K.: Macmillan Press, Ltd. and the U.S.: St. Martin's Press, Llc., 2000. 1-13.

Rijckeghem, Van & Beatrice Weder. "Sources of Contagion: Finance or Trade?" *IMF Working Paper* WP/99/146 (October 1999).

Rodríguez, Victoria E. and Peter M. Ward. "Introduction: Governments of the Opposition in Mexico." In *Opposition Government in Mexico*. Albuquerque: University of New Mexico Press,1995.

Roett, Riordan. "The Mexican Devaluation and the U.S. Response: Potomac Politics, 1995-Style." In *The Mexican Peso Crisis: International Perspectives*. Boulder and London: Lynne Rienner Publishers, 1996.

Root, Hilton L. "Suharto's Tax on Indonesia's Future." In *the East Asian Development Model: Economic Growth, Institutional Failure and the Aftermath of the Crisis*. The U.K.: Macmillan Press Ltd, and the U.S.: St. Martin's Press, Llc., 2000. 228-238.

Rosenau, James N. *Along the Domestic-Foreign Frontier: Exploring Governance in a Turbulent World*. Cambridge, U.K. and New York: Cambridge University Press, 1997.

_____."Toward the Study of National-International Linkages." In *The Scientific Study of Foreign Policy*. New York: Nichols Pub. Co., 1980.

Roubini, Nouriel. *Chronology of the Asian Currency Crises and its Global Contagion*. 1997-1998. Professor Nouriel Roubini's web page at New York University. http://www.stern.nyu.edu/~nroubini/asia/AsiaChronology1.html. Accessed October 12, 1999.

Rubin, Trudy. "Western Way not Always Right." *The State* (SC), September 30, 1999, A15.

Rubio, Luis. "Coping with Political Change." In *Mexico Under Zedillo*. Boulder and London: Lynne Rienner Publishers, 1998.

Russell, Philip L. *Mexico under Salinas*. Austin, TX: Mexico Resource Center, 1994.

Sabatier, Paul A. ed. *Theories of the Policy Process*. Boulder, CO: Westview Press, 1999.

Sachs, Jeffrey, Aarón Tornell, and Andrés Velasco *Financial Crises in Emerging Markets: The Lessons From 1995*. Working Paper 5576. National Bureau of Economic Research, May 1996a.

_____. "The Mexican Peso Crisis: Sudden Death of Death Foretold?" *Journal of International Economics* 41 (1996b):265-283.

_____. *The Collapse of the Mexican Peso: What Have We Learned?* Working Paper No. 5142. Cambridge, MA: National Bureau of Economic Research, June 1995.

Schlossstein, Steven. *Asia's New Little Dragons: the Dynamic Emergence of Indonesia, Thailand, and Malaysia*. Chicago: Contemporary Books, 1991.

Schulz, Donald E."Through a Glass Darkly: On the Challenges and Enigmas of Mexico's Future." In *Mexico Faces the 21ˢᵗ Century*. Westport, CT: Greenwood Press, 1995.

Schulz, Donald E. and Edward J. Williams. "Crisis of Transformation: The Struggle for the Soul of Mexico." In *Mexico Faces the 21ˢᵗ Century*. Westport, CT: Greenwood Press, 1995.

Shamsul A.B. "The Redefinition of Politics and the Transformation of Malaysian Pluralism." In *the Politics of Multiculturalism: Pluralism and Citizenship in Malaysia, Singapore, and Indonesia*. Honolulu: University of Hawai'i Press, 2001. 204-226.

Sharma, Shalendra. "The Missed Lessons of the Mexican Peso Crisis." *Challenge* 44, No.1 (January/February 2001).

Shin, Dongyoub. "Dual Sources of the South Korean Economic Crisis: Institutional and Organizational Failures and the Structural Transformation of the Economy." In *the East Asian Development Model: Economic Growth, Institutional Failure and the Aftermath of the Crisis*, The U.K.: Macmillan Press Ltd. and the U.S.: St. Martin's Press, Llc., 2000. 169-202.

Smith, Peter H. "Political Dimensions of the Peso Crisis." In *Mexico, 1994: Anatomy of an Emerging-Market Crash*. Washington, DC: Carnegie Endowment for International Peace, 1997.

Smith, Peter H. and Robert L. Bartley. "Mexico: A Chronology of Financial, Economic, and Political Events." In *Mexico 1994: Anatomy of an Emerging-Market Crash*. Washington, DC: Carnegie Endowment for International Peace, 1997.

Stiglitz, Joseph E. *Globalization and Its Discontents*. New York & London: W. W. Norton & Company, 2002.

Strange, Susan. *Mad Money*. Manchester: Manchester University Press, 1998.

_____. *The Retreat of the State: The Diffusion of Power in the World Economy*. Cambridge, the U.K. and New York: Cambridge University Press, 1996.

_____. *Casino Capitalism*. Oxfort, U.K. and New York: B. Blackwell, 1986.

Summers, Lawrence H. Testimony Before the Senate Committee on Banking, Housing, and Urban Affairs on March 10, 1995. U.S. Congress. Senate. Committee on Banking, Housing, and Urban Affairs. SUDOC: Y4.B22/3:S.HRG.104-164, 1995.

Teik, Khoo Boo. *Paradoxes of Mahathirism: An Intellectual Biograph of Mahathir Mohamad*. Kuala Lumpur: Oxford University Press, 1995.

The World Bank. "Mexican Exchange Rate Crisis: A Difficult Week." 1995. Mexican Economic Crisis Homepage. http://www.worldbank.org/wbi/edimp/mex/excri.ht ml Accessed December 4, 2000.

Tilly, Charles. *Big Structures, Large Processes, and Huge Comparisons*. New York: Russell Sage Foundation, 1984.

Toussaint, Eric. *Your Money or Your Life!: The Tyranny of Global Finance*. 1ˢᵗ English Language ed. London and Sterling, VA: Pluto Press, 1999.

Toyoda, A. Maria. "Malaysia: Ethnic Cleavages and Controlled Liberalization." In *The Political Economy of International Financial Crisis: Interest Groups, Ideologies, and Institutions*. New York and Oxford: Rowman & Littlefield Publishers, Inc., 2001. 91-110.

Trejo, Guillermo and Claudio Jones. "Political Dilemmas of Welfare Reform: Poverty and Inequality in Mexico."*Mexico Under Zedillo*. Boulder & London: Lynne Rienner Publishers, 1998.

Tsebelis, George. *Nested Games: Rational Choice in Comparative Politics*. Berkeley, Los Angeles, Oxford: University of California Press, 1990.

Verdier, Daniel. "Domestic Responses to Capital Market Internationalization Under the Gold Standard, 1870-1914." *International Organization* .52, No.1 (Winter 1998.): 1-34.

Wah, Frances Loh Kok and Joel S. Kahn. "Introduction: Fragmented Vision." In *Fragmented Vision: Culture and Politics in Contemporary Malaysia*. Honolulu: University of Hawaii Press, 1992.

Walsh, James I. *European Monetary Integration & Domestic Politics: Britain, France, and Italy*. Boulder and London: Lynne Rienner Publishers, 2000.

Waltz, Kenneth N. *Theory of International Politics*. Boston: Addison-Wesley, 1979.

Wei, Shang-Jin. *Negative Alchemy? Corruption and Composition of Capital Flows*. Technical Papers No.165. Paris: OECD Development Center, October 2000.

Wei, Shang-Jin and Sara E. Sievers. "The Cost of Crony Capitalism." In *the Asian Financial Crisis: Lessons for a Resilient Asia*. London & Cambridge, MA: 2000. 91-123.

Weintraub, Sidney. *Financial Decision-Making in Mexico: To Bet a Nation*. Pittsburgh, PA: University of Pittsburgh Press, 2000.

_____. "Mexico's Foreign Economic Policy: From Admiration to Disappointment." *Changing Structure of Mexico: Political, Social, and Economic Prospects.* New York & London: M.E. Sharpe, 1996.

Whitt, Joseph A., Jr. "The Mexican Peso Crisis." Federal Reserve Bank of Atlanta. *Economic Review* (January/February 1996).

Winters, Jeffrey A. "The Determinant of Financial Crisis in Asia." In *the Politics of the Asian Economic Crisis*. Ithaca & London: Cornell University Press, 1999. 79-97.

Wise, Carol, ed. *The Post-NAFTA Political Economy: Mexico and the Western Hemisphere*. University Park: Pennsylvania State University Press, 1998.

Woo-Cumings, Meredith. "The State, Democracy, and the Reform of the Corporate Sector in Korea." In *the Politics of the Asian Economic Crisis*. Ithaca & London: Cornell University Press, 1999. 116-142.

Woods, Ngaire. "International Financial Institutions and the Mexican Crisis." In *The Post-NAFTA Political Economy: Mexico and the Western Hemisphere*. University Park, PA: The Pennsylvania State University Press,1998.

Zapata, Francisco. "Mexican Labor in a Context of Political and Economic Crisis." In *Changing Structure of Mexico: Political, Social, and Economic Prospects*. New York and London: M.E. Sharpe, 1996.

Newspapers and Magazines:
(Accessed mostly via Lexis-Nexis)

Asian Business, June 1998, 25
Business and Industry, April 1996, 3.
Business Times, February 16, 1998, 4.
Business Times, August 20, 1998,18.
Business Week, July 17, 1995, 46.
Business Week, May 4, 1998, 58.
Business Week, September 21, 1998, 30.
Business Week, November 9, 1999.
Business Week, March 13, 2000, 140, E6.
Far Eastern Economic Review, December 18, 1997, 14-15.
Far Eastern Economic Review, February19, 1998, 15, 25.
Far Eastern Economic Review, March 5, 1998, 28.

Far Eastern Economic Review, April 16, 1998, 50-53
Far Eastern Economic Review, April 30, 1998, 60, 62.
Far Eastern Economic Review, May 21, 1998.
Far Easter Economic Review, June 18, 1998.
Far Eastern Economic Review, June 18, 1998, 21.
Far Eastern Economic Review, August 6, 1998, 72.
Far Eastern Economic Review, August 27, 1998.
Far Eastern Economic Review, September 17, 1998, 10,11, 13.
Far Eastern Economic Review, October 1, 1998, 18.
Far Eastern Economic Review, November 12, 1998,74.
Far Eastern Economic Review, December 10, 1998, 18
Far Eastern Economic Review, January 21, 1999.
Far Eastern Economic Review, May 6, 1999, 50.
Far Eastern Economic Review, August 12, 1999, 10.
Financial Times, "Special Report: Asia In Crisis," January 13, 1998, 08.
Financial Times, February 9, 1998, 02.
Financial Times, April 2, 1998, 36.
Financial Times, May 1, 1998, 15.
Financial Times, August 22, 1998.
Financial Times, August 28, 1998,.05.
Financial Times, May 10, 1999, 17, 28.
Financial Times, June 15, 1995, 22.
Financial Times, October 6, 2000, 18.
FT Asia Intelligence Wire (Bernama the Malaysian National News Agency). November 2, 1998.
FT Asia Intelligence Wire (Bernama the Malaysian National News Agency), April 17, 1998.
Global Intelligence Update, September 22, 1999, Internet.
Journal of Commerce, February 23, 1995, 1A.
Journal of Commerce, January 30, 1995, 2A.
Journal of Commerce, March 7, 1995, 1A
Los Angeles Times, January 14, 1995, B7.
Los Angeles Times, October 6, 1995, D12.
Los Angeles Times, January 16, 1997, A1.
Los Angeles Times, September 16, 1998, S3.
Malaysian Business, July 1, 2000, 18.
New Straits Times (Malaysia), July 14, 1998, 12.
New Straits Times (Malaysia), September 2, 1998, 23.
Pittsburgh Post-Gazette, December 24, 1994, A1.
South China Morning Post, March 17, 1999, 6.
South China Morning Post, September 7, 1998, 8
The Atlanta Journal and Constitution, December 24, 1994, D1.
The Baltimore Sun, December 23, 1994, 12A.
The Daily Telegraph, January 11, 1995, 31.
The Economist, April 12, 1997, S18.
The Economist, June 26, 1999.
The Houston Chronicle, January 5, 1995, A18.
The Houston Chronicle, January 6, 1995, 16.
The Houston Chronicle, April 22, 1995,1.
The Guardian, December 30, 1994, 12.

The Guardian, November 29, 1999, 19.
The New York Times, December 29, 1994, D18.
The New York Times, January 9, 1995, A5.
The New York Times, January 10, 1995, D1.
The New York Times, March 2, 1995, D1.
The New York Times, August 24, 1999, A15.
The Observer, September 12, 1999, 5.
The Phoenix Gazette, March 10, 1995, A10.
The Phoenix Gazette, "Editorial Opinion," December 26, 1994, B18.
The San Diego Union-Tribune, February 26, 1995, G-4.
The San Francisco Chronicle, January 8, 1998, A1.
The Star, January 23, 98, Internet.
The Star Online, Saturday, January 9, 1999. http://www.TheStar.com.my/current/09pg1.html.
The Star *Online,* Monday, December 20, 1999. http://www.TheStar.com.my/online/newsreport.
The Straits Times, "Regional News," April 30, 1998, Internet.
The Straits Times, "Region Business News," May 7, 1998, Internet.
The Straits Times, Interactive, May 16, 1998, Internet.
The Straits Times, May 26, 1999, Internet.
The Straits Times, Interactive, October 29, 1998.
The Washington Post, January 1, 1995, A29.
The Washington Post, February 13, 1995, A01.
The Washington Post, February 05, 1995, C02.
The Washington Post, July 02, 1998,.E01.
The Washington Post, July 12, 1995, F03.
The Washington Post, July 18, 1998, A08.
USA Today, February 22, 1995, 1A.
Wall Street Journal, January 5, 1995, A14.
Wall Street Journal, July 11, 1995, A2.

About the Author

Dr. Fahrettin Sümer earned his M.A. degree in Political Science from Rutgers University in New Jersey and his Ph.D. in International Studies from the University of South Carolina. During his doctoral training in the Department of Government and International Studies (currently the Department of Political Science), he earned a second M.A. degree in Economics from the Moore School of Business at the same university. Since completion of his Ph.D. in 2003, he has published several articles and taught multiple international relations, comparative politics, and economics courses in South Carolina and Virginia. He has recently been teaching international studies and comparative politics courses at Virginia Commonwealth University. His research interests include the causes and implications of globalization, financial crises and governmental responses, international political economy, international conflict, and international integration.